Welcome to

THESE HANDY, ACCESSIBLE BOOKS are designed to be the perfect travel companions. Whether you're traveling within a restricted budget or feeling the urge to splurge, you will find all you need to know to create the ideal vacation for yourself and your family.

These travel-friendly books present the latest information on hotel accommodations, restaurants, shopping, and transportation, as well as money-saving tips and strategies to beat the crowds and avoid the lines. Also included are detailed descriptions that help you make those tough decisions on which attractions to include in your travel itinerary.

Use these books to help you plan your vacation and then take them along with you for quick and easy reference. You can read them cover to cover or simply pick out the information you need. Let the *Everything® Travel Guides* pave the way for your fun-filled and exciting adventures!

##  TRAVEL TIP

Quick, handy tips

## ⊕ HOT SPOT

Places not to be missed

## ═FAST FACT

Important sound bytes of information

# THE
# EVERYTHING®
## — Travel Guides —

Dear Reader,

What you're about to read is the all-new third edition of this *Everything*®
travel guide about The Walt Disney World Resort, Universal Studios
Florida, and the other awesome attractions within greater Orlando. A lot
has happened in the world since the second edition of this book was
published—but the Orlando area remains one of the country's top tourist
and vacation destinations.

   If you'll be flying to the Orlando area, security at all of the major
airports and theme parks remains tight, but don't let this ruin your vacation. Now, more than ever, preplanning your vacation will save you time
and money, and this book will help!

   Since the tragedy of September 11th, things within the popular
theme parks remain as exciting as ever, be you now must pass through
metal detectors and have your bags searched as you enter each theme
park. This could result in a fifteen minute or so delay, especially if you
arrive to a park with the crowds, first thing in the morning.

   Once you pass through the main gates of any of Orlando's theme
parks, leave the pressures of the outside world behind as you enter into
a world of fantasy, adventure, excitement, and thrills. If you're about to
embark on your first trip to The Walt Disney World Resort, for example,
you're in for a vacation of a lifetime. For those of you returning, you'll
find a handful of new rides, shows, parades, and attractions within the
various parks. This edition also offers information about The Disney
Cruise Lines, which take the magic of a Disney World vacation and adds
a wonderful high-seas cruise adventure that's suitable for the entire family.

   Well, here's to you having a wonderful Orlando vacation! When
you get home, please feel free to email me at *jr7777@aol.com*, or visit
my Web site at *www.JasonRich.com*, and let me know how you
enjoyed your trip!

Sincerely,

# THE
# EVERYTHING®
## TRAVEL GUIDE TO
# THE WALT DISNEY WORLD RESORT,® UNIVERSAL STUDIOS,® AND GREATER ORLANDO
## THIRD EDITION

A complete guide to the best
hotels, restaurants, parks,
and must-see attractions

Jason Rich

Adams Media Corporation
Avon, Massachusetts

Publishing Director: Gary M. Krebs
Managing Editor: Kate McBride
Copy Chief: Laura MacLaughlin
Acquisitions Editor: Allison Carpenter Yoder
Development Editors: Lesley Bolton,
            Michael Paydos
Production Editor: Khrysti Nazzaro

Production Director: Susan Beale
Production Manager: Michelle Roy Kelly
Series Designer: Daria Perreault
Cover Design: Paul Beatrice, Frank Rivera
Layout and Graphics: Brooke Camfield,
Colleen Cunningham, Rachael Eiben
Michelle Roy Kelly, Daria Perreault

An Everything® Series Book.
Everything® and everything.com® are registered trademarks of Adams Media Corporation.

Published by Adams Media Corporation
57 Littlefield Street, Avon, MA 02322 U.S.A.
*www.adamsmedia.com*

ISBN: 1-58062-743-9
Printed in the United States.

J I H G F E D C B

**Library of Congress Cataloging-in-Publication Data**
available from the publisher.

This publication is designed to provide accurate and authoritative information with regard to the subject matter covered. It is sold with the understanding that the publisher is not engaged in rendering legal, accounting, or other professional advice. If legal advice or other expert assistance is required, the services of a competent professional person should be sought.
—From a *Declaration of Principles* jointly adopted by a Committee of the American Bar Association and a Committee of Publishers and Associations

The following are registered trademarks of The Walt Disney Company: California Adventure, Disneyland Resort, Main Street, U.S.A.

Although the author has taken care to ensure that this book accurately sets forth information as of the time it was prepared, prices, practices, and policies at Anaheim attractions may change at any time, and may be different from the information provided here.

Universal Studios is a registered trademark of Universal Studios, Inc.

Cover Illustrations by Barry Littmann.
Cartography by Creative Force, Inc.

*This book is available at quantity discounts for bulk purchases.*
*For information, call 1-800-872-5627.*

**Visit the entire Everything® series at everything.com**

# Contents

ACKNOWLEDGMENTS. . . . . . . . . . . . . . . . . . . . . . . . . . . . . . X

INTRODUCTION. . . . . . . . . . . . . . . . . . . . . . . . . . . . . XI

MAPS. . . . . . . . . . . . . . . . . . . . . . . . . . . . . . . . . . 1

CHAPTER 1 *Preparing for Your Vacation* . . . . . . . . . . . 13
Inside The WDW Resort . . . . . . . . . . . . . . . . . . . . . 13
Flying to Orlando . . . . . . . . . . . . . . . . . . . . . 15
Taking the Train . . . . . . . . . . . . . . . . . . . . . 21
Busing It to Orlando. . . . . . . . . . . . . . . . . . . . . 21
Renting a Car. . . . . . . . . . . . . . . . . . . . . . . . 22
Your Travel Budget. . . . . . . . . . . . . . . . . . . . . 27
Using a Travel Agent . . . . . . . . . . . . . . . . . . . . 31
Booking Your Vacation Online . . . . . . . . . . . . . . . . 32
Vacation Packages and When to Visit . . . . . . . . . . . . 33

CHAPTER 2 *Choosing Your Accommodations* . . . . . . . 39
Getting to the Theme Parks. . . . . . . . . . . . . . . . . . 39
Defining Your Needs . . . . . . . . . . . . . . . . . . . . 40
The WDW Resort Hotels. . . . . . . . . . . . . . . . . . . 41
Universal Orlando Accommodations . . . . . . . . . . . . . 54
Orlando-Area Accommodations . . . . . . . . . . . . . . . 57
Packing for Your Vacation . . . . . . . . . . . . . . . . . . 64
Before You Leave Home . . . . . . . . . . . . . . . . . . . 67

CHAPTER 3 *Admission to the Disney Theme Parks* . . . 69
Admission Prices and Passes. . . . . . . . . . . . . . . . . 69
Beware of Counterfeit Passes and Scams . . . . . . . . . . 74
Avoid Long Lines . . . . . . . . . . . . . . . . . . . . . 75
Travel Tips. . . . . . . . . . . . . . . . . . . . . . . . . 79
Guest Services . . . . . . . . . . . . . . . . . . . . . . 82
Gathering More Information . . . . . . . . . . . . . . . . 89

CHAPTER 4 *Orlando-Area Dining* . . . . . . . . . . . . . . . 91
Dining at Disney . . . . . . . . . . . . . . . . . . . . . . 91
Dining Outside of Disney Property . . . . . . . . . . . . . 93
Restaurants in Celebration . . . . . . . . . . . . . . . . . 97
Calculating the Tip. . . . . . . . . . . . . . . . . . . . . 97
The Ultimate Fine-Dining Experience . . . . . . . . . . . . 98

CHAPTER 5 *Introduction to The Magic Kingdom* . . . . 101
Getting to and from The Magic Kingdom . . . . . . . . . . . . . . . . . . . . . 101
First Things First . . . . . . . . . . . . . . . . . . . . . . . . . . 103
The Rating System . . . . . . . . . . . . . . . . . . . . . . . . . . 104
Kid Switch Policy. . . . . . . . . . . . . . . . . . . . . . . . . . 106
Dining in The Magic Kingdom . . . . . . . . . . . . . . . . . . . . 106
The Magic Kingdom and WDW Resort Tours . . . . . . . . . . . . . . . . . 112

CHAPTER 6 *Exploring The Magic Kingdom* . . . . . . . . . . 115
Park Overview . . . . . . . . . . . . . . . . . . . . . . . . . . . 115
Main Street, U.S.A. . . . . . . . . . . . . . . . . . . . . . . . . . . 117
Adventureland . . . . . . . . . . . . . . . . . . . . . . . . . . . 120
Frontierland . . . . . . . . . . . . . . . . . . . . . . . . . . . . 123
Liberty Square. . . . . . . . . . . . . . . . . . . . . . . . . . . 125
Tomorrowland . . . . . . . . . . . . . . . . . . . . . . . . . . . 128
Shop 'Til You Drop . . . . . . . . . . . . . . . . . . . . . . . . . . 134

CHAPTER 7 *Kid-Oriented Areas of
The Magic Kingdom* . . . . . . . . . . . . . . . . . . 141
Fantasyland . . . . . . . . . . . . . . . . . . . . . . . . . . . . 141
Mickey's Toontown . . . . . . . . . . . . . . . . . . . . . . . . . 147
Meet the Characters . . . . . . . . . . . . . . . . . . . . . . . . 150
Other Kid-Oriented Attractions . . . . . . . . . . . . . . . . . . . . . 151
Rides Not Suitable for Young Children . . . . . . . . . . . . . . . . . . . 151

CHAPTER 8 *All about Epcot* . . . . . . . . . . . . . . . . . . . 153
Park Overview. . . . . . . . . . . . . . . . . . . . . . . . . . . 153
The Rating System . . . . . . . . . . . . . . . . . . . . . . . . . 157
Future World. . . . . . . . . . . . . . . . . . . . . . . . . . . . 158
The World Showcase. . . . . . . . . . . . . . . . . . . . . . . . . 170
Leave a Legacy . . . . . . . . . . . . . . . . . . . . . . . . . . 182
What's Next?. . . . . . . . . . . . . . . . . . . . . . . . . . . . 183

CHAPTER 9 *The Disney-MGM Studios* . . . . . . . . . . . . . 185
Park Overview. . . . . . . . . . . . . . . . . . . . . . . . . . . 185
The Rating System . . . . . . . . . . . . . . . . . . . . . . . . . 189
The Studios' Rides and Attractions . . . . . . . . . . . . . . . . . . . 189
What's New at the Studios. . . . . . . . . . . . . . . . . . . . . . . 198
The Backstage Studio Tours . . . . . . . . . . . . . . . . . . . . . . 202
Dining at The Disney-MGM Studios . . . . . . . . . . . . . . . . . . 204
Shopping at The Studios . . . . . . . . . . . . . . . . . . . . . . . 207

## CHAPTER 10 *Disney's Animal Kingdom* . . . . . . . . . . . . . 213

Park Overview . . . . . . . . . . . . . . . . . . . . . . . . . . . . . 213
The Rating System . . . . . . . . . . . . . . . . . . . . . . . . . . 220
The Oasis . . . . . . . . . . . . . . . . . . . . . . . . . . . . . . . 220
Discovery Island . . . . . . . . . . . . . . . . . . . . . . . . . . . 221
Africa . . . . . . . . . . . . . . . . . . . . . . . . . . . . . . . . . 222
DinoLand U.S.A. . . . . . . . . . . . . . . . . . . . . . . . . . . . 225
Camp Minnie-Mickey. . . . . . . . . . . . . . . . . . . . . . . . . 228
Rafiki's Planet Watch . . . . . . . . . . . . . . . . . . . . . . . . . 230
Asia . . . . . . . . . . . . . . . . . . . . . . . . . . . . . . . . . . 231
Shopping at the Animal Kingdom . . . . . . . . . . . . . . . . . . 233
Dining at the Animal Kingdom . . . . . . . . . . . . . . . . . . . . 234

## CHAPTER 11 *Disney's Water Parks* . . . . . . . . . . . . . . . . 235

Water Park Information . . . . . . . . . . . . . . . . . . . . . . . . 235
Blizzard Beach. . . . . . . . . . . . . . . . . . . . . . . . . . . . . 237
Typhoon Lagoon . . . . . . . . . . . . . . . . . . . . . . . . . . . 238
River Country . . . . . . . . . . . . . . . . . . . . . . . . . . . . . 239
Other Area Water Parks . . . . . . . . . . . . . . . . . . . . . . . . 240

## CHAPTER 12 *Disney Nightlife* . . . . . . . . . . . . . . . . . . . 241

Nighttime Entertainment Overview . . . . . . . . . . . . . . . . . 241
Disney's West Side. . . . . . . . . . . . . . . . . . . . . . . . . . . 244
Pleasure Island . . . . . . . . . . . . . . . . . . . . . . . . . . . . 250
The Marketplace . . . . . . . . . . . . . . . . . . . . . . . . . . . 255
Disney's BoardWalk . . . . . . . . . . . . . . . . . . . . . . . . . . 261

## CHAPTER 13 *A High Seas Adventure* . . . . . . . . . . . . . . . 267

Disney Cruise Lines . . . . . . . . . . . . . . . . . . . . . . . . . . 267
The *Magic* and the *Wonder* . . . . . . . . . . . . . . . . . . . . 269
Pricing Your Vacation . . . . . . . . . . . . . . . . . . . . . . . . . 271
Children's Space . . . . . . . . . . . . . . . . . . . . . . . . . . . 272
Adult Activities. . . . . . . . . . . . . . . . . . . . . . . . . . . . . 272
Family Time . . . . . . . . . . . . . . . . . . . . . . . . . . . . . . 273
Dining Experiences. . . . . . . . . . . . . . . . . . . . . . . . . . . 274
Guest Services. . . . . . . . . . . . . . . . . . . . . . . . . . . . . 274

## CHAPTER 14 *The Universal Orlando Resort* . . . . . . . . . 277

Overview of the Resort . . . . . . . . . . . . . . . . . . . . . . . . 277
Driving Directions. . . . . . . . . . . . . . . . . . . . . . . . . . . 279
Parking at Universal Studios Escape . . . . . . . . . . . . . . . . . 280
Admission to Universal Studios Theme Parks . . . . . . . . . . . . 281
Universal Studios Florida VIP Tours . . . . . . . . . . . . . . . . . 282

Guest Services. . . . . . . . . . . . . . . . . . . . 285
Getting the Most out of Your Day . . . . . . . . . . . . . 285

## CHAPTER 15 *The Universal Studios*
### *Florida Theme Park* . . . . . . . . . . . . . . . . . **287**
Park Information . . . . . . . . . . . . . . . . . . . . . . 287
The Rating System . . . . . . . . . . . . . . . . . . . . . 288
The Rides . . . . . . . . . . . . . . . . . . . . . . . . . 289
Meet the Characters . . . . . . . . . . . . . . . . . . . . 304
Dining Opportunities . . . . . . . . . . . . . . . . . . . . 305
Shopping . . . . . . . . . . . . . . . . . . . . . . . . . 307
Special Events. . . . . . . . . . . . . . . . . . . . . . . 307

## CHAPTER 16 *Universal Escape's*
### *Islands of Adventure* . . . . . . . . . . . . . . . . **309**
Park Overview. . . . . . . . . . . . . . . . . . . . . . . 309
The Rating System . . . . . . . . . . . . . . . . . . . . . 311
Port of Entry. . . . . . . . . . . . . . . . . . . . . . . . 312
Seuss Landing . . . . . . . . . . . . . . . . . . . . . . . 314
The Lost Continent . . . . . . . . . . . . . . . . . . . . . 317
Jurassic Park. . . . . . . . . . . . . . . . . . . . . . . . 321
Toon Lagoon. . . . . . . . . . . . . . . . . . . . . . . . 325
Marvel Super Hero Island . . . . . . . . . . . . . . . . . 329

## CHAPTER 17 *Universal CityWalk*. . . . . . . . . . . . . **335**
An Overview of CityWalk. . . . . . . . . . . . . . . . . . 335
The Restaurants . . . . . . . . . . . . . . . . . . . . . . 336
The Universal Cineplex . . . . . . . . . . . . . . . . . . . 340
CityJazz. . . . . . . . . . . . . . . . . . . . . . . . . . 340
The Groove . . . . . . . . . . . . . . . . . . . . . . . . 341
CityWalk Shopping . . . . . . . . . . . . . . . . . . . . . 341

## CHAPTER 18 *SeaWorld and Discovery Cove*. . . . . . . . **343**
Park Overview. . . . . . . . . . . . . . . . . . . . . . . 343
The Rating System . . . . . . . . . . . . . . . . . . . . . 345
SeaWorld Highlights . . . . . . . . . . . . . . . . . . . . 346
Getting Hungry?. . . . . . . . . . . . . . . . . . . . . . 350
Become an Animal Trainer. . . . . . . . . . . . . . . . . . 351
Kids and SeaWorld . . . . . . . . . . . . . . . . . . . . . 351
Discovery Cove . . . . . . . . . . . . . . . . . . . . . . 352

## CHAPTER 19 *Exploring Greater Orlando* . . . . . . . . . . . 355
Resort Hotel Activities . . . . . . . . . . . . . . . . . . . . . . . . . . . . . . 355
The Town of Celebration . . . . . . . . . . . . . . . . . . . . . . . . . . . . 361
Tourist Information . . . . . . . . . . . . . . . . . . . . . . . . . . . . . . . . 362
Orlando-Area Activities . . . . . . . . . . . . . . . . . . . . . . . . . . . . . 363
The Orlando FlexTicket . . . . . . . . . . . . . . . . . . . . . . . . . . . . . 368

## CHAPTER 20 *Planning Your Trip* . . . . . . . . . . . . . . . . . . 369
Plan Accordingly . . . . . . . . . . . . . . . . . . . . . . . . . . . . . . . . . 369
Airline Information . . . . . . . . . . . . . . . . . . . . . . . . . . . . . . . . 370
Airport Ground Transportation Information . . . . . . . . . . . . . . . . . 371
Rental Car Information . . . . . . . . . . . . . . . . . . . . . . . . . . . . . . 371
Accommodation Information . . . . . . . . . . . . . . . . . . . . . . . . . . 372

## APPENDIX A *Important Phone Numbers* . . . . . . . . . . . . 373
## APPENDIX B *Attraction Selection Worksheet* . . . . . . . 379
## APPENDIX C *Daily Intinerary* . . . . . . . . . . . . . . . . . . . . 385

## INDEX . . . . . . . . . . . . . . . . . . . . . . . . . . . . . . . . . . . . 401

# Acknowlegments

Thanks to everyone at Adams Media for making this book a reality. Thanks also to Mark, Ellen, Sandy, Emily, Ferras, and my family for all of their love and support.

# Introduction

What you're about to read is the all-new third edition of *The Everything® Travel Guide to The Walt Disney World Resort,® Universal Studios,® and Greater Orlando*. This travel guide was written to help you make the most of your vacation experience. Unless you're planning to spend several weeks and an absolute fortune, there's no possible way that you'll be able to experience everything the Greater Orlando area has to offer. Therefore, you'll have to make decisions about which theme parks you want to visit, which attractions within those theme parks you want to experience, what shows and parades you want to see, and which restaurants you want to dine at.

The Walt Disney World (WDW) Resort, including the theme parks, resort hotels, restaurants, and other activities, offers the world-class service and hospitality that have become legendary. It's this hospitality that helps make everyone's vacation a truly memorable and enjoyable experience, and something that Walt Disney himself believed was so important.

The WDW Resort is a city unto itself, but it's a 30,500-acre (47-square mile) city unlike any other found on this planet. Yet, with everything that already exists in this ultimate vacation destination, less than one quarter of the total acreage of the resort complex has been developed. Thus, in the years and decades to come, you can bet that The WDW Resort will continue to evolve and provide many future generations with a taste of Disney magic and the wholesome family vacation experience that Walt Disney himself (along with his brother Roy) intended for all who visit this unique resort.

Located less than a thirty-minute drive from The WDW Resort is another fast-growing tourist destination, which is the second most popular theme park resort complex in the Greater Orlando area. Universal Studios Escape offers some of the most incredible rides, shows, and attractions found anywhere in the world, yet here you'll find a very different type of vacation experience than at The WDW Resort.

Originally, when Universal Studios Florida opened, it was a single, medium-sized theme park that could be experienced within one day. Now, this park has expanded dramatically, and as you'll read later in this book, it continues to undergo massive construction and development. As a result, vacationers can easily plan on spending two or three full days experiencing everything there is to see and do at Universal Studios Escape, which is now comprised of two theme parks, the CityWalk area, plus several resort hotels.

Located near Universal Studios Escape is the third most popular theme park attraction in Orlando—SeaWorld. This marine park offers an up close look at marine life, like dolphins and whales, plus it features an assortment of marine-related rides, shows, and attractions.

Inside this book, you will find detailed descriptions of all of the activities and things there are to see and do at The WDW Resort, Universal Studios Escape, SeaWorld, and other popular tourist attractions. There are also all sorts of tips and suggestions on how you can save time and money while making the most of your vacation.

As you read this book and start thinking about how exactly you want to spend your time, be sure to take notes. Keep track of which rides, shows, attractions, parades, and activities are of interest to you (and the people you'll be traveling with). Once you think you know what you want to experience, start planning out the actual days of your trip. While you're doing this, keep in mind that each of the various theme parks is massive. At The WDW Resort, for example, The Magic Kingdom is 107 acres, Epcot is 300 acres, The Disney-MGM Studios take up about 155 acres, and Disney's Animal Kingdom is spread across 500 acres, so plan on doing a lot of walking.

This book is "unofficial," which means that it is in no way authorized or sanctioned by The Walt Disney Company, Universal

Studios, SeaWorld, or any other Orlando attraction, travel agency, hotel chain, restaurant, or airline. Thus, this book has the freedom to tell it like it is, and to offer you money and timesaving advice that you won't find in any other travel guide or vacation-planning book.

As you'll read several times throughout this book, however, the various theme parks and resorts are always evolving. New rides, attractions, shows, parades, shops, restaurants, and activities are always being added, updated, or somehow changed, while outdated attractions are taken out of the various parks. Thus, when you actually visit Orlando, don't be surprised if you encounter something new or different that's not described in this book.

# The Magic Kingdom

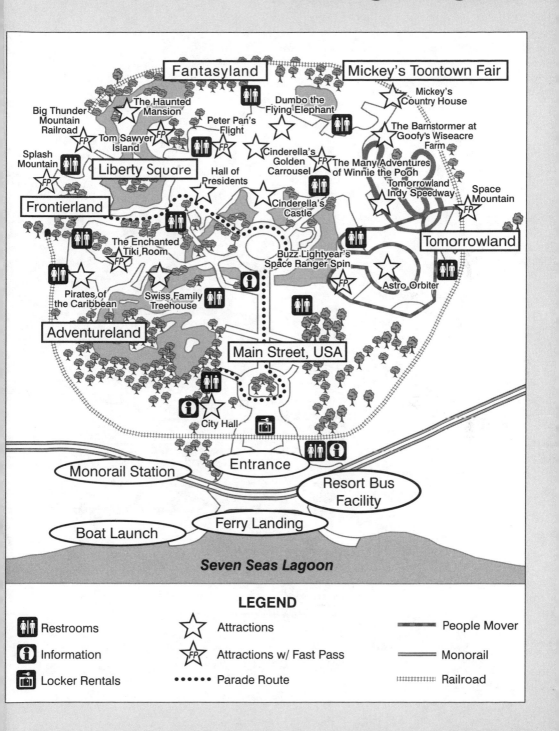

Fantasyland

Mickey's Toontown Fair

The Haunted Mansion

Dumbo the Flying Elephant

Mickey's Country House

Big Thunder Mountain Railroad

Peter Pan's Flight

Tom Sawyer Island

The Barnstormer at Goofy's Wiseacre Farm

Splash Mountain

Cinderella's Golden Carrousel

The Many Adventures of Winnie the Pooh

Liberty Square

Hall of Presidents

Tomorrowland Indy Speedway

Space Mountain

Frontierland

Cinderella's Castle

Tomorrowland

The Enchanted Tiki Room

Buzz Lightyear's Space Ranger Spin

Pirates of the Caribbean

Swiss Family Treehouse

Astro Orbiter

Adventureland

Main Street, USA

City Hall

Entrance

Monorail Station

Resort Bus Facility

Ferry Landing

Boat Launch

**Seven Seas Lagoon**

## LEGEND

| | | | | |
|---|---|---|---|---|
| Restrooms | Attractions | | | People Mover |
| Information | Attractions w/ Fast Pass | | | Monorail |
| Locker Rentals | Parade Route | | | Railroad |

# Epcot

Italy

"The American Adventure"

Japan

World Showcase

Morocco

"IllumiNations:
Reflections of Earth"

France

**World Showcase Lagoon**

United Kingdom

International Gateway

Canada

World Showplace Events Pavilion

| | Restrooms | | Attractions | ••••• | Parade Route |
|---|---|---|---|---|---|
| | Information | *FP* | Attractions w/ Fast Pass | ══ | Monorail |
| | Locker Rentals | | | | |

# The Disney-MGM Studios

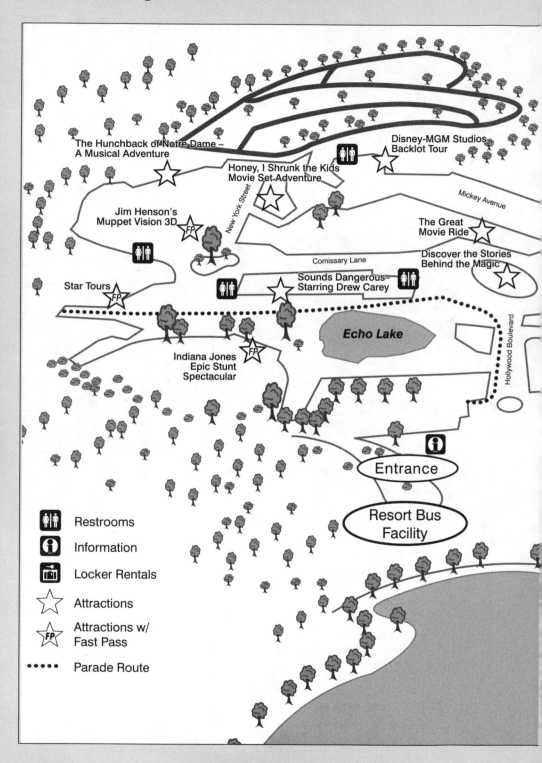

The Hunchback of Notre Dame – A Musical Adventure

Honey, I Shrunk the Kids Movie Set Adventure

Disney-MGM Studios Backlot Tour

Mickey Avenue

New York Street

Jim Henson's Muppet Vision 3D

The Great Movie Ride

Discover the Stories Behind the Magic

Comissary Lane

Sounds Dangerous– Starring Drew Carey

Star Tours

Echo Lake

Hollywood Boulevard

Indiana Jones Epic Stunt Spectacular

Entrance

Resort Bus Facility

Restrooms

Information

Locker Rentals

Attractions

Attractions w/ Fast Pass

Parade Route

Who Wants to be
a Millionaire–Play it!

Walt Disney:
One Man's Dream

Voyage of The
Little Mermaid

The Magic of
Disney Animation

Animation Courtyard

Playhouse
Disney

Rock 'n' Roller Coaster
Starring Aerosmith

Sunset Boulevard

Beauty and
the Beast
Live on Stage

The Twilight Zone
Tower of Terror™

Fantasmic!

Resort Boat
Facility

# Disney's Animal Kingdom

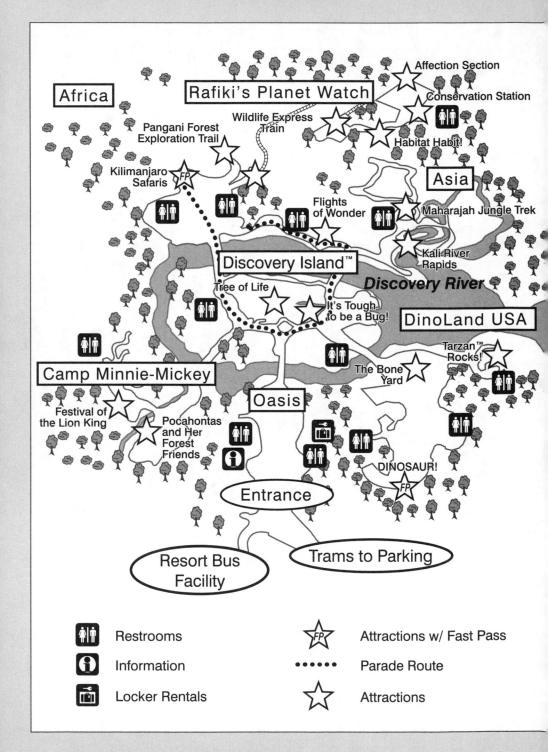

Africa

Rafiki's Planet Watch

Affection Section

Conservation Station

Wildlife Express Train

Pangani Forest Exploration Trail

Habitat Habit!

Kilimanjaro Safaris

Asia

Flights of Wonder

Maharajah Jungle Trek

Discovery Island™

Tree of Life

Kali River Rapids

Discovery River

It's Tough to be a Bug!

DinoLand USA

Tarzan™ Rocks!

Camp Minnie-Mickey

The Bone Yard

Festival of the Lion King

Oasis

Pocahontas and Her Forest Friends

DINOSAUR!

Entrance

Resort Bus Facility

Trams to Parking

Restrooms

Attractions w/ Fast Pass

Information

•••••• Parade Route

Locker Rentals

Attractions

# Downtown Disney

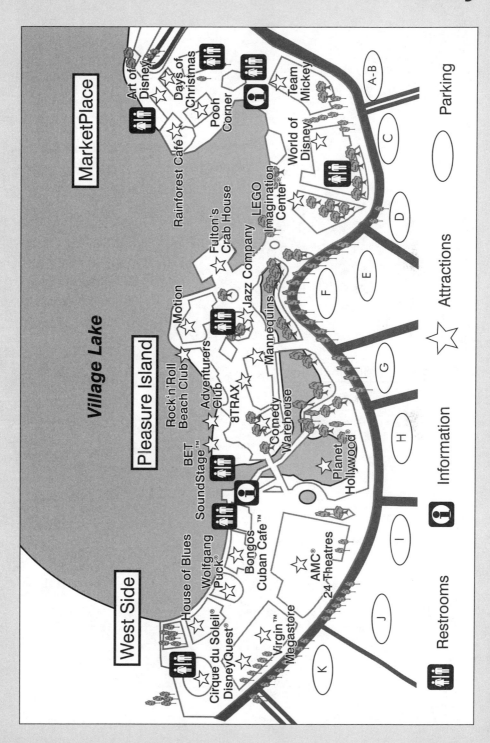

MarketPlace

Art of Disney
Days of Christmas
Pooh Corner
Rainforest Café
Team Mickey
World of Disney
LEGO Imagination Center®
Fulton's Crab House
Jazz Company

Village Lake

Pleasure Island

Motion
Rock'n'Roll Beach Club
Adventurers Club
8TRAX
BET SoundStage™
Mannequins
Comedy Warehouse
Planet Hollywood®

West Side

House of Blues
Wolfgang Puck®
Bongos Cuban Cafe™
AMC® 24-Theatres
Cirque du Soleil®
DisneyQuest®
Virgin™ Megastore

A-B
C
D
E
F
G
H
I
J
K

Parking

Attractions

Information

Restrooms

# Universal Studios Florida

New York

Kongfrontation®

42nd St

Canal St

The Blues Brothers

Delancey St

South St

TWISTER...
Ride It Out®

57th St

Park Ave

7th Ave

South St

Amblin Ave

The Bone Yard

Stage 54

Battery Park

Production Central

8th Ave

Hollywood

Nickelodeon
Studios®

The Funtastic World
of Hanna-Barbera™

Alfred Hitchcock:
The Art of Making Movies

Hollywood Blvd

Nickelodeon Way

Plaza Of The Stars

Rodeo Dr

Lucy—A Tribute℠

The Gory, Gruesome
& Grotesque
Horror Make-Up Show

Hard Rock
Cafe

TERMINATOR 2:
3-D BATTLE ACROSS TIME™

Entrance

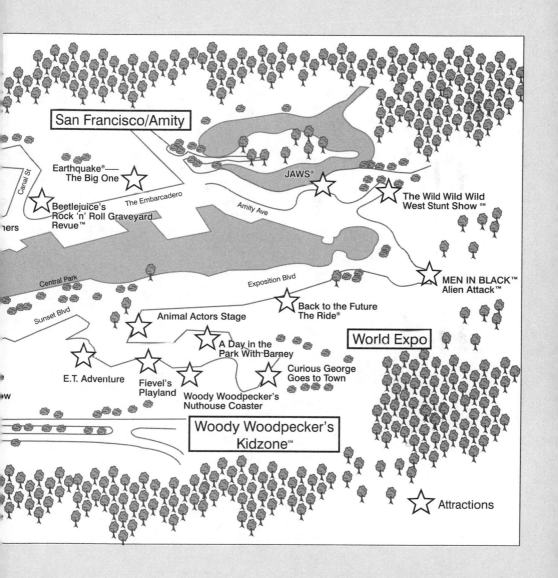

San Francisco/Amity

Canal St

Earthquake® —
The Big One

Beetlejuice's
Rock 'n' Roll Graveyard
Revue™

ners

The Embarcadero

Amity Ave

JAWS®

The Wild Wild Wild
West Stunt Show ℠

Central Park

Exposition Blvd

MEN IN BLACK™
Alien Attack™

Sunset Blvd

Back to the Future
The Ride®

Animal Actors Stage

World Expo

A Day in the
Park With Barney

E.T. Adventure

Fievel's
Playland

Curious George
Goes to Town

Woody Woodpecker's
Nuthouse Coaster

w

Woody Woodpecker's
Kidzone℠

Attractions

# Universal Escape's Islands of Adventure

Jurassic Park River Adventure℠

Camp Jurassic®

Pteranodon Flyers®

Triceratops Encounter℠

Popeye & Bluto's Bilge Rat Barges℠

Dudley Do-Right's Ripsaw Falls®

Toon Trolley Beach Bash

Toon Lagoon®

Me Ship, The Olive℠

The Amazing Adventures of Spider–Man℠

Port of Entry®

Doctor Doom's Fearfall®

Marvel Super Hero Island®

Incredible Hulk Coaster®

Storm Force Accelatron℠

# Greater Orlando Metro Area

# CHAPTER 1

# Preparing for Your Vacation

YOUR FIRST STEP IN PLANNING A DISNEY VACATION is to determine how long your vacation is going to last and how much money you have in your travel budget. Next, you'll need to book your airfare and hotel accommodations, and possibly reserve a rental car. This chapter will help you save money and time as you take care of these initial vacation-planning steps.

## Inside The WDW Resort

 The WDW Resort has become much more than just another theme park. This 30,500-acre resort located near Orlando, Florida, is the single, most popular vacation destination in the world, and one that over 100 million guests have experienced since the resort opened in 1971. Within The WDW Resort are activities galore. So, no matter who you are or where your interests lie, you'll be able to spend every minute of your vacation participating in exciting activities or, if you choose, kicking back at your hotel's swimming pool, relaxing, and getting a tan.

Listed in alphabetical order, The WDW Resort consists of:

**Blizzard Beach**—One of Disney's wettest and wildest water parks.

**Championship Golf Courses**—If you enjoy playing golf, The WDW

Resort offers your choice of award-winning eighteen-hole courses, putting greens, and driving ranges.

**Disney-MGM Studios**—Get a peek at Disney's motion picture and animation production studios and experience some awesome rides, shows, and attractions, like Tower of Terror and Star Tours.

**Disney's Animal Kingdom**—Disney's newest and biggest theme park.

**Disney's BoardWalk**—A nightspot that's jam-packed with restaurants, clubs, bars, shops, and activities.

**Disney's Vacation Club**—Disney's time-share vacation opportunity.

**Disney's West Side**—Disney comes to life after dark with clubs, restaurants, bars, shops, and activities.

**Disney's Wide World of Sports Complex**—A huge sports facility designed for amateur and professional athletes alike.

**Epcot**—The Disney theme park that offers both Future World and the World Showcase.

**Fort Wilderness Campground**—In addition to resort hotels, The WDW Resort complex offers plenty of fully equipped campsites and special activities at this campground area.

**The Magic Kingdom**—This is the theme park that started it all. Experience the classic Disney attractions and make your own Disney memories. This theme park includes many of the attractions that Walt Disney himself created or helped to develop before his death.

**On-Property Resort Hotels**—Each of the award-winning resort hotels has its own special theme, and all offer some of the most incredible customer service and hospitality that you'll find anywhere in the world.

**Pleasure Island**—For one admission price, guests have a chance to experience a handful of hot clubs and celebrate New Year's Eve every night of the year. This area of Downtown Disney offers the world's largest street party, and the action all starts after the sun goes down.

**Restaurants**—No matter what type of food you're looking for or how much you have to spend, chances are you'll find it somewhere on Disney property.

**River Country**—This is Disney's original water park.

**Typhoon Lagoon**—Another family-oriented water park that offers gallons and gallons of fun and surprises.

## 💼 TRAVEL TIP

To make your vacation the best it can possibly be, you'll want to invest some time before you depart to properly plan your trip. Especially if you're traveling with children or a group of people, the more planning you do now, the more organized and relaxing your trip will be when it actually begins.

## Flying to Orlando

 All of the airlines listed in this section (and possibly a few others) offer competitive rates and travel packages to the Orlando International Airport, so be sure to shop around for the best airfares and flights. Not all of the airlines, however, will offer service from your home city.

As a general rule, you want to book your airfare as far in advance as possible. Many airlines offer the best prices if you book and pay for your tickets twenty-one days in advance. You can, however, also obtain good fares if you make your reservations (and pay for your airline tickets) fourteen or seven days early. When making your travel plans, try to have the most flexible schedule possible, and if your schedule permits, you'll almost always get a better airfare if your stay includes a Saturday night.

Keep in mind, with "discounted" or "special" airfares, the tickets will not be refundable, and there will be a fee to change the travel dates the airline ticket is good for. The change fee is usually between $100 and $150, plus the price difference in the airfare itself. To avoid this change fee, most airlines will allow you to fly standby; however, this does not guarantee you a seat on a specific flight, and if you're traveling with a family and the flight you're trying to get onto is close to capacity, your chances of all getting on the same flight are slim, especially during peak travel periods.

If you choose to use your frequent-flier miles to book your airline ticket to Orlando, keep in mind that seats may be difficult to reserve during peak travel periods, so make your reservations early. The advantages of using a frequent-flier ticket are that it's free and most airlines allow you to change your travel plans at the last minute with no penalties or fees.

 **TRAVEL TIP**

If you're traveling cross-country, red-eye (overnight) flights that leave the West Coast between 10:00 P.M. and midnight and arrive in Orlando the following morning are almost always the cheapest flights available. While most people hate flying all night, you can sometimes save up to several hundred dollars when traveling between the West Coast and the East Coast via a red-eye flight on any airline.

Always ask the airline reservation representative you speak with for the absolutely lowest airfare available. After an airfare is quoted to you, ask again if it is the best deal. Next, ask if there are flights to and from Orlando at around the same times as the ones quoted to you that would make the airfare less expensive. You won't often be quoted the absolute lowest prices the first time you ask.

Also, check the travel section of your local newspaper for advertised special fares and promotions. You can make a reservation that will be held for twenty-four hours without having to pay for the ticket, so make an unpaid reservation and then shop around by calling additional airlines.

## Strategies for the Best Airfare

There are several alternatives available to you when it comes to shopping around for the best airfares. You can go to the airport and visit a ticket counter, or book your travel directly with the airline via the telephone.

You can also surf the Internet and visit the various travel-related Web sites such as ✎ Travelocity.com, ✎ Priceline.com, ✎ LastMinuteTravel.com, or ✎ Orbitz.com (described later in this chapter). The Web sites of individual airlines can also be used to research and reserve travel. For example, the Web site for US Airways is ✎ *www.usairways.com*.

Another alternative is to call a travel agent and have them do the busywork for you. Travel agents have computer systems that allow them to search for flight availability on all airlines at once. Most travel agents will be happy to work with you over the telephone, so it's not necessary to take time out of your busy schedule during business hours to visit a travel agent's office in person.

## 🧳 TRAVEL TIP

To save money, consider using public transportation to get to the airport. It'll almost always be cheaper than parking your car at the airport. The cheapest option is to have a friend or family member drop you off at the airport and pick you up when you return. Another option is to use a door-to-door shuttle bus service, which is almost always cheaper than a taxi, limo, or town car service.

When choosing a travel agent, find someone who comes highly recommended by someone you trust. Travel agents can be extremely helpful and save you money, but some will purposely quote you higher-priced airfares since they're receiving a commission from the airline based on the price of the ticket they sell. If you're a member of AAA or have an American Express card, both of these companies offer highly reputable travel agencies that offer their services either in person or by telephone to members.

Finally, you might want to look into package deals offered by the various airlines. Many packages include airfare, hotel, rental car, and perhaps meals or show tickets. Most airlines have a separate "Vacation Package" reservation department that's different from the regular airline reservation department. The Walt Disney Travel Company also offers a handful of discounted packages to The WDW Resort ✆ (407) 939-7675.

## The Orlando International Airport

The Orlando International Airport is the closest major airport to all of the theme parks, resorts, and attractions within the Greater Orlando area. If you'll be flying to Orlando, chances are this is the airport you'll be flying into. While this list is subject to change, the major airlines that service this airport include:

**AeroMexico:** ✆(800) 237-6639

**Air Canada:** ✆(800) 247-2262

**AirJamaica:** ✆(800) 523-5585

**AirTran Airways:** ✆(800) AIR-TRAN

**American Airlines:** ✆(800) 433-7300

**AmericaWest Airlines:** ✆(800) 235-9292

**ANA:** ✆(800) 235-9262

**Bahamasair:** ✆(800) 222-4262

**British Airways:** ✆(800) AIR-WAYS

**Carnival:** ✆(800) 274-6140

**ComAir:** ✆(800) 354-9822

**Continental:** ✆(800) 523-3273

**Delta Airlines/Delta Express:** ✆(800) 221-1212

**El Al:** ✆(800) 223-6700

**Icelander:** ✆(800) 223-5500

**Jet Blue:** ✆(800) 538-2583

LTU: ☎(800) 888-0200

Midway: ☎(800) 44-MIDWAY

Mortinair: ☎(800) 627-8462

Northwest Airlines/KLM: ☎(800) 225-2525

Saudia: ☎(800) 472-8342

Southwest Airlines: ☎(800) 435-9792

Spirit Airlines: ☎(800) 772-7117

United: ☎(800) 241-6522

US Airways: ☎(800) 428-4322

US Airways Vacation Packages: ☎(800) 455-0123

Vanguard Airlines: ☎(800) 826-4827

Varig Brazil: ☎(800) 468-2744

Virgin Atlantic: ☎(800) 862-8621

*Note:* A handful of other airlines also operate charter flights to and from Orlando and other major U.S. cities and foreign countries.

The Orlando International Airport is in the process of completing a $1.2 billion upgrade and expansion. For more information about this airport, you can call ☎(407) 825-2001 or visit the airport's Web site at ✑ *www.orlandoairports.net.*

If you're driving from the airport to The WDW Resort, there are multiple routes that'll get you there. One direct route is to take the North exit from the airport to the Beeline Expressway West (Route 528). Get onto I-4 West and then follow signs to The WDW Resort. You'll want to exit I-4 at either Exit 26B or Exit 25, depending on your final destination within the huge resort complex. The trip is less than 25 miles and should take about thirty minutes (without traffic).

Mears Motor Shuttles offers van service to the various hotels at The WDW Resort (as well as nearby areas) from the Orlando airport (and back). The cost is $14 each way or $25 round trip for adults, $10 one way or $17 round trip for kids (ages four to eleven), and free to kids under age four. These shuttles leave the airport every fifteen minutes or so and can be picked up right outside of the airport terminals. For reservations, call ☎(407) 423-5566.

Taxi service is available outside of the airport's main terminals, but this is one of the more expensive ways to reach The WDW Resort. Check with the Ground Transportation Information Desk located inside the airport for various other transportation options to get you from the airport to your hotel in the Orlando area.

##  TRAVEL TIP

If you're planning to meet people in Orlando, be sure they're provided with the appropriate airline, flight number, and departure time/date. With this information, anyone can contact your airline for arrival information or use one of these Web sites: *www.thetrip.com*, *www.travelocity.com*, or *www.flightprogress.com*.

### Airport Security Information

All of the airports in America have adopted much stricter security. Be sure to arrive at the airport at least ninety minutes prior to your scheduled departure time and have your driver's license, military ID, or passport ready to show multiple times at various security checkpoints, including the airline ticket counter.

The following items cannot be taken past the security checkpoint at any airport, nor can they be kept in a carry-on bag taken onto an airplane. The majority of these items, however, can be packed within the suitcases that you'll be checking with the airline.

- Aerosol cans, i.e., hairspray
- Baseball bats
- Carpet knives
- Corkscrews
- Cutting instruments
- Golf clubs
- Hockey sticks
- Ice picks
- Knitting/crochet needles

- Knives of any size
- Pepper spray
- Pool cues
- Scissors of any size
- Ski poles
- Straight razors

If you live in a city with multiple airports, or you live between two cities that both have airports, price your airline tickets going to and from the airports closest to you. Airlines often offer special deals and promotions from specific airports.

## Taking the Train

Located extremely close to The WDW Resort, there's an Amtrak station in Kissimmee, Florida (Amtrak Station Code: KIS). Information about taking an Amtrak train from anywhere in the country to WDW can be obtained by calling ✆ (800) USA-RAIL or by visiting the Web site ✍ *www.amtrak.com*.

Amtrak offers travel discounts to all students and veterans, as well as to AAA and AARP members who present their membership card when purchasing a train ticket. Amtrak train tickets can be purchased from many travel agents, by visiting any Amtrak ticket office, or by calling Amtrak directly and using a major credit card.

## Busing It to Orlando

**Greyhound** has two bus terminals close to The WDW Resort: one in **Orlando** (✉ 555 North John Young Parkway, Orlando, ✆ (407) 292-3440) and the other in **Kissimmee** (located at ✉ 103 East Dakin Avenue, Kissimmee, ✆ (407) 847-3911). From these bus terminals, taxi service is available to The WDW Resort, Universal Studios, or any other nearby hotel or destination.

## Renting a Car

 Just like when making airline reservations, there are several tricks to use when reserving a rental car that will help ensure that you get the lowest rate possible. For starters, reserve your rental car as far in advance as possible (seven days in advance, minimum), and if you can, try to get the weekly rate instead of the daily rate offered by the car rental company. Most rental car companies will apply their weekly rates to five-, six-, or seven-day rentals.

### Finding the Best Rate

Especially in tourist areas, like Orlando, the various rental car companies are always running special promotions, so be sure to ask about them, and keep your eyes open for ads from the rental car companies in your local newspaper and in your favorite magazines. In addition, many of the rental car companies provide a discount to AAA members, so after getting the rental car company's best rate, ask for a AAA member discount. The Entertainment Book (described later in this book) also has discount coupons and special offers that apply to many of the popular rental car companies.

## TRAVEL TIP

If you're a member of any airline's frequent-flier program, you can often receive a rental car discount from promotional partners of that airline. Check your monthly frequent-flier statement from the airline for information about special rental car offers.

Some popular credit cards have special promotional deals with the major rental car companies, so call the customer service phone number listed on your credit cards and inquire about what deals they offer for renting a car. While you're on the phone with the credit card company, also ask if your credit card automatically provides rental car insurance if you use that credit card to pay for the rental. American Express, Diner's Club, and virtually all Visa and MasterCards (issued as part of an airline's frequent-flier program) automatically offer rental car insurance.

If you think you've found a great rental car rate, reserve the car, but continue to shop around. Call three or four other rental car companies and see if they'll beat the deal you've been offered. Many travelers believe that the best known rental car companies are always the most expensive, but this isn't always the case. You'll often be pleasantly surprised to discover that companies like Hertz, Avis, and National offer highly competitive rates once you take advantage of their special promotional deals, airline frequent-flier discounts, and/or a AAA (or any auto club) member discount.

When making a rental car reservation, make sure unlimited mileage is included in the rental price. Some rental car companies charge by the mile, in addition to the daily rental fee, so make sure you understand what's included in the price you're being quoted. Extremely low daily or weekly rental rates often do not include unlimited mileage, and once you travel above the allowed miles, you're charged a hefty fee per mile.

## Insurance

No matter what hourly, daily, or weekly rate you're quoted by the rental car companies you call, these rates do not include the various types of optional insurance options that are offered, nor is tax included in the quoted rate. If you choose to pay for all of the different insurance options, the quoted rate for the rental car often more than doubles. What most travelers don't know, however, is that they do not need all of the optional insurance, because their own regular insurance policies, as well as the travel insurance provided free of charge by some credit card companies, offer more than adequate protection.

Prior to renting a car, call the customer service number for your auto insurance company as well as your home owner's insurance company. Ask if rental car insurance is automatically offered under your existing policy. If so, you probably don't need any of the insurance offered by the rental car companies. If you rely on your existing insurance, however, and you're forced to make a claim due to an accident in the rental car, your regular insurance rates could go up in the future.

## ≡FAST FACT

One benefit of purchasing the optional insurance from the rental car companies is that your existing policies won't be affected if a claim has to be made (assuming any damage or injury claims are under the limit of the insurance you purchase).

### Rental Car Companies

The following are rental car companies in the Orlando area. When reserving your vehicle, make sure the rental car company offers airport service (either pickup at the airport or a free shuttle to their nearby pickup location). All of the nationally known car rental companies including Hertz, Avis, National, Alamo, and Budget are located within a five-minute free shuttle bus ride from the Orlando airport.

**Alamo:** ✆(800) 354-2322
**Avis:** ✆(800) 331-1212
**Budget:** ✆(800) 527-0700
**Dollar:** ✆(800) 800-4000
**Enterprise:** ✆(800) RENT-A-CAR
**Hertz:** ✆(800) 654-3131
**Hertz Gold Club Reservations:** ✆(800) CAR-GOLD
**National:** ✆(800) 227-7368
**Payless Car Rental:** ✆(800) PAY-LESS
**Rent A Wreck:** ✆(407) 823-8388
**Thrifty:** ✆(800) 367-2277

If you want to enjoy the luxury and novelty of renting a flashy sports car, such as a Jaguar, Hummer, BMW, Porsche, Mercedes,

Viper, Rolls Royce, Ferrari, Lamborghini, or Aston Martin, for example, call **Dream Cars Unlimited** at ✆ (866) 624-6396. Rentals are available by the day, week, or month. By visiting the company's Web site at ✑ *www.dreamcarsunlimited.com*, you can download and print a discount coupon. Renters must be at least twenty-five years of age, have proof of insurance coverage, and have a major credit card in their name.

## Special Services

Most of the rental car companies will provide child safety seats, either free of charge or for a small daily fee, but these seats must be reserved in advance. This will save you the hassle of having to bring your own child safety seats with you on your trip. However, you must bring your own if you want your child to sit in one on the airplane.

If you're a nonsmoker, be sure to ask for a nonsmoking vehicle when you make your reservation. Otherwise, you could get stuck with a car that reeks of smoke.

When you pick up your rental car at the airport, computer-generated driving directions and maps are often provided free of charge from the airport to virtually any location in Florida, including all of the popular hotels and attractions.

 **TRAVEL TIP**

Many rental car companies now offer cellular phone rentals; however, the rates are extremely high. If you have a handheld or transportable cellular phone that you can bring with you to Orlando, you're better off paying the roaming charges than the high daily rental and per-minute service fees associated with renting a cellular phone.

When you pick up the rental car, ask about the rental car company's policy for additional drivers. Typically, when you rent a car, only the person whose name appears on the rental agreement is legally permitted to drive the car, unless additional paperwork is completed. Some rental car companies charge to add additional names to the rental contract, allowing for multiple drivers. The following are often exempt from additional driver charges (but check with the rental car company): the renter's employer or regular fellow employee when on company business; the renter's spouse; the renter's mate, life companion, significant other, or live-in; and disabled renters who have completed a special form.

## Final Suggestions

First, ask if you're required to return the car with a full tank of gas, or if you're paying for the gas in advance. If you're required to return the car with a full tank of gas and you fail to do so (which many people do), you'll be billed up to three times the going rate per gallon of gas needed to fill the tank. Before returning the car, find a low-priced gas station and fill the tank with basic unleaded gasoline (the cheapest stuff you can find). This will fulfill your obligation to return the car with a full tank of gas.

If you pick up the car at 3:00 P.M., for example, you must return the car before 3:00 P.M. on the day your rental agreement ends or you'll automatically be billed for additional hours at a high rate. When you pick up the car, ask what time the car must be returned by to ensure that you won't be billed overtime hours, and ask what the overtime rate is.

When returning your car, plan on arriving at the airport about ninety minutes (or even two hours) prior to your scheduled flight time. You will most likely be returning your car several miles from the actual airport, and you'll need to allow ample time to return the car, take the complimentary shuttle bus to your airline terminal, check in at the airline terminal, check your bags, and get to the actual gate. It's a common problem for travelers to miss their flight because they didn't allow enough time to return their rental car, so plan accordingly.

As soon as you pick up your car, before leaving the rental car company's parking lot, make sure there is nothing obviously wrong with the vehicle. If there's a problem, report it immediately. Once you leave the rental car company's parking lot, if you notice a problem, call the rental car company and report it. Likewise, if you get stuck on the road, call the rental car company and report your situation. Free assistance, often including towing services, will be provided, and you'll often be given a replacement rental car.

Finally, after a long flight, you'll land in Orlando, pick up your rental car, and be driving in unfamiliar territory while you're tired. This increases the possibility of your becoming involved in an auto accident, so before getting behind the wheel, make sure you're totally awake and alert and that you have detailed driving directions for reaching your destination. If you're too tired to be driving, take a taxi or shuttle bus to your hotel and pick up your rental car later in the day or the following day, but be sure to call the rental car company and mention your change of plans to avoid being charged.

 **TRAVEL TIP**

If you're worried about getting lost, Hertz offers an (optional) feature in some of its rental cars, called NeverLost. The NeverLost unit identifies exactly where you are at any time, and shows and tells you how to get wherever you want to go. The additional daily cost is about $6 per day.

## Your Travel Budget

 As you begin to plan your trip, it's important to establish a basic travel budget for yourself and to stick to that budget. Once you reach your destination, you'll no doubt be tempted to dine at fancy restaurants, buy extravagant souvenirs, and participate in costly activities. When creating your budget, you'll want to make allowances for these unplanned splurges, but you'll want to maintain control over your spending at all times. Otherwise, you could easily end up with massive credit card bills after your vacation.

The first step in planning a budget is to figure out how much money you have to spend on your upcoming vacation. Next, determine how many people you'll be traveling with (and paying for), how many days you'll be away, and what you want your travel itinerary to be.

Based on this information, start pricing out airfares, hotel/motel accommodations, rental cars, and the cost of various activities (such as admission to the theme parks and dining). The checklist later in this chapter will help you predict some of the costs.

## Saving Money

Hopefully, once you've priced out everything, the total price of your planned vacation will be within your proposed budget. Before making your reservations, however, invest some time in shopping around for money-saving deals and/or packages. Finding a coupon or utilizing a deal that'll save you $50 on a hotel, for example, is money that can be used for souvenirs or kept in your bank account.

Also, you can save money by eating outside of the theme parks. Instead of having the fancy (and sometimes costly) breakfast at your Disney-owned hotel every morning during your trip, consider experiencing that breakfast once, then eating off-property on the rest of the mornings to save some money. Obviously, there's something very special (especially for kids) about eating Mickey Mouse–shaped waffles with the Disney characters roaming the dining room and meeting guests. However, this is something that doesn't need to be experienced every morning.

## ▣ TRAVEL TIP

Unless your budget is unlimited, chances are, once you get to Orlando, you will not be able to afford to do absolutely everything you'd like to during a single trip. Thus, you'll want to use this book (and your firsthand experience) to determine which activities you'd most enjoy, and focus on those to start off with.

If this isn't your first trip to The WDW Resort, you can save a lot of money by staying at a non-Disney-owned hotel/motel that's close to the theme parks. While you won't experience the legendary Disney service or the perks associated with staying at a Disney-owned hotel, the financial savings will add up quickly.

## Budget Checklist

Use this form to help you approximate the cost of your trip to The WDW Resort/Greater Orlando area in advance. Planning your schedule/itinerary before you leave and setting budgetary spending limits will help you enjoy your vacation without going into unexpected debt or spending outside of your budget.

| BUDGET CHECKLIST | | |
|---|---|---|
| Expense | Calculation | Totals |
| Adult airfare | $ _____ per ticket × <br> $ _____ (# of adults) | $ _____ |
| Child airfare | $ _____ per ticket × <br> $ _____ (# of children) | $ _____ |
| Rental car | $ _____ per day/week × <br> $ _____ (# of days/weeks) | $ _____ |
| Insurance/gas | $ _____ per day × <br> $ _____ (# of days) | $ _____ |
| Transportation <br> (taxi, bus, etc.) | $ _____ per trip × <br> $ _____ (# of people) × <br> $ _____ (# of trips) | $ _____ |
| Hotel/motel | $ _____ per night × <br> $ _____ (# of rooms) × <br> $ _____ (# of nights) | $ _____ |
| Adult Disney ticket | $ _____ per ticket × <br> $ _____ (# of people) × <br> $ _____ (# of days) | $ _____ |
| Child Disney ticket | $ _____ per ticket × <br> $ _____ (# of people) × <br> $ _____ (# of days) | $ _____ |
| Adult Universal <br> Studios ticket | $ _____ per ticket × <br> $ _____ (# of people) × <br> $ _____ (# of days) | $ _____ <br> (continued) |

## BUDGET CHECKLIST (continued)

| Expense | Calculation | Totals |
|---|---|---|
| Child Universal Studios ticket | $ _____ per ticket ×<br>$ _____ (# of people) ×<br>$ _____ (# of days) | $ _____ |
| Other attraction | $ _____ per ticket ×<br>$ _____ (# of people) ×<br>$ _____ (# of days) | $ _____ |
| Other attraction | $ _____ per ticket ×<br>$ _____ (# of people) ×<br>$ _____ (# of days) | $ _____ |
| Adult nighttime entertainment | $ _____ per person ×<br>$ _____ (# of nights) | $ _____ |
| Child nighttime entertainment | $ _____ per person ×<br>$ _____ (# of nights) | $ _____ |
| Show/movie | $ _____ per person ×<br>$ _____ (# of shows) | $ _____ |
| Total meal budget | $ _____ per person ×<br>$ _____ (# of meals) ×<br>$ _____ (# of days) | $ _____ |
| Snack/drink budget | $ _____ per person ×<br>$ _____ (# of days) | $ _____ |
| Souvenir budget | $ _____ per person | $ _____ |
| Child care | $ _____ per hour ×<br>$ _____ (# of hours) ×<br>$ _____ (# of children) | $ _____ |
| Kennel costs | $ _____ per day ×<br>$ _____ (# of days) ×<br>$ _____ (# of pets) | $ _____ |
| Airport parking | $ _____ per day ×<br>$ _____ (# of days) | $ _____ |
| Other | _____ | $ _____ |
| Other | _____ | $ _____ |
| Other | _____ | $ _____ |
| Approximate Vacation Expenses Total: | | $ _____ |

# Using a Travel Agent

 Utilizing a full-service travel agency to plan your trip and make your travel reservations will typically save you a lot of time, but not necessarily a lot of money. Most travel agents these days specialize in corporate travel or high-priced vacations and earn their income by taking a commission of the total price of the trip they coordinate for you. Thus, unless you have an established relationship with a travel agent, they're not always apt to find you the lowest possible rates. Of course, there are plenty of exceptions.

If you don't already have a reliable travel agent that you use, consider seeking out a favorable recommendation from a friend or relative as opposed to opening the telephone book. When choosing a travel agent, make sure he or she specializes in planning family vacations and is familiar with Orlando.

Hotel room brokers, discount travel agents, and hotel reservation services in the Orlando area include:

**Accommodations Express:** ☏(800) 971-7666,
  🖱 www.Accommodationsexpress.com
**Central Reservation Service:** ☏(800) 548-3311
**Check-In Reservation Services:** ☏(800) 237-1033
**Destinations Travel Service:** ☏(407) 859-3501
**Eventures Unlimited, Inc.:** ☏(800) 356-7891 (This service offers special package deals designed specifically for senior citizens interested in vacationing at The WDW Resort.)

## ≡FAST FACT

The Hotel Reservations Network in Orlando advertises up to 60 percent off hotel rates at over 300 hotels and motels in the Orlando area. This company will also help you find available hotel rooms during peak travel periods. For more information, call ☏(800) 511-5321.

# Booking Your Vacation Online

 If you have some time to invest when planning your vacation, and you have access to the Internet, you can save an absolute fortune by planning and booking your travel arrangements online. Airfares, hotels, and rental cars can all be reserved and paid for using the Web and a major credit card.

When using the Internet to plan and book your own travel, you have three primary options:

1. Visit the Web site of the specific airline, hotel chain, and/or rental car company. For example, if you're booking your airfare on **US Airways,** you'd visit ✐ *www.usairways.com.* Often, each individual airline offers discounted online-only fares and specials that cannot be obtained anywhere else. The drawback to using an airline's Web site is that to shop around for the best fares, you'll need to visit the Web sites of multiple airlines.

2. Utilize the services of an online travel-related Web site, such as **Travelocity** (✐ *www.travelocity.com*), **Expedia** (✐ *www.expedia.com*), **Orbitz** (✐ *www.orbitz.com*), or **Yahoo! Travel** (✐ *http://travel.yahoo.com*). These services allow you to quickly search all of the major airlines for the best flights and fares. You'll also find great deals on hotels, rental cars, and travel packages. When using one of these services, the more time you spend exploring them, the better your chances of saving a lot of money will be. Once you know when you want to travel, try searching for better fares by altering your travel dates slightly. Sometimes, leaving a day earlier or later, for example, can save you money. You can also try looking up various airport combinations. For example, if you're flying from New York's LaGuardia Airport to Orlando International Airport, you can also look up departing flights from Newark Airport and New York's Kennedy Airport. Checking each variable takes

only seconds using one of these online travel services.

3. If you have a somewhat flexible travel schedule, you can save between 30 and 70 percent off of airfares, hotels, and rental cars using a service such as **Priceline.com** ( *www.price line.com*), **Last Minute Travel** ( *www.lastminutetravel.com*), or **Travel Hub** ( *www.travelhub.com/airfares*).

## 📰 TRAVEL TIP

If you're planning to book your airfare, hotel, and rental car through Priceline, do so as three separate transactions, starting with your airfare. For people who book their airfares through Priceline, the company typically offers special "Insider Rates" for hotels and rental cars.

## Vacation Packages and When to Visit

 There are a variety of organizations that offer various types of discounts and travel packages to The WDW Resort, Universal Studios, and other Orlando-area destinations. A travel package might consist of any or all of the following: airfare, hotel accommodations, meals, rental car, and admission to one or more theme parks. Using the budget checklist in this chapter, calculate what it will cost you to plan your own vacation, then compare those rates with those offered by comparable travel packages from an airline or one of the following travel organizations.

In addition to contacting the various airlines directly about individual airfares or travel packages, contact organizations such as the **AAA,** which has a travel department (☎ (800) 222-7448,  *www.aaa.com*), or the **AARP** (☎ (800) 424-3410,  *www.aarp.org*).

Two travel agencies that offer an assortment of different travel packages for people interested in The WDW Resort include:

**American Express Travel:** ☎(800) 346-3607,  *www.itn.net*
**Walt Disney Travel Company:** ☎(800) 225-2024

## The Disney Club

**The Disney Club** (✆ (800) 654-6347, ✎ *www.disneyclub.com*) is a program sponsored by The Walt Disney Company that offers its members discounts on theme park tickets, Disney merchandise, and Disney-owned/operated hotel accommodations. There's an annual membership fee of $35. This program should not be confused with the Disney Vacation Club (which offers time-shares) or the Walt Disney Travel Company (which is a full-service travel agency).

## ≡FAST FACT

If you're planning a trip to The WDW Resort, plan on staying at a Disney-owned hotel, eating within Disney-owned restaurants, buying Disney merchandise, and/or visiting the theme parks, not only will you recoup the annual Disney Club membership fee, but you'll most likely save considerable money on your purchases. The discount also applies to purchases from the Disney stores as well as the Disney Store Catalog and DisneyStore.com.

## The Entertainment Book

**Entertainment Books** (✆ (800) 933-2605, ✎ *www.entertainment. com*) offer 50 percent off and two-for-one discounts at your favorite places for dining and shopping, at attractions, for sports, and for services like dry cleaning and movie rentals. Entertainment Books also include discounts at hotels and other travel services.

The Entertainment Ultimate Hotel & Travel, Dining Advantage, and National Value directories offer deep discounts toward worldwide hotels, travel, dining, retail, and services. The travel and hotel directories contain helpful amenity icons, so you can choose the hotel that best meets your needs. The pages of these directories also include bonus value savings on airlines, cruises, car rentals, and attractions.

The Entertainment Book is an extremely useful resource for finding restaurants in the Orlando area that are not located on Disney property. The book typically offers sample menus as well as money-saving offers. People with access to a rental car who can travel freely around the Orlando area will get the most out of this discount book.

## ≡FAST FACT

The 2002 Entertainment Book, which covers Orlando, offers discounts and money-saving coupons for 303 local area restaurants, over 5,000 hotels (nationwide), and special deals from rental car companies and various retail stores and tourist attractions. The Orlando edition of the Entertainment Book is priced at $35.

### The Best Times to Visit

During The WDW Resort's peak summer season (and during major holidays), you could be sharing your vacation with 40,000 to 65,000 other visitors in each theme park. Throughout the year, Saturday is each theme park's busiest day of the week. Around noon, the park is usually the most crowded. On Sundays and during the week, the park is less crowded. The drawback to visiting The WDW Resort on a weekday is that the parades and shows happen less frequently, and sometimes not at all.

As soon as you arrive at the Disney theme park of your choice (Magic Kingdom, Epcot, Disney-MGM Studios, or Disney's Animal Park), pick up a copy of the free guide-map booklet given out at the main entrances of each park. These colorful booklets contain the times for all parades and shows, describe the times and places to meet the Disney characters, and offer a detailed map of the park that lists all of the major attractions, restaurants, and amenities (restrooms, public phones, ATMs, etc.).

Anytime during the year, if it's raining, you can count on much smaller crowds than usual. Bring along rain gear (avoid umbrellas), or pick up one of the plastic Mickey Mouse rain ponchos sold throughout the park on rainy days. Expect all parades, outdoor shows, and a few outdoor rides to be cancelled or closed on rainy days. Much of the park (including most of the attractions) will, however, be open, and the lines will be far shorter.

# ⊕ HOT SPOT

Within The Magic Kingdom, you can find out exactly what the lines are like for every attraction by visiting the Information Desk/Wait Board. Similar Information Desks/Wait Boards can be found at each of the Disney theme parks and at other popular theme parks (including Universal Studios and Islands of Adventure).

For the shortest lines, visit the Disney theme parks during any weekday in the off-season. If you happen to visit on a busy day, go against the crowds. For example, you'll notice that in the morning, most people race toward the most popular rides and attractions, and these same people stake out a prime viewing spot for a parade up to two or three hours before show time. Most of the park's most popular parades happen twice each afternoon or evening. During the first parade presentation is the best time to visit all of the most popular attractions. You can catch the second showing of the parade when the crowds are greatly reduced. Likewise, when most people break for lunch or dinner, many of the lines for attractions are shorter.

The very best times to visit The WDW Resort, due to lack of crowds, are:

- The week after Thanksgiving through the week before Christmas
- The week after Labor Day until Thanksgiving week
- The second week of January through the beginning of February

Attendance is considered "average" during the following times of year. If you're planning to travel during one of these times, expect to experience lines for the most popular WDW theme park attractions between thirty minutes and ninety minutes long.

- The first week of January
- Early February until Presidents' week
- Late February until mid-March
- Late April until early June
- Late August until Labor Day
- Thanksgiving week

## Busiest Times of Year

The WDW Resort and all of the Orlando-area theme parks are the busiest during the following times of year. These times are considered "peak" travel periods. The good news is that the theme parks are open longer hours and more parades and shows are held per day, but you can expect long waits for the major theme park attractions, and you'll have to deal with relatively large crowds, even if the weather is bad.

- Presidents' week
- Late March until late April
- Mid-June until late August (the summer season)
- Christmas through New Year's Day

## Hours of Operation

Prior to choosing the exact dates for your trip (if you have flexibility), call The WDW Resort's main reservations number (☎ (407) W-DISNEY) and inquire about each theme park's hours of operation during the dates of your proposed visit. During the "off-peak" times, the parks tend to close around 7:00 P.M. or 9:00 P.M. as opposed to 11:00 P.M. or midnight during "peak" periods. The hours of operation for each theme park are also posted at the official Disney World Web site (✍ *www.disneyworld.com*).

If the parks will be closing early during off-peak times, you probably won't have to wait in any really long lines to experience attractions, so you'll get to experience a lot more each day. You will, however, have to plan evening and nighttime activities that don't include the theme parks. If you want to stay on Disney property, spending evenings and nights at Pleasure Island and/or Disney's BoardWalk will provide plenty of dining and entertainment options until as late as 2:00 A.M. (throughout the year).

##  TRAVEL TIP

When you attempt to make your hotel reservation, if your first choice for accommodations is already booked solid, make alternate reservations, but keep checking back with your first-choice hotel. Even during the busy times of year, last-minute cancellations are common.

If you're planning your Disney vacation during one of the busy periods, book your reservations as early as possible, especially if you hope to stay at one of the more popular Disney-owned hotels.

# Choosing Your Accommodations

WHILE YOU PROBABLY WON'T BE SPENDING too much time in your hotel or motel room while on vacation, you'll definitely want accommodations that are comfortable and that offer the amenities you need and want, at a price that's within your budget. This chapter will help you select the accommodations that are most suited to your needs within the Orlando area.

## Getting to the Theme Parks

 From any of the hotels and resorts on Disney property, reaching any of the Disney theme parks is as easy as catching a bus that stops in front of the hotel. The complimentary Disney Bus Service transports guests from the various hotels to the Disney theme parks and attractions (including the water parks and Downtown Disney areas). The buses typically run every fifteen to twenty minutes.

In some cases, a Disney hotel may be within walking distance to one or more of the Disney theme parks. Monorail, boat, or other transportation may also be available. When using the bus service, allow approximately thirty to forty-five minutes (including wait time) to reach your destination. All of the buses are handicap accessible and air conditioned. You'll also find that the drivers are extremely knowledgeable about the theme parks and events happening at The WDW Resort.

 **TRAVEL TIP**

For hotels, motels, and resorts located off-property, contact the hotel's front desk or concierge to determine if complimentary shuttle service is available to the parks.

## Defining Your Needs

To experience the ultimate Disney vacation and the superior service and hospitality Disney is known for, you'll probably want to stay at one of The WDW Resort's hotels. If, however, you're looking for a clean, fully functional hotel room or suite, or even a less expensive motel, either of which will save you a lot of money, staying at a non-Disney hotel is an excellent idea, especially if you're planning on renting a car.

As you make your hotel reservation, shop around for the best room rates. Non-Disney hotel rates are often negotiable, plus most will honor some type of discount program (AAA, the Entertainment Book, etc.). Before mentioning that you're a member of any discount program, ask the hotel for its best rate and negotiate the best deal you can, then mention that you'd like the added discount.

To ensure that you'll get the best room selection and best rates, make your hotel reservations as far in advance as possible and be prepared to guarantee your reservation using a major credit card. If you're having trouble locating a hotel with rooms available that offers the accommodations you're looking for, consider using the services of a travel agent.

If you need help finding accommodations and making a reservation, especially during peak travel times, consider contacting any of these organizations:

**The Kissimmee-St. Cloud Convention & Visitors Bureau:**
 ☎(407) 847-5000
**Official Visitor Center:** ☎(407) 363-5872,
 ✆ www.goflorida.com/orlando
**The Orlando/Orange County Convention & Visitors Bureau:**
 ☎(407) 363-5871

##  TRAVEL TIP

In addition to the hotel room's nightly charge, determine in advance any extra charges you'll incur, such as phone surcharges, parking charges, shuttle bus charges, an extra fee for a roll-away bed, and so on. All of these charges can easily add up.

## The WDW Resort Hotels

 As you'll discover, there are several advantages to staying at one of The WDW Resort's on-property resort hotels (accounting for over 33,000 guest rooms).

If you stay at one of the Disney-owned and -operated resort hotels, you'll be staying on Disney property and you'll be treated to the world-class service and hospitality that Disney is known for. Guests of The WDW Resort hotels have full access to the WDW Transportation bus service to travel around the resort complex. Some of the Disney resort hotels also offer their own special attractions and activities for guests that add to the overall Disney vacation experience.

### Prices

The WDW Resort hotels are divided into price-based categories. The following ranges are based on 2002 prices:

- Campground facilities (located on property) range from $34 to $77 per night.
- Value hotel rooms range from $77 to $109 per night.

- Moderate-priced hotel rooms range from $129 to $209 per night.
- Home Away From Home hotel rooms range from $279 up to over $1,800 per night.
- Deluxe hotels range from $279 to $800 (and up) per night.

## Resort Perks

The following are some of the perks you'll receive by staying on Disney property, at a WDW Resort hotel:

*Easy access to the theme parks.* No need to deal with parking your car at the theme parks: Complimentary transportation via boats, buses, and monorails carries Disney's resort guests directly to any area in the entire WDW Resort.

*Advance dining reservations.* Resort guests can make advance dining reservations for priority seating up to sixty days before their arrival at many of the more than 200 restaurants throughout The WDW Resort. Call ✆ (407) WDW-DINE to make reservations.

*Character dining opportunities.* Here's your chance to meet and dine with Mickey and his friends. Disney's famous character break-fasts are held daily at Disney's Grand Floridian Resort & Spa, Disney's Beach Club Resort, Disney's Polynesian Resort, Disney's Contemporary Resort, and Disney's Old Key West Resort.

*Preferred tee times.* If you're visiting The WDW Resort to play golf, you'll receive preferred tee times at Disney's six courses, which total ninety-nine holes of championship golf.

*Child-care services.* Enjoy a break away from your kids! Resort guests can drop off the kids at one of Disney's child-care facilities, available to resort guests for a nominal fee.

*On-property sports and recreation.* A variety of playtime activities, including tennis, swimming, and golf, are available to resort guests. Several WDW hotels offer workout facilities and full-service spas. Additional activities available to resort guests include canoeing, fishing, sailing, horseback riding, playgrounds, croquet, and shuffleboard.

*Free movies.* Complimentary Disney cartoons and full-length Disney films are shown nightly at Fort Wilderness to all resort guests.

## ≡FAST FACT

To make reservations or request color brochures, a free Disney vacation video, or other information about any of The WDW Resort hotels, call 📞(407) W-DISNEY or visit ✉ *www.disney world.com* on the Internet.

*Guaranteed entry into the theme parks.* Even on the busiest days, when the parking lots are full, resort guests using Disney transportation are guaranteed entry to all Walt Disney World theme parks and water parks.

*Central billing.* The WDW Resort identification cards, which can be used to charge food and merchandise, now also have guests' ticketing options encoded on the back. The resort ID cards are issued upon check-in, and all purchases are charged to guests' resort hotel accounts.

*Disney's Character Caravans.* Guests staying at a WDW Resort don't have to go far to say "good morning" to their favorite Disney characters. Created as a surprise send-off for guests heading to Walt Disney World theme parks, water parks, and other attractions, Disney's Character Caravans are the newest enhancement for guests staying at the Disney resorts. Three mornings each week, the characters head to various resorts in a custom-painted motorcoach to visit guests. Disney tunes are played to signal the arrival of the caravan. Following a brief welcome, the characters enter the resort lobby to meet and greet guests.

## All-Star Resorts

### Hotel Rate Classification: Value

The All-Star Music Resort, All-Star Sports Resort, and All-Star Movies Resort hotels are the least expensive on Disney property. Each of these complexes has 1,920 nice, but no-frills rooms, consisting of two double beds, a color TV, a small amount of furniture, and a bathroom. The rooms aren't very large (260 square feet), but if you're looking to stay on Disney property and don't want to spend a fortune, these no-frills hotels are your best bet.

Transportation to all theme parks and attractions is available via the WDW Transportation buses. Expect to spend between thirty and forty-five minutes (each way) traveling from these WDW hotels to most of the Disney attractions via the WDW Transportation Bus service.

To reach guests staying at the **All-Star Music Resort,** call ✆ (407) 939-6000. Guests staying at the **All-Star Sports Resort** can be reached by calling ✆ (407) 939-5000. You can reach people at the **All-Star Movies Resort** by calling ✆ (407) 939-7000, or ask the Disney operator to connect you if you're calling from a courtesy phone or WDW Resort hotel room phone.

## Beach Club and Yacht Club

### Hotel Rate Classification: Deluxe

Located along a lovely twenty-five-acre lake, these are two of the nicest Disney resort hotels, both inside and out. The Beach Club and the Yacht Club are modeled after New England seashore hotels from the 1880s. Both are full-service hotels that are within walking distance from Epcot.

The Beach Club offers 583 guest rooms, while the Yacht Club offers 630 guest rooms. Both have a nautical theme and absolutely fabulous outdoor pool/beach areas. Whether or not you're staying at one of these two hotels, checking out these hotels' joint 750,000-gallon pool area is worthwhile. Both hotels also offer a variety of indoor and outdoor activities such as boat rentals, tennis, a video arcade, a playground, and a full-service health club.

The **Beach Club** resort's phone number is ☎ (407) 934-8000. The phone number for the **Yacht Club** is ☎ (407) 934-7000. To reach a guest at one of these hotels, call the number directly or ask the Disney operator to connect you if you're calling from a courtesy phone or another WDW Resort hotel room phone.

## BoardWalk Inn

### Hotel Rate Classification: Deluxe

This hotel offers 378 rooms, all decorated with cherry wood furniture. All rooms have two double beds or one king-size bed and a daybed. Room rates are based on the view offered. If you want the best view, be sure to request a room overlooking the Seven Seas Lagoon.

The hotel offers several restaurants, plus the restaurants at Disney's BoardWalk, a full health club facility, day care and children's programs, tennis courts, swimming pool, and all sorts of other amenities that you'd expect from one of Disney's full-service resorts.

To reach guests staying at this resort, call ☎ (407) 939-5100 or ask the Disney operator to connect you if you're calling from a courtesy phone or WDW Resort hotel room phone.

## ═FAST FACT

One of the nicest features of this hotel is that all rooms also have a private balcony or patio. This hotel is located in the heart of Disney's BoardWalk, so it overlooks the Seven Seas Lagoon and is within walking distance of Epcot.

## BoardWalk Villas

### Hotel Rate Classification: Home Away From Home

While The BoardWalk Villas are part of Disney's Vacation Club time-share program and are typically available only to members, when vacancies exist (especially during off-peak times), these villas are offered as hotel rooms to the general public. Studio, one-, two-, and three-bedroom villas include kitchenettes, or kitchens are available, with amenities that typical hotel rooms don't offer. The BoardWalk Grand Villas offer the ultimate in comfort and luxury for couples and families (up to twelve people). These Grand Villas are also among the most expensive accommodations you'll find anywhere within The WDW Report complex.

To reach guests staying at this hotel, call ✆ (407) 939-6200 or ask the Disney operator to connect you if you're calling from a courtesy phone or WDW Resort hotel room phone.

### Caribbean Beach
#### Hotel Rate Classification: Moderate
Located within The WDW Resort complex, the Caribbean Beach Resort is a 200-acre resort unto itself, complete with its own indoor and outdoor activities. The 2,000-plus rooms offered here, however, are pretty basic. Most rooms contain two double beds and are designed to sleep four people. The entire resort consists of two-story buildings that are divided into clusters. Each group of buildings has its own pool and beach area, named after an island in the Caribbean. The resort has a central check-in area and food court. Everything has a tropical island feel.

 **TRAVEL TIP**

> One of the biggest problems with this massive hotel is that all of the buildings look identical, so it's easy to get lost. If you're staying here, make sure you don't forget what section you're in as well as your room number.

This is one of The WDW Resort's moderately priced hotels. If you're staying here, however, you'll save time each day by renting a car. If you rely on WDW Transportation buses to get you to and from the various theme parks, you'll wind up spending a considerable amount of time each day commuting.

To reach guests staying at this hotel, call ✆ (407) 934-3400 or ask the Disney operator to connect you if you're calling from a courtesy phone or WDW Resort hotel room phone.

## Contemporary Resort

### Hotel Rate Classification: Deluxe

This was the very first WDW Resort hotel and is the only one that the Disney monorail system passes directly through. This fifteen-story A-frame tower has 1,041 rooms, six shops, three restaurants, two snack shops, two lounges, its own marina, a manmade beach, a full health club, a pool (complete with water slide), two Jacuzzis, and an arcade. It's also one of the most centrally located hotels to most of the resort's attractions.

To reach guests staying at this hotel, call ✆ (407) 824-1000 or ask the Disney operator to connect you if you're calling from a courtesy phone or WDW Resort hotel room phone.

## Coronado Springs Resort

### Hotel Rate Classification: Moderate

The Coronado Springs Resort features 1,967 moderately priced guest rooms that encircle a fifteen-acre lagoon. This resort is divided into three two-story guest buildings, each with its own pool. The hotel also features a food court area, a lounge, a salon, and a health club. In addition to the basic rooms, which are equipped with two double beds (designed to sleep four people), a coffee maker, and ironing equipment, the hotel also has a limited number of executive suites, VIP suites, and junior suites.

To reach guests staying at this hotel, call ✆ (407) 939-1000 or ask the Disney operator to connect you if you're calling from a courtesy phone or WDW Resort hotel room phone.

## Port Orleans Riverside

### Hotel Rate Classification: Moderate

Disney's Port Orleans Riverside (formally Dixie Landings) is divided into two primary sections, the Mansion area and the Bayou. In all, there are 2,048 rooms within this property. Most of the rooms have two double beds; however, some are furnished with a king-size bed and have space for portable twin beds that can be brought into the room for children (for a small extra fee).

To reach guests staying at this hotel, call ☎ (407) 934-6000 or ask the Disney operator to connect you if you're calling from a courtesy phone or WDW Resort hotel room phone.

## ≡FAST FACT

Transportation via the WDW Transportation bus system is provided to all of the theme parks and attractions throughout the resort complex. The Downtown Disney area, however, can only be reached via a shuttle boat.

## Walt Disney Dolphin and Swan Resorts
### Hotel Rate Classification: Moderate/Deluxe

Unlike many of the other official WDW Resort hotels that are owned and operated by Disney, the Swan is operated by Westin Hotels, while the Dolphin is operated by ITT Sheraton. Each room at the Swan offers one king-size bed or two queen-size beds, although special suites are available. The Dolphin rooms are furnished with two double beds or one king-size bed, and suites are available.

Both hotels have full-service restaurants and a wide range of activities and amenities, including a full-service health club, a salon, tennis, swimming pools, children's programs, and shopping. These hotels also have a special Web site: ✑ *www.swandolphin.com.*

To reach guests staying at the **Swan** or **Dolphin**, call ☎ (407) 934-4000, or ask the Disney operator to connect you if you're calling from a courtesy phone or WDW Resort hotel room phone.

## Fort Wilderness Resort & Campground
### Hotel Rate Classification: Home Away From Home

In addition to providing 784 campsites (between 25 and 65 feet in length), Fort Wilderness offers 408 Wilderness Homes and Cabins (which have air conditioning and full amenities).

Many of the sites offer cable TV connections (for RVs), electricity and water hookups, and sanitary disposal. The sites also feature a picnic table, a paved driveway pad, and a charcoal grill. Restrooms, showers, ice machines, telephones, and a laundry room are available at the campsites.

The Wilderness Homes are designed to hold up to six people (four adults and two children). The log cabins are more rustic in design than other Disney Resort hotel accommodations, but each has a private deck.

Fort Wilderness is located within walking distance from the River Country water park. Transportation to and from the other theme parks is available via the WDW Transportation bus system or water shuttle (which is faster). Golf carts can also be rented for use around the campground facility.

To reach guests staying at this hotel, call ✆ (407) 824-2900 or ask the Disney operator to connect you if you're calling from a courtesy phone or WDW Resort hotel room phone.

# ⊕ HOT SPOT

The campsites offer the cheapest way to stay on Disney property. Campsites with partial hookup start at around $35 per night.

## Grand Floridian Resort and Spa
### Hotel Rate Classification: Deluxe

Located along the Seven Seas Lagoon, the Grand Floridian is a 900-room resort with a Victorian theme that truly defines the word "elegance." In addition to offering elegant décor, full-service restaurants, and top-quality Disney service, this resort also offers business services for guests, a health club, a luxurious full-service day spa, and plenty of on-site activities. The Grand Floridian is located along the Disney monorail system, so getting to and from The Magic Kingdom, Epcot, and the Ticket and Transportation Center is easy and fun.

To reach guests staying at this hotel, call ☎ (407) 824-3000 or ask the Disney operator to connect you if you're calling from a courtesy phone or WDW Resort hotel room phone.

## Old Key West Resort

**Hotel Rate Classification: Home Away From Home**

This resort complex is considered the main flagship property of Disney's Vacation Club time-share. While membership is normally required, when vacancies are available, especially during the off-peak season, villas can be rented by nonmembers. Studios as well as one-, two-, and three-bedroom villas are available. All offer a kitchenette, a living room, and a bathroom in addition to the bedroom(s). Guests also enjoy the villas' whirlpool tubs and over-size showers.

If you're not a member of Disney's Vacation Club, call the regular reservation number ☎ (407) W-Disney for room availability. To reach guests staying at this hotel, call ☎ (407) 827-7700 or ask the Disney operator to connect you if you're calling from a courtesy phone or WDW Resort hotel room phone.

## Polynesian Resort

**Hotel Rate Classification: Deluxe**

This hotel offers guest rooms and has a monorail stop right outside the door, providing easy access to The Magic Kingdom, Epcot, and the Ticket and Transportation Center. The Polynesian also has multiple restaurants, two swimming pools, an arcade, and a playground.

To reach guests staying at this hotel, call ☎ (407) 824-2000 or ask the Disney operator to connect you if you're calling from a courtesy phone or WDW Resort hotel room phone.

## ≡FAST FACT

One of the classic nighttime attractions offered at this resort is the Polynesian Luau, presented nightly at 6:45 P.M. and 9:30 P.M. This dinner show is open to everyone and is priced at $47.80 per adult and $24.81 per child. Reservations are required.

## Port Orleans Resort-French Quarter
### Hotel Rate Classification: Moderate
Modeled after the historic French Quarter of New Orleans, the Port Orleans resort offers 1,008 rooms located in seven three-story buildings. Most of the rooms offer two double beds and are designed to accommodate families of four. Adjoining rooms are available but can't be guaranteed when you make your reservation. WDW Transportation buses take guests to and from all of the Disney theme parks and attractions; however, water shuttle service is available to the Downtown Disney area.

To reach guests staying at this hotel, call ✆ (407) 934-5000 or ask the Disney operator to connect you if you're calling from a courtesy phone or WDW Resort hotel room phone.

## Villas at the Disney Institute
### Hotel Rate Classification: Home Away From Home
The Villas at the Disney Institute are for guests of the Disney Institute and are located within walking distance of the Disney Institute's main activity areas. All of these villas are designed to accommodate families (up to five or six people) and offer full kitchen facilities. One-bedroom bungalows as well as one- and two-bedroom townhouses are available. For the ultimate in style and luxury, the Villas at the Disney Institute offer Grand Vista Homes, which easily accommodate up to eight people, but are priced between $1,000 and $1,300 per night.

Unless you're planning to spend most of your time at the Disney Institute itself, you'll probably want to rent a car in order to get to and from the various Disney theme parks and attractions, although WDW Transportation bus service is provided.

To reach guests staying at this hotel, call ☎ (407) 827-1100 or ask the Disney operator to connect you if you're calling from a courtesy phone or WDW Resort hotel room phone.

## Disney's Wilderness Lodge

### Hotel Rate Classification: Deluxe

This hotel looks like a giant log cabin with two authentic totem poles in the front and offers 728 rooms, many of which are equipped with queen-size beds and bunk beds, or two sets of bunk beds, which is a favorite among kids/teens.

The Villas at Disney's Wilderness Lodge offer more family-oriented Home Away From Home accommodations.

To reach guests staying at this hotel, call ☎ (407) 824-3200 or ask the Disney operator to connect you if you're calling from a courtesy phone or WDW Resort hotel room phone.

##  TRAVEL TIP

You'll probably want to have a rental car available if you're staying here, in order to avoid the daily commute time associated with riding the WDW Transportation buses from the hotel to the various theme parks and back. This rustic-looking hotel with a full complement of modern amenities is truly in the woods, so it isn't within walking distance of any of the theme parks.

## Shades of Green on Walt Disney World Resort

Formally known as the Disney Inn, this 288-room complex is located along one of Disney's popular PGA championship eighteen-hole golf courses. Golf, tennis, swimming, a fitness center, and a game room are among the activities offered.

This resort is operated as an Armed Forces Recreation Center for the exclusive use of military members and their families. For reservations, call ☎ (407) 824-3600. (Reservations for this property cannot be booked through ☎ (407) W-DISNEY.)

## The Celebration Hotel

While not located on The WDW Resort's property, the Celebration Hotel can be found in the heart of Celebration, Florida—the town that Disney built. This independently owned, 150-room hotel reflects the charm of historic America's small-town inns, yet offers top-notch amenities. Room rates begin at around $100 per night for this quiet and elegant resort hotel. It's about a ten-minute drive (5 miles) to the various Disney theme parks and transportation is provided.

The Celebration Hotel is located at 700 Bloom Street, Celebration, Florida. The hotel's main number is ☎ (407) 566-6000; for reservations call ☎ (888) 499-3800, or check out their Web site at ⌨ www.celebrationhotel.com.

## Animal Kingdom Lodge
### Hotel Rate Classification: Deluxe

This is a 1,307-room, African themed (and decorated) resort featuring deluxe guest rooms and luxury suites. Rates start at just over $200 per night, but the atmosphere alone makes these accommodations worth every penny. What make this resort so special are the wild animals that coexist with the guests. To reach guests staying at this unique hotel, call ☎ (407) 934-7639.

## ⊕ HOT SPOT

Over 1,000 exotic animals live at Disney's Animal Kingdom, and guests of this resort will find themselves overlooking a thirty-three-acre African savanna. So, instead of looking out the window or off the balcony and seeing a parking lot, swimming pool, or golf course, what guests see are incredible views of real-life giraffes, zebras, antelopes, and other wild animals.

## Pop Century Resort

### Hotel Rate Classification: Value

A new, 5,760-room resort is currently being built that will send guests on a trip back through American popular culture with over-size icons representing each decade of the twentieth century. This new resort complex will open in phases, starting in 2002.

## Vacation Club at Eagle Pines

### Hotel Rate Classification: Home Away From Home

This new resort property will feature 600 villas designed to complement and enhance the beautiful setting found at Disney's Eagle Pines golf course. The atmosphere and elegance found in the coastal communities of Southeast Florida (Palm Beach and Boca Raton) will be re-created in the resort's design and tropical landscaping. This resort will open in spring/summer 2004.

## ≡FAST FACT

One of the benefits of staying at a WDW Resort is that as a guest, you can take advantage of the amenities at other WDW Resorts. You can use The WDW Resort bus transportation system (for free) to travel from location to location within Disney property.

# Universal Orlando Accommodations

If you choose to stay near Universal Studios Escape (where you'll find Universal Studios Florida, Islands of Adventure, and CityWalk), this area also contains several conveniently located, on-property hotels. In conjunction with your stay at any of these properties, special theme park admission deals and travel packages are available.

Following in the footsteps of The WDW Resort, Universal Studios Escape is quickly becoming a stand-alone vacation desti-nation, complete with theme parks, restaurants, resorts, activities, and just about everything else a vacationer could possibly want—all offered on-property.

Now that Universal Studios Florida, Islands of Adventure, and CityWalk are in full operation, travelers to Orlando can complete their vacation by staying at one of the on-property resorts.

## The Portofino Bay Hotel

**Reservations:** ☎ (888) 322-5541

✍ *www.uescape.com*

The first Universal Studios Escape on-property resort to open was the Portofino Bay Hotel (owned and operated by Loews Hotels), which is within walking distance from the theme parks and CityWalk (however, complimentary transportation is provided). This resort opened in the summer of 1999 and offers Mediterranean architecture and landscaping. The buildings surround a beautiful manmade bay.

The Portofino Bay Hotel contains 750 guest rooms, all featuring a state-of-the-art security system. In addition to offering all of the amenities you'd expect from a prestigious resort, the Portofino Bay Hotel offers several advantages to Universal Studios Escape guests. For example, guests of the hotel are invited to enter the theme parks one hour before the general public. This means that for the first hour, there are virtually no lines for any of the most popular rides and attractions offered within either theme park.

## ═FAST FACT

A wide range of room rates are available, based on season, type of guest room (or suite), and the room's view. Room rates begin around $250 per night and go up to over $2,500 per night for a multibedroom suite.

The Portofino Bay Hotel is an upscale, family-oriented resort with eight restaurants (with many more dining options available at CityWalk). There's also a 10,600-square-foot, fully equipped spa (offering Swedish massage, wraps, aromatherapy tubs, and a full-service salon). Outdoor activities include a Roman aqueduct-styled pool with a water slide, a private villa pool, three whirlpools, and a children's pool. In addition, you'll find an outdoor jogging, walking, and bicycle path and two bocci ball courts.

## The Hard Rock Hotel

Reservations: ☏ (888) 322-5541

🖳 www.uescape.com

Rock legends and families alike will receive superstar treatment at the Hard Rock Hotel, which opened in late 2000. Designed in the architectural style of a California mission, this resort caters to a hip crowd, offering 654 guestrooms, suites, and bungalows. The resort also offers two restaurants and bars, a music-filled pool area, a fitness center, retail shops, and a children's activity center.

Guests of this resort receive early admission to the theme parks, priority seating at certain restaurants, plus the ability to purchase length-of-stay theme park tickets. This is definitely a more adult-oriented hotel and will appeal to guests looking for an upbeat party atmosphere. It's ideal for spring breakers, young business travelers, honeymooners, and adults traveling alone.

## Royal Pacific Resort

Reservations: ☏ (888) 322-5541

🖳 www.uescape.com

The 1,000-guest room property offers elaborate landscaping, waterfalls, and lagoons, plus it provides a unique design that will make guests feel as if they've been transported to the enchanted isles of the South Pacific. The resort offers world-class Loews Hotel service and accommodations, plus a wide range of amenities. A variety of dining options includes a restaurant, a pool snack bar, and the Village Bazaar featuring a medley of fast-food options. There are retail shops, a business center, fitness and children's activity centers, plus meeting and function facilities including a 28,000-square-foot ballroom.

Resort guests will also enjoy an exclusive theme park benefits package including front-of-the-line access, early theme park admission, complimentary on-site transportation, priority restaurant seating, character dining opportunities, destination-wide charging privileges, and more.

## ≡FAST FACT

At the time this book was written, room rates were not yet available. Call ✆(888) 322-5541 for details.

## Orlando-Area Accommodations

 In the Orlando area, there are literally hundreds of motels and hotels, as well as luxury suites where you can stay. These facilities are located outside of Disney property, but some offer free shuttle service to and from Disney and other nearby attractions.

Many non-Disney hotels are substantially cheaper than the Disney resort hotels, or at the very least offer a better value. If you're a AAA member, be sure to check out the *TourBook* for Florida (available free of charge at any AAA office or by calling ✆(800) AAA-HELP). This book lists Orlando-area hotels rated by AAA, many of which offer discounts to members. Be sure to inquire about additional AAA discounts when renting a car or visiting any Orlando-area attraction.

For about the same price as a "value" or "moderate" room at a WDW Resort hotel, you could enjoy a stay at a top-rated and often luxury hotel or resort that's located outside of Disney property but only a few minutes' drive away via a complimentary shuttle bus that's provided by the hotel or via rental car.

In fact, the independent hotels located outside of Disney property are so competitive that basic rooms are available for as little as $50 per night. A deluxe two-bedroom suite that's complete with a kitchen, living room, and plenty of amenities and hotel services can be easily found starting as low as $150 per night (less if you receive a discount using the Entertainment Book or another discount hotel program).

## Benefits

By staying at an independent or chain hotel outside of The WDW Resort, you'll get more for your money (or save money). You can have a full apartment-style suite for the same price as a "moderately" priced room at a WDW Resort hotel. These suites and apartment-style accommodations offer multiple bedrooms, giving the people you're traveling with some added privacy and more personal space. (This will result in a more stress-free vacation for everyone and could reduce the arguments that are common when family members travel together.) Plus, with a fully equipped kitchen or kitchenette, you can make your own breakfasts and/or lunches and save on meal expenses.

If you want to experience the ultimate Disney vacation and the superior service and hospitality that Disney is known for, stay at one of The WDW Resort hotels. If, however, you're looking for a clean, fully functional hotel room or suite that'll save you a lot of money, staying at a non-Disney hotel is an excellent idea, especially if you're planning on renting a car.

## ═══FAST FACT

The Orlando/Orange County Convention & Visitors Bureau (☎(407) 363-5871) reports that in the Orlando area, there are more than 82,000 hotel rooms available. For a complete listing of hotels, call this visitors bureau.

## Area Hotels

The following are hotels, motels, and resorts located in the Orlando, Lake Buena Vista, or Kissimmee areas that are close to The WDW Resort, Universal Studios Escape, and/or other popular attractions. The rates for these hotels vary based on season and room availability, so contact each hotel directly for exact rates and availability for the dates you plan on visiting. All rates listed are approximations (subject to change) and are based on double occupancy.

---

**KEY:**

🛏 = Hotel/Motel Name

☎ = Phone Number

**$** = Price Range per Night
 **$:** $0–$50 per night
 **$$:** $51–$75 per night
 **$$$:** $76–$99 per night
 **$$$$:** $100–$150 per night
 **$$$$$:** $151–$200 per night
 **$$$$$$:** $201+ per night

🚗 = Distance from The Disneyland Resort by Car

---

🛏 **Adam's Mark of Orlando,** ☎ (407) 859-1500 or (800) 231-7883, 🚗 20 minutes, **$$$/$$$$**

🛏 **Arnold Palmer's Bay Hill Club & Lodge,** ☎ (407) 876-2429 or (800) 523-5999, 🚗 20 minutes, **$$$/$$$$**

🛏 **Baymont Inn,** ☎ (407) 240-0500 or (800) 428-3438, 🚗 15 minutes, **$$/$$$**

🛏 **Best Western Kissimmee,** ☎ (407) 846-2221 or (800) 944-0062, 🚗 20 minutes, **$**

🛏 **Best Western Lake Buena Vista Hotel,** ☎ (407) 828-2424 or (800) 348-3765, 🚗 On WDW Resort property, **$$$$/$$$$$$**

🛏 **Best Western Orlando West,** ☎ (407) 841-8600 or (800) 645-6386, 🚗 25 minutes, **$**

🛏 **Best Western Plaza International,** ☎ (407) 345-8195 or (800) 645-7160, 🚗 10 minutes, **$/$$$**

**Buena Vista Suites,** (407) 239-8588 or (800) 537-7737, 5 minutes, **$$$$**

**Caribe Royale Resort Suites,** (407) 238-8000 or (800) 823-8300, 5 minutes, **$$$$**

**The Castle Doubletree Hotel,** (407) 345-1511 or (800) 952-2785, 20 minutes, **$$$$/$$$$$$**

**Clarion Maingate,** (407) 396-4000 or (800) 568-3352, 3 minutes, **$$/$$$$**

**The Clarion Universal of Orlando,** (407) 351-5009 or (800) 445-7299, 15 minutes, **$/$$$**

**Comfort Suites Orlando,** (407) 351-5050, 10 minutes, **$/$$$**

**Courtyard By Marriott,** (800) 223-9930, On WDW Resort property, **$$$$/$$$$$**

**Courtyard Marriott,** (407) 239-6900 or (800) 635-8684, 10 minutes, **$$/$$$$**

**Days Inn Colony Plaza,** (407) 656-3333, 30 minutes, **$$/$$$**

**Days Inn Convention Center/Sea World,** (407) 352-8700 or (800) 224-5055, 15 minutes, **$$/$$$**

**Days Inn East of Universal Studios,** (407) 351-3800, 20 minutes, **$$/$$$**

**Days Inn Lake Buena Vista,** (407) 239-4441 or (800) 224-5058, 3 minutes, **$$/$$$**

**Delta Orlando Resort,** (407) 351-3340 or (800) 634-4763, 15 minutes, **$$$$**

**Doubletree Guest Suites,** (407) 934-1000 or (800) 222-8733, On WDW Resort property, **$$$$/$$$$$$**

🛏 **Doubletree Hotel,** ✆ (407) 239-4646 or (800) 521-3297, 🚗 3 minutes, **$$$$**

🛏 **Econolodge Maingate Hawaiian Resort,** ✆ (407) 396-2000 or (800) 365-6935, 🚗 3 minutes, **$$/$$$**

🛏 **Embassy Suites International Drive/Jamaican Court,** ✆ (407) 345-8250 or (800) 327-9797, 🚗 10 minutes, **$$$$**

🛏 **Embassy Suites International Drive South,** ✆ (407) 352-1400 or (800) 433-7275, 🚗 20 minutes, **$$$$/$$$$$**

🛏 **Embassy Suites Lake Buena Vista Resort,** ✆ (407) 239-1144 or (800) 257-8483, 🚗 5 minutes, **$$$$**

🛏 **Fairfield Inn By Marriott,** ✆ (407) 363-1944 or (800) 363-1944, 🚗 10 minutes, **$$/$$$**

🛏 **Grosvenor Resort,** ✆ (407) 828-4444 or (800) 624-4109, 🚗 On WDW Resort property, **$$$$/$$$$$$**

🛏 **Hampton Inn at Universal Studios,** ✆ (407) 351-6716 or (800) 231-8395, 🚗 15 minutes, **$$/$$$**

🛏 **Hampton Inn–International Drive Area,** ✆ (407) 363-7886, 🚗 10 minutes, **$$/$$$**

🛏 **Hampton Inn Maingate Hotel,** ✆ (407) 396-8484 or (800) 243-8440, 🚗 5 minutes, **$$/$$$**

🛏 **Hampton Inn South of Universal Studios,** ✆ (407) 345-1112 or (800) 763-1100, 🚗 15 minutes, **$$/$$$**

🛏 **Hilton,** ✆ (407) 827-4000 or (800) 782-4414, 🚗 On WDW Resort property, **$$$$$$**

🛏 **Holiday Inn Express International Drive,** ✆ (407) 351-4430 or (800) 365-6935, 🚗 15 minutes, **$$/$$$**

🛏 **Holiday Inn International Drive Resort,** ✆ (407) 351-3500 or (800) 206-2747, 🚗 15 minutes **$$/$$$**

**Holiday Inn Main Gate East,** ☎ (407) 396-4488 or (800) 366-5437, 🚗 5 minutes, **$$/$$$$**

**Holiday Inn Sunspree,** ☎ (407) 239-4500 or (800) 366-6299, 🚗 5 minutes, **$$$/$$$$**

**Holiday Inn Universal Studios,** ☎ (407) 351-3333 or (800) 327-1364, 🚗 15 minutes, **$$/$$$**

**Homewood Suites Maingate at the Parkway,** ☎ (407) 396-2229 or (800) 255-4543, 🚗 5 minutes, **$$$$**

**Howard Johnson Inn Maingate East,** ☎ (407) 396-1748 or (800) 288-4678, 🚗 5 minutes, **$$/$$$**

**Howard Johnson's Plaza Resort,** ☎ (407) 351-2000 or (800) 327-3808, 🚗 20 minutes, **$$/$$$$**

**Hyatt Regency Grand Cypress Hotel,** ☎ (407) 239-1234 or (800) 233-1234, 🚗 3 minutes, **$$$$$/$$$$$$**

**Kingstonian Resort,** ☎ (407) 846-1530 or (800) 816-1530, 🚗 20 minutes, **$$/$$$**

**Knights Inn Maingate,** ☎ (407) 396-4200 or (800) 944-0062, 🚗 5 minutes, **$/$$**

**Magic Castle Inn**, ☎ (407) 396-1212 or (800) 446-5669, 🚗 10 minutes, **$$/$$$**

**The Omni Rosen Center Hotel,** ☎ (407) 354-9840 or (800) 204-7234, 🚗 15 minutes, **$$$$$/$$$$$$**

**Parc Corniche Resort,** ☎ (407) 239-7100 or (800) 446-2721, 🚗 6 minutes, **$$/$$$$$$**

**Peabody Orlando,** ☎ (407) 352-4000 or (800) 732-2639, 🚗 20 minutes, **$$$$$$**

**Quality Inn Plaza,** ☎ (407) 345-8585 or (800) 999-8585, 🚗 15 minutes, **$$/$$$**

**Radisson Barcelo Hotel Orlando,** ☎ (407) 345-0505 or (800) 333-3333, 🚗 15 minutes, **$$$$**

**Radisson Inn Lake Buena Vista,** ☎ (407) 239-8400 or (800) 333-3333, 🚗 5 minutes, **$$$$**

**Ramada Plaza Gateway,** ☎ (407) 396-4400 or (800) 327-9170, 🚗 3 minutes, **$$/$$$$$$**

**Ramada Suites by SeaWorld,** ☎ (407) 239-0707 or (800) 633-1405, 🚗 10 minutes, **$$$$**

**Rosenpleza Hotel,** ☎ (407) 352-9700 or (800) 627-8258, 🚗 15 minutes, **$$$$/$$$$$$**

**Royal Plaza Hotel,** ☎ (407) 828-2828 or (800) 248-7890, 🚗 On WDW Resort property, **$$$$/$$$$$$**

**Sheraton Four Points Lakeside,** ☎ (407) 396-2222 or (800) 848-0801, 🚗 5 minutes, **$$/$$$**

**Sheraton Studio City,** ☎ (407) 239-3100 or (877) 668-9330, 🚗 15 minutes, **$$$$$/$$$$$$**

**Sheraton World Resort,** ☎ (407) 352-1100 or (800) 325-3535, 🚗 12 minutes, **$$$$**

**Summerfield Suites Hotel,** ☎ (407) 352-2400 or (800) 830-4964, 🚗 20 minutes, **$$$$$/$$$$$$**

**Summerfield Suites Lake Buena Vista,** ☎ (407) 238-0777 or (800) 830-4964, 🚗 6 minutes, **$$$$$/$$$$$$**

**Travel Lodge Maingate Hotel,** ☎ (407) 396-0100 or (800) 327-9151, 🚗 5 minutes, **$**

**Travel Lodge Orlando South,** ☎ (407) 345-8000 or (800) 346-1551, 🚗 20 minutes, **$$/$$$**

**Universal Tower Resort Hotel,** ☎ (407) 351-2100 or (800) 327-1366, 🚗 20 minutes, **$$$$**

*Note:* Travel times, as reported by each hotel, motel, or resort, are approximate and will vary based on traffic and weather conditions.

### Time-Shares

No matter where you go in Orlando, various companies, including the Walt Disney Company, will try hard to get you interested in purchasing time-share vacation packages. If you're interested in learning more about some of the time-share vacation opportunities available in the Orlando area, contact these companies:

**A Time Share Resale Broker:** ☎(407) 273-0559
**All Timeshare Services, Inc.:** ☎(800) 266-8735
**Disney Vacation Club:** ☎(800) 500-3990,
   🖰 *www.disneyvacationclub.com*
**Hilton Grand Vacations Club:** ☎(407) 238-2600
**Sheraton/Vistana Resort:** ☎(407) 239-3100
**Time Share Resales of America:** ☎(800) 789-2718
**Time Share Re-Sellers:** ☎(800) Own-4-Fun

## ≡FAST FACT

Just for sitting through a sales presentation, you'll be offered all sorts of incentives, ranging from free (or discounted) admission to popular attractions, free (or discounted) hotel accommodations, free meals, and/or other incentives.

# Packing for Your Vacation

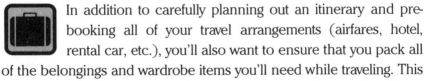 In addition to carefully planning out an itinerary and pre-booking all of your travel arrangements (airfares, hotel, rental car, etc.), you'll also want to ensure that you pack all of the belongings and wardrobe items you'll need while traveling. This section will help you actually put together the ultimate packing list.

### The Orlando Climate

To find out the current weather in Orlando, be sure to watch

The Weather Channel, check the weather map in *USA Today*, or visit the WDW Web site at ✑ *www.disneyworld.com* for an up-to-date weather report. You can also call ✆ (407) 824-4104 for Walt Disney Resort weather. Another option is to visit one of these Web sites:

**MSNBC Weather:** ✑ *www.msnbc.com*

**USA Today:** ✑ *www.usatoday.com/weather*

**Weather Channel Online:** ✑ *www.weather.com*

**Yahoo! Weather:** ✑ *http://weather.yahoo.com*

| AVERAGE TEMPERATURES AT THE WALT DISNEY WORLD RESORT | | | |
|---|---|---|---|
| Month | Average High Temperature (°F) | Average Low Temperature (°F) | Average Rainfall |
| January | 70 | 50 | 2.2" |
| February | 72 | 51 | 2.9" |
| March | 77 | 56 | 3.3" |
| April | 82 | 61 | 2.2" |
| May | 88 | 66 | 4.0" |
| June | 90 | 71 | 7.4" |
| July | 92 | 73 | 7.8" |
| August | 92 | 73 | 6.3" |
| September | 90 | 73 | 5.6" |
| October | 84 | 65 | 2.8" |
| November | 78 | 57 | 1.8" |
| December | 71 | 54 | 1.8" |

## Theme Park Attire

The trick to dressing appropriately at any theme park is not to wear the trendiest or most stylish outfits. Comfort and protection from the sun are the key! On hot days, wear light and comfortable clothing. On cooler days, wear layers that can be removed and that aren't too bulky. (You can always store clothing items in the lockers available at the theme parks.)

A hat and sunglasses are virtually always a must. Even if the skies are overcast, it's still possible to get sunburned, so make sure that you use powerful sunblock on all exposed skin. This is particularly important with kids.

Finally, comfortable shoes should round out your theme park attire. If you're traveling with kids, or plan to experience rides where you get wet, bring along an extra change of clothes for everyone and store it in a locker (or within your car) until it is needed. Ideally, you'll want to keep your hands as free as possible, so try to avoid heavy purses, backpacks, and shoulder bags. Waist packs are an excellent solution for storing smaller items such as wallets, glasses, keys, and small cameras.

On rainy days, many people are inclined to bring an umbrella to the theme parks. This is a bad idea. Navigating around within the theme parks (among the crowds) is particularly difficult with an open umbrella. You're better off wearing a waterproof hat, raincoat, or one of the plastic rain ponchos sold at the theme parks for about $5 each.

Before getting dressed in the morning, find out what the weather will be like for the day and dress accordingly, keeping in mind that at night the temperature may drop.

## ≡FAST FACT

Due to heightened security measures, all bags you carry into a theme park will be hand-searched by security personnel at the park, so plan accordingly.

### What to Carry with You

All of the airlines have changed their policies regarding carry-on luggage. This is what you physically carry onto the airplane with you and store either under the seat or in the overhead compartment. Virtually all of the airlines are now strict about allowing only one or two carry-on bags (including a purse or laptop case) per passenger, and the size requirements for each bag continue to change. The following table describes basic guidelines for some of the major air-lines in terms of what's allowed to be taken onto the plane.

| BAGGAGE SIZE RESTRICTIONS | |
|---|---|
| Airline | Carry-On Bag Size (inches) |
| American | 9 × 13 × 23 |
| Continental | 45 linear inches |
| Delta | 9 × 14 × 22 |
| Northwest | 9 × 14 × 22 |
| Southwest | 10 × 16 × 24 |
| TWA | 10 × 16 × 24 |
| United | 9 × 14 × 22 |
| USAir | 10 × 16 × 24 (overhead) |
| USAir | 8 × 16 × 21 (under seat) |

# Before You Leave Home

 As you get ready to leave your home and depart on your vacation, here's a quick checklist of things you might want to do prior to leaving. Due to the increased security within airports, make sure to arrive at the airport at least ninety minutes (or even two hours) prior to your flight's scheduled departure. With this in mind, plan your schedule accordingly.

Here are a few things to do before leaving your home to go on a vacation:

- Arrange for someone to care for your pets and plants.
- Ask a friend, relative, or neighbor to check on your home or apartment while you're gone.
- Ask the post office to hold your mail (and fill out the appropriate form).
- Clean all dirty dishes.
- Close and lock all windows and close the blinds/curtains.
- Contact your child's teacher if he/she will be missing classes.

- Empty your refrigerator of perishable items.
- Empty your trash.
- Get a haircut, manicure, etc.
- Give a copy of your house keys to a nearby friend or relative.
- Leave your contact information with coworkers, friends, relatives, or anyone who might need to reach you in case of an emergency.
- Pay your mortgage, rent, credit card bills, and other bills.
- Refill all prescription medications.
- Stop daily newspaper delivery or arrange for newspapers to be placed in an area that's out of sight. You don't want to make it obvious that you're on vacation.
- Turn down the heat or air conditioning.
- Turn on your telephone answering machine, but don't announce that you're on vacation.
- Unplug electrical appliances.
- Visit a bank to get cash and traveler's checks.

# Admission to the Disney Theme Parks

ONCE YOU DEVELOP A PRELIMINARY ITINERARY for your trip, decide how many days you'll spend exploring the various Disney theme parks. There are one-park/one-day tickets that provide unlimited admission to one of Disney's theme parks for a single day. Other options include multiday/single-park passes, multiday/multipark passes, multiday "Park Hopper" passes, and annual passes.

## Admission Prices and Passes

 Admission to the various theme parks at WDW can be purchased per park, by the day. If you're planning to stay at WDW for multiple days, however, you'll save money by purchasing multiday Park Hopper passes that give you full access to all of the WDW theme parks.

The primary Disney theme parks include:

- The Magic Kingdom
- Epcot
- The Disney-MGM Studios
- Disney's Animal Kingdom

Unless you purchase a 5-Day Park Hopper Plus Pass or Premium Annual Pass, separate admission is required for:

- Blizzard Beach
- Discovery Island Park
- DisneyQuest
- Disney's Wide World of Sports complex
- Pleasure Island
- River Country
- Typhoon Lagoon

An alternative to purchasing single-day/single-park passes or multiday Park Hopper passes is to purchase a complete vacation package from Walt Disney Travel Company, any travel agent, or most major airlines. Package prices and what the packages include vary greatly.

##  TRAVEL TIP

You can save time when you first visit the theme parks (and avoid lines) by purchasing your admission tickets in advance, through any Disney Store or from a travel agent, for example.

The following are some of the admission prices for the WDW theme parks. (All prices are subject to change.) For more information about park admission prices or to prepurchase your passes, call ✆ (407) W-DISNEY, visit **Disney World's Web site** (✑ *www. disneyworld.com*), or visit any Disney Store. If you're a member of the **Disney Club** (✑ *www.disneyclub.com*), be sure to inquire about special discounts that are offered.

## 1 Day/1 Park Ticket

These tickets are good for admission to any one of the primary WDW theme parks for one day.

| 1 DAY/1 PARK TICKET | | |
|---|---|---|
| Number of Days | Adult Pass | Child Pass (ages 3 to 9) |
| 1 | $48 | $38 |

## Water Park One-Day Admission

Admission to **Typhoon Lagoon** or **Blizzard Beach** is included with this ticket.

| TYPHOON LAGOON OR BLIZZARD BEACH | | |
|---|---|---|
| Duration | Adult Pass | Child Pass (ages 3 to 9) |
| 1 Day | $29.95 | $24 |
| Annual Pass | $99.95 | $80.50 |

| RIVER COUNTRY ONLY | | |
|---|---|---|
| Duration | Adult Pass | Child Pass (ages 3 to 9) |
| 1 Day | $15.95 | $12.50 |

## Pleasure Island Admission

During the day, Pleasure Island, which is located between the Downtown Disney shopping area and Disney's West Side, is open to the public. There is no admission fee. In the evenings and at night, however, when the Pleasure Island clubs open, there is a separate admission fee that includes admission to all of the clubs and attractions within this area. (Drinks and food, however, are sold separately.)

| PLEASURE ISLAND | | |
|---|---|---|
| Duration | Adult Pass (18+ only) | Child Pass |
| 1 Night | $19.81 | Not Available |
| Annual Pass | $54.95 | Not Available |

Note that for special events at Pleasure Island (such as New Year's Eve), an additional admission fee and advance reservations may be required.

## Disney's Wide World of Sports

For sports fans of all ages who wish to explore **Disney's Wide World of Sports** complex, there is a separate admission fee.

| DISNEY'S WIDE WORLD OF SPORTS | | |
|---|---|---|
| Duration | Adult Pass | Child Pass (ages 3 to 9) |
| 1 Day | $9.75 | $7.50 |

## DisneyQuest

Within Disney's West Side area is an indoor, high-tech interactive attraction called **DisneyQuest,** which combines video arcade games with state-of-the-art virtual reality rides and attractions. While **DisneyQuest** will appeal primarily to boys between the ages of ten and twenty-one, there is plenty to do here for everyone. The all-inclusive, one-day pass includes unlimited use of all rides and attractions within **DisneyQuest.**

| DISNEYQUEST | | |
|---|---|---|
| Duration | Adult Pass | Child Pass (ages 3 to 9) |
| 1 Day | $29 | $23 |
| Annual Pass | $79 | $63 |

## 4-Day or 5-Day Park Hopper Pass

This pass allows you to visit **The Magic Kingdom, Epcot, The Disney-MGM Studios,** and **Disney's Animal Kingdom** only. You enter and exit these parks as often as you'd like during any four or five days. In most cases, unused days do not expire and the days do not have to be consecutive.

| PARK HOPPER PASS | | |
|---|---|---|
| Duration | Adult Pass | Child Pass (ages 3 to 9) |
| 4 Days | $192 | $152 |
| 5 Days | $217 | $172 |

## 5-Day Park Hopper Plus Pass

This pass allows you to visit **The Magic Kingdom, Epcot, The** Disney-MGM Studios, and **Disney's Animal Kingdom,** and enter and exit these parks as often as you'd like during any five days. In addition to the primary theme parks, this type of ticket also grants the holder the choice of admission to two of the following: **Blizzard Beach, Typhoon Lagoon, River Country, Pleasure Island,** or **Disney's Wide World of Sports.** Unused days do not expire.

| PARK HOPPER PASS PLUS | | |
|---|---|---|
| Duration | Adult Pass | Child Pass (ages 3 to 9) |
| 5 Days | $247 | $197 |
| 6 Days | $277 | $222 |
| 7 Days | $307 | $247 |

## Annual Pass

If you plan on visiting The WDW Resort multiple times in any twelve-month period, consider purchasing an annual pass. These passes provide unlimited admission to **The Magic Kingdom, Epcot, The Disney-MGM Studios,** and **Disney's Animal Kingdom** during normal operating hours. Parking and unlimited use of WDW Transportation is included. Special discounts are also offered for food and merchandise. The twelve-month period begins on the first day the pass is used to enter a theme park (not when it's issued).

| ANNUAL PASS | | |
|---|---|---|
| Status | Adult Pass | Child Pass (ages 3 to 9) |
| Nonresident | $349 | $297 |
| Florida Resident | $289 | $246 |

## Premium Annual Pass

These twelve-month passes offer unlimited admission to **The Magic Kingdom, Epcot, The Disney-MGM Studios, Disney's Animal Kingdom,** plus **Pleasure Island, Discovery Island, Typhoon Lagoon, River Country, Blizzard Beach, Disney's Wide World of Sports** complex, and **DisneyQuest** during normal operating hours.

Parking and unlimited use of WDW Transportation is included. Special discounts are also offered for food and merchandise.

| PREMIUM ANNUAL PASS | | |
|---|---|---|
| Status | Adult Pass | Child Pass (ages 3 to 9) |
| Nonresident | $469 | $399 |
| Florida Resident | $389 | $331 |

## Length of Stay Pass

If you're staying at The WDW Resort for a number of days that isn't included in one of the pass options, you can purchase a special Length of Stay Pass that offers you unlimited access to all of the theme parks during your entire stay. These passes are good from the moment you check in at your WDW Resort hotel until midnight of the day you check out of the hotel. These passes give guests total freedom to go from park to park at will, and use all WDW Transportation. The price for this type of pass varies based on the length of your stay. For more information, call ☎ (407) W-DISNEY.

## ≡FAST FACT

As part of special travel packages, an Ultimate Park Hopper pass is available for the length of your stay. This pass includes unlimited admission to all of the primary Disney theme parks and water parks, plus unlimited admission to **Pleasure Island, Disney's Wide World of Sports,** and **DisneyQuest** during the length of your stay. Call ☎ (407) W-DISNEY for details.

## Beware of Counterfeit Passes and Scams

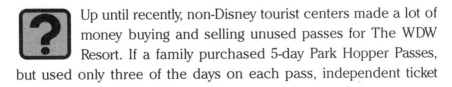 Up until recently, non-Disney tourist centers made a lot of money buying and selling unused passes for The WDW Resort. If a family purchased 5-day Park Hopper Passes, but used only three of the days on each pass, independent ticket

agencies would purchase the unused days at a fraction of the true value, and then resell those passes to other tourists to earn a profit.

Recently, however, the Walt Disney Company began using new technology to print and issue passes for the Disney theme parks that prevents counterfeiting, unauthorized ticket brokering, or illegal ticket scalping. As a result, to protect yourself, do not purchase any admission passes to any Disney theme park (for any price) from any unauthorized ticket agent. The safest places to purchase your admission passes for the Disney theme parks are from your own travel agent, directly from any WDW Resort ticket counter (on Disney property), from a Disney Store, or from Disney Online. American Express Travel Services, AAA Travel Services, and Delta Airlines Vacation Packages are among the agencies that are allowed to sell admission tickets to the Disney theme parks. If someone tries to sell you highly discounted admission tickets to the Disney theme parks, or asks to purchase your used or unused passes, walk away.

## ≡FAST FACT

Some unofficial tourist information centers will offer legitimate discount tickets to the Disney theme parks; however, you must first submit yourself to a ninety-minute sales presentation for local time-share vacation/investment opportunities.

## Avoid Long Lines

It's everyone's dream to visit one of the Disney World theme parks and discover the place is absolutely empty—with none of those dreaded lines to wait in, even for the most popular rides. Well, the chances of that dream coming true, no matter how much pixie dust you use, are slim. Thanks to WDW's FASTPASS, however, visitors don't have to wait hours at a time to experience the most popular rides within the various Disney theme parks.

Combine careful planning with the new FASTPASS system, and you'll be able to enjoy most or all of each park's most popular rides, without having to wait for hours at a time in line to experience each of them. FASTPASS use is free of charge to all theme park visitors.

When you approach a ride that supports FASTPASS, you'll see two clocks located near the ride's entrance. One clock displays the estimated wait time in the regular line. (For a popular ride during a peak vacation period, the wait could be sixty to ninety minutes or more.) The second clock displays the current return time for people using FASTPASS.

If you choose to use FASTPASS, simply insert your theme park admission ticket (passport or annual pass) into the special kiosk located near the ride's entrance. A special pass will be printed explaining what time to return to the ride. For example, if it's 1:00 P.M. when you approach the ride for the first time, and you insert your ticket into the FASTPASS turnstile, you may be told to return to the ride at 2:30 P.M., at which time you can proceed directly to the ride's preshow or boarding area. There will then be little or no wait.

Using FASTPASS is like making a reservation to experience a ride, without having to wait in line. While guests can't specify a specific time they'd like to experience a ride, it is possible to save considerable time and avoid waiting in long lines. While you're waiting for your designated FASTPASS time, you're free to experience other rides, shows, and attractions within the theme park.

## TRAVEL TIP

Guests are given a one-hour window during which they can return to experience the ride once they take advantage of FASTPASS. So, if the printed FASTPASS ticket you receive indicates you should return at 2:00 P.M., for example, you can arrive at the ride's entrance anywhere between 2:00 P.M. and 3:00 P.M.

Guests can activate FASTPASS for only one ride at a time. So, if you're waiting to experience Splash Mountain, for example, and you have ninety minutes until your designated boarding time, you can't race over to Space Mountain and also take advantage of FASTPASS until after you've experienced Splash Mountain.

Using FASTPASS within any of the Disney theme parks is easy. It all starts by purchasing an admission ticket for The Magic Kingdom, Epcot, The Disney-MGM Studios, or Disney's Animal Kingdom. Once you're in one of the parks, follow these steps:

1. Proceed to the ride of your choice that supports FASTPASS (a list follows).
2. Check the clocks located near the ride's entrance to determine the wait time without using FASTPASS and what time you could experience the ride if you obtain a FASTPASS ticket.
3. Based on your schedule, if you choose to request a FASTPASS ticket, insert your theme park admission ticket into the ride's special turnstile. You will then receive a printed ticket indicating what time you should return to the ride. (Keep in mind, you have a one-hour window from the time printed on the ticket.)
4. When the designated time to return to the ride arrives, proceed directly to the ride's preshow or boarding area. At this point, you can expect little or no wait.

## 🧳 TRAVEL TIP

If used correctly, FASTPASS can save you up to two hours each day. This gives you up to 25 percent more time to experience rides and attractions, as opposed to waiting in long lines for the popular attractions.

Since FASTPASS works with many of the most popular rides within each of Disney's theme parks, you can use this free feature to help plan your day and ensure that you're able to experience everything you'd like to during your visit to each park. FASTPASS is particularly useful if you're traveling with young kids, who are typically impatient and hate waiting in lines, especially on a hot day.

The following rides currently support FASTPASS within the various Disney theme parks. Due to the success of this program, new rides are always being added.

### The Magic Kingdom
- Big Thunder Mountain Railroad
- Buzz Lightyear's Space Ranger Spin
- The Haunted Mansion
- The Jungle Cruise
- The Many Adventures of Winnie the Pooh
- Peter Pan's Flight
- Space Mountain
- Splash Mountain

### Epcot
- Honey I Shrunk the Audience
- Living with the Land
- Maelstrom
- Test Track

## ⊕ HOT SPOT

Test Track is one of Epcot's newest and most popular rides; therefore, there's almost always a long wait. If you don't want to take advantage of FASTPASS, consider experiencing this ride as a single person and getting into the special singles' line located near the ride's entrance—the wait will typically be considerably shorter.

### The Disney-MGM Studios
- Indiana Jones Epic Stunt Spectacular!
- *Jim Henson's Muppet*Vision 3-D*
- Rock 'n' Roller Coaster Starring Aerosmith
- Star Tours
- Tower of Terror

- Voyage of the Little Mermaid
- Who Wants to Be a Millionaire–Play It!

### Disney's Animal Kingdom
- DINOSAUR
- *It's Tough to Be a Bug*
- Kali River Rapids
- Kilimanjaro Safaris

##  TRAVEL TIP

The Kali River Rapids is an exciting, rather turbulent river rafting ride. While it's not dangerous, people who experience this ride can get very wet. Thus, plan your day accordingly. You probably don't want to experience this ride first thing in the morning and then have to wait for several hours until you dry off.

## Travel Tips

 As you read this book and start thinking about how exactly you want to spend your time, be sure to take notes and keep track of which rides, shows, attractions, parades, and activities are of interest to you and the people you'll be traveling with. Once you think you know what you want to experience, start planning out the actual days of your trip. While you're doing this, keep in mind that each of the various theme parks is massive, so plan on doing a lot of walking.

Make sure everyone you're traveling with gets to experience activities that he or she is most excited about. This may mean making compromises or separating at various times. There's no reason why every family member should be dragged to activities that others aren't interested in. While you'll definitely want to plan some "quality family time," that time together will be more thoroughly enjoyed if everyone you're traveling with is happy and excited about the activities he or she has experienced during the vacation.

##  TRAVEL TIP

To save yourself a considerable amount of time traveling between theme parks and activities, plan out your itinerary in half-day chunks. Also, when making up your schedule, don't forget to leave time to eat, rest, experience the popular rides and attractions, and also wait in line to experience those attractions.

### For Single Travelers

Unfortunately, The WDW Resort was designed as a family vacation destination, so there aren't too many opportunities for singles to meet other singles (after all, this isn't the Love Boat). If you're single, you might consider inviting a friend or relative along with you on your vacation. Otherwise, your best chances for meeting other singles is to partake in the nighttime activities at Downtown Disney and Disney's BoardWalk, where you'll find bars, restaurants, and dance clubs that are frequented by Disney guests as well as Orlando residents, especially on weekends.

If you're a college student, Spring Break is an ideal time to meet other young people at The WDW Resort, since Disney World tends to attract groups of Spring Breakers traveling together and looking to meet and party with others.

### For Seniors

One of the nicest things about vacationing at The WDW Resort is that there's so much to do, yet you can set your own pace. Senior citizens should consider staying at one of the resort hotels that attract primarily adults (as opposed to families), such as the Grand Floridian or the BoardWalk Inn. As for the activities, The WDW Resort complex offers several golf courses, plus many other activities for older guests.

Seniors interested in exploring the various theme parks should not get too overwhelmed by the large size of the parks. Instead of visiting one park per day, seniors should consider taking a more casual approach and spend more time at places like Epcot. A senior citizen could easily spend two or three full days at Epcot alone. Anyone who tires easily or doesn't enjoy a lot of walking should seriously consider renting a wheelchair or electronic convenience vehicle. Also, spend more time enjoying the various fine-dining experiences available throughout the resort complex. Take time in the middle of the day to relax and enjoy a two-hour lunch. You might also consider arriving at a park early in the morning, exploring for three or four hours, taking several hours to relax in the afternoon, and then venturing back out in the late afternoon or evening for several more hours.

 **TRAVEL TIP**

In order to help pace yourself, seniors should consider participating in the various Disney World tours of the theme parks that are offered. Seniors should also consider planning their vacation to The WDW Resort during the off-peak season, so that they won't have to deal with large crowds and long lines for the attractions.

In addition to a lot of walking, one of the biggest concerns older people should have when visiting The WDW Resort is dealing with the heat and sun. Overexposure to the sun can cause health problems. Be sure to wear plenty of sunblock, a hat, sunglasses, and light clothing that covers your entire body. Also, drink plenty of fluids and take rests often. During the afternoon hours (when the weather is the hottest), plan to visit the indoor, air-conditioned attractions. At Epcot, these include Innoventions, the Living Seas, Wonders of Life, and Universe of Energy. You can easily plan on spending between one and three hours at each of these indoor attractions.

# Guest Services

 Within each of the Disney theme parks (The Magic Kingdom, Epcot, The Disney-MGM Studios, Disney's Animal Kingdom, the water parks, etc.), you find the following guest services designed to make your visit to the parks more comfortable and enjoyable.

## Automated Teller Machines

Within the Disney theme parks, as well as within Downtown Disney, you'll find multiple automated teller machines (ATMs). Ask any Disney cast member for directions to the closest machine, or check the map located within the souvenir guide map and daily schedule brochures. Your bank many charge a transaction/withdrawal fee for using an ATM that's outside of your bank's own network.

Throughout The WDW Resort, cash (U.S. currency), traveler's checks, Disney Dollars, personal checks, debit cards, Visa, MasterCard, American Express, JCB, the Disney Credit Card, and Discover Card are accepted. Credit cards are not accepted at the various food and merchandise kiosks located throughout the parks. If you're staying within a Disney hotel/resort, your room key can also be used as a charge card within the parks. Your purchases will be billed directly to your hotel room.

Within The WDW Resort, there's a full-service SunTrust bank that's located across the street from Downtown Disney. The branch is open on weekdays between 9:00 A.M. and 4:00 P.M. (6:00 P.M. on Thursdays). Call ✆ (407) 237-4786 or ✆ (800) 432-4760 for details. At this branch, you can obtain a cash advance from a major credit card, receive a wire transfer, and perform many other banking functions.

## Child Care

Baby Service areas can be found within each of the primary Disney theme parks. Private rooms are available for nursing and feeding. Highchairs, bibs, plastic spoons, and diaper changing rooms are provided. Additional baby-care products (disposable diapers, formula, etc.) can be purchased. Baby changing tables are available in all public restrooms throughout the theme parks.

In-room babysitting service is available by calling your hotel's front desk or concierge. There is an hourly (per child) charge. In addition, there are child care programs available at several of the Disney hotels. Call ☎ (407) 939-3463 for details, hours of operation, and fees.

## ≡FAST FACT

The Den's Club at the Wilderness Lodge offers child care between 4:30 P.M. and midnight, for a fee of $8 per hour, per child. This facility is open to kids between the ages of four and twelve, who are toilet trained. Similar services are available at Disney's Polynesian Resort, Disney's Beach Club Resort, Disney's Contemporary Resort, Disney's Grand Floridian Resort & Spa, Disney's BoardWalk, and the Disney Animal Kingdom Lodge.

### Emergency Services

No matter what type of emergency you experience, medical or otherwise, contact the nearest Disney cast member immediately. Those who work at The WDW Resort and the theme parks are highly trained to deal with virtually any type of emergency, such as lost children, medical-related problems, and/or lost/stolen items.

Within all of the Disney theme parks, you'll find fully equipped first aid stations. Various amenities such as pain relievers, sunblock, and bandages can be purchased at many of the gift shops, including those along Main Street, U.S.A. (within The Magic Kingdom) or D-TV (within Pleasure Island).

When adults get separated, messages can be left at the Guest Relations desk (typically located near the entrance to each park). It's highly recommended, however, that you predetermine a location and time to meet if you get separated within the theme parks. Many travelers also resort to cell phones and/or walkie-talkies to stay in contact with one another. Numeric or alphanumeric pagers can be rented from all of the Disney hotels/resorts. Check with the front desk at your hotel for details.

## Health-Related Services

Aside from the first aid stations located within each of the theme parks, there are walk-in medical facilities (operated by Florida Hospital) located just outside of The WDW Resort area. For information about these medical facilities, call ☎ (407) 238-2000 or ☎ (407) 239-6463. Complimentary transportation to these walk-in medical centers is available.

To receive an in-room visit from a doctor (at your Disney hotel), call the Doctors-On-Call service at ☎ (407) 399-3627. This service is available twenty-four-hours per day. Two of the closest hospitals to The WDW Resort are Sandlake Hospital ☎ (407) 351-8500 and Celebration Health ☎ (407) 303-4000.

 **TRAVEL TIP**

Before leaving on your vacation, make sure to obtain a copy of your prescription to take with you, along with contact information for your doctor and medical insurance company. Thus, if you need to have your prescription refilled, it will be much less of a hassle.

To arrange to have a prescription delivered to your hotel room, call Centra Care at ☎ (407) 239-7777. There are also three Walgreens pharmacies (☎ (800) 289-2273) located near The WDW Resort (near the Downtown Disney area).

Refrigeration facilities for prescription medications (such as insulin or antibiotics) are available, free of charge, within the theme parks and Disney hotels. Contact the First Aid office or Guest Relations for more information.

## Religious Services

To find a house of worship or nearby religious services, check any local Orlando-area telephone book or ask the front desk (or concierge) at your hotel. In many cases, free shuttle service is available from The WDW Resort to the house of worship of your choice.

## Lockers

Lockers are available for rent within all of the Disney theme parks. These are excellent for storing an extra change of clothing, jackets, or camera equipment during the day until they're needed. While visiting the parks, you'll want to keep your hands as free as possible. Storing items you bring into the park or that you purchase (souvenirs) is an excellent strategy. Renting a locker is a lot more convenient than running back and forth to your parked car or hotel room, which will typically require a long walk and/or a tram ride. The daily charge for unlimited use of a locker within each of the Disney theme parks is $6 (plus a $1 refundable deposit).

## Lost and Found

There's a Lost and Found office located within each theme park. If you lose an item, report it missing as quickly as possible. If someone returns the item quickly, you can pick it up at the Lost and Found office. If the item is found after your departure from the park, the Walt Disney Company will mail the item to you at whatever address you provide.

If you find someone else's lost item, bring it to one of the park's Lost and Found offices. If the item is not claimed within sixty days, you have the option of keeping it. Ask any Disney cast member for the location of the Lost and Found desk within the Disney theme park or Disney resort you're visiting.

## Package Express Service

If you're staying at one of the Disney hotels, one of the perks is that whenever you make a purchase (of a souvenir, for example), you can have the purchased item delivered directly to your hotel room, free of charge. This means you won't have to carry around your purchases or store them in lockers.

For those who aren't staying at one of the Disney hotels, you can arrange to have your purchases delivered and held at the Package Express Pickup Window, located just outside the main entrance to the theme parks. You can pick up your items at the end of the day. This is a complimentary service.

## Pet Care

The WDW Kennels can be found adjacent to the Transportation and Ticket Center, at the entrance to Epcot, at the entrances to The Disney-MGM Studios and Disney's Animal Kingdom Park, and near the entrance to Disney's Fort Wilderness Resort & Campground.

## ≡FAST FACT

Keep in mind that all dogs and cats are required to have a certificate of vaccination signed by a licensed veterinarian (rabies, parvo, DHLP, Bordetella for dogs; rabies, FPRC for cats).

The daily fee is $6 per day (per pet) and/or $9 per night (per pet). When you leave your pet within the kennels, you will be required to drop in for a visit at least once per day. Dog owners, for example, are required to walk their own dogs at least twice daily (or three times daily for puppies).

Kennel space is somewhat limited, especially during peak travel times, so be sure to reserve space in advance. Making a hotel reservation is separate from reserving space for your pet within one of the kennels. In addition to housing dogs, the kennels will also accept cats, birds, ferrets, small rodents, and nonvenomous snakes (if in their own carriers).

## Public Telephones

Throughout The WDW Resort (in public areas of the hotels, as well as within the theme parks and in the Downtown Disney area), you'll find an abundance of public telephones. The majority of the pay telephones accept coins, credit cards, or prepaid phone cards.

You'll find that virtually all of the nationwide cellular services work within the Orlando area (and within The WDW Resort); however, depending on your cellular service or digital PCS contract, you may be charged per-minute roaming fees, so contact your cellular service provider for details.

Long-distance rates vary. If you can find a good deal on a calling card (with no per-call surcharge and only a per-minute rate), this will probably be the least expensive option when using a pay phone or making calls from a hotel room.

Before making calls from your hotel room, determine what the surcharges will be. Some hotels charge $1 or more every time you pick up the phone to make an outgoing call, even if you're calling locally or using a toll-free phone number.

## Restaurant Priority Seating/Reservations

Many of the upscale, sit-down restaurants within the Disney theme parks, the Disney hotels, and in the Downtown Disney area accept reservations. You can call ☎ (407) WDW-DINE to make a restaurant reservation, drop into the restaurant in person, visit the guest relations desk within the theme parks, or ask the concierge at your hotel to make the reservation for you.

## 💼 TRAVEL TIP

When choosing where to dine, keep in mind that the majority of restaurants and eating establishments within the entire resort complex offer specially priced children's menus. If you're an annual pass holder or Disney Club member, additional discounts will often be available.

For those restaurants that do accept lunch and dinner reservations (especially those within the parks), space fills up quickly, so make your reservations as early as possible. Group reservations (or plans for a special event or private party) should be made well in advance.

## Services for the Disabled

The WDW Resort offers a wide range of services for physically disabled guests. Manually operated wheelchairs and electric convenience vehicles can both be rented (for a small daily fee) near the entrance of each theme park. If you're staying at a Disney hotel, complimentary wheel chairs are available from the hotel. See the front desk for details. The buses that transport guests throughout The WDW Resort are all wheelchair accessible.

For guests with visual disabilities, a special Braille guidebook is available, free of charge, from Guest Relations at any of the theme parks. For those with hearing impairments, closed-captioning is available on many of the movie/video-based attractions, written storylines are available for virtually all of the rides and attractions, and some of the rides and attractions utilize Assistive Listening Systems. (The receiver is available from Guest Relations within the theme parks.)

## ≡FAST FACT

Throughout your visit to The WDW Resort, guests with almost any type of disability will find that their needs will be met. In some cases, however, preplanning is required to ensure the proper accommodations and/or services will be available at the time of your visit.

For additional information about all of the various services available for disabled guests, call **Guest Relations** at ☎ (407) 824-4321. A free publication, called *The Guidebook for Guests with Disabilities*, offers information about accessibility to the various rides, shows, attractions, shops, and restaurants within the theme parks. This guide is available from Guest Relations.

If you have special dietary needs, speak with the chef at any of the sit-down (full-service) restaurants within The WDW Resort. Whenever possible, your special needs will almost always be met.

All of the Disney hotels also offer special accommodations for the disabled. These accommodations must be reserved in advance, when making your actual reservation.

### Stroller Rentals

Within the theme parks, stroller rentals are available for $7 per day (plus a $1 refundable deposit). The rental locations are near the entrances of The Magic Kingdom, at the base of Spaceship Earth within Epcot, within Oscar's Super Service at The Disney-MGM Studios, and at the entrance to Disney's Animal Kingdom.

When renting a stroller, be sure to keep the receipt with you at all times. If you park your stroller in order to experience an attraction, and your stroller is gone when you return, simply go to a stroller replacement center or the main rental area for a replacement. Ask any Disney cast member for the location of the nearest replacement center.

Because you'll be leaving the stroller unattended (parked outside of each attraction you experience), it's an excellent idea to rent a stroller when you get to one of the theme parks. Do not plan on bringing your own. Also, never leave anything valuable within the storage compartments of the stroller.

## Gathering More Information

If you still have questions regarding your travel plans and making reservations at The Walt Disney World Resort, call the appropriate telephone number listed here:

**Disney Club Membership Information:** ☎(800) 49-DISNEY

**Disney Cruise Lines:** ☎(888) DCL-2500

**Disney Restaurant Advance "Priority Seating" Reservations:** ☎(800) WDW-DINE

**Disney Tour Information:** ☎(800) WDW-TOUR

**Walt Disney Travel Company:** ☎(800) 828-0228

**Walt Disney World Guest Information:** (407) 824-4321

**The Walt Disney World Resort Information Line:** (407) W-DISNEY

# Orlando-Area Dining

CHANCES ARE, visiting the various Orlando-area theme parks and tourist attractions is going to make you hungry. Well, when it comes to dining out, your choices in the Orlando area are extensive! No matter what type of food you enjoy, chances are you'll find it within The WDW Resort or in a nearby area.

## Dining at Disney

In addition to the many fast-food and sit-down (full-service) eating establishments within each of the theme parks (described in Chapters 6, 8, 9, and 10), there is also a handful of excellent restaurants within the Downtown Disney, Disney's West Side, and Disney's BoardWalk areas (see Chapter 12), plus each of the Disney resorts offers at least several dining options for breakfast, lunch, dinner, and snacks. When you head over to Universal Studios Escape, you'll also find a handful of excellent restaurants within the CityWalk area (described in Chapter 17).

You'll find that the various dining establishments offer diverse menus and cater to different needs. For example, there are fast-food dining options, moderately priced full-service restaurants, fine-dining (expensive) restaurants, plus family-oriented theme dining options available—all on WDW property and easily accessible using the Disney bus system, monorails, boats, or other forms of transportation.

On WDW Resort property alone, there are dozens upon dozens of restaurants. For dining suggestions, contact the front desk (or concierge) of your hotel, or call ☎ (407) WDW-DINE. Keep in mind, many of the full-service restaurants, especially those within the theme parks, tend to be crowded during peak mealtimes. To avoid long waits, it's best to make reservations.

## International Dining Options

While not cheap, the various fine-dining restaurants located with the World Showcase at Epcot offer a wide range of international, authentic, and delicious dining options, whether you're in the mood for Japanese, Chinese, Italian, German, Moroccan, French, English, or Mexican cuisine. See Chapter 8 for details.

## Theme Dining

When it comes to theme dining, people of all ages will enjoy Planet Hollywood, located within the West Side area of Downtown Disney. Just look for the giant globe. This is the world's largest Planet Hollywood restaurant. It's jam-packed with all kinds of Hollywood memorabilia, plus it features an extensive menu. There's also the Rainforest Café in the Downtown Disney area, the ESPN Café at the Disney Wide World of Sports, the Hard Rock Café within Universal's CityWalk, and many other exciting themed dining experiences waiting for you.

## ⊕ HOT SPOT

If you're in the mood for an elegant dining experience without leaving the park, the place to visit is the Brown Derby at Disney-MGM Studios. This restaurant is a re-creation of the original Brown Derby restaurant, located in Hollywood, California, where the Cobb Salad (the house specialty) was originally created. All of the food here is top-notch, whether you enjoy a full lunch or dinner.

# Dining Outside of Disney Property

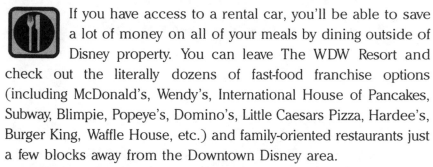 If you have access to a rental car, you'll be able to save a lot of money on all of your meals by dining outside of Disney property. You can leave The WDW Resort and check out the literally dozens of fast-food franchise options (including McDonald's, Wendy's, International House of Pancakes, Subway, Blimpie, Popeye's, Domino's, Little Caesars Pizza, Hardee's, Burger King, Waffle House, etc.) and family-oriented restaurants just a few blocks away from the Downtown Disney area.

Within minutes of The WDW Resort (and even closer to Universal Orlando and SeaWorld), there are countless dining options along International Drive. You can enjoy top-quality food at many of these restaurants, without having to pay a premium for eating at a theme park.

For dining suggestions, visit the **icFlorida** Web site (✑ *www.icflorida.com/restaurants*). From this Web site you can print out discount coupons for a handful of restaurants, compliments of Val-Pak. Restaurant reviews and listings can also be obtained at the **Orlando Weekly** Web site (✑ *www.orlando weekly.com/dining*).

##  TRAVEL TIP

To save money when dining at participating non-Disney restaurants, take advantage of the Entertainment Book for the Orlando area (☎(800) 374-4464), or the Dining-A-La-Card program offered free with the Diner's Club credit card (☎(800) 2-DINERS).

The following franchise and independently owned restaurants are located within 2 miles of The WDW Resort.

## RESTAURANTS WITHIN 2 MILES OF THE WDW RESORT

**Arthur's 27** 🏠 1900 Buena Vista Drive 📞(407) 827-2727

**Bahama Breeze** 🏠 8615 Vineland Avenue 📞(407) 938-9010

**Baskervilles** 🏠 1850 Hotel Plaza Blvd. 📞(407) 828-44

**Bongos Cuban Café** 🏠 Downtown Disney West Side
📞(407) 828-0999

**C&N Steakhouse** 🏠 8460 Palm Parkway 📞(407) 239-7256

**Cascade Restaurant** 🏠 1 Grand Cypress Blvd. 📞(407) 239-1234

**The Cheesecake Factory** 🏠 1486 E. Buena Vista Drive
📞(407) 828-8066

**La Coquina Restaurant** 🏠 1 Grand Cypress Blvd. 📞(407) 239-1234

**Crab House** 🏠 8496 Palm Parkway 📞(407) 239-1888

**Denny's Restaurant** 🏠 12375 State Road 525 📞(407) 239-7900

**Domino's Pizza** 🏠 8542 Palm Parkway 📞(407) 239-1221

**Emily's Restaurant** 🏠 8607 Palm Parkway 📞(407) 239-4999

**Finn's Grill** 🏠 1751 Hotel Plaza Blvd. 📞(407) 827-3838

**Fortune Court** 🏠 8607 Palm Parkway 📞(407) 239-4999

**Hana Café & International Market** 🏠 8546 Palm Parkway
📞(407) 238-9006

**Havana Café** 🏠 8544 Palm Parkway 📞(407) 238-5333

**Hemingway's Restaurant** 🏠 1 Grand Cypress Blvd.
📞(407) 239-1234

**House of Blues** 🏠 Downtown Disney West Side 📞(407) WDW-2NITE

**JR Steakery** 🏠 8200 Vineland Avenue 📞(407) 239-9066

**Jungle Jim's** 🏠 12501 State Road 📞(407) 827-1257

**Landry's Seafood House** 🏠 8800 Vineland Avenue
📞(407) 827-6466

**Lone Star Steakhouse** 🏠 8850 Vineland Avenue 📞(407) 827-8225

**Lower East Side Restaurant** 🏠 8548 Palm Parkway
📞(407) 465-0565

**Max Orient** 🏠 8200 Vineland Avenue 📞(407) 239-4139

**McDonald's** 🏠 12549 State Road 525 📞(407) 827-1030

## RESTAURANTS WITHIN 2 MILES OF THE WDW RESORT

**McDonald's** 🖃 1674 E. Buena Vista Drive ✆(407) 828-0224

**Nothing But Dessert** 🖃 8629 Palm Parkway ✆(407) 239-8897

**Olive Garden Restaurant** 🖃 12361 Apopka Vineland
✆(407) 239-6708

**Outback Restaurant** 🖃 1900 Buena Vista Drive ✆(407) 827-2727

**Perkins Family Restaurant** 🖃 12559 State Road 535
✆(407) 827-1060

**Pizzeria Uno** 🖃 12553 State Road 535 ✆(407) 827-0022

**Planet Hollywood** 🖃 Downtown Disney West Side
✆(407) 827-7827

**Ponderosa Steakhouse** 🖃 14407 International Drive
✆(407) 238-2526

**The Rainforest Café** 🖃 Disney's Animal Kingdom ✆(407) 938-9100

**The Rainforest Café** 🖃 Downtown Disney ✆(407) 827-8500

**Red Lobster Restaurant** 🖃 12557 State Road 535 ✆(407) 827-1045

**Shoney's Restaurants** 🖃 12204 S. Apopka-Vineland Road
✆(407) 239-5416

**Subway** 🖃 8200 Vineland Avenue ✆(407) 238-7706

**Taco Bell** 🖃 12555 State Road 535 ✆(407) 827-8226

**TGI Friday's** 🖃 12543 State Road 535 ✆(407) 827-1020

**Tropix Grille** 🖃 8100 Lake Avenue ✆(407) 239-7151

**Waffle House** 🖃 12805 State Road 535 ✆(407) 239-6444

**Watercress Café** 🖃 1900 N. Buena Vista Drive ✆(407) 827-3440

**Wolfgang Puck** 🖃 Downtown Disney West Side
✆(407) WDW-2NITE

The following are other nearby upscale restaurants, many of which offer a family-oriented dining experience in addition to full bar service. Reservations should be made for any of these restaurants, which are ideal for celebrating special occasions.

## ORLANDO RESTAURANTS

**Benihana Japanese Steak House** ▦ 1751 Hotel Plaza Blvd.
☎(407) 827-4865

**The Butcher Shop Steakhouse** ▦ 8445 International Drive
at The Mercado ☎(407) 363-9727

**Charley's Steakhouse** ▦ 8255 International Drive
☎(407) 363-0228

**Charlie's Lobster House** ▦ 8445 International Drive
at The Mercado ☎(407) 352-6929

**Christini's Ristorante Italiano** ▦ 7600 Dr. Phillips Blvd.
☎(407) 345-8770

**Del Frisco's Prime Steak & Lobster** ▦ 729 Lee Road
☎(407) 645-4443

**DiVino's Italian Restaurant** ▦ 8445 International Drive
at The Mercado ☎(407) 345-0883

**Dux** ▦ 9801 International Drive ☎(407) 345-4550

**FishBones** ▦ 6707 Sand Lake Road ☎(407) 352-0135

**Kobe Japanese Steakhouse** ▦ 8350 International Drive
☎(407) 352-1811

**Kobe Japanese Steakhouse** ▦ 5606 Kirkman Road
☎(407) 248-1978

**Palm Restaurant of Orlando** ▦ 5800 Universal Blvd.
☎(407) 503-3463

**Ruth Chris Steak House** ▦ 610 N. Orlando Avenue
☎(407) 662-2444

# Restaurants in Celebration

 Celebration, Florida, is the city conceived and designed by Walt Disney. It was built about ten minutes away from The WDW Resort and is an absolutely charming area to shop, dine, and explore. For additional information, visit *www.celebrationfl.com.*

Some of the dining options within Celebration, Florida, include:

| CELEBRATION, FL RESTAURANTS |
| --- |
| Café D'Antonio  &(407) 566-2233 |
| Celebration Town Tavern: Seafood, Steaks & More<br>&(407) 566-2526 |
| Columbia Restaurant  &(407) 566-1505 |
| Herman's Ice Cream Shoppe  &(407) 566-1300 |
| Market Street Café  &(407) 566-1144 |

## ⊕ HOT SPOT

The main street area of Celebration, called Market Street, features several upscale, fine-dining restaurants well worth experiencing. Make sure, however, that you leave ample time to explore the nearby shops when you visit Celebration.

# Calculating the Tip

 At any full-service restaurant, you're expected to leave a tip for your server. The customary amount to leave is 15 percent of the total bill; however, you may choose to leave slightly more or less depending on the quality of service you receive.

Many restaurants automatically add a gratuity to the bill for groups, so be sure to determine if a gratuity has already been added to your meal bill if you're dining with a group of people. The following table will help you quickly calculate the appropriate tip amount (based on 15 or 20 percent):

| SUGGESTED TIP AMOUNTS | | |
| --- | --- | --- |
| Meal Price | 15% Tip Amount | 20% Tip Amount |
| $5.00 | $.75 | $1.00 |
| $10.00 | $1.50 | $2.00 |
| $12.00 | $1.80 | $2.40 |
| $14.00 | $2.10 | $2.80 |
| $16.00 | $2.40 | $3.20 |
| $18.00 | $2.70 | $3.60 |
| $20.00 | $3.00 | $4.00 |
| $25.00 | $3.75 | $5.00 |
| $30.00 | $4.50 | $6.00 |
| $35.00 | $5.25 | $7.00 |
| $40.00 | $6.00 | $8.00 |
| $45.00 | $6.75 | $9.00 |
| $50.00 | $7.50 | $10.00 |
| $55.00 | $8.25 | $11.00 |
| $60.00 | $9.00 | $12.00 |
| $65.00 | $9.75 | $13.00 |
| $70.00 | $10.50 | $14.00 |
| $75.00 | $11.25 | $15.00 |
| $80.00 | $12.00 | $16.00 |
| $85.00 | $12.75 | $17.00 |
| $90.00 | $13.50 | $18.00 |
| $95.00 | $14.25 | $19.00 |
| $100.00 | $15.00 | $20.00 |
| $125.00 | $18.75 | $25.00 |
| $150.00 | $22.50 | $30.00 |

# The Ultimate Fine-Dining Experience

 Located less than thirty minutes away from The WDW Resort is what could easily be called the very best restaurant in Orlando. While this fine-dining establishment isn't cheap, it offers the best steak and lobster entrees that you can imagine. Del Frisco's Prime Steak & Lobster is the perfect restaurant if you're looking to add an extremely memorable dining experience to your vacation. It's the ideal place to celebrate a birthday, anniversary, or any special occasion, and is where many of Orlando's residents choose to dine.

Owned and operated by Russ and Carole Christner, the secret of this restaurant's incredible success is that Russ, Carole, or one of their sons or son-in-laws can always be found in the kitchen whenever food is being prepared. This is to ensure that the restaurant's award-winning recipes are being followed to the letter, and that the food is being prepared with the freshest ingredients and with absolute quality consistency.

## ≡FAST FACT

According to Russ and Carole, about 80 percent of the restaurant's patrons begin their meal with one of the shrimp cocktail appetizers. Microwave ovens are never used when preparing the food. To ensure that food is served promptly, the servers use a team approach.

While everything served at Del Frisco's Prime Steak & Lobster is delicious, the specialties of the house are the 8-ounce and 12-ounce filet mignons, the prime porterhouse steak, and the lobster. The beef is prime, aged, corn-fed, and imported from the Midwest. The beef is never frozen, and each steak is cut to order right off the loin when the ticket enters the kitchen. The tenderloins are graded U.S.D.A. Choice and up. Steak knives aren't provided, because the meat is so tender, it cuts easily with a butter knife.

The lobsters are cold water Australian tails, broiled golden. Of course, the bread that's served before the meal is baked fresh daily and served piping hot to your table, and the vegetables are all fresh and seasoned to perfection. Entrees from the restaurant's a-la-carte menu are priced between $17.95 and $25.95 each. Appetizers, salads, soups, vegetables, and desserts, all made fresh daily in the

Del Frisco's kitchen, are priced from $3.50 to $10 each. All portions are extremely generous and can be shared; however, house rules state that each person must order one entree.

In addition to serving some of the best food you'll experience anywhere, the service at Del Frisco's is prompt and friendly. The décor of the restaurant is elegant, featuring fine wood paneling and antiques. There's also a full bar, which features a wine cellar that's extensive and the biggest selection of single malt Scotch in the country, including a bottle that sells for $6,000.

Del Frisco's does no advertising, yet it's crowded virtually every night of the week due to word of mouth and frequent returns by Orlando-area residents. From the moment you step into this restaurant, you'll quickly discover why it has won several awards and has been rated one of the country's top-ten steak houses. Great food, an upbeat and friendly atmosphere, and top-notch service—what more could anyone ask for?

Del Frisco's is open for dinner only, Monday through Thursday, between 5:00 P.M. and 10:00 P.M., and on Friday and Saturday, between 5:00 P.M. and 11:00 P.M. Reservations are definitely recommended, and valet parking is available. Private rooms are available for parties, business meetings, and banquets of up to fifty people.

**Del Frisco's Steak House** is located at ⌨ 729 Lee Road, Orlando, FL 32810. The phone number is ✆ (407) 645-4443.

CHAPTER 5

# Introduction to The Magic Kingdom

IF THIS ISN'T YOUR FIRST TRIP to The Magic Kingdom, but you haven't been to this park in years (or decades), what awaits you is a combination of nostalgic rides, shows, and attractions and a whole new set of entertaining experiences. This chapter provides information that will help you get ready to visit The Magic Kingdom.

## Getting to and from The Magic Kingdom

 Getting to The Magic Kingdom is easy, especially if you're staying at one of The WDW Resort Hotels. Ferryboats and other types of ships cross the Seven Seas Lagoon and take guests to and from nearby hotels and the Ticket and Transportation Center. The resort's famous monorail system stops right in front of The Magic Kingdom and also picks up and drops off guests at several Disney hotels, as well as the Ticket and Transportation Center (TTC). After you arrive at the Ticket and Transportation Center (either by car or by WDW Transportation bus), the ride to The Magic Kingdom will take about four to six minutes once you board a ferryboat or the monorail. A monorail departs from the Ticket and Transportation Center to The Magic Kingdom every three minutes or so.

101

When attempting to take the monorail service or ferryboat to The Magic Kingdom, if there's a long wait, get yourself to Disney's Contemporary Resort, then walk to The Magic Kingdom (it's about a ten- to fifteen-minute walk). At the end of the day, you can avoid long exit lines by walking to Disney's Contemporary Resort and then hopping in your car or taking the WDW Transportation bus to your own hotel or back to the TTC.

The WDW Transportation bus system takes guests to and from all of the Disney hotels as well as the various other theme parks and attractions located in the entire resort. While the bus system will, in fact, take you anywhere within the resort complex that you need to go, it's not a terribly fast service, so plan on spending at least thirty minutes to one hour traveling each time you need to use this free bus service.

Having a rental car to get around the resort is a much faster (and less crowded) mode of transportation, but there are parking fees if you want to park at The Magic Kingdom or the other theme parks. Independent taxi service is available (for a fee, of course). Taking taxis eliminates the wait times involved with taking a WDW Transportation bus, as well as parking hassles, but it is very expensive compared to the other options.

Especially during holiday and peak seasons, those traveling by car should plan on arriving at the Ticket and Transportation Center (the parking area for The Magic Kingdom) early to ensure you'll get a parking spot before the lot gets too jammed. Daily parking fees are $6 per car. (It's free if you're staying at a WDW Resort Hotel; however, you'll have to pay a daily parking fee at the hotel.)

If you're being dropped off by someone (in a car), you'll need to go to the parking lot of the Ticket and Transportation Center, and then take the monorail or ferry boat to The Magic Kingdom. The driver will have to pay the daily parking fee; however, this fee will be refunded if the driver stops at the Exxon gas station near the exit of the parking lot and presents the parking receipt to the attendant within one hour.

## ═══FAST FACT

No matter where you need to get to within The WDW Resort, the WDW bus system will get you there. This complimentary service features over 230 buses that operate continuously in order to transport guests between theme parks, the Disney hotels/resorts, and around the resort property.

# First Things First

 Admission to The Magic Kingdom (or any theme park) requires a ticket. For details about the various ticket and pricing options for visiting The Magic Kingdom and all of the theme parks within The WDW Resort, see Chapter 3.

Whenever you leave The Magic Kingdom, be sure to have your hand stamped as you exit in order to be granted readmission into the park later that day or evening. In addition to the hand stamp, be sure to retain your ticket stub. The hand stamps are designed to be water-resistant, so don't worry if your hand gets wet if you choose to return to your hotel in the middle of the day to go swimming, and then want to return to The Magic Kingdom later that evening. Try to refrain, however, from scrubbing your hands clean with soap until your day's visit to The Magic Kingdom is totally complete.

## What to Bring

Make sure you wear comfortable shoes! Depending on the weather, you might want to take along a jacket (you can always store it in a locker). Try to avoid carrying too much stuff with you. You'll enjoy your visit more if your hands are as free as possible. Don't forget to bring your camera, along with plenty of film and batteries. Avoid having to purchase high-priced film, batteries, or camera supplies in the park.

In case of rain, plan on getting a bit wet. Wear a raincoat or plan to purchase a bright yellow Mickey Mouse poncho (for about $5). Avoid bringing an umbrella into the park. You'll find it frustrating trying to walk around the crowded park with an open umbrella. During a rainstorm, crowds will be less; however, some outdoor rides and attractions will be closed, and some parades and shows might be cancelled.

##  TRAVEL TIP

One good rule is to always travel against the crowds. For example, many rides and attractions will have two lines. Most people automatically head to the right. You'll probably find that the line to the left will be shorter.

### Choose a Place to Meet

As soon as you arrive at The Magic Kingdom, choose a place where you'll meet up with the other people in your group if you get separated. Two ideal meeting places are in front of City Hall or at the Hub (in front of the Walt Disney and Mickey Mouse statue). Decide to meet on the half-hour if you become separated. Adults can leave written messages for each other at City Hall.

If you're traveling with children, upon arriving at The Magic Kingdom, set some ground rules. Instruct the kids to stay close to you (the parent or adult) at all times. They should know that if they get lost, they should immediately contact any Disney cast member.

## The Rating System

To help you choose which rides, shows, and attractions are most worth experiencing while visiting The Magic Kingdom (and all of the theme parks at The WDW Resort), this book offers a star-based ratings system. The ratings are based on the age group each will most appeal to. For each ride, you'll see a chart listing several age groups, plus a one- to three-star rating for that attraction.

Thus, if a rating chart for an attraction has three stars under each age group this ride, show, or attraction is suitable for the entire family and should not be missed.

| | |
|---|---|
| Ages 2–4: | ★★★ |
| Ages 5–10: | ★★★ |
| Ages 11–15: | ★★★ |
| Ages 16–Adult: | ★★★ |
| Senior Citizens: | ★★★ |

If a specific ride, show, or attraction receives two or three stars, but only under one age-group category, that's who will enjoy it the most. In some cases, it may not be suitable for other age groups. In the case of a thrill ride, such as Magic Mountain, it may be a "must-see" ride for the Ages 11–15 and Ages 16–Adult age groups, but it's not suitable for young kids, senior citizens, or anyone else who doesn't enjoy thrill rides. An "N.S." rating indicates that a specific ride, show, or attraction is not suitable for a specific age group. The following is what a rating chart might look like for a highly turbulent thrill ride.

| | |
|---|---|
| Ages 2–4: | N.S. |
| Ages 5–10: | N.S. |
| Ages 11–15: | ★★★ |
| Ages 16–Adult: | ★★★ |
| Senior Citizens: | N.S. |

Here's a brief summary of how each ride, show, and attraction is rated within this book, and what the difference is between one, two, and three stars. These ratings are only recommendations. If you have a mature nine-year-old, he or she may very well enjoy a ride, show, or attraction that's more suitable for an eleven- to fifteen-year-old. As a parent, that's a judgment call you'll need to make based on the information provided within this book and after seeing the ride, show, or attraction for yourself once you get to the theme park.

| | |
|---|---|
| ★ | = Rides and attractions that earned just one star aren't worth waiting for and could be skipped, especially if your time within the theme park is limited. |
| ★★ | = Rides and attractions that earned two stars are good, but they don't fall into the "must-see" category. |
| ★★★ | = The rides and attractions that earned three stars are definitely worth seeing and should not be missed. |
| N.S. | = This denotes rides and attractions that are "Not Suitable" for a specific age group. |

TRAVEL TIP

The very best time to visit the park and not have to deal with huge crowds is on Sunday morning.

## Kid Switch Policy

 Not all of the rides and attractions within The Magic Kingdom are suitable for young children. If two adults are traveling with young kids, but both adults want to experience a ride that's not suitable for the kids, they can take advantage of the Kid Switch policy offered at all of the Disney theme parks.

The Kid Switch policy gives both adults (Mom and Dad, for example) the opportunity to enjoy the various thrill ride attractions that aren't suitable for kids, without the double wait. To take advantage of this policy, one parent waits in line with a small child while the other parent rides the attraction. When the first adult exits the attraction and returns to the loading area, he/she takes custody of the child while the second parent rides—without having to wait in line.

## Dining in The Magic Kingdom

 If you're looking for a fine dining experience, you'll find fancy restaurants located in many of The WDW Resort hotels, as well as in Epcot, The Disney-MGM Studios, Pleasure Island, Downtown Disney, and Disney's BoardWalk. The Magic Kingdom does not have as many restaurants geared to adults looking for a fine dining experience as some of the other parks. For a basic, family-oriented dining experience, The Magic Kingdom offers a variety of restaurants and snack shops. Smoking is not permitted in any of the park's eating establishments.

The restaurants in The Magic Kingdom will be the most crowded every day between 11:00 A.M. and 2:00 P.M. (for lunch) and between 5:00 P.M. and 7:00 P.M. (for dinner). If you don't mind having a flexible eating schedule and you want to avoid the crowds, your best bet is to hit The Magic Kingdom's most popular attractions during these times, and eat during the nonbusy periods. It's always a good idea to experience the more turbulent rides (Magic Mountain, Big Thunder Mountain Railroad, Splash Mountain, etc.) before eating a big meal.

For additional information about the dining options available in **The Magic Kingdom,** call ✆ (407) WDW-DINE. At some of these restaurants, special meals can be ordered to accommodate most dietary restrictions. If you need special meals prepared, however, you're better off eating at one of the restaurants located elsewhere in The WDW Resort. Salads as well as low-salt, vegetarian, and low-cholesterol meals are available at many of the following snack shops and full-service restaurants in The Magic Kingdom.

 TRAVEL TIP

At all of the full-service snack shops and restaurants, be sure to ask about children's portions or special children's menus.

## Fast-Food Snack Shops

These eating establishments are considerably cheaper than the full-service restaurants in The Magic Kingdom. With a few exceptions, hamburgers, hot dogs, chicken strips/nuggets, salads, soft drinks, bottled water, and ice cream are the typical menu offerings at the following fast-food snack shops.

**Aloha Isle** (*Adventureland*)—Dole pineapple "whips" are the snack food available from this kiosk. Plan on spending under $7 per person for a snack.

**Auntie Gravity's Galactic Goodies** (*Tomorrowland*)—If you're looking for frozen yogurt and fruit juices that are out of this world, park your rockets here for a snack. Plan on spending under $7 per person for a snack.

**Aunt Polly's Dockside Inn** (*Frontierland*)—This is the only place on Tom Sawyer's Island where you can purchase food, including "picnic lunches" featuring a ham-and-cheese sandwich. Plan on spending under $12 per person for a meal.

**Casey's Corner** (*Main Street, U.S.A.*)—Hot dogs (with many different toppings), french fries, soft drinks, and a wide range of desserts are available for lunch and dinner. Plan on spending under $12 per person for a meal.

**Columbia Harbor House** (*Liberty Square*)—Fried chicken strips and fried fish, clam chowder, sandwiches, and other fast-food items are on the menu. Plan on spending under $12 per person for a meal.

**Cool Ship** (*Tomorrowland*)—This is a drink-only kiosk. Coca-Cola and other sodas are served. Plan on spending under $4 per person for a drink. Because this is a kiosk and not a restaurant, only cash is accepted here.

**Cosmic Ray's Starlight Café** (*Tomorrowland*)—Traditional burgers; vegetarian burgers; chicken entrees; soups; tossed, chef, and Caesar salads; and sandwiches are available at this cafeteria-style dining location. On the stage in this indoor (air-conditioned) café is an Audio-Animatronic alien (Sonny Eclipse) who performs an ongoing musical act that kids will enjoy watching while they eat. Plan on spending under $12 per person for a meal.

**Diamond Horseshoe Saloon Review** (*Liberty Square*)—Sandwiches, soft drinks, and snacks are served here. Kick back and enjoy the show while you chow down on snacks in the comfort of an air-conditioned theater. Plan on spending under $12 per person for a meal.

**Enchanted Grove** (*Fantasyland*)—Slushes and soft-serve ice cream may be the perfect snack on a hot day. Plan on spending under $7 per person for a snack.

**Frontierland Fries** (*Frontierland*)—In addition to a variety of cold drinks, this is one of the few places within The WDW Resort where McDonald's french fries are available. They're a favorite snack among kids. Plan on spending under $7 per person for a snack.

**Launching Pad at Rockettower Plaza** (*Tomorrowland*)—Various snack-food items, beverages, and smoked turkey legs are available. Plan on spending under $7 per person for a snack.

**Main Street Bakery** (*Main Street, U.S.A.*)—Freshly baked goods, including cookies and pastries; various flavored gourmet coffees; and cold beverages are available here. If you choose to order a bagel and cream cheese, you'll be given an extremely small amount of cream cheese. Additional cream cheese costs extra, and you'll quickly discover that while the baked goods are fresh, the bagels aren't made on-site. Plan on spending under $7 per person for a snack.

**Mrs. Potts' Cupboard** (*Fantasyland*)—Slushes, soft-serve ice cream, and sundaes are served. Plan on spending under $7 per person for a snack.

**Pecos Bill Café** (*Frontierland*)—Burgers, BBQ chicken, hot dogs, wrap sandwiches, and salads are the main entrees available. Plan on spending under $12 per person for a meal.

**Pinocchio Village Haus** (*Fantasyland*)—Hamburgers, cheeseburgers, hot dogs, and salads are among this snack shop's most popular selections. Plan on spending under $12 per person for a meal.

**El Pirata Y El Perico** (*Adventureland*)—It's not Taco Bell, but if you're in the mood for tacos, nachos, hot dogs, and the like, this is the place to stop for a quick Mexican lunch or dinner. Plan on spending under $12 per person for a meal.

**Plaza Ice Cream Parlor** (*Main Street, U.S.A.*)—Carnation ice cream is the most popular item. Plan on spending under $7 per person for a snack.

**The Plaza Pavilion** (*Tomorrowland*)—Individual pan pizzas, fried chicken strips, and salads are among the main entrees served at this location. Plan on spending under $12 per person for a meal.

**Scuttle's Landing** (*Fantasyland*)—Shaved ice and drinks are available. Plan on spending under $5 per person for a snack. This is a favorite snack stop among kids with a sweet tooth looking to cool down on a hot day.

**Sleepy Hollow** (*Liberty Square*)—Various types of snacks and beverages can be consumed here if a light, informal snack or meal is what you're looking for. Cappuccino, espresso, and gourmet coffee are served. Plan on spending under $7 per person for a snack.

**Sunshine Tree Terrace** (*Frontierland*)—Nonfat frozen yogurt, cappuccino, espresso, and various citrus drinks and snacks are available. Plan on spending under $7 per person for a snack.

**Toontown Farmer's Market** (*Toontown*)—Fresh fruit, snacks, and drinks are served. This is one of the few places where truly healthy snacks can be purchased within The Magic Kingdom. Plan on spending under $6 per person for a snack.

Also located throughout the park are wagons and snack kiosks that serve a variety of specialty items, including sodas, bottled water, juices, popcorn, ice cream, turkey legs, eggrolls, pretzels, and fresh fruit. The turkey legs are extremely popular. Genuine McDonald's french fries can also be purchased from a kiosk across from Pecos Bill Café in Frontierland.

## Restaurants

If you're looking for a complete meal in a full-service, sit-down restaurant, the following eating establishments are offered within The Magic Kingdom. Plan on spending between $15 and $25 per person when eating at any of these restaurants. To make a same-day lunch or dinner **"Preferred Seating"** reservation, call ☎ (407) WDW-DINE, visit City Hall, or drop by the individual restaurants as early in the day as possible.

**Cinderella's Royal Table at King Stefan's Banquet Hall** (*Fantasyland,* inside the castle)—Chicken, prime rib, salads, and a few different seafood dishes are the primary dinner entrees at this restaurant. There's also a "Once Upon A Time" character breakfast, served every morning between 8:00 A.M. and 10:00 A.M. that allows you and your family to dine with popular Disney characters. Reservations are suggested.

**Crystal Palace** (*Main Street, U.S.A.*)—You'll probably run into several popular Disney characters as you dine at this all-you-can-eat buffet. The menu at this restaurant changes throughout the year; however, American cuisine and seafood are served. Reservations are suggested.

**Liberty Tree Tavern** (*Liberty Square*)—If you have about an hour to spend eating, this full-service restaurant offers a large menu of American favorites. During the dinner hours, you'll often find Disney characters wandering around this restaurant mingling with guests. Reservations are suggested.

**Plaza Restaurant** (*Main Street, U.S.A.*)—An ideal place to stop for lunch, this restaurant offers a large selection of salads, grilled deli-style sandwiches, gourmet burgers, and other light entrees. For dessert, ice cream sundaes, milkshakes, and old-fashioned ice cream sodas are served. A full dinner menu is available. The service is fast, so you can get back into The Magic Kingdom quickly and continue enjoying your day. Reservations are suggested.

**Tony's Town Square** (*Main Street, U.S.A.*)—Italian lunch and dinner entrees are what you'll find at this "old New York"–style restaurant. Reservations are suggested.

Just outside of The Magic Kingdom, picnic facilities are available (free of charge) if you bring your own food to the park.

Guests, however, are not encouraged to bring their own food or drinks into The Magic Kingdom. If you happen to hide a sandwich, piece of fruit, or a candy bar in your jacket pocket or purse, you're not going to be arrested. But, if you get caught trying to smuggle a picnic basket of goodies into the park, you'll be asked to store it in a locker or return it to your car.

Chewing gum is not sold anywhere in The Magic Kingdom. If you choose to bring your own chewing gum, please be considerate of other guests and dispose of it in a trash can when you're done chewing it.

## ⊕ HOT SPOT

For breakfast, head over to Cinderella's Royal Table. This breakfast with the Disney characters fills up fast, so make reservations! For lunch, join Winnie the Pooh and other characters at the Crystal Palace: A Buffet with Character. For dinner with the characters, the Liberty Tree Tavern is the place to dine, starting at 4:00 P.M.

## The Magic Kingdom and WDW Resort Tours

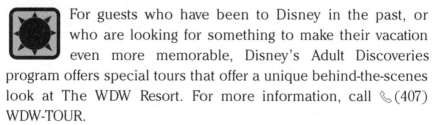

For guests who have been to Disney in the past, or who are looking for something to make their vacation even more memorable, Disney's Adult Discoveries program offers special tours that offer a unique behind-the-scenes look at The WDW Resort. For more information, call ☎ (407) WDW-TOUR.

The Backstage Magic tour is held every Monday, Wednesday, Thursday, and Friday and is a seven-hour look at The Magic Kingdom, including a special look at the park's underground tunnels. This tour also takes guests to see backstage at Epcot and The Disney-MGM Studios. Lunch is included. This tour is open to people over the age of sixteen and costs $160 per person.

The Keys to the Kingdom tour is offered every day and provides a four-hour behind-the-scenes look at The Magic Kingdom. Tour guides explain the history of the park and offer guests a special look at the underground tunnel system. This tour begins promptly at 10:00 A.M. from The Magic Kingdom's City Hall and costs $45 per person (minimum age is sixteen), plus the cost of admission to the park.

If you have a green thumb, or wish you did, Disney's Gardens of the World tour is presented every Tuesday and Thursday by a member of Disney's horticultural team. The three-hour tour includes a walk around Epcot, with detailed descriptions and information about the exotic plants, trees, and landscaping. The cost is $25 per person, plus the price of admission to the park.

Aside from the forty-five-minute Animation tour offered to everyone at The Disney-MGM Studios, there's a special two-and-a-half-hour Inside Animation tour that goes into far more detail about how Disney creates its animated features. Guests who participate in this tour will meet some of the talented Disney animators responsible for creating Disney's most popular animated features. The cost of this tour is $45 per person, plus the price of admission to The Disney-MGM Studios.

## ⊕ HOT SPOT

In addition to being able to meet the various Disney characters in Mickey's Toontown Fair and at other predetermined locations within the park, "Cinderella's Surprise Celebration" offers a musical show and a chance to meet over twenty of your favorite Disney characters afterward. This musical celebration takes place daily in the Castle forecourt.

Hidden Treasures of World Showcase offers a special look at the various pavilions at Epcot's World Showcase. There are three separate tours available; each is two hours in length. Each costs $25 per person, plus the price of admission to the park. Every Wednesday, a complete, five-hour tour of all eleven pavilions is offered for $65 per person. (Admission to Epcot and lunch is included in the price of this tour.)

For a chance to interact with the dolphins at the Living Seas pavilion of Epcot, the Dolphins In Depth tour is offered. If you're a certified scuba diver, the DiveQuest program allows you to take a dive into the Living Seas tank and interact with the thousands of sea creatures living within it. Both of these programs are described in greater detail in Chapter 8 of this book. The prices for these tours are $140 per person.

All of these tours are given by extremely knowledgeable Disney cast members and are limited to small groups in order to ensure personalized attention. No matter which of these tours you partici-pate in, you're sure to have a memorable experience designed to make your vacation even more exciting. Taking pictures during many of these tours is not permitted.

# *Exploring The Magic Kingdom*

THE HEART AND SOUL of The Walt Disney World Resort is the place that probably most resembles Walt Disney's original dream for a theme park—The Magic Kingdom. This chapter will provide you with an attraction-by-attraction tour of the family-oriented rides, shows, and attractions within The Magic Kingdom, plus explain how you can make the most of your time visiting this popular theme park.

## Park Overview

This area of the resort is modeled after Disneyland (in Anaheim, California), and while it's only one of several theme parks that now make up the entire WDW resort, this theme park can easily provide at least one or two full days (and evenings) of fun-filled entertainment, especially if you're traveling with kids. Out of all of the theme parks and activities available at The WDW Resort, The Magic Kingdom is most likely what kids will enjoy the most, since most of the rides and attractions, especially in Fantasyland and Mickey's Toontown Fair, are designed with kids in mind.

Like Disneyland, Walt Disney considered The Magic Kingdom to be a giant stage, in which guests participate in every aspect of their entertainment. Many of the rides, shows, and attractions in The Magic Kingdom are based on classic Disney stories and movies, and like Disneyland (which was build first), The Magic Kingdom is divided up into distinctly themed lands—Adventureland, Liberty Square, Frontierland, Fantasyland, Mickey's Toontown Fair, Tomorrowland, and Main Street, U.S.A. These lands are comprised of rides, shows, attractions, restaurants, snack shops, gift shops, outdoor entertainers, and specially designed architecture that make you feel totally immersed in the theme park experience.

Guests enter through the Main Entrance, pass under the Walt Disney World Railroad, and find themselves on Main Street, U.S.A This street, which is The Magic Kingdom's parade route, is lined with shops, restaurants, and plenty of delightful surprises, like the Main Street vehicles, street performers, and musicians.

## ≡FAST FACT

This park opened on October 1, 1971; however, the official grand-opening ceremony took place October 22 through 24 and was televised nationally on NBC. At the time, The Magic Kingdom contained twenty-two major attractions.

As guests wander down Main Street, U.S.A., the sight ahead is Cinderella's Castle—the most famous landmark in The WDW Resort. This 180-foot-tall castle is the entrance to Fantasyland and is located just past the Hub, where an almost life-size statue of Walt Disney and Mickey Mouse is displayed. This circular park (complete with benches and beautiful landscaping) is known as the Hub, because it's located in the center of The Magic Kingdom. From this location, guests can easily locate the entrances to each of The Magic Kingdom's themed lands (with the exception of Mickey's Toontown Fair).

# Main Street, U.S.A.

 Located along Main Street, U.S.A. are all sorts of interesting shops that offer a wide selection of souvenirs, gifts, and memorabilia, along with film and various other necessities. These shops are most crowded first thing in the morning and just before the park closes. Don't forget, anything you purchase can be held at a pickup location near the exit of The Magic Kingdom, stored in a locker, or delivered to your WDW Resort hotel. You probably don't want to carry around your purchases throughout the day.

## ⟰FAST FACT

City Hall is The Magic Kingdom's main information and reservation center as well as the Lost and Found. Tickets to the walking tour of The Magic Kingdom can also be purchased here. For adults who get separated during their visit to this park, messages can be left at City Hall.

Many of these shops are fully air-conditioned, so if the sun and heat outside become too overwhelming, come inside, browse, and cool off. For your convenience, the shops along Main Street, U.S.A. tend to stay open up to one hour later than the rest of the park.

### Boulevard Entertainment

Throughout the day, guests are entertained by sidewalk performers, including Dapper Dan's Barbershop Quartet, Rhythm Rascals Band, Casey's Corner Piano, and other talented performers who all add ambiance to Main Street, U.S.A. and surrounding areas.

## Fantasy in the Sky Fireworks

| | |
|---|---|
| Ages 2–4: | ★★★ |
| Ages 5–10: | ★★★ |
| Ages 11–15: | ★★★ |
| Ages 16–Adult: | ★★★ |
| Senior Citizens: | ★★★ |

This fireworks show takes place each night high above Cinderella's Castle. The fireworks are choreographed and synchronized to popular Disney tunes. This is a ten-minute show that the entire family will love, so don't miss it! The best viewing locations can be found along Main Street, U.S.A., toward (and around) the Hub. Basically, if you have a good view of the top of the castle, you'll see the entire fireworks show clearly.

👍 This is a must-see attraction.

## Main Street Cinema

| | |
|---|---|
| Ages 2–4: | ★ |
| Ages 5–10: | ★ |
| Ages 11–15: | ★★ |
| Ages 16–Adult: | ★★ |
| Senior Citizens: | ★★★ |

If you're in the mood to catch Mickey Mouse in his very first animated features, drop into this old-fashioned cinema located along Main Street, U.S.A. Mickey's movies are shown continuously, so you're free to come and go as you please. There's seldom a crowd at this attraction, and since the theater is air-conditioned, dropping in for a few minutes is a great way to cool off and experience some of Walt Disney's classic animation. There are no seats in this small theater, but there is an area where kids can sit on the floor.

## Main Street Railroad Depot

| | |
|---|---|
| Ages 2–4: | ★★ |
| Ages 5–10: | ★★ |
| Ages 11–15: | ★★ |
| Ages 16–Adult: | ★★ |
| Senior Citizens: | ★★ |

This is the main station for the Walt Disney World Railroad, which follows a circular track around the perimeter of The Magic Kingdom. Here's your chance to ride in an authentic 1920s steam train and get a tour of The Magic Kingdom at the same time. You can get on and off at any of the train stations, or take a ride completely around the park. (It takes about twenty minutes to complete the 1.5-mile journey.)

## ⊕ HOT SPOT

Take a ride on a horseless carriage, an old-fashioned fire engine, trolleys drawn by beautiful Belgian and Percheron horses, and other vehicles that provide free transportation from one end of Main Street, U.S.A to the other.

### SpectroMagic Parade

| | |
|---|---|
| Ages 2–4: | ★★★ |
| Ages 5–10: | ★★★ |
| Ages 11–15: | ★★★ |
| Ages 16–Adult: | ★★★ |
| Senior Citizens: | ★★★ |

In 1991, the Main Street Electrical Parade was replaced by the SpectroMagic Parade. Floats and popular Disney characters are covered with thousands of fiber-optic lights that flash in a rainbow of colors as this parade travels down Main Street, U.S.A. accompanied by popular Disney music.

This is a family-oriented parade that's presented in the evenings and shouldn't be missed. One good viewing location is from the porch of the Visitor's Center, located near the train station, opposite City Hall. Otherwise, you can catch this parade from anywhere along Main Street, U.S.A. Be sure to arrive early to stake out your viewing location, especially if the park is crowded. If two shows are presented the evening of your visit, the crowd for the second performance will be much smaller.

👍 This is a must-see attraction.

### The Afternoon Disney Character Parade

| | |
|---|---|
| Ages 2–4: | ★★ |
| Ages 5–10: | ★★★ |
| Ages 11–15: | ★★★ |
| Ages 16–Adult: | ★★ |
| Senior Citizens: | ★★ |

Each day, there's a parade during the day that features some of your all-time favorite Disney characters riding on colorful floats and dancing to popular Disney tunes. This parade is more kid-oriented, although it'll appeal to people of all ages and help get you into the Disney spirit as you spend your day in The Magic Kingdom.

The best viewing spots are anywhere along Main Street, U.S.A, like in front of the Plaza Ice Cream Parlor. As with any parade or show, you'll want to arrive early to stake out the best viewing location.

Performed daily, typically at 3:00 P.M., this parade lasts about fifteen minutes and features over 110 cast members, including many of your favorite Disney characters.

## ≡FAST FACT

Every day, you'll see concerts presented by the official Walt Disney World Marching Band as it travels up and down Main Street, U.S.A and also performs live in Town Square.

### The Welcome Center

Located on the right side of Main Street, U.S.A, just after you pass under the train tracks, you'll find the Welcome Center. What's offered within this attraction changes periodically. The movie theater in the Welcome Center is fully air-conditioned and comfortable seating is provided. There's also a AAA Travel Center/Information Desk inside this building.

## Adventureland

As you already know, The Magic Kingdom is divided into various themed areas. Starting with Adventureland, here's a rundown of the rides, shows, and attractions you'll find in this area of the theme park. Anything that's specifically targeted to young kids (and not necessarily teens or adults), however, is described in the next chapter.

## The Jungle Cruise

| | |
|---|---|
| Ages 2–4: | ★ |
| Ages 5–10: | ★★ |
| Ages 11–15: | ★★ |
| Ages 16–Adult: | ★★★ |
| Senior Citizens: | ★★★ |

This is one of The Magic Kingdom's original rides that opened in 1971. Safari boats carry guests down a manmade river that resembles a scene right out of Africa. You'll see life-size Animatronic animals as you embark on a ten-minute journey. Don't worry, this ride is pretty mellow (you won't get wet, and the boat travels slowly). You should definitely experience the Jungle Cruise during daylight hours. Be prepared to hear corny jokes from your tour guide.

## Pirates of the Caribbean

| | |
|---|---|
| Ages 2–4: | ★ |
| Ages 5–10: | ★★★ |
| Ages 11–15: | ★★★ |
| Ages 16–Adult: | ★★★ |
| Senior Citizens: | ★★★ |

Since 1973, this boat ride has taken guests on a magical journey to a port on the Spanish Main. You'll be singing "Yo ho, yo ho; a pirate's life for me" along with the life-size Audio-Animatronic pirates as you experience this enjoyable ten-minute cruise. While it's no longer state-of-the-art and isn't a thrill ride, Pirates of the Caribbean is one of The Magic Kingdom's most popular rides.

 This is a must-see attraction.

## ═FAST FACT

As with many of the rides located throughout WDW, this one has several hidden Mickey ears that are visible if you're looking for them during the cruise, so keep your eyes peeled for the ears.

## Swiss Family Treehouse

| | |
|---|---|
| Ages 2–4: | N.S. |
| Ages 5–10: | ★★★ |
| Ages 11–15: | ★★★ |
| Ages 16–Adult: | ★★ |
| Senior Citizens: | N.S. |

Inspired by the 1960 Disney film *Swiss Family Robinson*, this is a giant tree house that guests of all ages are welcome to climb and explore. This tree contains over 300,000 lifelike polyethylene leaves that appear to grow on 1,400 man-made branches. Children in particular will enjoy exploring the hidden areas located in this tree house.

## The Enchanted Tiki Room—
## Under New Management

| | |
|---|---|
| Ages 2–4: | ★ |
| Ages 5–10: | ★★★ |
| Ages 11–15: | ★★ |
| Ages 16–Adult: | ★★★ |
| Senior Citizens: | ★★★ |

Originally, this was one of the first Disney attractions ever to utilize Audio-Animatronics (robotic characters that seem lifelike). A version of this show was first introduced at Disneyland back in 1963. It featured 225 Audio-Animatronic birds that sang and entertained guests during a seventeen-minute performance that was extremely cute.

Back in 1998, however, this attraction was reworked. While the concept is pretty much the same, this attraction is now "hosted" by Audio-Animatronic adaptations of Iago (from Disney's *Aladdin*) and Zazu (from *The Lion King*). The music that's performed has also been updated. So, if you haven't visited The Magic Kingdom in the past few years, seeing this new show will provide a new entertainment experience, yet rekindle a touch of Disney nostalgia.

# ⊕ HOT SPOT

Throughout the day, at specific times that are listed within *The Magic Kingdom Guide Map,* the Disney characters will make appearances throughout the park. Two of the appearance locations within Adventureland are in front of Pirates of the Caribbean and near the Magic Carpets of Aladdin.

## The Magic Carpets of Aladdin

| | |
|---|---|
| Ages 2–4: | N.S. |
| Ages 5–10: | ★★★ |
| Ages 11–15: | ★★★ |
| Ages 16–Adult: | ★★ |
| Senior Citizens: | ★★ |

This is The Magic Kingdom's newest attraction! Here's your chance to hop aboard a magic carpet and see Agrabah in style. Based on Disney's *Aladdin*, guests climb aboard moving vehicles (four people per carpet), which they then control. Carpets can move up and down, plus pitch forward and backward. During the ride, water gets shot at guests by spitting camels. (Don't worry, you'll hardy get wet.)

# Frontierland

Here's a rundown of what you'll experience in this area of The Magic Kingdom, which was inspired by America's early days of exploration and expansion.

## Big Thunder Mountain Railroad

| | |
|---|---|
| Ages 2–4: | N.S. |
| Ages 5–10: | ★★ |
| Ages 11–15: | ★★★ |
| Ages 16–Adult: | ★★★ |
| Senior Citizens: | N.S. |

Don't confuse this fast and furious runaway train ride with the Walt Disney Railroad. This is a four-minute, high-speed, fast-turning thrill ride up, down, and around a manmade mountain. Along this ride's 2,780 feet of roller coaster track, over twenty Audio-Animatronic characters and over $300,000 worth of genuine mining antiques help to add a sense of authenticity to this exciting ride. To truly experience this ride, check it out after dark. Guests must be at least 40 inches tall to experience Big Thunder Mountain Railroad, and anyone who suffers from heart or back problems or is pregnant should skip it. This is one of the attractions in The Magic Kingdom that teens and adults won't want to miss.

👍 This is a must-see attraction.

## Big Thunder Shooting Arcade

| | |
|---|---|
| Ages 2–4: | N.S. |
| Ages 5–10: | ★ |
| Ages 11–15: | ★ |
| Ages 16–Adult: | ★ |
| Senior Citizens: | ★ |

Replica rifles that use infrared bullets are used in this old Western-style shooting gallery. Get ready for the unexpected if you hit your targets. (If you want to test your aim, it'll cost you fifty cents. Like all of the arcades, shooting costs aren't included in the price of your admission to The Magic Kingdom.)

## Country Bear Jamboree

| | |
|---|---|
| Ages 2–4: | ★★ |
| Ages 5–10: | ★★★ |
| Ages 11–15: | ★★★ |
| Ages 16–Adult: | ★ |
| Senior Citizens: | ★ |

Country music is performed by a group of about twenty life-size Audio-Animatronic bears and creatures. Young kids and adults will find this show charming, while the teen set will probably find it a bit hokey. This seventeen-minute show will have you singing and clapping along. Shows are continuous, and there's excellent visibility from all seats in the theater, so don't worry about trying to get preferred seating in the front or center of the auditorium.

## Splash Mountain

| | |
|---|---|
| Ages 2–4: | N.S. |
| Ages 5–10: | ★★★ |
| Ages 11–15: | ★★★ |
| Ages 16–Adult: | ★★★ |
| Senior Citizens: | ★ |

This light-hearted flumelike boat ride starts out totally calm and mellow, as guests are entertained by dozens of singing Audio-Animatronic characters from Disney's animated classic *Song of the South*. "Zip-A-Dee-Doo-Dah" is the theme song of this ride, which tells the story of Brer Rabbit as he tries to locate his "laughing place."

Brer Rabbit gets the last laugh, however. At the end of this ride, you'll be sent cruising down a 52-foot drop at a 45-degree angle, traveling in excess of 40 miles per hour. In all, this is a rather calm eleven-minute boat ride. It's only the very last few seconds that constitute the thrill-ride element. Splash Mountain is definitely one of The Magic Kingdom's very best attractions, from both an entertainment and a thrill-providing standpoint. It's not suitable for young children (under 44 inches tall), nor should it be experienced by anyone with back or heart problems or who can't endure the final drop at the end of the ride.

 This is a must-see attraction.

## ═FAST FACT

Chances are, you will get a bit wet at the end of this ride, so be sure that you cover up your camera equipment and snuggly stow your belongings. As you're taking the final plummet, be sure to smile! Color 8" × 10" photos of your plunge are available as you exit this ride, for an additional fee of about $12.

### Tom Sawyer Island

| | |
|---|---|
| Ages 2–4: | ★ |
| Ages 5–10: | ★★ |
| Ages 11–15: | ★★★ |
| Ages 16–Adult: | ★★ |
| Senior Citizens: | ★ |

This manmade island is located in the center of the Rivers of America. To reach this island, you'll need to hop aboard one of the Tom Sawyer log rafts that departs regularly. The island is open during daylight hours only. Kids especially will love exploring Injun Joe's Cave, Harper's Mill, and Ft. Sam Clemens. The island is filled with dirt paths to follow, bridges to cross, and lots of places to explore. Kids who know the story of Tom Sawyer and Huck Finn will enjoy this attraction the most.

## Liberty Square

 Give me liberty or give me Mickey! Patriotic tourists, thrill seekers, and fun-loving vacationers alike will find a lot to experience in this area of The Magic Kingdom.

## The Diamond Horseshoe Saloon Revue

| | |
|---|---|
| Ages 2–4: | ★ |
| Ages 5–10: | ★★ |
| Ages 11–15: | ★★ |
| Ages 16–Adult: | ★★ |
| Senior Citizens: | ★★ |

Seven times a day, this live musical review features dancing girls, comedians, and singers, plus other entertaining acts all with a Western flare. Each show is one hour in length; however, guests are welcome to come and go as they please (providing seats are available). Food service is available.

## Davy Crockett Keel Boats

| | |
|---|---|
| Ages 2–4: | N.S. |
| Ages 5–10: | ★ |
| Ages 11–15: | ★★ |
| Ages 16–Adult: | ★★ |
| Senior Citizens: | ★ |

Head for the dock near the Haunted Mansion and climb aboard one of these keel boats for a ride around Tom Sawyer's Island (along the Rivers of America).

## Liberty Square Riverboat

| | |
|---|---|
| Ages 2–4: | ★★ |
| Ages 5–10: | ★★ |
| Ages 11–15: | ★★ |
| Ages 16–Adult: | ★★ |
| Senior Citizens: | ★★★ |

The Richard F. Irvine is a real stern-wheeler steamboat that was built at Disney World and named after one of its designers. This boat picks up passengers and takes them for a fifteen-minute ride around the Rivers of America (a one-half-mile-long cruise), giving a great view of Tom Sawyer's Island and many other sites in The Magic Kingdom.

## ≡FAST FACT

This ship has been cruising since 1971 and makes trips regularly throughout the day. Since this ship holds a huge number of passengers, you're almost always guaranteed to get aboard on the cruise of your choice with a minimal wait.

For the best view of the park, climb to the upper deck during the cruise. This is a relaxing experience and a great way to kick back and get off your feet for a while, and at the same time, experience the ambiance of The Magic Kingdom. This is one of The Magic Kingdom's original attractions.

## The Hall of Presidents

| | |
|---|---|
| Ages 2–4: | N.S. |
| Ages 5–10: | ★ |
| Ages 11–15: | ★★ |
| Ages 16–Adult: | ★★★ |
| Senior Citizens: | ★★★ |

This attraction is sort of like visiting a high-tech museum in which Audio-Animatronic re-creations of America's presidents actually teach guests history. Kids will most likely get bored by this twenty-minute presentation; however, adults will find it both highly patriotic and extremely interesting. Advanced Audio-Animatronic technology is used to make several of the presidents, including George W. Bush (the newest addition to this attraction), come to life on the stage. President George W. Bush makes an inspirational ninety-second speech (which he actually recorded for this attraction) about freedom to create, to prosper, and to dream.

This presentation is shown in an air-conditioned theater. In fact, even the waiting room is air-conditioned. As you're spending time in the waiting room, browse around and check out the historical paintings on the walls. Take a look back at American history in this educational and inspirational attraction.

## The Haunted Mansion

| | |
|---|---|
| Ages 2–4: | N.S. |
| Ages 5–10: | ★★ |
| Ages 11–15: | ★★★ |
| Ages 16–Adult: | ★★★ |
| Senior Citizens: | ★★★ |

Yes, this is a haunted house that's jam-packed with all sorts of awesome special effects, but this ride is designed to provide family-oriented entertainment, so don't expect anything too scary. During much of your eight-minute tour of this mansion, you'll be riding in a moving love seat. This is definitely one of The Magic Kingdom's most technologically advanced rides in terms of the special effects. As you enter the house, be sure to read the rather bizarre inscriptions on the tombstones.

As you wait outside of the mansion for your tour, you'll be covered by an awning, so you won't be exposed to direct sun or rain. Be sure to notice the somber costumes worn by Disney cast members working at this attraction. When you're escorted into a small room that appears to stretch, be sure to look upward, especially just after the lights go out. The ride portion of this attraction begins as you exit the small room (which is really an elevator). You'll be loaded into two-person love-seat-like vehicles.

When your tour begins, check out the "animated" statues in the library. Other wonderful effects to be on the lookout for are the woman's head in a crystal ball and the ghosts in the ballroom (be sure to look all around this room, including near the floor and the ceiling). Near the very end of your tour, look into the mirror to see who (or what) is sitting between you and the living person you're sitting next to as you see this final haunting special effect.

 This is a must-see attraction.

## ═══ FAST FACT

This is another one of The Magic Kingdom's classic attractions that has been entertaining guests since the park first opened.

# Tomorrowland

 When The Magic Kingdom first opened in 1971, this land was designed to offer guests a peek into the future. As the years have gone by, Tomorrowland has evolved, with older (outdated) rides and attractions being replaced by newer, more state-of-the-art rides and attractions that continue to offer a futuristic theme. In 1996, Tomorrowland received a major overhaul, when the ExtraTERRORestrial Alien Encounter, the Timekeeper, and the Astro

Orbiter ride opened to the public. The most recent addition to this area of The Magic Kingdom is Buzz Lightyear's Space Ranger Spin, which opened in 1998 (replacing the Take Flight attraction).

### The ExtraTERRORestrial Alien Encounter

| | |
|---|---|
| Ages 2–4: | N.S. |
| Ages 5–10: | N.S. |
| Ages 11–15: | ★★★ |
| Ages 16–Adult: | ★★★ |
| Senior Citizens: | ★★ |

Believe it or not, this is one of the scariest attractions at WDW from a sci-fi/horror point of view. While not exactly a thrill ride, rather elaborate special effects are used to make guests feel like they're about to be attacked by evil aliens.

George Lucas worked with Disney's Imagineers to create this rather bizarre attraction. As this attraction begins, guests are actually restrained in their seats, which adds to the intensity. Remember, this isn't a roller coaster, nor is it an extremely bumpy ride, so don't get too nervous. This entire attraction lasts about twenty minutes and involves a rather elaborate preshow.

 This is a must-see attraction.

## ⊕ HOT SPOT

Alien Encounter is far scarier and more intense than the Haunted Mansion and is not suitable for young children and most senior citizens. For teens and adults, this is definitely something that should not be missed. As soon as the park opens, race over to this ride for the shortest wait.

### The Timekeeper

| | |
|---|---|
| Ages 2–4: | ★ |
| Ages 5–10: | ★★ |
| Ages 11–15: | ★★ |
| Ages 16–Adult: | ★★ |
| Senior Citizens: | ★★ |

Are you ready to take a twenty-minute tour through time? That's the theme of this attraction, which combines Audio-Animatronic characters with an impressive 360-degree movie experience. Jules Verne and H. G. Wells are just some of the "people" you'll meet as you trek through time and around the world.

This is an exciting attraction that's suitable for people of all ages. Even with your feet planted firmly on the ground, the 360-degree movie makes you feel like you're actually moving. If this experience gets too real or too intense, simply shut your eyes to re-establish your equilibrium. This attraction currently operates on a seasonal basis. Consult *The Magic Kingdom Guide Map* for details.

 This is a must-see attraction.

## Space Mountain

| Ages 2–4: | N.S. |
|---|---|
| Ages 5–10: | ★★ |
| Ages 11–15: | ★★★ |
| Ages 16–Adult: | ★★★ |
| Senior Citizens: | N.S. |

Since 1975, this has been one of the most popular rides in all of WDW, and with good reason. Space Mountain is a high-speed roller coaster that uses some special effects to make you feel like you're seated in a rocket that's racing through space. In reality, you'll be traveling about 28 miles per hour.

This entire ride is experienced in almost total darkness, so you won't see what's coming. This is an awesome thrill ride. For those who don't normally enjoy roller coasters, this one offers a lot of high-speed sharp turns, but very few drops, making it exciting, but a bit tamer than a typical roller coaster. The ride itself lasts under three minutes, but the wait is usually about one hour (or more). Space Mountain is one of those rides you don't want to miss, so plan your time in The Magic Kingdom accordingly.

The best times to experience this ride are during one of the parades, or during peak lunch or dinner hours. Space Mountain is not suitable for very young children (there is a height restriction of 44 inches and children under the age of seven need an adult to ride with them) or anyone with heart, back, or other medical problems. Pregnant women should also sit this one out. As soon as the park opens, race to this ride for the shortest wait.

 This is a must-see attraction.

## ≡FAST FACT

While experiencing Space Mountain, and all of the other rides at WDW, guests are under constant video surveillance. The Walt Disney Company is extremely safety conscious. Guests who act in a manner that endangers themselves or others will be dealt with accordingly.

## Astro Orbiter

| | |
|---|---|
| Ages 2–4: | N.S. |
| Ages 5–10: | ★★ |
| Ages 11–15: | ★★ |
| Ages 16–Adult: | ★ |
| Senior Citizens: | N.S. |

Here's one way to get a great view of Tomorrowland and at the same time enjoy a mild thrill ride. Guests sit in rocket-shaped cars that go up and down as they travel around in circles high above ground level. The line for this ride moves very slowly. If there's a long wait, either return later in the day or skip this ride.

## Walt Disney's Carousel of Progress

| | |
|---|---|
| Ages 2–4: | ★ |
| Ages 5–10: | ★★ |
| Ages 11–15: | ★★★ |
| Ages 16–Adult: | ★★★ |
| Senior Citizens: | ★★★ |

This classic WDW attraction was revamped in 1996 but is still as charming as when it first began entertaining guests in 1975. Guests are seated in a theater-like room that actually rotates around a 360-degree stage. Each time the theater moves, a new scene featuring an Audio-Animatronic American family is seen. Guests follow this family through the twentieth century and explore some of the major technological advances that have occurred in the home during the early 1900s, 1920s, 1940s, and present day. The final scene depicts technology that we might be seeing in the not-too-distant future. "A whole new century is waiting for us" and "Tomorrow is just a dream away" are two of the themes of this attraction.

This is a twenty-minute show for the entire family that shouldn't be missed. The theater is air-conditioned, and guests get to sit down and relax as the show takes place. The waiting area is outside, but covered. There are only two benches to sit down on, so plan on standing as you wait to enter into the theater.

 This is a must-see attraction.

# ═══FAST FACT

Walt Disney himself created this attraction, which has been seen by more people than any other show in U.S. history. As you're waiting to go into the revolving theater, you'll see a video presentation (on monitors) that features Walt Disney and provides some history behind this unique attraction.

## Tomorrowland Transit Authority

| | |
|---|---|
| Ages 2–4: | ★ |
| Ages 5–10: | ★ |
| Ages 11–15: | ★★ |
| Ages 16–Adult: | ★★ |
| Senior Citizens: | ★★★ |

For a ten-minute, rather relaxing tour of Tomorrowland, climb aboard Tomorrowland's energy-efficient, pollution-free mass-transit system that travels about 10 miles per hour and follows a mile-long track. You'll get a sneak peek inside Space Mountain and pass by just about all of Tomorrowland's other rides and attractions.

## Tomorrowland Indy Speedway

| | |
|---|---|
| Ages 2–4: | N.S. |
| Ages 5–10: | ★★★ |
| Ages 11–15: | ★★★ |
| Ages 16–Adult: | ★ |
| Senior Citizens: | ★ |

People of all ages (who meet the 52-inch height restriction)—whether or not they have a real-life driver's license—can drive these sports cars along a 2,000-foot-long track. These gasoline-powered cars have rack-and-pinion steering and disc brakes, but they're confined to a track that keeps the driver totally safe. Drivers can reach cruising speeds of about 7 miles per hour as they take a single lap around the track.

The ride lasts about five minutes and gives young people a true feeling of being in the driver's seat of a car. Drivers beware: Even in these cars, minor fender benders are common, especially if you get stuck behind a slow driver. Instead of spending time at this raceway, teens and adults looking for a real thrill should steer over to Epcot (or take the monorail) and experience Test Track.

## Buzz Lightyear's Space Ranger Spin

| | |
|---|---|
| Ages 2–4: | ★★ |
| Ages 5–10: | ★★★ |
| Ages 11–15: | ★★★ |
| Ages 16–Adult: | ★ |
| Senior Citizens: | ★ |

Designed with kids in mind, this attraction lets young guests take on the role of Space Rangers as they join their hero, Buzz Lightyear, on an adventure to save the universe's crystollic fusion cell supply (i.e., batteries). Riders climb aboard a ZP-27 space cruiser and take a light-hearted voyage through ten interactive scenes. While the vehicles move forward by themselves as the adventure unfolds, riders can make their vehicle spin around, since there are things to see all around. The final scene of the adventure features stunning laser effects.

## The Galaxy Palace Theater

| | |
|---|---|
| Ages 2–4: | ★★ |
| Ages 5–10: | ★★★ |
| Ages 11–15: | ★★★ |
| Ages 16–Adult: | ★ |
| Senior Citizens: | ★ |

Mickey Mouse and his Disney pals entertain guests with plenty of colorful costumes, singing, and dancing. Performances are held throughout the day, but show times vary based on the time of year and on weather conditions. On sunny days, make sure you apply plenty of sunblock (and wear a hat). This is an outdoor amphitheater, so you'll be exposed to the sun. Be sure to arrive about twenty minutes early to ensure that you'll get a good seat.

 **TRAVEL TIP**

The show offered here changes periodically. Consult *The Magic Kingdom Guide Map* for show details and times.

# Shop 'Til You Drop

Located throughout The Magic Kingdom are dozens of shopping opportunities, including specialty shops, general gift shops, and plenty of souvenirs to choose from. All of the shops in The Magic Kingdom offer complimentary package delivery to your WDW Resort hotel. For an additional fee, your purchases can be shipped (via FedEx) to any location worldwide. Keep in mind that even though FedEx is being used for shipping, it could take up to two weeks for your items to arrive at their destination, due to order processing delays at Disney World. Before shipping your items, ask how long it'll take for the order to be processed.

## ⩵FAST FACT

Members of the Disney Club (⌨ *www.disneyclub.com*) will receive a 10 percent discount on any items purchased from the Disney Store or the Disney Catalog, but not on anything purchased at the shops located at The WDW Resort theme parks. Disney Club discounts are, however, honored in the Marketplace area of Downtown Disney.

If you find something you really like but can't afford at the moment, or you don't want to lug it home, you can order any item available from any WDW shop by calling ✆ (407) 363-6200 during business hours. Many of the items available at Walt Disney World are not sold at any of the Disney Stores and are not available from the Disney Catalog. To order a free copy of the Disney Catalog, or to place an order from it, call ✆ (800) 237-5751.

Sometimes finding the perfect souvenir or the ideal gift is a difficult task. To help you find exactly what you're looking for, drop by City Hall for recommendations on where you can find specific gift and souvenir items. You can also call ✆ (407) 824-5566 and speak with someone working at the Disney merchandise hotline.

## Shops along Main Street, U.S.A

**The Chapeau**—Monogrammed Mickey ears (like the ones worn by the original Mouseketeers on *The Mickey Mouse Club*) can be purchased here. This is the only place in The Magic Kingdom where you can get the ears monogrammed while you wait. The cost of monogrammed Mickey or Minnie ears is $5.30.

**Crystal Arts**—Handmade crystal items (many with a Disney theme) and unique and beautiful handblown glass objects are available here. Many different monogrammed gifts and souvenirs are available.

**Disneyana Collectibles**—An assortment of Disney memorabilia and collectibles, including animation cells and limited-edition items, are sold here. The Disney Gallery (located above the Pirates of the Caribbean attraction) is also a popular stop for Disneyana enthusiasts.

**Disney & Company**—Children's clothing and other souvenirs for kids are the main inventory at this shop.

**Disney Clothiers**—Disney character–based clothing (T-shirts, sweatshirts, ties, etc.) is available.

**Emporium**—This large shop offers a wide range of Disney merchandise, clothing, books, videos, plush toys, and souvenirs of interest to guests of all ages.

**Harmony Barber Shop**—This old-fashioned barbershop is more something to see, but various items are available to purchase. At times, a real-life barber is even on hand. Men's haircuts cost $15. Boys' haircuts cost $12.

**Kodak Camera Center**—Disposable cameras, Kodak film, batteries, and other camera accessories are sold here. Two-hour film developing is available from this location, and camcorders can also be rented. If you bring your own camcorder and the battery dies, one free service available at the Kodak Camera

Center is that they'll recharge your battery for you.

**Main Street Athletic Store**—A large assortment of sports-related Disney and ESPN clothing, as well as autographed sports collectibles are available. At this shop, a football helmet signed by Joe Montana sells for $395, while an autographed photo/plaque of this sports legend carries a price tag of $225.

**Main Street Confectionery**—Homemade chocolates, cookies, fudge, and other sweets are available.

**Market House**—Candy and other gift items are available.

**Newsstand**—Sorry, but you won't find any newspapers or magazines. What you will find, however, is a selection of souvenirs that you can purchase from this small store located near The Magic Kingdom's exit.

**The Shadow Box**—Handmade silhouettes of guests are created and sold.

**Uptown Jewelers**—Looking for a Mickey Mouse watch, some type of 14-karat gold jewelry, or fine china? That's what you'll find at this shop.

## Shops in Adventureland

**Agrabah Bazaar**—Themed merchandise and other colorful wares are sold at this open-air marketplace.

**Bwana Bob's**—Themed toys and film are among the souvenir offerings.

**Elephant Tales**—The theme of this store is an African safari marketplace, so what you'll discover is clothing, plush toys, and other items with an animal theme.

**House of Treasure**—After experiencing the Pirates of the Caribbean, you'll have a chance to walk through a marketplace that offers an assortment of pirate products and other gifts.

**Island Supply**—Gardeners and those who appreciate spending time outdoors will find a nice selection of gardening tools, wind chimes, and shirts made of unbleached cotton. Some of these products even have a Disney theme.

**Plaza Del Sol Caribe Bazaar**—Pick up some candy and snacks, plus some authentic Caribbean gifts, like piñatas, pottery, straw bags, and even some clothing items.

**Tiki Tropics**—The Magic Kingdom has a surf shop, and here you'll find all sorts of surfing clothing and accessories, plus T-shirts and other goodies for beach lovers.

**Traders of Timbuktu**—In this shop, you'll find handcrafted carved wooden animals, ethnic jewelry, and African clothing.

## ⊕ HOT SPOT

If you're a coin collector or looking for a unique jewelry gift, look for the kiosk in Adventureland that sells handcrafted coin art. Designs are carved into real coins using a jeweler's saw. Prices for these souvenirs range from $10 to $400 (for a minted gold piece).

### Shops in Frontierland

**Big Al's**—There are a few basics that everyone exploring the frontier should have—a coonskin cap, leather goods, a harmonica, and a gun (or at least a toy replica). You'll also find more useful items here, like sunblock.

**Briar Patch**—Once you've taken the plunge and have experienced Splash Mountain, you'll probably want to pick up a few souvenirs to remind you of the lovable characters you saw before that mega-drop. Winnie the Pooh items are also sold here, so it's a great place to pick up a gift for a young child.

**Frontier Trading Post**—Jewelry, leather goods, and clothing, all with a Western theme, are among the offerings available from this shop.

Here you can get a leather bracelet imprinted with your name. This is a popular souvenir among kids.

**Frontier Wood Carving**—If you're looking for handcrafted wooden gifts, many of which can be personalized on the spot, this is the place to shop. Three-dimensional wood carvings of someone's name (or carved wooden letters on a plaque) are available for $1.50 per letter, plus the price of the plaque, which ranges from $2 to $5.50.

**Prairie Outpost & Supply**—This turn-of-the-century general store stocks a wide selection of candy and rather unusual food items. Anyone hungry for alligator meat? Of course, some of the products also have a Disney theme.

**Trail Creek Hat Shop**—This shop offers hats of every size, shape, color, and description, from Disney-themed hats and caps to Western-style hats.

## Shops in Liberty Square

**Heritage House**—Located next to the Hall of Presidents, this shop is stocked with an assortment of unusual souvenirs and gift items, many with a patriotic flair. (The Statue of Liberty never looked so Disney-esque.)

**Ichabod's Landing**—Once you see what this shop has to offer, it'll come as no surprise that the Haunted Mansion is located right next door. You'll certainly be able to scare up some freaky masks and ghostly gifts.

**Liberty Square Portrait Gallery**—A team of talented artists are on hand to create a hand-drawn portrait of you and your family while you wait. This is a wonderful one-of-a-kind souvenir that you can take home, frame, and display proudly in your home.

**The Yankee Trader**—For chefs and those who enjoy working in the kitchen, at this shop you'll discover cooking tools with a

Disney theme. Everything from a Mickey Mouse waffle iron to Mickey plates and cups can be acquired.

**Ye Olde Christmas Shop**—This colorful shop offers a vast selection of Christmas items, many with a Disney theme. Dolls and tree ornaments are just a sampling of what's available.

 TRAVEL TIP

To avoid long lines for The Magic Kingdom's most popular rides and attractions, be sure to take advantage of FASTPASS at Big Thunder Mountain Railroad, Buzz Lightyear's Space Ranger Spin, the Haunted Mansion, Jungle Cruise, the Many Adventures of Winnie the Pooh, Peter Pan's Flight, Space Mountain, and Splash Mountain.

# Kid-Oriented Areas of The Magic Kingdom

WHILE THE ENTIRE WDW RESORT WAS CREATED TO entertain and inspire people of all ages, there are certain lands within The Magic Kingdom specifically designed for young children, under the age of twelve (along with their parents). Thus, if you're traveling with young people, plan on spending extra time within these areas.

## Fantasyland

 This area of The Magic Kingdom offers many attractions specifically for young kids that feature some of Disney's classic characters from movies like *Snow White and the Seven Dwarfs, Cinderella, Peter Pan, Alice in Wonderland,* and *The Lion King.* With the exception of the *Legend of the Lion King* stage show and the Many Adventures of Winnie the Pooh, all of the attractions in Fantasyland were among the park's offerings from the time it first opened (back in 1971). Anyone traveling with young kids should plan on spending at least several hours experiencing everything that Fantasyland has to offer. Teens and adults traveling alone should definitely not miss "It's a Small World" and the Legend of the Lion King.

**TRAVEL TIP**

During peak travel times (especially holidays), plan on allocating an average of forty-five minutes per ride or attraction. This includes wait times.

## Cinderella's Castle

| | |
|---|---|
| Ages 2–4: | ★★★ |
| Ages 5–10: | ★★★ |
| Ages 11–15: | ★★★ |
| Ages 16–Adult: | ★★★ |
| Senior Citizens: | ★★★ |

This is the best-known landmark in all of The WDW Resort, and one that people from all over the world come to see. It's also the most photographed building in the park. Inside the castle is a glass tile mosaic mural that tells the story of Cinderella. This castle is 180 feet tall and is twice the height of Sleeping Beauty's Castle located at Disneyland.

Kids especially will enjoy eating breakfast, lunch, or dinner with Cinderella in the castle at Cinderella's Royal Table. Make your breakfast reservations several days early. Whether or not you decide to eat inside the castle, you'll definitely want to wander through it.

👍 This is a must-see attraction.

## Cinderella's Surprise Celebration

| | |
|---|---|
| Ages 2–4: | ★★★ |
| Ages 5–10: | ★★★ |
| Ages 11–15: | ★★ |
| Ages 16–Adult: | ★ |
| Senior Citizens: | ★ |

Several times throughout the day (see *The Magic Kingdom Guide Map* brochure for details), Cinderella's Surprise Celebration takes place on the castle's front stage. This is a musical show that stars Cinderella and other classic Disney characters. After the show, there's a meet-and-greet opportunity that provides an awesome chance for parents to photograph their kids in front of the castle with the various characters. It's also an opportunity for kids to collect autographs of the popular Disney characters.

## Cinderella's Golden Carrousel

| | |
|---|---|
| Ages 2–4: | ★★ |
| Ages 5–10: | ★★★ |
| Ages 11–15: | ★★ |
| Ages 16–Adult: | ★ |
| Senior Citizens: | ★ |

This is one of the world's largest carrousels, and one of The Magic Kingdom's original attractions. Cinderella's Golden Carrousel holds seventy-two hand-carved horses that are truly works of art that guests of all ages can ride upon. Along with the exquisitely decorated horses, the entire carrousel features medieval decor. This ride was built in 1917 and acquired from an amusement park in New Jersey that's no longer in existence. It has since been totally refurbished and modernized, but it still has its original beauty and charm. The ride itself lasts about two minutes.

# ≡FAST FACT

Most families (with kids) visit the park in the morning. As the day progresses, however, kids get hungry and tired, so as evening rolls around, most families with kids tend to leave the park. Thus, late afternoons, evenings, and at night are the best times for adults to experience the areas of The Magic Kingdom described within this chapter.

## Dumbo the Flying Elephant

| | |
|---|---|
| Ages 2–4: | ★★ |
| Ages 5–10: | ★★★ |
| Ages 11–15: | ★★ |
| Ages 16–Adult: | ★ |
| Senior Citizens: | ★ |

The Magic Kingdom's younger guests can fly high above Fantasyland in cars shaped like Dumbo (the elephant), who uses his oversized ears to fly. Inspired by Disney's animated movie *Dumbo*, this two-minute ride is for kids only.

If the line is very long for Dumbo the Flying Elephant, a similar ride is offered within Disney's Animal Kingdom, called TriceraTop Spin. Instead of featuring Dumbo, this ride's vehicles are shaped like friendly triceratops.

## It's a Small World

| | |
|---|---|
| Ages 2–4: | ★★★ |
| Ages 5–10: | ★★★ |
| Ages 11–15: | ★★★ |
| Ages 16–Adult: | ★★★ |
| Senior Citizens: | ★★★ |

Whether you're spending one hour or several days exploring The Magic Kingdom, this is one attraction that nobody should miss. It's been called the "happiest cruise that's ever sailed," and you'll quickly discover that this description is totally accurate.

This is a colorful, ten-minute boat ride that takes guests through several large indoor areas filled with Audio-Animatronic children from around the world, all singing "It's a Small World" in different languages. It's a Small World is absolutely delightful and is well worth waiting in line to experience. (There's almost always a shorter wait if you get into the left line queue.) During the ride, be sure to look upward as well as to the sides, because there are exciting and adorable things happening all around you. Kids love the laughing hyenas, about five minutes into the ride, while adults will find the final scene on the ride extremely heartwarming.

As they leave, many people feel inclined to toss a coin into the water and make a wish. If you're traveling with someone in a wheelchair, special boats are available (upon request) to accommodate wheelchairs.

 This is a must-see attraction.

## ═══FAST FACT

It's a Small World was created by Walt Disney and his team of Imagineers for the 1964–1965 New York World's Fair, and was later added to Disneyland, and then to The Magic Kingdom at WDW, where it continues to entertain guests.

## Mad Tea Party (a.k.a. The Teacups)

| | |
|---|---|
| Ages 2–4: | N.S. |
| Ages 5–10: | ★★★ |
| Ages 11–15: | ★★★ |
| Ages 16–Adult: | ★★ |
| Senior Citizens: | N.S. |

Inspired by Disney's *Alice in Wonderland,* this ride is virtually guaranteed to make you totally dizzy. It's the type of ride that most kids love, but only suitable for anyone who has the stomach for it. Guests sit in oversized teacups that spin around each other. At the same time, individual guests can make their own teacup spin around its own axis. The ride lasts about two minutes and is best experienced on an empty stomach.

## Mr. Toad's Wild Ride

| | |
|---|---|
| Ages 2–4: | ★ |
| Ages 5–10: | ★★★ |
| Ages 11–15: | ★★★ |
| Ages 16–Adult: | ★ |
| Senior Citizens: | ★ |

Here's another ride for the younger crowd that's based on one of Disney's classic animated films, in this case, *The Adventures of Ichabod and Mr. Toad.* Guests ride in cars that make sharp turns, but as whole, it's not too turbulent and really pretty tame. If you're traveling with kids (twelve and under), you'll want to experience this ride, otherwise, skip it.

## Peter Pan's Flight

| | |
|---|---|
| Ages 2–4: | N.S. |
| Ages 5–10: | ★★★ |
| Ages 11–15: | ★★★ |
| Ages 16–Adult: | ★ |
| Senior Citizens: | ★ |

Guests ride in pirate galleons over London on a nonstop, three-minute journey to Never Never Land, where Captain Hook and the Lost Boys will be waiting. Think of this ride as an animated, three-dimensional storybook that tells a condensed version of the Peter Pan story. This ride is definitely kid-oriented and will be of little interest to adults traveling without young kids. Don't be surprised if this ride has one of the longest lines in Fantasyland. This attraction may be too scary for very young children.

## Snow White's Scary Adventures

| | |
|---|---|
| Ages 2–4: | N.S. |
| Ages 5–10: | ★★★ |
| Ages 11–15: | ★★★ |
| Ages 16–Adult: | ★ |
| Senior Citizens: | ★ |

Young guests in particular will enjoy this three-minute ride that depicts several popular scenes from Disney's *Snow White and the Seven Dwarfs* animated classic. The Audio-Animatronic dwarfs are really cute, but kids might get a bit scared by the wicked witch's multiple appearances, so it's a good idea to prepare children by telling them what to expect. Once again, this ride should be experienced by people traveling with kids, otherwise could be skipped. This attraction may be too scary for very young children.

## The Many Adventures of Winnie the Pooh

| | |
|---|---|
| Ages 2–4: | ★★★ |
| Ages 5–10: | ★★★ |
| Ages 11–15: | ★★ |
| Ages 16–Adult: | ★ |
| Senior Citizens: | ★ |

This colorful ride takes guests on a whirlwind visit with the classic *Winnie the Pooh* characters from the Hundred Acre Wood. As guests ride in honey pot–shaped vehicles, they bounce along with Tigger, float through a floody place with Piglet, and then enter the mysterious world of Heffalumps and Woozles. Colorful Animatronic figures and three-dimensional sets are used to convey the storyline of this adventure.

## ═FAST FACT

This is one of the newest rides within Fantasyland. It's designed specifically for young children (and their parents). Since this is an extremely popular ride, be sure to take advantage of FASTPASS to avoid waiting in long lines.

## The Legend of the Lion King

| | |
|---|---|
| Ages 2–4: | ★★★ |
| Ages 5–10: | ★★★ |
| Ages 11–15: | ★★★ |
| Ages 16–Adult: | ★★★ |
| Senior Citizens: | ★★★ |

This, too, is one of the newest attractions in Fantasyland, and definitely one that should be experienced by everyone—not just kids. Disney's Imagineers have taken the animated *The Lion King* movie and transformed it into a twenty-five-minute show featuring a colorful cast of life-size puppets, costumed characters, and special effects that tell a condensed version of the story.

This show is presented continuously throughout the day, but closes about forty-five minutes before the designated park closing time, so don't wait until the last minute to see this show. The entire presentation, including the preshow and the preshow waiting area, is indoors. The theater is air-conditioned.

 This is a must-see attraction.

## ═FAST FACT

The show features multiple songs from the movie. All of the celebrity actors and actresses who provided voices for the animated characters in the original film, reprise their roles for this extremely impressive presentation. Even if you've already seen the animated movie and/or *The Lion King* Broadway musical, this is yet another totally unique and highly impressive rendition of the story of Simba the lion cub.

# Mickey's Toontown

 People traveling with young children (ages three to twelve) will definitely want to check out The Magic Kingdom's newest land, which was designed specifically for kids. This area features many of Disney's classic characters, including Mickey Mouse, Minnie Mouse, Donald Duck, and Goofy.

Mickey's Toontown Fair is a colorful, cartoonlike town that's a blast for kids, but it offers little of interest to adults. Near the entrance of this area, you'll find Pete's Garage. Here you'll find rest rooms and public phones. If you want to meet Mickey Mouse and Minnie, Donald, and Goofy, the best place to do this is within Mickey's Toontown Fair.

## Donald's Boat

| | |
|---|---|
| Ages 2–4: | ★★★ |
| Ages 5–10: | ★★★ |
| Ages 11–15: | ★ |
| Ages 16–Adult: | N.S. |
| Senior Citizens: | N.S. |

Kids get to explore this boat-shaped playground with a nautical theme. This boat is hardly seaworthy, however. In fact, it has so many leaks, kids who explore it are virtually guaranteed to get a bit wet. The shooting fountains offer an excellent way for kids to cool off on a hot day. On cooler days, you might want to instruct your kids to stay dry by avoiding the shooting water. (A cold and wet kid is an unhappy kid.) Otherwise, have a dry change of clothes on hand.

## ≡FAST FACT

Mickey's Toontown typically opens a little later than the rest of the park and sometimes closes earlier. Be sure to check *The Magic Kingdom Guide Map* brochure or the Information Board (at the end of Main Street, U.S.A) for details and plan your day accordingly.

## Mickey's Country House and Judge's Tent

| | |
|---|---|
| Ages 2–4: | ★★★ |
| Ages 5–10: | ★★★ |
| Ages 11–15: | ★★★ |
| Ages 16–Adult: | N.S. |
| Senior Citizens: | N.S. |

After exploring Mickey's yellow, green, and red country home and yard, young visitors get to meet Mickey in person. This is an excellent photo opportunity and a chance for your children to meet the Mouse one-on-one. While Disney characters make appearances every day throughout Walt Disney World, if you want to be guaranteed that your child will get a chance to meet Mickey (and shake hands, etc.), this is the place to visit. The wait, however, could be up to one hour. Mickey's Country House is a colorful four-room cottage where Mickey lives. Guests can explore it before meeting Mickey.

## Minnie's Country House

| | |
|---|---|
| Ages 2–4: | ★★★ |
| Ages 5–10: | ★★★ |
| Ages 11–15: | ★★★ |
| Ages 16–Adult: | N.S. |
| Senior Citizens: | N.S. |

Young guests get to explore Minnie's pink-and-purple country home, and then explore the backyard, where Minnie herself will be waiting to greet guests in her gazebo. This is another excellent photo opportunity and a chance to interact with one of Disney's most popular characters. Be prepared to experience a wait to meet Minnie in person.

## The Barnstormer at Goofy's Wiseacre Farm

| | |
|---|---|
| Ages 2–4: | N.S. |
| Ages 5–10: | ★★★ |
| Ages 11–15: | ★★★ |
| Ages 16–Adult: | N.S. |
| Senior Citizens: | N.S. |

Young people will love Toontown's only thrill ride—a roller coaster with a "car-toon" twist that's fast enough to give young people a bit of excitement, without being too scary. Near the exit of the Barnstormer is a fun snack shop where guests can make their own strawberry shortcake. Kids must be at least 35 inches tall to experience this mild thrill ride.

## Toon Park

| | |
|---|---|
| Ages 2–4: | N.S. |
| Ages 5–10: | ★★★ |
| Ages 11–15: | ★★ |
| Ages 16–Adult: | N.S. |
| Senior Citizens: | N.S. |

This playground looks like a 3-D cartoon, and virtually everything within it is made out of foam, including the grass and animal statues. Toon Park is a fun and safe place for your kids to have fun while the adults sit on the sidelines.

## Toontown Fair Hall of Fame

| | |
|---|---|
| Ages 2–4: | N.S. |
| Ages 5–10: | ★★★ |
| Ages 11–15: | ★★ |
| Ages 16–Adult: | N.S. |
| Senior Citizens: | N.S. |

This gallery features many of Disney's most popular characters from popular animated movies. Guests can also meet and greet multiple Disney characters who appear throughout the day.

## Toontown Fair Railroad Station

| | |
|---|---|
| Ages 2–4: | ★★ |
| Ages 5–10: | ★★ |
| Ages 11–15: | ★★ |
| Ages 16–Adult: | ★★ |
| Senior Citizens: | ★★★ |

Climb aboard the WDW Railroad, which makes stops at Main Street, U.S.A and Frontierland.

## ⊕ HOT SPOT

Within Mickey's Toontown Fair, the main shopping opportunity can be found in County Bounty, a gift shop that sells an assortment of Disney-themed merchandise.

# Meet the Characters

 Located between Fantasyland and Tomorrowland, Ariel's Grotto is where you'll usually find Ariel and possibly other characters from Disney's *The Little Mermaid*, who meet guests, take pictures, and sign autographs in an area that's designed to look like Ariel's undersea home. It's an excellent photograph and autograph opportunity, and the line typically isn't too long.

The Fantasyland Character Festival is where you'll find a handful of Disney characters who will be on hand to meet and greet guests, sign autographs, and take pictures. While you typically won't find Mickey or Minnie, at least a few other classic characters can typically be found here throughout the day.

Within the Fairytale Garden in Fantasyland, at several times throughout the day, young guests can hang out with Belle (from *Beauty and the Beast*) as she tells a story about her adventures within a small and intimate setting. Show times are listed in *The Magic Kingdom Guide Map* brochure. Be sure to arrive early, since space is limited.

## Other Kid-Oriented Attractions

 The other lands within The Magic Kingdom also offer kid-oriented attractions. In addition, all of the parades and shows will appeal to the younger crowd. If you're traveling with kids, the following rides, shows, and attractions (highlighted in the previous chapter) should not be missed:

**Astro Orbiter** (Tomorrowland)

**Buzz Lightyear's Space Ranger Spin** (Tomorrowland)

**Country Bear Jamboree** (Frontierland)

**The Magic Carpets of Aladdin** (Adventureland)

**Swiss Family Treehouse** (Adventureland)

**Tomorrowland Indy Speedway** (Tomorrowland)

**Tom Sawyer Island** (Frontierland)

## Rides Not Suitable for Young Children

 Due to the turbulent, thrill-ride nature or themes presented within some of the rides and attractions within The Magic Kingdom, some simply aren't suitable for young kids (under age six). Some of these rides and attractions include Splash Mountain, Big Thunder Mountain Railroad, the Haunted Mansion, Peter Pan's Flight, Snow White's Scary Adventures, Space Mountain, and The ExtraTERRORestrial Alien Encounter.

As a parent, you'll need to make a judgment call based on the information provided within this book after seeing the ride, show, or attraction for yourself once you get to the theme park.

# All about Epcot

OUT OF ALL OF THE THEME PARKS and things to do
and see at The WDW Resort, Epcot is probably the most un-Disney.
In other words, you won't be seeing flashy parades. What you will
find, however, is that Epcot is a theme park designed primarily for
teens and adults that offers attractions that will both entertain and
educate.

## Park Overview

Epcot is really two totally different theme parks in one.
There's Future World, which offers rides and attractions,
each showcasing or demonstrating man's progress in science and technology. And then there's the World Showcase, which
is designed to examine the cultural achievements, food, artistic
products, and classic architecture of eleven countries from around
the world.

Guests of all ages, especially adults, will find Epcot to be educational and thought provoking. This theme park takes an extremely
innovative and entertaining approach to teaching people about the
world we live in. Make sure that you wear comfortable shoes when
you visit Epcot, because a considerable amount of walking is
required.

There's an awful lot to see and do at Epcot. In order to see everything, plan on spending a minimum of two days visiting this park. Ideally, you'll want to spend one full day exploring Future World, and one day visiting the World Showcase pavilions. If you can't allocate this much time to visiting this park, choose a handful of attractions that are of interest to you from each area.

Looking at a map of Epcot, you'll discover that the park is laid out in the shape of an eight. The bottom loop comprises the attractions, shops, restaurants, and rides in Future World. The top loop comprises the World Showcase pavilions, which circle around the World Showcase Lagoon. For parents and educators, Epcot features two Discover Centers in Future World that offer educational resources and products.

## Getting to Epcot

Just like The Magic Kingdom, Epcot is connected to the WDW monorail system, so you can reach this park via monorail by departing from the Ticket and Transportation Center. If you're staying at the Grand Floridian, the Contemporary, or the Polynesian (all WDW Resort hotels along a monorail route), take the monorail from the hotel to the Ticket and Transportation Center, then switch monorails and take the one that goes directly to Epcot's main entrance.

To reach Epcot's World Showcase entrance (a.k.a. The International Gateway entrance), take a short walk along a paved pathway from the Disney Yacht and Beach Club, Swan, Dolphin, and BoardWalk hotels. Instead of entering through Epcot's main entrance, which puts you in Future World (in front of Spaceship Earth), you'll enter the park from the back, in between the France and United Kingdom pavilions.

From all other WDW Resort hotels, you can take a WDW bus to Epcot's main entrance. If you're arriving at Epcot by car, there are several parking lots located near the main entrance. Follow the directions given by the parking attendants, write down the exact location where you parked your car, then hop aboard the free tram that'll take you to the park's main entrance. Parking costs $6 per day. Keep your parking ticket so that you can leave and re-enter the parking lot during a single day. Guests who are staying at any WDW Resort hotel and are already paying for parking at their hotel will receive free parking at any of Epcot's parking lots.

##  TRAVEL TIP

To go against the crowds and thus cut down the amount of waiting time you'll experience at each attraction, consider visiting Future World in the afternoon or evening, when it is the least crowded. The best time to visit the pavilions in the World Showcase is as soon as this part of the park opens in the morning.

## Admission to Epcot

Admission to Epcot requires a ticket. For details about the various ticket and pricing options for visiting Epcot and all of the theme parks within The WDW Resort, see Chapter 3.

## Same-Day Re-entry

As you leave Epcot, be sure to have your hand stamped as you exit in order to be granted readmission into the park later that day or evening. In addition to the hand stamp, be sure to retain your ticket stub. The hand stamps are designed to be water-resistant, so don't worry if your hand gets wet if you choose to return to your hotel in the middle of the day to go swimming, and then want to return to Epcot later that evening. Try to refrain, however, from scrubbing your hands clean with soap until your day's visit to the park is complete.

## Hours of Operation

The hours Epcot is open vary throughout the year; however, during much of the year, the park is open from 9:00 A.M. to 9:00 P.M., but there are exceptions. Future World is typically open from 9:00 A.M. to 7:00 P.M.; however, the popular Spaceship Earth and

Innoventions attractions remain open until 9:00 P.M. The World Showcase, on the other hand, typically opens daily at 11:00 A.M. and remains open until 9:00 P.M. If you're visiting Epcot during the summer or during a peak holiday period, Epcot's hours are extended. To obtain the exact park operating hours for the dates of your visit, call ☎ (407) 824-4321.

## What to Bring

Make sure you wear comfortable shoes! Depending on the weather, you might want to take along a jacket (you can always store it in a locker). Try to avoid carrying too much stuff with you. You'll enjoy your visit more if your hands are as free as possible.

Don't forget to bring your camera, along with plenty of film and batteries. Avoid having to purchase high-priced film, batteries, or camera supplies in the park.

In case of rain, plan on getting a bit wet. Wear a raincoat or plan on purchasing a Mickey Mouse poncho ($5 each). Avoid bringing an umbrella into the park. You'll find it frustrating trying to walk around the crowded park with an open umbrella. For an up-to-the-minute weather report for the Orlando area, call ☎ (407) 824-4104.

## ═FAST FACT

Most of the things to see and do within Epcot are located inside. In fact, many of the attractions even allow you to wait in line indoors. You will, however, have to walk outside to go from attraction to attraction in Future World and from pavilion to pavilion in the World Showcase.

## Choose a Place to Meet

As soon as you arrive at either Future World or the World Showcase at Epcot, choose a place where you'll meet up with the other people in your group if you happen to get separated. Choose to meet on the half hour or on the hour, after being separated.

If you're traveling with children, upon arriving at Epcot, set some ground rules. Instruct your kids to stay close to you at all times. They should know that if they get lost, they should immediately contact any Disney cast member.

There are several good meeting locations in Future World, such as in front of Spaceship Earth or in front of the fountain near Epcot's main entrance. While visiting the World Showcase, you can choose a meeting location in front of a particular pavilion, such as The American Adventure, which is located exactly halfway around World Showcase Lagoon (opposite Future World).

## Guest Relations

Located near Spaceship Earth is the Epcot Guest Relations building. The Disney cast members here are exceptionally helpful and will answer any and all of your questions regarding what to see and do at Epcot or anywhere at The WDW Resort. You can also make dining reservations here, or rent a special translator device that will translate the audio portion of many attractions within Epcot into Spanish, German, or French. The rental fee for one of these translator devices is $4 per day (with a refundable $40 deposit).

## ═══FAST FACT

All of the guest services found at The Magic Kingdom, The Disney-MGM Studios, and Disney's Animal Kingdom are also available at Epcot, including ATMs, first aid, telephones, water fountains, locker rentals, and rest rooms (with baby-changing stations). See Chapter 3 for details.

## The Rating System

 To help you choose which rides, shows, and attractions are most worth seeing while visiting Epcot's Future World and World Showcase, this book offers star-based ratings for each ride and attraction based on the age group each will most appeal to. Each ride and attraction has earned between one and three stars.

| | |
|---|---|
| ★ | = Rides and attractions that earned just one star aren't worth waiting for and could be skipped, especially if your time within the theme park is limited. |
| ★★ | = Rides and attractions that earned two stars are good, but they don't fall into the "must-see" category. |
| ★★★ | = The rides and attractions that earned three stars are definitely worth seeing and should not be missed. |
| N.S. | = This denotes rides and attractions that are "Not Suitable" for a specific age group. |

# Future World

 Epcot's Future World comprises multiple large buildings that house the various shows, rides, and attractions. This section provides information about everything there is to see and do in this portion of Epcot. Plan on spending between forty-five minutes and three hours at each of these attractions. As you'll see, some of the attractions contain multiple rides, shows, or things to experience. (If the park is extremely crowded, more time may be required.)

## Spaceship Earth

| | |
|---|---|
| Ages 2–4: | N.S. |
| Ages 5–10: | ★★ |
| Ages 11–15: | ★★★ |
| Ages 16–Adult: | ★★★ |
| Senior Citizens: | ★★★ |

Whether you approach Epcot via car, bus, or monorail, you can't miss seeing this 16-million-pound, 180-foot-tall, silver landmark as you approach the park. Inside this oversize golf ball-like object is an entertaining and informative attraction that explores the history of communication.

Spaceship Earth is the first major attraction you reach once you enter into Epcot's Future World from the main entrance. As a result, the line to experience Spaceship Earth's fifteen-minute-long ride is usually long. Once guests board the Omni-Mover transport inside the geosphere, they're seemingly transported back in time to discover how humans first learned to communicate. Throughout the attraction, Audio-Animatronics, lasers, and all sorts of other special effects are used to showcase communication and communication technology past, present, and future.

As the ride comes to an end, guests disembark from the Omni-Mover and find themselves in the AT&T Global Neighborhood. Guests can also enter this area through a separate entrance. This is a hands-on exhibit that showcases up-and-coming communication technology and offers a firsthand look at equipment like video telephones, and state-of-the-art ways of surfing the Internet.

The best time to experience Spaceship Earth is late afternoon or during the last ninety minutes before Epcot's Future World closes for the day.

## ⊕ HOT SPOT

Located in Innoventions plaza is the digital Epcot Tip Board. This information board lists the current wait times for all of the major attractions at Epcot, so you can better plan your day at the park. Show times are also available at this location.

## Innoventions

| | |
|---|---|
| Ages 2–4: | N.S. |
| Ages 5–10: | ★★ |
| Ages 11–15: | ★★★ |
| Ages 16–Adult: | ★★★ |
| Senior Citizens: | ★★★ |

The purpose of Innoventions is to showcase technologically advanced products and services from many of the world's technology leaders. Innoventions is a large hands-on and visually exciting exhibit that's constantly changing. Its goal is to offer guests a preview of consumer electronics and computer technology that's new, but not necessarily currently available in American homes. What sets Innoventions apart from other attractions at Epcot is that almost everything that's on display is interactive, so you actually get to try things out, not just look at products or see someone else demonstrate them.

Whether you're a computer guru or totally computer illiterate, Innoventions gives people of all ages a chance to learn about current and future technology in a fun, but casual, setting. You're free to visit and walk through only the areas of Innoventions that are of interest to you, and spend as much or as little time as you want in each area. If you happen to see a product you're interested in, helpful people are available at each area of the pavilion to answer your questions or supply you with free informational brochures.

 This is a must-see attraction.

## The Land

| | |
|---|---|
| Ages 2–4: | N.S. |
| Ages 5–10: | ★★ |
| Ages 11–15: | ★★ |
| Ages 16–Adult: | ★★★ |
| Senior Citizens: | ★★★ |

The overall theme of the Land is an exploration of our planet and how it produces food to support humanity and all of the other creatures living on Earth. The Land is divided up into four separate attractions: Living with the Land, Circle of Life, Food Rocks, and a Greenhouse Tour. Once you enter into this six-acre complex, plan on spending a minimum of one to three hours here.

**Living with the Land** is a fourteen-minute boat ride that takes guests through a manmade rain forest as well as the Land's massive greenhouses where plant research is being conducted. All of the plants you see in the greenhouses are alive and real. Along the boat ride, however, to create some of the scenes you'll be seeing, artificial plants and special effects are used. This ride will appeal to people of all ages and is meant to be highly educational as well as entertaining.

| | |
|---|---|
| Ages 2–4: | ★★★ |
| Ages 5–10: | ★★★ |
| Ages 11–15: | ★★ |
| Ages 16–Adult: | ★★ |
| Senior Citizens: | ★★ |

The **Circle of Life** attraction located in the Land pavilion is a twenty-minute movie shown on a massive screen (23" × 60") that combines live action with animation. This movie stars characters from *The Lion King*. Designed to appeal to younger guests, the attraction focuses on the many dangers that face our environment. Environmental responsibility, demonstrated in ways that kids and adults alike will understand, is a central theme of this movie.

| | |
|---|---|
| Ages 2–4: | ★★★ |
| Ages 5–10: | ★★★ |
| Ages 11–15: | ★★ |
| Ages 16–Adult: | ★★ |
| Senior Citizens: | ★★ |

**Food Rocks** is another kid-oriented attraction within the Land pavilion that offers a fifteen-minute concert featuring upbeat and original music. The setting is a kitchen, and the performers include vegetables, a milk carton, and silverware. While guests will recognize many of the songs that are performed, all of the lyrics have been changed, giving each song a food theme. We're all taught never to play with food, but until you experience this show, you probably haven't thought too much about how entertaining food can be.

| | |
|---|---|
| Ages 2–4: | N.S. |
| Ages 5–10: | N.S. |
| Ages 11–15: | ★★ |
| Ages 16–Adult: | ★★★ |
| Senior Citizens: | ★★★ |

If you have a green thumb, enjoy gardening as a hobby, or just want to get a close-up look at the exotic plants growing within the **Land's Greenhouses** and see how they're maintained, one-hour guided tours are offered throughout the day.

Reservations for this tour can be made only on the day of your visit, and must be made in person by visiting the tour desk located at the **Green Thumb Emporium** (found inside the Land pavilion). There's a small fee (under $10 per person) to participate. The tour, however, will appeal mainly to adults interested in gardening and agriculture.

##  TRAVEL TIP

Space for these walking tours is extremely limited, but guests have the unique opportunity to see firsthand how plants are being grown without soil, and learn how NASA and the U.S. Department of Agriculture are working together on research being conducted at Epcot.

## The Living Seas

| | |
|---|---|
| Ages 2–4: | ★★★ |
| Ages 5–10: | ★★★ |
| Ages 11–15: | ★★★ |
| Ages 16–Adult: | ★★★ |
| Senior Citizens: | ★★★ |

Unless you've had the opportunity to ride in a real-life submarine or go scuba diving in the Caribbean, you haven't seen what life is truly like in the ocean. The Living Seas is much more than just the world's largest fish tank. Some of the world's most renown oceanographers, researchers, and scientists, along with Disney's Imagineers, have created an attraction that allows guests to get a close-up view of life under the sea without ever having to get wet. What you'll see when you enter this pavilion is nothing short of spectacular.

The attraction begins with a walking tour through a gallery that chronicles man's journey into the oceans, using submarines and deep-sea diving equipment. Next, you'll see a short, two-and-a-half-minute movie that shows some of the deep-sea diving and ocean exploration equipment that's currently being used for research.

Your next stop is Sea Base Alpha, the world's largest aquarium, in which guests travel through glass tunnels that allow them to see ocean wildlife in its natural environment—a coral reef on the ocean floor. The reef you'll be seeing, however, is manmade, but the fish and exotic marine life are all real. Sea Base Alpha also offers hands-on activities and interactive video screens that help to explain various oceanographic topics. Once you enter into the Living Seas, plan on spending at least thirty to sixty minutes here.

On some evenings around 7:00 P.M., if you're lucky you'll get to see Mickey Mouse in scuba gear diving into the tank and swimming with the sea life.

👍 This is a must-see attraction.

## ⊕ HOT SPOT

For $140 per person, guests can participate in two very special tours. The Dolphins in Depth program is three-and-a-half hours long and allows guests to interact directly with dolphins and meet the researchers who work at the Living Seas pavilion. For those who are certified scuba divers, DiveQuest allows guests to rent scuba-diving equipment and explore the six-million-gallon tank with a guide. Advanced reservations are required to participate in either the Dolphins in Depth or DiveQuest programs. Call ☎(407) WDW-TOUR.

## Universe of Energy

| | |
|---|---|
| Ages 2–4: | ★★ |
| Ages 5-10: | ★★ |
| Ages 11–15: | ★★★ |
| Ages 16–Adult: | ★★★ |
| Senior Citizens: | ★★★ |

The Universe of Energy was one of the original pavilions in Epcot's Future World. In 1996, however, it was totally revamped to provide guests with an entirely new and far more entertaining experience. So, if you're making a return visit to Epcot, this is one of the newer attractions you should make a point of experiencing.

As you might have gathered from the name, this attraction explores how energy is created and used around the world. In all, plan on spending about forty minutes experiencing this attraction's three movies and ride (not including waiting time to enter the attraction). Not only does this attraction explain all of the different options available for creating energy now and in the future, but it does so in a way that's entertaining and not preachy.

👍 This is a must-see attraction.

## Wonders of Life

| | |
|---|---|
| Ages 2–4: | ★★ |
| Ages 5–10: | ★★ |
| Ages 11–15: | ★★ |
| Ages 16–Adult: | ★ |
| Senior Citizens: | ★ |

This attraction takes a look at life on the planet Earth and examines health and fitness issues facing busy humans. In addition to all sorts of high-tech hands-on displays and exercise equipment for guests to try out, the Fair Grounds area of this pavilion features three theaters.

An eight-minute multimedia show, called *Goofy About Health,* features the classic Disney character Goofy. This movie is shown continuously in a 100-seat theater designed so guests can come and go as they please. This movie is informative, entertaining, and is suitable for people of all ages.

| | |
|---|---|
| Ages 2–4: | ★ |
| Ages 5–10: | ★★ |
| Ages 11–15: | ★★ |
| Ages 16–Adult: | ★★ |
| Senior Citizens: | ★★ |

Also in this area of the pavilion is the **AnaComical Players Theater,** the home of an improvisational acting troupe that performs a comical show utilizing audience participation. Performances are held at predefined times throughout the day.

## ⊕ HOT SPOT

Plan on spending between two and four hours here if you want to experience all of the shows, movies, and attractions within Wonders of Life.

| | |
|---|---|
| Ages 2–4: | ★ |
| Ages 5–10: | ★★ |
| Ages 11–15: | ★★ |
| Ages 16–Adult: | ★★ |
| Senior Citizens: | ★★ |

In a third theater, *The Making of Me* movie is shown. Featuring actor/comedian **Martin Short,** this fourteen-minute film focuses on Martin's character, who contemplates where he came from. As part of this presentation, Martin's character travels back in time to witness his parents grow up, meet, and get married. Ultimately, he even watches his own birth. For this scene, footage of an actual birth is shown. While this entire movie discusses sexual intercourse, it does so in a nongraphic and extremely tasteful and nonoffensive way. Parents should decide for themselves if this material is suitable for their children to see.

## ⊕ HOT SPOT

In the Wonders of Life pavilion, computers are available where guests can enter their age, weight, height, how much they exercise, and other information. This information is used by the computer to suggest various ways guests can reduce the stress in their lives and at the same time become more physically fit.

| | |
|---|---|
| Ages 2–4: | ★★ |
| Ages 5–10: | ★★★ |
| Ages 11–15: | ★★★ |
| Ages 16–Adult: | ★★ |
| Senior Citizens: | ★★ |

Another attraction in the Wonders of Life pavilion is **Cranium Command,** a seventeen-minute show that uses movie footage and Audio-Animatronics to take guests into the mind of a twelve-year-old boy. This comical and extremely creative show examines how the brain works, and features the voice talents of well-known celebrities like John Lovitz, Charles Grodin, George Wendt, Dana Carvey, and Kevin Nealon. Cranium Command is suitable for people of all ages.

| | |
|---|---|
| Ages 2–4: | N.S. |
| Ages 5–10: | ★★ |
| Ages 11–15: | ★★★ |
| Ages 16–Adult: | ★★★ |
| Senior Citizens: | ★★ |

**Body Wars** uses flight-simulator technology (like Star Tours at The Disney-MGM Studios) to send guests on a turbulent thrill ride inside the human body. The five-minute ride makes guests feel like they've been shrunk to a size smaller than a single cell and placed inside a ship capable of exploring the human body. This ride explains how the human immune system works and uses realistic special effects to make guests feel like they're actually traveling inside of a body. This ride is extremely turbulent, so make sure your seatbelt is securely fastened and that your belongings are all safely stowed. This ride is exciting, but not suitable for young kids (under 40 inches tall) or anyone with heart problems or back problems or who suffers from motion sickness. This is the most popular attraction in the Wonders of Life pavilion, so expect to wait between twenty minutes and one hour to experience it.

## Imagination!

| | |
|---|---|
| Ages 2–4: | ★ |
| Ages 5–10: | ★★ |
| Ages 11–15: | ★★ |
| Ages 16–Adult: | ★★ |
| Senior Citizens: | ★★ |

The Epcot ride/attraction **Journey Into Your Imagination,** which opened in conjunction with this theme park, has been totally revamped, creating a totally different attraction. While the result isn't as impressive as it could have been, guests who experience this ride are encouraged to expand their own imaginations as they experience an onslaught of sights and sounds designed to stimulate their senses. Rooms turn upside down and normal turns inside out as guests are challenged to increase their I.Q. (Imagination Quotient). At the end of the ride, visitors enter into a hands-on interactive area featuring various activities.

Also located in the **Journey Into Imagination** pavilion is the **Honey, I Shrunk the Audience show,** which is loosely based on Disney's *Honey, I Shrunk the Kids* movie. Rick Moranis and Marcia Strassman, along with the kids from this movie series, reprise their roles for this comical fourteen-minute 3-D movie.

| | |
|---|---|
| Ages 2–4: | ★★ |
| Ages 5–10: | ★★★ |
| Ages 11–15: | ★★★ |
| Ages 16–Adult: | ★★★ |
| Senior Citizens: | ★★ |

Ultimately, after the theater is invaded by 3-D movie mice, and you see the on-screen characters miniaturized, the audience itself becomes the unwilling victim of Professor Wayne Szalinski's shrinking machine. This movie is exciting, extremely entertaining, and offers lots of surprises. While you'll be handed special 3-D glasses as you enter into the theater, do not place them over your eyes until you're seated and instructed to do so. The 3-D glasses can be placed directly over prescription eyeglasses.

☞ This is a must-see attraction.

## ⊕ HOT SPOT

What used to be a highly enjoyable and lighthearted ride for people of all ages (before it was revamped) has been transformed into an entertainment experience that by Disney standards is average. Imagination! is more suitable for kids and teens than adults.

### Test Track

| | |
|---|---|
| Ages 2–4: | N.S. |
| Ages 5–10: | ★★ |
| Ages 11–15: | ★★★ |
| Ages 16–Adult: | ★★★ |
| Senior Citizens: | ★ |

When you experience this attraction, you take on the role of a test driver for General Motors. Your responsibilities include testing new models of automobiles while they're still in the concept phase. This is a challenging job that takes skill, guts, and a love for speed. That's the premise behind Epcot's thrill ride Test Track.

The preshow/line queue takes place within an industrial looking test laboratory filled with equipment and vehicle components. There are simulated brake, wheel, suspension, airbag, seat belt, and windshield tests.

As the ride begins, get ready to buckle up and travel along bumpy terrain, through hairpin turns, into freezing cold chambers, and along 50-degree banked curves at speeds up to 65 miles per hour. Guests experience this ride in specially designed six-passenger vehicles that travel along the mile-long track.

☞ This is a must-see attraction.

##  TRAVEL TIP

Due to its popularity, be prepared for a long wait or take advantage of FASTPASS. If you don't mind experiencing this ride without the people you're traveling with, take advantage of the singles' line. This line tends to move much quicker, but you'll wind up riding with strangers. Guests must be at least 40 inches tall to experience Test Track.

## Innoventions Fountain

| | |
|---|---|
| Ages 2–4: | ★★ |
| Ages 5–10: | ★★ |
| Ages 11–15: | ★★ |
| Ages 16–Adult: | ★★ |
| Senior Citizens: | ★★ |

Every fifteen minutes, a computer-controlled, fully choreographed shooting water performance is presented at this fountain, located outside in Innoventions Plaza. This short show is nothing compared to IllumiNations (presented nightly), but it offers a nice diversion as you're walking by.

## Dining in Future World

| | |
|---|---|
| Ages 2–4: | ★★ |
| Ages 5–10: | ★★ |
| Ages 11–15: | ★★ |
| Ages 16–Adult: | ★★ |
| Senior Citizens: | ★★ |

These restaurants and snack shops located in Epcot's Future World are open during park hours (but most close at 7:00 P.M.). For exact hours or to make a reservation at any of the fine-dining establishments, call ☎ (407) WDW-DINE. The following are dining options available at Epcot's Future World:

**Coral Reef**—This is a full-service restaurant located in the Living Seas pavilion. The backdrop for this dining room is the attraction's 6-million-gallon aquarium. The majority of the menu items served at this restaurant are seafood dishes. Priority Seating reservations are definitely recommended. Lunch and dinner are served daily.

**Garden Grill**—This full-service restaurant serves breakfast, lunch, and dinner hosted by Disney characters, including Mickey Mouse and Minnie Mouse. Lunch and dinner entrees include chicken, fish, and steak dishes.

**Electric Umbrella**—Located near Innoventions, this is Future World's largest fast-food dining establishment. Entrees include hamburgers, cheeseburgers, hot dogs, sandwiches, salads, and a variety of snack items and beverages.

**Fountain View Espresso & Bakery**—Freshly baked items such as croissants and a wide range of extremely tasty desserts are offered at this dining spot located near Innoventions. Espresso, cappuccino, coffee, wine, beer, and other beverages are available.

**Pure & Simple**—This snack shop, located within the Wonders of Life pavilion, offers a selection of healthy snack foods, like fresh fruit, salads, frozen yogurt, muffins, juices, and oat bran waffles with fruit toppings. Breakfast, lunch, and dinner are served, and counter service is available.

**Sunshine Season Food Fair**—Located on the lower level of the Land pavilion in Future World, this food court offers soups and salads, as well as baked goods, bagels, fresh fruit, cinnamon rolls, Danish, and other breakfast treats. There's also a barbecue stand, Chinese food stand, a sandwich shop, and the Potato Store. The Beverage House offers a large list of tropical (alcoholic and nonalcoholic) frozen drinks, plus beer, wine, bottled water, and soda.

## ═FAST FACT

Throughout Epcot, you'll find snack carts that sell ice cream, snack foods, and beverages.

## Shopping in Future World

As you probably expect, gift shops and souvenir stands are located throughout Epcot's Future World. **Gateway Gifts** and the **Camera Center** are located near the park's main entrance. Here you can pick up souvenirs or film for your camera. Video cameras can be rented at the **Camera Center,** and same-day film processing is available. You will, however, pay a premium if you purchase film or batteries anywhere at WDW or have your film developed at the park.

**The Centorium** is located in the midst of Innoventions and offers a large selection of Disney character merchandise, gifts, and souvenirs with the Epcot logo. This is the largest gift shop in Epcot. Smaller gift shops can be found near **Journey Into Your Imagination** and in the **Wonders of Life** pavilions.

For Disney fans and collectors, the **Art of Disney Epcot Gallery** is one of the most exciting shops at Epcot, because on display (and available for purchase) is Disney animation artwork, including actual production animation cells and limited edition cells. Other Disney collectibles are also displayed in a museum gallery–like setting. Whether you're looking to add to your Disney art collection, you're hoping to start a collection, or you just want to see some of the stunning artwork that's on display, be sure to stop by this gallery for a visit. It'll appeal mainly to adults.

# The World Showcase

Each of the pavilions in the World Showcase represents a country and showcases its culture, architecture, food, art, music, and history. These pavilions are staffed by natives of the featured country and offer an authentic look at what each country has to offer. To make your trip around the world more exciting, many of the pavilions offer live shows, musical performances, and some type of ride or movie attraction. Specialty shops are also featured within the pavilions, so you can pick up unique souvenirs that were handcrafted or manufactured in the featured country.

The World Showcase as a whole is designed more for adults than children, although there's always so much to see and do in this area of Epcot, people of all ages will enjoy the experience of traveling to exotic countries without ever stepping foot on an airplane. These pavilions are described in the order that you'll encounter them if you begin at the main entrance of the World Showcase (approached by coming through Future World) and proceed in a clockwise direction (traveling tfrom the left side).

## ⊕ HOT SPOT

The full-service, fine-dining restaurants within these pavilions offer some of the best food available anywhere in WDW. Reservations for these relatively high priced restaurants are strongly recommended. Call ✆ (407) WDW-DINE as far in advance as possible. Same-day reservations are also available, but if you don't mind waiting, you can simply show up for a meal at one of the full-service restaurants.

### Mexico

A large pyramidlike structure is the home of the Mexico pavilion, where you can experience **El Rio Del Tiempo: The River of Time**. This is a six-minute boat ride that takes a look at life in Mexico past and present. Movies, animated sets, and Audio-Animatronics are used to provide the visuals along the boat trip. The lines for this attraction will probably be long in the morning, so if you wait until late in the day or evening, your wait will be less. Live entertainment is provided both inside and outside of the pavilion throughout the day.

At the **Plaza Del Los Amigos** marketplace area, you can shop for piñatas, sombreros, pottery, colorful paper flowers, and other genuine Mexican souvenirs. For a higher-priced selection of merchandise, visit **Artesanias Mexicanas.** Products from northern Mexico are showcased at **El Ranchito Del Norte,** while **La Familia Fashions** offers clothing and accessories for women and children, along with jewelry.

As for the Mexican dining experience offered at this pavilion, **San Angel Inn** is a second location for a famous restaurant located in Mexico City. Here you'll be able to choose from an assortment of delicious Mexican entrees, including tacos as well as fish, meat, and chicken dishes. This is a full-service restaurant and reservations are strongly recommended. Lunch and dinner are served daily.

A less expensive dining option at the Mexico pavilion is offered at **Cantina de San Angel.** Here you can snack on various types of filled soft tortillas and other fast-food items. Lunch, dinner, and snacks are served, and counter service is offered. Nearby outdoor tables are provided, or you can enjoy your food as you walk around the **World Showcase Promenade.**

## Norway

This pavilion offers you the opportunity to learn about some of the history, culture, and folklore of Norway. The architecture of this pavilion depicts several different styles from around the country, plus from the country's past. For example, one of the main structures is a Norwegian castle that was modeled after a fourteenth-century fortress that can still be seen in Oslo's harbor.

The main attraction of the Norway pavilion is the **Maelstorm,** a ten-minute ride that uses boats modeled after those used by Vikings over 1,000 years ago. Your journey begins with a look at the country's past and at its ancient folklore. After the boat ride, your look at Norway continues in a theater, where a movie depicting life in modern Norway is presented. This is a popular attraction that's often less crowded in the evenings.

One of the buildings that make up this pavilion is a re-creation of a wooden stave church. Inside you'll discover a gallery that offers scenes and objects designed to help guests better understand this country's culture.

**The Puffin's Roost** is a shop that displays an assortment of Norwegian gifts, handmade items, clothing, jewelry, toys, and other souvenirs.

At the **Akershus** restaurant, located inside the castle, guests are treated to an authentic royal Norwegian (all-you-can-eat) buffet, which includes a wide array of hot and cold dishes. This is considered a fine-dining experience. Norwegian hosts and hostesses are always on hand to answer questions and add to the ambiance. Lunch and dinner are served daily. Reservations are strongly recommended.

##  TRAVEL TIP

This part of Epcot requires a lot of walking. If you have physical limitations that might keep you from being able to walk around the entire World Showcase Lagoon and explore the pavilions, you should seriously consider renting a wheelchair so that you don't miss any part of this fascinating area of Epcot.

**Kringla Bakeri og Kafe** offers less expensive snacks and candies as well as open-faced smoked salmon, roast beef, and turkey sandwiches. One treat that's sold here is kringles, which are candied pretzels that Norwegians eat on special occasions. Beers from Norway are served. Counter service is available, and nearby outdoor seating is provided.

### China

As you approach the China pavilion, you'll quickly notice the authentic architecture and hear the Chinese music that's played constantly near the pavilion so passersby can get a taste of China, even without dropping into the pavilion. Inside the pavilion's **Temple of Heaven,** live music is performed almost continuously, while in the nearby courtyard, you can catch a performance by a team of highly talented acrobats. This courtyard features landscaping made up of plants that are native to China.

In addition to the live performances, the China pavilion features a Circle-Vision 360 movie, *Wonders of China: Land of Beauty, Land of Time.* This nineteen-minute presentation shows locations in China that foreigners had never seen prior to this movie's premier at

Epcot. You'll see stunning footage of Beijing's Forbidden City, the Great Wall of China, and many other beautiful locations.

As you leave the movie theater, you'll have a chance to walk through an exhibit of Chinese art. The gallery exhibit changes every six months but always includes pieces from well-known artists that are on loan from private collectors and world-renowned museums.

Your visit to the China pavilion can also include a shopping excursion to the **Yonh Feng Shangdain Shopping Gallery,** located on the **Street of Good Fortune.** Here you can purchase authentic Chinese merchandise like silk robes, paper fans, and umbrellas, as well as antiques and other souvenirs.

If you're in the mood for a tasty Chinese lunch or dinner, the **Nine Dragons** restaurant offers a wonderful full-service dining experience. The food is prepared in a variety of different cooking styles, including Mandarin, Hunan, Cantonese, and Szechuan. On the menu, you'll find a wide range of entrees listed, along with Chinese teas, beers, and wines. Reservations are strongly recommended.

For lunch or dinner, **The Lotus Blossom Café** is Epcot's answer to Chinese fast food. Nearby outdoor seating is provided. The food served here is considerably less expensive than the full-service **Nine Dragons** restaurant, and you'll finish eating much faster, allowing you to continue exploring the World Showcase.

 **TRAVEL TIP**

To help make the trek around the lagoon a bit easier, water taxis are available that depart from docks located near several of the pavilions. In addition, double-decker buses continuously travel around the lagoon, making stops at all of the pavilions.

## Germany

The Germany pavilion is a re-creation of a small German village, although the architecture of the various buildings and structures was borrowed from many different areas of the country. On the hour, a glockenspiel located within the pavilion can be heard playing an original tune, and throughout the day, live musical entertainment is often featured.

By exploring the pavilion, you'll encounter several small shops, each featuring unique German items. At **Der Bucherwurm,** you'll find books about Germany, artwork, and souvenir items. **Volkskunst** is a small shop that sells clocks and watches, as well as other handcrafted items. If you're looking for a special gift for a child (or a collectible doll for yourself), check out what's offered at **Der Teddybar,** a lovely toy shop.

Participate in a daily wine tasting or take home a bottle of German wine by visiting **Weinkeller,** a wine shop that offers over 250 varieties of German wine that were produced and bottled by **H. Schmitt Sohne.** Crystal jewelry and glass items are offered at **Kunstarbeit In Kristal.** You'll be able to satisfy your sweet tooth at **Sussigkeiten,** a confectionery shop that offers many German sweets.

## ⊕ HOT SPOT

No matter what time of year you're visiting Epcot, it's always the Christmas holiday season at Die Weihnachts Ecke, a German Christmas shop that sells ornaments, holiday decorations, and holiday-oriented gift items. Those who collect tree ornaments will be able to purchase some wonderful and very unique additions for their collection here.

At **Glas Und Porzellan,** you'll find glass and porcelain items made by Goebel. Collectors of Hummel figurines will find a huge assortment of these collectibles on display, plus there's often a Goebel artist on hand answering questions and demonstrating how these statues are hand-painted. This is a wonderful shop to browse through, even if you have no intention of making a purchase.

Lunch and dinner are served daily at the German pavilion's

fine-dining restaurant, called **Biergarten.** Guests sit at large tables (often with total strangers) and can enjoy a selection of authentic German cuisine and drink Beck's beer. During dinner hours, live entertainment is offered every hour on the half hour, so be sure to time your dining experience accordingly. Reservations are strongly recommended.

At **Sommerfest,** bratwurst sandwiches are the specialty, but you'll also find treats like soft pretzels, apple strudel, and other German snacks. Counter service is provided and nearby outdoor seating is available. Located in between the Germany and China pavilions is a snack shop that offers soda, bottled water, frozen yogurt, and ice cream.

## Italy

In addition to fine Italian food, guests get a true taste of Italy when they visit this pavilion. In the courtyard of this pavilion, not only will you see and hear live music performed, but you'll also get a chance to see the **Living Statues.** Performers stand motionless and periodically change positions. Despite the best efforts of guests to distract these performers, they remain expressionless and motionless except to change positions.

**Delizie Italiane** is a marketplace area that sells chocolates and other sweets, while **La Cucina Italiana** is a gourmet shop that offers Italian pastries and dessert items. Take-home gourmet food items and accessories are also sold here. For more expensive gifts, such as glassware or porcelain figurines, be sure to visit **La Bel Cristallo** ("The Beautiful Crystal"). Jewelry made from silver and gold, along with other items, is sold at **La Gemma Elegante.**

An authentic and delicious Italian dining experience is offered during lunch and dinner hours at **L'Originale Alfredo di Roma Ristorante.** The special of the house is fettuccine, although you'll find a range of Italian entrees available. The kitchen of this restaurant is located behind a large glass window, so guests can see the chefs at work.

## The American Adventure

Located halfway around the World Showcase Lagoon is the **American Adventure.** A large colonial-style building is the main structure of this pavilion. Inside, guests are invited to see a twenty-nine-minute attraction called the **American Adventure Show,** which features Audio-Animatronic characters that bring some of America's heroes and most famous historical figures and entertainers to life.

Live music is presented at the **American Adventure pavilion,** which is almost always crowded. Outside of the main pavilion, located in front of the **World Showcase Lagoon,** the **America Gardens Theater** offers various concerts and performances that constantly change. Show times and details about the various shows are posted in front of the theater, at Guest Relations, and at the Tip Board. The nearby **All-American Red, White & Blue** gift shop sells items that are patriotic and that represent the country. American flags, clothing, books, and other products are available, along with Coca-Cola merchandise.

## ≡FAST FACT

Guests are invited to walk through the Hall of Flags, where forty-four flags that at some point in American history represented our country (or various parts of it) are displayed.

There is no full-service restaurant in this pavilion, but the **Liberty Inn** offers all-American food like hamburgers, hot dogs, salads, soda, and cookies. Counter service is available, and nearby seating is provided. Lunch, dinner, and snack items are served. People traveling with children will find food here that their children will recognize and will relate to, since many of the pavilions in this part of Epcot offer food that is totally foreign to most young people.

If you're lucky enough to travel to WDW during the Christmas holiday season (late November through late December), you won't want to miss the Candlelight Processional, which is held two or three times per night at the **America Gardens Theater.** This magical and heart-warming holiday performance lasts about one hour, and features a 450-voice choir, a fifty-piece orchestra, and a celebrity narrator.

## Japan

The **Imperial Palace** is the main focal point of this pavilion. Outside, you'll see and hear Japanese music performed, and you might even get to see stilt-walkers dressed like exotic birds perform. Native landscaping is seen around the pavilion. The **Bijutsu-Kan Gallery** offers an ever-changing exhibit of traditional and more modern Japanese art.

The **Mitsukoshi Department Store** offers a huge assortment of Japanese products, gifts, and souvenirs offered at a range of prices from extremely affordable to extremely expensive. This is definitely one of the most interesting shops to browse through at Epcot.

One of the very best restaurants in Epcot's World Showcase is **Mitsukoshi,** a Japanese steak house where your food is prepared by talented chefs right at your table. The **Tempura Kiku** area of this restaurant serves batter-dipped, deep-fried entrees made from beef, chicken, and seafood. The main dining room offers a full menu of Japanese dishes, all cooked at your table in an extremely entertaining style. At the large tables, you'll probably be seated with strangers as you enjoy this fine-dining experience. Lunch and dinner are served daily. Reservations are strongly suggested.

**Yakitori House** offers less expensive Japanese cuisine that can be enjoyed for lunch, dinner, or a snack. Guydon and yakitori are among the main menu selections served here.

## Morocco

Inside the **Gallery of Arts and History,** guests have the opportunity to see authentic Moroccan artwork. Also on hand at the **Moroccan National Tourist Office** within this pavilion are travel experts who can help you plan your next vacation to their country. Be sure to take a few minutes to watch the slide show that's presented at this office continuously.

If you're in the market for a hard-to-find fez or another article of Moroccan clothing, drop by the **Tangier Traders** shop. The **Marketplace in the Medina** shop sells handcrafted baskets and other handmade items. If it can be made out of brass, you'll find it at a shop called the **Brass Bazaar.** Additional brass items can be purchased at **Berber Oasis,** a smaller gift shop also found in this pavilion. Kids are sure to find a toy or souvenir at **Medina Arts,** a shop that sells toys, clothing, and other items featuring characters from Disney's *Aladdin* motion picture.

As you dine at **Marrakesh,** you'll be entertained by belly dancers and live musical performances. The food served is genuine Moroccan cuisine, which includes chicken brochette, couscous, and roast lamb. The live entertainment makes this dining experience extremely memorable and enjoyable. Reservations are strongly recommended. Lunch and dinner are served daily.

## ═FAST FACT

The buildings that make up this pavilion are designed to showcase the authentic architecture of Morocco, and the insides of these building are true works of art. Disney reports that over nine tons of handcrafted tiles were imported and laid inside this pavilion.

### France

A re-creation of the Eiffel Tower is the prominent landmark at this pavilion. The main attraction here is the *Impressions de France* movie that offers a comprehensive and visually stunning look at France in eighteen minutes.

**Plume Et Palette** is a beautiful shop that sells cosmetics, fragrances, and bath products imported from France. There's also an area that sells oil paintings and prints by well-known French artists. At **La Signature,** an assortment of gift items is available, including collectibles and tapestries. The **Galerie Des Halles** also sells an assortment of affordable souvenirs from France, including musical

CDs. Posters, prints, and other items imprinted with artwork from famous artists like Monet and Renoir are available from **La Casserole.**

If you're in the mood for fine French food for lunch or dinner, make a reservation to eat at **Bistro de Paris,** a full-service restaurant that's located one flight above **Chefs de France.** Here, a traditional French bistro menu is served daily. Downstairs at Chefs de France, some of the country's finest chefs are invited to showcase their talent at this posh restaurant. This, however, is one of the most expensive restaurants at Epcot. A special children's menu is available, and lunch or dinner reservations are strongly recommended.

## ⊕ HOT SPOT

France produces over 20 percent of the wine consumed in the world. Wine collectors and connoisseurs will find a vast selection of French wines on sale at La Maison Du Vin. Daily wine tastings are held here. There's a small fee to participate in a wine tasting, but you'll receive a special souvenir glass that's yours to keep.

### The United Kingdom

Guests who visit this pavilion get to enjoy the authentic architecture, landscaping, and shops. There's even a hedge maze that's located just outside of the pavilion's cottage. **At the Pooh Corner** shop, you'll find an incredible assortment of merchandise based on Winnie the Pooh. Meanwhile, at the **Crown & Crest,** you'll find dart boards, chess sets, and other unique gifts and items. The beautiful chess sets range in price from $250 to $900. Sweaters made of lamb's wool are available at Pringle of Scotland.

**Lords & Ladies** is the home of china products manufactured and sold by Royal Doulton, Ltd. Figurines and fine china are available at a wide range of prices, but even if you don't want to buy anything, this store is worth visiting just to browse. For handmade products from Wales, visit the **Magic of Wales** shop. English teas, teapots, biscuits, and fine candies are sold at the **Tea Caddy.**

When you're ready to eat lunch, dinner, or a snack, check out the menu at **Rose & Crown Pub and Dining Room.** This authentic English pub offers fish and chips and an assortment of other entrees. Seating in the pub area is available on a first-come-first-served basis; however, reservations are suggested for the dining room.

## Canada

If you're traveling around Epcot's World Showcase Lagoon clockwise, then your trip around the world ends at Canada. A seventeen-minute movie, *O Canada!* is shown in Circle-Vision 360 and offers a visual tour of this country. There are no seats in this theater, so be prepared to stand while the movie is shown all around you.

At the **Northwest Mercantile,** a selection of Canadian clothing, like lumberjack shirts, as well as other items and handcrafted products can be purchased. **Le Cellier** is open only during certain times of the year but offers a selection of Canadian food in a casual environment that's not too expensive compared to the other restaurants located in the World Showcase pavilions.

Lunch, dinner, and snacks are served in a cafeteria-style setting. For a quick snack, consider stopping at the **Refreshment Port.** Canadian beer and wine are available, along with frozen yogurt, fresh fruit, and ice cream.

Outside of the Canadian pavilion, you're likely to see live performances by Canadian folk dancers and the **Caledonia Bagpipe Band.**

## IllumiNations

| | |
|---|---|
| Ages 2–4: | ★ |
| Ages 5–10: | ★★★ |
| Ages 11–15: | ★★★ |
| Ages 16–Adult: | ★★★ |
| Senior Citizens: | ★★★ |

Every evening (just after dark), thousands of people gather around the World Showcase Lagoon for an incredible display of fireworks, lasers, and dancing fountains, all synchronized to music. This show can be seen from anywhere around the lagoon, but you'll want to stake out your viewing location up to one hour early if the park is extremely crowded. This is one of the most spectacular nighttime shows presented anywhere at WDW, so if you're visiting Epcot, plan on staying into the evening so you don't miss this magical and visually stunning show.

☞ This is a must-see attraction.

## 💼 TRAVEL TIP

IllumiNations changes every year, so if you're making a return visit to Epcot, the show you saw during your last visit will be different. Check with Guest Relations or the Tip Board for specific show times. You can also call ☎(407) 824-4321.

### Tapestry of Dreams Parade

In addition to the nighttime IllumiNations performance, Epcot now has its own parade, which pays tribute to children from around the world, and the dreams and legacy of Walt Disney. This thirty-minute parade features colorful floats; larger-than-life puppets; and 112 cast members who sing, dance, and entertain guests who line the parade route.

Featuring original music, Tapestry of Dreams is presented twice every evening. The parade travels between the Mexico and Morocco pavilions within Epcot's World Showcase. Unlike the parades within The Magic Kingdom and Disney's Animal Kingdom, for example, this one is more adult-oriented, because there's less of an emphasis on the Disney characters. Instead, the large puppets, beautiful floats, and costumed performers are showcased. People of all ages will enjoy this parade.

## Leave a Legacy

 Epcot offers guests the opportunity to leave their legacy in the form of a digital photo that gets mounted on a series of sculptures located near the main entrance to the park. Guests have an opportunity to purchase "memory tiles" upon which a digital photograph (taken at the park) is etched. One or two images can be included on each tile.

The cost of one image is $35. For two images on one tile, the price is $38. With every tile purchased, a verification certificate gets mailed to the purchaser that lists the exact location of the tile on the Legacy Sculpture.

## ≡ FAST FACT

From home, people can view the sculpture and the individual tiles at a specially created Web site (✐ *www.disney.go.com/ millenniumlegacy*).

## What's Next?

Like the other theme parks, Epcot (especially Future World) is always evolving. The displays and interactive areas of Innoventions are constantly being revamped and updated, while new rides, shows, and attractions are being created elsewhere within the park. The next big addition to Epcot will be Mission: SPACE, slated to open in 2003.

According to Walt Disney Imagineering, this new thrill-ride attraction will offer guests a one-of-a-kind "astronaut-like" experience that will take participants on a simulated space adventure—from liftoff to the weightlessness of outer space.

Mission: SPACE is being created in conjunction with Compaq Computer Corporation but is taking full advantage of NASA advisors, as well as astronauts and scientists, to create a new and ultra-realistic experience. Those who experience Mission: SPACE will be transported decades into the future, where they'll find they've become recruits at an International Space Training Center.

Al Weiss, president of Walt Disney World Resort, explained, "The combination of Disney magic and Compaq technology will create a truly one-of-a-kind experience. Epcot is the perfect setting, continuing the park's dedication to the explorer in all of us with its unique attractions that inspire us to discover new worlds."

Michael Capellas, CEO of Compaq Computer Corporation, added, "Computers are vital in developing space programs today and well into the future. With some of the most advanced technology ever produced, Mission: SPACE will provide guests with a rare glimpse into a world where the possibilities for computers and space flight are endless."

Construction of Mission: SPACE is well under way. You'll find the construction site located next to Test Track, which is currently Epcot's newest and most exciting attraction (from a thrill-ride standpoint). For a sneak preview of this new attraction, be sure to visit Innoventions East.

# The Disney-MGM Studios

THE DISNEY-MGM STUDIOS THEME PARK offers at least one day's worth of quality entertainment for adults as well as entire families. This chapter describes all of the shows, attractions, rides, restaurants, shops, and guest services available at The Disney-MGM Studios, and will help you plan an exciting visit to this popular WDW Resort theme park.

## Park Overview

 The Disney-MGM Studios is the home to many highly popular attractions and shows suitable for the entire family. The theme park portion of this complex, where the rides and attractions are located, was inspired by the Golden Age of Hollywood.

The Studios opened to the public in 1989. Since then, millions of tourists, not to mention hundreds of the world's most famous celebrities, have visited this working studio facility/theme park. Even on the busiest of days, you should be able to see most of the shows and attractions, plus experience most (if not all) of the rides and tours that are of interest to you and your family, during one full day at The Disney-MGM Studios.

## Getting to the Studios

If you're arriving at the studios by car, you'll want to park in the specified lot, which costs $6 per day for non-WDW Resort hotel guests. Since this parking lot is huge, be sure to write down the exact location where your car is parked, and then take the free tram to the park's entrance. Once you pay for parking, you're allowed to exit the parking lot during the day, and re-enter later that day at no charge. Guests of WDW Resort hotels who are already paying for parking at their hotel receive free parking at the studios. If you arrive midday and the parking lot is full, proceed to the nearby Dolphin or Swan hotel and take the water shuttle to the Studios.

A free water launch from several WDW Resort hotels, including the Dolphin, Swan, Yacht Club, Beach Club, and BoardWalk, goes directly to the studio's entrance. The boats go back and forth throughout the day and are the quickest way to reach the studios from the above-mentioned hotels.

Those coming from The Magic Kingdom, Epcot, and all other WDW resorts, take the specially marked WDW bus directly to the Studios. Guests traveling to this park from the Fort Wilderness Hotel, the Disney Village Marketplace, or Pleasure Island must take a WDW bus to the Transportation and Ticket Center, and then switch buses to get to the Studios.

## ≡FAST FACT

Admission to The Disney-MGM Studios requires a ticket. For details about the various ticket and pricing options for visiting this theme park, and all of the theme parks within The WDW Resort, see Chapter 3.

## Same Day Re-entry

As you leave The Disney-MGM Studios, be sure to have your hand stamped as you exit in order to be granted readmission into the park later that day or evening. In addition to the hand stamp, be sure to retain your ticket stub. The hand stamps are designed to be water-resistant, so don't worry if your hand gets wet if you choose to return to your hotel in the middle of the day to go swimming, and then want to return to the Studios later that evening. Try to refrain, however, from scrubbing your hands clean with soap until your day's visit to the studios is complete.

## Hours of Operation

The Disney-MGM Studios are open seven days per week, typically from 9:00 A.M. to 7:00 P.M. During the summertime and on certain holidays and peak periods, the Studios remain open later. To determine the hours of operation on the date(s) you're planning to visit the park, call ✆ (407) 824-4321.

## What to Bring

Make sure you wear comfortable shoes! Depending on the weather, you might want to take along a jacket (you can always store it in a locker). Try to avoid carrying too much stuff with you. You'll enjoy your visit more if your hands are as free as possible.

 **TRAVEL TIP**

In case of rain, plan on getting a bit wet. Wear a raincoat or plan to purchase a Mickey Mouse poncho. Avoid bringing an umbrella into the park. You'll find it frustrating trying to walk around the crowded park with an open umbrella. For an up-to-the-minute weather report for the Orlando area, call ✆ (407) 824-4104.

Don't forget to bring your camera, along with plenty of film and batteries. The Disney-MGM Studios is a working motion picture and television studio, so you might run into some popular celebrities as well as your favorite Disney characters. Avoid having to purchase high-priced film, batteries, or camera supplies in the park.

## The Tip Board

Located at the junction of Hollywood and Sunset Boulevard is the Studios Tip Board. This information board lists the current wait times for all of the major attractions in The Disney-MGM Studios. Stationed at this board is a Disney cast member who is in constant contact with the operators of all of the park's major attractions. Accurate wait times for each ride are posted, so you can better plan your day. Show and parade times are also available at this location. The very best time to visit the park and not have to deal with huge crowds is on Sunday morning.

As a general rule, if you're planning on focusing your attention on experiencing only The Disney-MGM Studios' most popular rides and attractions, it'll take you an average of forty-five minutes per attraction. This, however, depends on how crowded the park is and which attractions and rides you're trying to experience. If you're heading to one popular ride but notice that a line is particularly short for another attraction that you were planning to check out later in the day, adjust your schedule and go where the lines are the shortest.

Another good rule to follow is to always travel against the crowds. For example, many rides and attractions will have two lines. Most people automatically head to the right. You'll probably find that the lines to the left will be shorter.

 TRAVEL TIP

If you're traveling with children, upon arriving at this park, set some ground rules. Instruct them to stay close to you at all times. Young people should know that if they get lost, they should immediately contact any Disney cast member.

## Choose a Place to Meet

As soon as you arrive at the Studios, choose a place where you'll meet up with the other people in your group if you happen to get separated. Two ideal meeting places are in front of the Mann's Chinese Theater and at the Crossroads to the World (located near the park's main entrance).

## The Rating System

 To help you choose which rides and attractions are most worth seeing while visiting The Disney-MGM Studios, this book offers star-based ratings for each ride and attraction, based on the age group each will most appeal to. Each ride and attraction has earned between one and three stars.

★ = Rides and attractions that earned just one star aren't worth waiting for and could be skipped, especially if your time within the theme park is limited.

★★ = Rides and attractions that earned two stars are good, but they don't fall into the "must-see" category.

★★★ = The rides and attractions that earned three stars are definitely worth seeing and should not be missed.

N.S. = This denotes rides and attractions that are "Not Suitable" for a specific age group.

## The Studios' Rides and Attractions

 Like all of the Disney theme parks, there's a lot to see and do at The Disney-MGM Studios. Here's a rundown of what you'll discover as you explore this fun-filled "Hollywood"-themed theme park.

### Hollywood Boulevard

As soon as you enter The Disney-MGM Studios, you'll find yourself on Hollywood Boulevard, which is lined with a wide assortment of shops. To add to the overall atmosphere of Hollywood in the 1940s, you'll find an assortment of "Streetmosphere" performers who interact with guests while staying in character. Since the shops on Hollywood Boulevard are open thirty minutes after the park's official closing time, save your shopping for later in the day. The daily character parade goes down Hollywood Boulevard. For parade times, visit the Tip Board.

## ═FAST FACT

As you go down Hollywood Boulevard, you can walk to the right and follow Sunset Boulevard, which leads directly to the Tower of Terror, one of the most popular thrill rides at the park. Along Sunset, you'll also find additional shops, plus the Theater of the Stars, home of the Beauty and the Beast stage show.

### The Twilight Zone: Tower of Terror

| | |
|---|---|
| Ages 2–4: | N.S. |
| Ages 5–10: | N.S. |
| Ages 11–15: | ★★★ |
| Ages 16–Adult: | ★★★ |
| Senior Citizens: | N.S. |

The Hollywood Tower Hotel cost the Walt Disney Company more to build than virtually all of the other WDW Resort hotels, only this one won't ever be used to accommodate living guests. This hotel looks like it's from Hollywood's Golden Age, but one that hasn't been maintained too well over the years. The Hollywood Tower Hotel is where you can experience the Twilight Zone: Tower of Terror, which is arguably the most thrilling of thrill rides in all of Walt Disney World.

The attraction starts with a preshow and a brief tour of the hotel. Guests then board the elevator, which is rather unique, because you get to sit down as you ride upward. When you reach one of the top floors, you'll experience some of the most incredible visual special effects you've ever seen. That is, just before you plummet down thirteen floors (157 feet) in what feels like a free fall. The drop lasts about three seconds, but it's very intense. Just when you think the thrill is over after the massive drop, the elevator starts rising upward again, only to drop guests a second time.

To experience Tower of Terror, guests must be at least 40 inches tall. This ride is not recommended for anyone with heart or back problems, nor should it be experienced by pregnant women. Whatever you do, avoid eating before experiencing this ride or you'll be sorry. As you take the thirteen-floor drop, a photo will be taken of you, which can be purchased as a souvenir as you leave the hotel.

 This is a must-see attraction.

## The Great Movie Ride

| | |
|---|---|
| Ages 2–4: | ★★★ |
| Ages 5–10: | ★★★ |
| Ages 11–15: | ★★★ |
| Ages 16–Adult: | ★★★ |
| Senior Citizens: | ★★★ |

"Hooray for Hollywood" is the theme of this twenty-two-minute ride that utilizes over fifty Audio-Animatronic characters to re-create scenes from some of the most famous motion pictures of all time. This ride is located inside the Mann's Chinese Theater. As you're waiting to board the ride, once inside the theater, you'll see many authentic props and costumes from classic movies, and then when the ride begins, the movies will come to life before your eyes as you ride in a vehicle that takes you from scene to scene. The Great Movie Ride is thoroughly entertaining for people of all ages.

 This is a must-see attraction.

## Jim Henson's Muppet*Vision 3-D

| | |
|---|---|
| Ages 2–4: | ★★★ |
| Ages 5–10: | ★★★ |
| Ages 11–15: | ★★★ |
| Ages 16–Adult: | ★★★ |
| Senior Citizens: | ★★★ |

Kermit, Miss Piggy, and all of the classic Muppet characters are featured in this attraction's twelve-minute preshow that's followed by a comical and rather bizarre twelve-minute 3-D movie. Muppet fans of all ages will truly love this attraction.

 This is a must-see attraction.

## ≡FAST FACT

The theater itself was designed for this show, and it looks a lot like the set from *The Muppet Show* television series. During the movie, the theater itself actually becomes part of the show.

### Star Tours

| | |
|---|---|
| Ages 2–4: | N.S. |
| Ages 5–10: | ★★★ |
| Ages 11–15: | ★★★ |
| Ages 16–Adult: | ★★★ |
| Senior Citizens: | ★★ |

What happens when you combine the creative talent of Disney's Imagineers with the imagination of George Lucas? The result is Star Tours, a ride based on the original *Star Wars* movies and features characters like R2-D2 and C3-PO. As an intergalactic tourist, you and thirty-nine other guests will board a StarSpeeder and experience a whirlwind tour of the galaxy. Using flight-simulator technology, the StarSpeeder is on hydraulics and is perfectly synchronized with the movie you'll be watching on the ship's main view screen.

You'll feel like you're actually traveling at ultrafast speed through space, when, in reality, your StarSpeeder is only a few feet off the ground. Star Tours is a fast-paced and turbulent roller coaster–like ride. Be prepared for a long wait to ride this attraction, but while you're waiting to board the StarSpeeder, you'll be entertained by an elaborate preshow that includes Audio-Animatronic characters from the *Star Wars* movies.

This ride is suitable for people of all ages, except very young children (under the age of three) and people who suffer from back problems, heart conditions, motion sickness, etc. Once you board the StarSpeeder, stow all of your loose clothing, purse, camera bag, etc., and fasten your seatbelt. This ride is bumpy, but not scary. The best time to ride this attraction is late in the evening. If the line for this ride doesn't go outside of the building, the wait will be less than twenty minutes.

 This is a must-see attraction.

## "Honey I Shrunk the Kids" Movie Set Adventure

| | |
|---|---|
| Ages 2–4: | N.S. |
| Ages 5–10: | ★★★ |
| Ages 11–15: | ★★★ |
| Ages 16–Adult: | N.S. |
| Senior Citizens: | N.S. |

This playground looks like a scene from the popular live-action Disney movie, *Honey, I Shrunk the Kids*, because everything is extremely over-sized, making young guests feel incredibly small as they climb, crawl, jump, and slide around. If you're traveling with kids, this attraction offers adults a chance to sit down and relax, while the children have fun exploring this playground.

## ⊕ HOT SPOT

Located on the cement ground in front of the Mann's Chinese Theater, the home of the Great Movie Ride, are actual hand imprints, and in some cases, foot imprints, from real-life celebrities who have visited The Disney-MGM Studios since 1989. Spend a few minutes to check out which stars have left their permanent mark imprinted in the sidewalk.

## Voyage of the Little Mermaid

| | |
|---|---|
| Ages 2–4: | ★★★ |
| Ages 5–10: | ★★★ |
| Ages 11–15: | ★★★ |
| Ages 16–Adult: | ★★★ |
| Senior Citizens: | ★★★ |

Here's an exciting opportunity to go under the sea without ever getting wet. Voyage of the Little Mermaid is an extremely innovative, fifteen-minute live show that features costumed characters and unique life-size puppets, along with special effects. Scenes from the animated Disney movie *The Little Mermaid* are re-created. This is an extremely popular attraction, especially among kids, so be prepared to wait up to one hour to experience this show.

👍 This is a must-see attraction.

## American Film Institute Showcase

| | |
|---|---|
| Ages 2–4: | ★ |
| Ages 5–10: | ★ |
| Ages 11–15: | ★★ |
| Ages 16–Adult: | ★★ |
| Senior Citizens: | ★★ |

This museumlike attraction displays props, costumes, and sets from many popular and classic television shows and movies. Movie and television buffs will appreciate this ever-changing exhibit.

## Indiana Jones Epic Stunt Spectacular

| | |
|---|---|
| Ages 2–4: | ★ |
| Ages 5–10: | ★★ |
| Ages 11–15: | ★★★ |
| Ages 16–Adult: | ★★★ |
| Senior Citizens: | ★★★ |

This live-action stunt show was choreographed by Glenn Randall, who was the stunt coordinator for all of the *Indiana Jones* movies. While you won't see Harrison Ford, you will see talented stuntpeople re-create scenes from this movie series. Fireworks, explosions, and other special effects are used to add extra drama to this exciting show.

The Indiana Jones Epic Stunt Spectacular is presented several times throughout the day (show times are listed in front of the theater and at the Tip Board). About 2,000 people fit into the theater, so if you arrive between fifteen and thirty minutes early, you're virtually guaranteed a seat for this high-action thirty-minute show. A few brave guests are selected at the start of each show to be "extras." Not only do audience members get to see dozens of stunts performed, they also learn how many stunts are actually performed in movies so that nobody gets injured.

## Beauty and the Beast

| | |
|---|---|
| Ages 2–4: | ★★ |
| Ages 5–10: | ★★★ |
| Ages 11–15: | ★★★ |
| Ages 16–Adult: | ★★ |
| Senior Citizens: | ★★ |

After Disney's *Beauty and the Beast* animated movie was released and became an instant classic, a live adaptation of this movie was created for guests of The Disney-MGM Studios. This thirty-minute live-action performance stars actors and costumed characters. The show re-creates several scenes from the movie.

This show inspired the hit Broadway musical and is presented several times throughout each day. Show times are displayed in front of the theater and at the Tip Board. While the theater holds over 1,500 people, be sure to arrive between fifteen and thirty minutes early to get the best seats (depending on how crowded the Studios are on the day of your visit).

## Sorcery in the Sky Fireworks Spectacular

| | |
|---|---|
| Ages 2–4: | ★ |
| Ages 5–10: | ★★★ |
| Ages 11–15: | ★★★ |
| Ages 16–Adult: | ★★★ |
| Senior Citizens: | ★★★ |

This incredible fireworks presentation is shown at night, but only during WDW's peak seasons (during the holidays and during certain times in the summer). The fireworks are launched from above the Mann's Chinese Theater, so the best viewing location is from Hollywood Boulevard, in front of the Mann's Chinese Theater. When you're facing the theater, the clearing to the left is an excellent viewing location.

All of the fireworks are choreographed to music from *Fantasia* as well as other classic Disney films. The entire show lasts about ten exciting minutes.

 This is a must-see attraction.

##  TRAVEL TIP

Check with the Tip Board for the exact show times, and be sure to stake out your viewing spot between thirty minutes and one hour early. (You want an unobstructed view looking over the Mann's Chinese Theater.)

## The Hunchback of Notre Dame: A Musical Adventure

| | |
|---|---|
| Ages 2–4: | ★★ |
| Ages 5–10: | ★★★ |
| Ages 11–15: | ★★★ |
| Ages 16–Adult: | ★★★ |
| Senior Citizens: | ★★★ |

This thirty-minute live-action show features actors, dancers, giant puppets, and costumed characters who re-create popular scenes from Disney's animated *Hunchback of Notre Dame* film. This show is presented at the Backlot Theater, which is covered, keeping the audience out of the sun.

Several songs from the movie are performed as guests see their favorite characters from the film come to life in an upbeat and entertaining performance that kids especially will enjoy. This show is presented multiple times throughout the day. Check the Tip Board for exact show times, and be sure to arrive between thirty minutes and one hour early to ensure you'll get a seat of your choice for the performance.

## ≡FAST FACT

These actors take on the roles of a wide range of characters, from movie starlets to crazed fans who will mistake a guest as a big-name celebrity and seek that guest's autograph. When you're visiting The Disney-MGM Studios, everyone becomes part of the show.

## Streetmosphere Performers

One of the goals of The Disney-MGM Studios is to re-create the Golden Age of Hollywood and make visitors to this Orlando attraction feel like they've been transported across the country and back in time. As you wander down Hollywood and Sunset Boulevards, don't be surprised if you come across "Streetmosphere Performers"—professional actors and actresses who help to add ambiance. The performers roam freely around the park and interact with guests, while constantly staying in character.

### Fantasmic!

| | |
|---|---|
| Ages 2–4: | ★★★ |
| Ages 5–10: | ★★★ |
| Ages 11–15: | ★★★ |
| Ages 16–Adult: | ★★★ |
| Senior Citizens: | ★★★ |

Adopted from the highly popular show that was originally created for Disneyland, this nighttime spectacle combines lasers, special effects, dancing waters, fiber-optic effects, classic Disney animated movie footage, Disney characters, a cast of over fifty performers, and plenty of Disney music. This is all choreographed perfectly into a twenty-five-minute performance that you'll remember forever. This is perhaps the most spectacular show at The WDW Resort. Fantasmic! should not be missed. To stake out a good location to watch this show from, arrive at least one hour early for the performance.

 This is a must-see attraction.

## ⊕ HOT SPOT

The Disney Radio Studios is where several national radio programs originate from. Since these studios feature large glass windows and speakers outside, you can spend a few minutes watching a live radio broadcast take place.

### Rock 'n' Roller Coaster Starring Aerosmith

| | |
|---|---|
| Ages 2–4: | N.S. |
| Ages 5–10: | N.S. |
| Ages 11–15: | ★★★ |
| Ages 16–Adult: | ★★★ |
| Senior Citizens: | ★★ |

The latest ride added to The Disney-MGM Studios is a state-of-the-art roller coaster with a musical twist. As you experience this high-speed indoor coaster, 125 speakers will rock your world with Aerosmith music. When this coaster launches, you'll go from zero to 60 miles per hour in under two seconds, but that's just the start of the experience, which offers plenty of unexpected turns, loops, and twists.

The entire experience (including preshow) lasts about ten minutes. Having quickly become one of the most popular attractions at this park, a sixty- to ninety-minute wait for it is typical. To save time, be sure to take advantage of FASTPASS. Riders must be at least 48 inches tall.

## What's New at the Studios

 Like all of the Disney theme parks, The Disney-MGM Studios is always growing and evolving. Here's a look at what's been added to this theme park recently.

### Mickey's Sorcerer's Hat— 100 Years of Magic Tribute

| | |
|---|---|
| Ages 2–4: | N.S. |
| Ages 5–10: | ★ |
| Ages 11–15: | ★ |
| Ages 16–Adult: | ★★ |
| Senior Citizens: | ★★ |

Starting in December 2001, a giant sorcerer's hat (adapted from the hat Mickey Mouse wore in *Fantasia*) was built directly in front of the Mann's Chinese Theater to commemorate Walt Disney's 100th birthday. Using interactive kiosks located behind this giant hat, guests get a peak at events in Disney history. Mickey's 122-foot tall, 156-ton Sorcerer's Hat is slated to remain as a prominent fixture within the theme park at least through 2002.

### Sounds Dangerous: Starring Drew Carey

| | |
|---|---|
| Ages 2–4: | N.S. |
| Ages 5–10: | ★ |
| Ages 11–15: | ★★ |
| Ages 16–Adult: | ★★ |
| Senior Citizens: | ★★ |

This interactive show stars comedian Drew Carey and showcases how audio special effects are created for television shows and motion pictures. For this presentation, you're invited to a taping of a fictional television series pilot (that stars Drew Carey). The show lasts about twelve minutes and takes place within an indoor theater (The ABC Sound Studio). Keep in mind, a portion of this comedy show, which focuses on audio, is done in complete darkness. While this isn't meant to be scary, it might not be suitable for very young children.

## Disney Stars and Motor Cars Parade

| | |
|---|---|
| Ages 2–4: | ★ |
| Ages 5–10: | ★★ |
| Ages 11–15: | ★★ |
| Ages 16–Adult: | ★★ |
| Senior Citizens: | ★★ |

In this twenty-five-minute daily parade, guests have a chance to see some of Disney's most famous characters as they ride down Hollywood Boulevard in a fleet of custom automobiles. The parade route begins near Star Tours and ends near the Crossroads (at the entrance of the studios). In all, sixty-three Disney characters are featured, along with a handful of Disney-MGM Studios guests who are preselected to participate in this upbeat parade. By sitting along the curb of Hollywood Boulevard, guests will have a chance to interact with some of the characters as they pass by, so have your camera ready.

## Who Wants to Be a Millionaire—Play It!

| | |
|---|---|
| Ages 2–4: | N.S. |
| Ages 5–10: | ★ |
| Ages 11–15: | ★★★ |
| Ages 16–Adult: | ★★★ |
| Senior Citizens: | ★★★ |

America's attention has been captivated by a television game show that asks a simple question, "Who wants to be a millionaire?" Well, in addition to being one of ABC-TV's most popular game shows, Who Wants to Be a Millionaire—Play It! is one of the park's most popular interactive attractions. Due to its popularity, you'll definitely want to take advantage of FASTPASS to experience it.

As soon as you step into the soundstage that houses this attraction, you'll find yourself sitting in the midst of a faithful re-creation of the *Who Wants to Be a Millionaire* T.V. studio set. While Regis is in New York hosting the actual game show, a stand-in host is on hand as you experience what it would be like to watch a taping of the real-life game show.

The big difference, however, is that every seat in the theater is interactive, which means you can play along. And, if you're quick (and accurate) when it comes to providing answers, you may find yourself in the famous "hot seat" competing for prizes. (Sorry, in this version of the game, no cash is awarded.)

 This is a must-see attraction.

## FAST FACT

This interactive attraction lasts about thirty minutes and is extremely faithful to the format of *Who Wants to Be a Millionaire,* with a few minor exceptions that allow the entire "studio audience" to be involved in the game.

### Walt Disney: One Man's Dream

| | |
|---|---|
| Ages 2–4: | N.S. |
| Ages 5–10: | ★ |
| Ages 11–15: | ★ |
| Ages 16–Adult: | ★★★ |
| Senior Citizens: | ★★★ |

In conjunction with Walt Disney's 100th birthday celebration, which kicked off in December 2001, The Disney-MGM Studios created a self-paced, walk-through exhibit that showcases the life of Walt Disney and pays tribute to his many achievements. This exhibit contains extensive memorabilia from the Walt Disney archives, much of which has never been displayed to the public before.

According to Disney Imagineer Roger Holzberg, the senior show producer/director of this attraction, "When we were researching the attraction, we found that many of our guests under the age of fifteen did not know Walt Disney was a real person. They thought it was just a company name."

Walt Disney: One Man's Dream features a short film of Walt Disney's life that explores the extraordinary hardships he overcame. "He is an individual, not an icon," added Holzberg. "This tells the story of Walt the man, and we hope that guests will be moved by the scope of his imagination, what he accomplished, and what he inspired."

Anyone who truly appreciates the accomplishments of Walt Disney as a television and motion picture producer, animator, and theme park creator will enjoy this museumlike exhibit, which is not particularly kid-oriented.

## Playhouse Disney—Live on Stage!

| | |
|---|---|
| Ages 2–4: | ★★★ |
| Ages 5–10: | ★★★ |
| Ages 11–15: | ★ |
| Ages 16–Adult: | ★ |
| Senior Citizens: | ★ |

Designed specifically for the under-ten crowd that watches *Playhouse Disney* on The Disney Channel, this live musical show features characters from *Bear in the Big Blue House, Rolie Polie Olie, Stanley,* and stars from *The Book of Pooh.* This is a twenty-minute show that's colorful, upbeat, and will provide plenty of entertainment for kids (especially those familiar with the characters from the various TV shows on The Disney Channel). If you're traveling with young kids, this adorable show should not be missed!

On days when the park is crowded, be sure to arrive at the theater at least twenty to thirty minutes prior to the posted show time. To ensure that kids, in particular, get the best view of the action, audience members sit on a carpeted floor.

 This is a must-see attraction.

## ═FAST FACT

Multiple shows are presented throughout the day. Check The Disney-MGM Studios *Guide Map* for show times.

## The Osborne Family Spectacle of Lights

| | |
|---|---|
| Ages 2–4: | ★★★ |
| Ages 5–10: | ★★★ |
| Ages 11–15: | ★★★ |
| Ages 16–Adult: | ★★★ |
| Senior Citizens: | ★★★ |

Between late November and early January, The Disney-MGM Studios celebrate the holiday season by transforming the "backlot" area of the working motion picture studio portion of the theme park into a holiday winter wonderland. Opening every evening after dark, this walk-through attraction is absolutely breathtaking and is suitable for the entire family.

One of the primary focal points of this extravagant light display is a 70-foot-tall Christmas tree that's adorned with over 58,000 lights. In all, however, over 350 miles of Christmas lights are used to create this attraction, which requires 800,000 watts of electricity to bring it to life. As you explore this holiday attraction, be on the lookout for the over forty hidden Mickeys that can be found within the decorative display. Even if you don't celebrate Christmas, this attraction is still worth experiencing.

 This is a must-see attraction.

## ⊕ HOT SPOT

At several times throughout each day, you can meet Mickey, Minnie, and other popular Disney characters. While the characters sometimes wander around the park interacting with guests, you can also find them along Mickey Avenue and also near the entrance to Disney's Hunchback of Notre Dame: A Musical Adventure.

## The Backstage Studio Tours

 One of the things that makes a trip to The Disney-MGM Studios so special is that you actually have the opportunity to visit an actual motion picture, television, and animation studio, where movies and television programs are being produced. The actual studios can be seen by taking any of the two main tours that are available throughout the day.

## The Magic of Disney Animation

| | |
|---|---|
| Ages 2–4: | N.S. |
| Ages 5–10: | ★ |
| Ages 11–15: | ★★★ |
| Ages 16–Adult: | ★★★ |
| Senior Citizens: | ★★★ |

While not an attraction per se, this thirty-five-minute movie/tour combination offers guests a walking tour of the working Disney Animation Studios facility in Orlando. Not only will you learn how animated movies and television shows are created, but you'll also see animation artwork and have a chance to see actual animators at work. The best time to experience this tour is on a week day, during business hours (because that's when the animators will be working).

Disney's *Mulan* is the first full-length animated feature to be produced entirely at the Orlando animation facility, although the animators here contributed to *The Lion King, Aladdin, Pocahontas, Beauty and the Beast, The Hunchback of Notre Dame,* and other, more recent, films. Chances are you'll get a chance to see many of the animators who worked on these movies, plus get a sneak peak at future animation projects that Walt Disney Animation is working on.

👍 This is a must-see attraction.

## The Studio Backlot Tour

| | |
|---|---|
| Ages 2–4: | ★ |
| Ages 5–10: | ★★ |
| Ages 11–15: | ★★★ |
| Ages 16–Adult: | ★★★ |
| Senior Citizens: | ★★★ |

Guests ride in trams that take them on a twenty-five-minute tour of the actual working Disney-MGM Studios facilities (a.k.a. the Backlot). You'll see sets from movies that are in production, outdoor "facades," as well as soundstages where movies and TV shows are filmed. During this tour, you might even get a glimpse of a well-known celebrity.

You'll also see the studio's wardrobe/costume facility, plus get a chance to see costumes from classic movies.

For anyone interested in a behind-the-scenes look at how movies are made, this tour offers this and more. Tours are given throughout the day. Check with the Tip Board for departure times.

## ⊕ HOT SPOT

> To make this attraction even more entertaining, there are also a few surprises. For example, you'll see how special effects are created firsthand, as water and fire (pyrotechnics) effects are demonstrated in Catastrophe Canyon.

## Dining at The Disney-MGM Studios

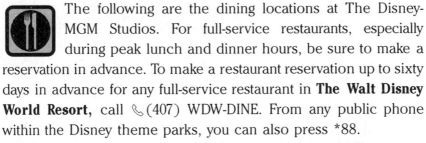 The following are the dining locations at The Disney-MGM Studios. For full-service restaurants, especially during peak lunch and dinner hours, be sure to make a reservation in advance. To make a restaurant reservation up to sixty days in advance for any full-service restaurant in **The Walt Disney World Resort,** call ✆ (407) WDW-DINE. From any public phone within the Disney theme parks, you can also press *88.

For same-day reservations, visit the restaurant of your choice, or stop at the Tip Board. While several of these restaurants offer somewhat fancy atmospheres and are considered fine-dining experiences, casual attire is acceptable. (After all, you're on vacation at a theme park. Throw on your favorite T-shirt and shorts, but don't forget your wallet.)

### Hollywood Brown Derby

This full-service restaurant is a re-creation of the Brown Derby in Hollywood, where some of Hollywood's biggest and most famous stars used to dine. This is one of the very best restaurants located anywhere in The WDW Resort. While it's rather expensive, it's a wonderful place to enjoy lunch or dinner. Live piano entertainment (with an accompanying singer) is continuous. Reservations are strongly recommended, and a children's menu is available.

The original Brown Derby is where owner Bob Cobb created the now-popular Cobb Salad in the 1930s. Comprising salad greens, bacon, turkey, tomato, egg, avocado, and blue cheese, this is one of the restaurant's most popular dishes. While the lunch and dinner entrees are incredible, just wait until you see what's offered for dessert. The Hollywood Brown Derby is located in the heart of The Disney-MGM Studios, along Hollywood Boulevard, and like the original restaurant, it is a popular dining location for visiting celebrities and dignitaries.

## Mama Melrose's Ristorante Italiano

Open for lunch (and dinner during WDW's busy seasons), this Italian restaurant serves pizzas cooked in a wood-burning oven. Seafood, steak, and chicken dishes (grilled on a hardwood charbroiler) are also popular entrees. Although this is one of the Studios' more expensive restaurants, the food is delicious. Reservations are strongly recommended.

## 50's Prime Time Café

This 1950s-style diner features television monitors located throughout the restaurant (and on the tables) that show black-and-white clips from popular 1950s sitcoms. Instead of serving food on traditional plates, the meals, while cooked fresh, are presented like old-fashioned TV dinners. Hamburgers, turkey burgers, roast beef sandwiches, salads, and other staple diner items can be found on the menu of this theme restaurant that will appeal to the entire family.

## ≡FAST FACT

The food here isn't cheap, because you're paying for the atmosphere. A special children's menu is available. In addition to serving lunch and dinner, this is a great place to stop for a snack. Reservations are strongly recommended, or you'll find yourself waiting for a table.

## Sci-Fi Dine-In Theater

This full-service theme restaurant simulates a 1950s drive-in movie theater. The tables are in the shapes of popular cars, and fiber-optic special effects are used to simulate stars on the ceiling as guests dine and watch a movie screen that shows continuous science fiction movie trailers and cartoons from the 1950s. Lunch and dinner are served daily, and popcorn is always served as an appetizer. Reservations are strongly recommended.

## Fast Food

If you're not looking for a full-service restaurant, the following options are available for lunch, dinner, and snacks throughout the day. These dining locations are considerably less expensive than the above-listed restaurants.

**Backlot Express**—Another fast and inexpensive dining choice at the Studios is the Backlot Express, which also offers counter service and a Hollywood studio theme. Hamburgers, hot dogs, salads, dessert items, fresh fruit, and soda are among the most popular menu selections. Beer and wine are also available.

**Commissary**—All of the major Hollywood studios offer a commissary, where actors, actresses, and motion picture or television crews can grab a quick bite to eat on the studio lot. What you will find is fast food: hamburgers, hot dogs, chicken sandwiches, salads, sodas, bottled water, and ice cream are among the menu options.

**Dinosaur Gertie's**—This snack shop looks like a giant dinosaur located along Echo Lake. What you'll find here is frozen slush in a variety of flavors—the perfect way for your kids to cool down and get a sugar rush on a hot day.

**Hollywood & Vine Buffeteria**—Serving breakfast, lunch, and dinner, this cafeteria offers a wide selection of inexpensive menu items. As for the décor, you'll find a huge mural depicting Hollywood landmarks such as several major studios.

**Min & Bill's Dockside Diner**—Soft-serve ice cream and sandwiches are available at this lakeside diner.

**Soundstage Restaurant**—This is one of the few places in The Disney-MGM Studios where you're virtually guaranteed to see Disney characters and have a chance to meet them, get autographs, and take pictures. You'll have the opportunity to dine at the all-you-can-eat buffet. Chicken, beef, salads, and seafood dishes are usually among the offerings.

**Starring Rolls Bakery**—This is the perfect place to stop for breakfast if you're on the go and don't want to waste a minute sitting around eating when you could be experiencing a show, ride, or attraction at the Studios. For lunch, a variety of sandwiches (served on freshly baked croissants) are available.

**Studio Catering Co.**—Snacks and desserts are the specialty of this eating establishment, which you'll come across at the end of the Studio Backlot Tour tram ride. Beer is available here.

**Sunset Ranch Market**—This area comprises several food stands along Sunset Boulevard (located on the way to the Tower of Terror). Hot dogs, frozen yogurt, popcorn, assorted fresh fruit, and all sorts of soda, juice, and bottled water are available.

**Toy Story Pizza Planet**—This themed restaurant will remind guests of Disney's *The Toy Story* movie. Individual pizzas are the featured items, although salads, Italian ices, and other snacks are also available.

# Shopping at the Studios

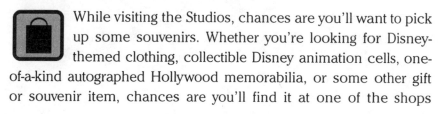

While visiting the Studios, chances are you'll want to pick up some souvenirs. Whether you're looking for Disney-themed clothing, collectible Disney animation cells, one-of-a-kind autographed Hollywood memorabilia, or some other gift or souvenir item, chances are you'll find it at one of the shops located within this park. If you're looking for something in particular, but don't know where to find it, call the **Disney Merchandise Hotline** at ✆ (407) 824-5566.

## 💼 TRAVEL TIP

For those visiting Orlando during the rainy season, which many people believe lasts most of the year, you can purchase a bright yellow Mickey Mouse rain poncho at virtually all of the shops located within the park. These vinyl ponchos are available for kids and adults.

**Animation Courtyard Shops**—Located right near the Voyage of the Little Mermaid attraction in the Animation courtyard, you'll find gifts, souvenirs, toys, clothing, and all sorts of other stuff with a Little Mermaid theme. Young girls especially will enjoy shopping.

**Animation Gallery**—Limited-edition Disney animation cells, original Disney artwork, and other collectibles are available here. This gallery is located in the Animation building. While most of the artwork and collectibles are rather expensive, you can also purchase books and posters.

Even if you're not in the buying mood, if you're interested in Disney animation, you'll want to drop into this air-conditioned gallery and enjoy what's on display. A Disney animator/artist is usually on hand to answer questions and to demonstrate how animation cells are created. This gallery will appeal more to adults, Disneyana collectors, and Disney animation fans.

**Celebrity 5 & 10**—While this shop looks like a Woolworth's store from the 1940s, you'll be extremely hard pressed to find anything for five or ten cents. In addition to Disney-themed merchandise, this is the place to go for movie-biz souvenirs like clapboards.

**Cover Story**—Connected to the Darkroom photo-supply shop, Cover Story offers personalized photographic souvenirs that put you (or the people you're with) on the cover of a popular magazine.

**Crossroads of the World**—Located at the Studios' main entrance, this kiosk offers a small selection of souvenir merchandise and sundries but is staffed by knowledgeable Disney cast members who can answer just about all of your questions.

**The Darkroom**—In addition to being able to rent video camcorders from this shop, you can also purchase Kodak film, batteries, disposable cameras, and just about any photographic accessory you need. Two-hour photo processing is also available from here, as well as from several other shops within the Studios that have a sign to this effect in the window or on the counter.

**Fototoons**—At this souvenir stand, which you'll come across after participating in the Studio Backlot Tour, you'll have a chance to purchase a photo of yourself (or someone you're with) posing with a popular character.

## ≡FAST FACT

A selection of Disney character merchandise can be found at Golden Age Souvenirs.

**Indiana Jones Adventure Outpost**—You'll find this gift shop located right near the Indiana Jones Epic Stunt Spectacular theater. What's offered here is a variety of souvenir items such as hats, shirts, and toys, all with an *Indiana Jones* theme or logo.

**It's a Wonderful Shop**—No matter what day of the year it is, it's always beginning to look a lot like Christmas at this gift shop. You'll find this Christmas shop, which is filled with tons of tree ornaments, located near the Muppet*Vision 3-D theater.

**Keystone Clothiers**—Disney-themed fashions for women are in abundance at Keystone Clothiers. Whether you're looking for character clothing and accessories suitable for vacation or beach wear, or something more suitable for the work environment, you'll find it here.

**L.A. Cinema Storage**—Disney clothes for kids, featuring the classic Disney characters as well as characters from the recent Disney animated features, are sold here.

**Lakeside Newsstand**—All sorts of clothing, gifts, souvenirs, trinkets, and other stuff, all imprinted with The Disney-MGM Studios logo, are available.

**Legends of Hollywood**—Books, videos, compact discs, and all sorts of other classic Hollywood memorabilia and souvenirs can be found here.

**The Loony Bin**—Roger Rabbit merchandise and gag gifts are sold at this shop, which you'll find near the exit of the Studio Backlot Tour. Be sure to check out the props from the *Who Framed Roger Rabbit?* movie, which are on display (but not for sale) in this shop.

## ≡FAST FACT

Merchandise, clothing, and toys based on Disney's latest animated features are sold at the Studio Store.

**Mickey's of Hollywood**—Logo-imprinted Mickey Mouse, Walt Disney Studios, and Disney-MGM Studios merchandise and clothing are the main thrust of what's offered at this shop.

**Mouse About Town**—Men's apparel featuring Mickey Mouse and other Disney characters is available at this shop.

**Movieland Memorabilia**—Located just outside of the Studio's main entrance (to the extreme left), this kiosk is both your first and last chance to pick up a souvenir as you enter or leave the park.

**Once Upon A Time**—This gift shop looks just like the movie theater where *Snow White* premiered in 1937. Instead of watching a movie, however, what you'll see inside are collectibles (and limited-edition merchandise) that feature the classic Disney characters.

**Oscar's Classic Car Souvenirs**—You'll find this old-fashioned gas station located to the right as you enter the park's main entrance. Instead of your basic selection of Disney stuff, this shop offers automotive memorabilia.

## ⊕ HOT SPOT

This is also the place where you can rent wheelchairs, strollers, or Electronic Convenience Vehicles. Behind this service station, you'll find lockers that can be rented by the day, as well as an ATM, rest rooms, a stamp machine, and public telephones.

**Planet Hollywood Super Store**—Theme dining Hollywood-style is possible only at Planet Hollywood restaurants. For souvenirs from Planet Hollywood, drop into this popular shop.

**Sid Cahuenga's One-of-a-Kind**—Out of all the shops within this park, with the exception of the Animation Gallery, this one offers extremely interesting and very unique merchandise that's non–Disney related. What you'll find here are one-of-a-kind autographed photos, posters, and books, plus items once owned by celebrities.

**Stage 1 Company Store**—Located near the Muppet*Vision 3-D attraction, Muppetmania is the theme of this shop, which offers all sorts of Muppet-themed toys and souvenirs. Of course, you'll also find classic Disney character merchandise available.

**Sunset Club Culture**–Dozens of Disney watches, including collectibles and limited-edition watches, are on display and available for purchase. These watches are available in a wide range of styles, and the prices vary greatly. Disney-themed jewelry is also available here, but this is definitely the place to go if you're shopping for a watch.

**Sunset Ranch**–Film, batteries, hats, sunblock, sundries, and souvenirs are available.

**Sweet Success**–The key ingredient of virtually everything sold here is sugar. Candies and other goodies are in abundance. If you're on a diet, do not enter!

**Tatooine Traders**–As you exit the popular Star Tours ride, you'll find yourself in the middle of this souvenir shop that sells a variety of *Star Wars* toys and products, as well as other space-themed merchandise.

**The Writer's Shop**–This small shop is a bookstore where The Disney-MGM Studios often hosts well-known authors for special book-signing events. There's also a gourmet coffee kiosk within the shop.

## ═FAST FACT

As a working television studio, some of the shows that have been produced here include *The New Mickey Mouse Club*, *Sheena*, *Full House*, *Wheel of Fortune*, *World Championship Wrestling*, *ESPN College Football Awards*, *Talk Soup*, *Step By Step*, and *Barbara Walters Special*, and *Live! With Regis & Kathie Lee*.

# Disney's Animal Kingdom

BY COMBINING THE TALENTS OF ZOOKEEPERS, wildlife experts, and Disney Imagineers from around the world, Disney's Animal Kingdom has become a unique collection of innovative rides, shows, parades, and attractions that combine the thrill of a Disney theme park with the unpredictable excitement of seeing exotic wild animals up close in re-creations of their natural habitats.

## Park Overview

 Several years ago, the Walt Disney Company set aside 500 acres of The Walt Disney World Resort to create a totally new type of theme park—one that features a lively cast of animals, but that would be unlike any zoo or wildlife sanctuary. Construction of this theme park began in August 1995. Disney's Animal Kingdom is now larger than The Magic Kingdom, Epcot, and The Disney-MGM Studios, and offers what the company calls "a new species of theme park entertainment."

So, what's Disney's Animal Kingdom all about? It's about seeing the animals that live on our planet in a whole new light and learning about them. It's also about fun, exploration, and excitement.

On April 22, 1998, the hard work and dreams of thousands of Disney Imagineers and cast members came to fruition as Disney's

Animal Kingdom opened to the public. Here, guests come face-to-face with over 1,500 animals (representing over 250 species) in a theme park that only Disney's Imagineers could conceive.

While guests will see Mickey and his pals in the park, Disney's Animal Kingdom is designed to educate as well as entertain, in an environment that is less commercial than The Magic Kingdom. Messages and lessons about wildlife preservation and conservation are intertwined into virtually every experience that guests have while visiting this exiting theme park.

## Area Divisions

Located in the center of this theme park is Safari Village, which contains the Tree of Life (a 145-foot masterpiece with 325 animals carved into its trunk). Just like The Magic Kingdom, Disney's Animal Kingdom is divided into areas, which include: Discovery Island, Camp Minnie-Mickey, Africa, the Oasis, Rafiki's Planet Watch, Asia, and DinoLand U.S.A. Each of these areas has a totally different theme, yet all involve interaction with animals that are either alive, from the past, or from the imagination of Disney's Imagineers.

## ══FAST FACT

Disney's Animal Kingdom offers beautiful landscaping that includes 600 species of trees, 350 species of grasses, along with 1,800 species of shrubs, vines, ferns, mosses, epiphytes, and perennials. More than 100,000 trees and over 4 million individual plants, trees, grasses, and shrubs have been planted on the park's 500 acres.

Throughout this park, you'll find many rides, shows, and attractions suitable for young kids (under age twelve); however, Camp Minnie-Mickey and, more recently, DinoLand U.S.A. have become the kid-oriented areas of this theme park.

## Animal Care

To ensure that the animals living in this theme park are always given the best care, the Walt Disney Company has hired hundreds of animal specialists, curators, animal keepers, veterinarians, and animal behavioral specialists from over 200 leading zoos, educational institutions, and wild animal parks from around the world.

Depending on when you visit Disney's Animal Kingdom and how crowded the park is, you'll easily be able to spend between one and one-and-a-half full days experiencing everything this theme park has to offer.

## Animal Viewing

As you plan your time at Disney's Animal Kingdom, pace yourself—lots of walking is required. Since some of the park's most popular attractions involve seeing live animals, keep in mind that many of the animals tend to be more active and visible to the public in the mornings and late afternoons when the temperature is cooler. The majority of the animals are allowed to roam freely in their habitats, so at times they may not be visible to guests, simply because they're napping in the shade. Thus, try to experience the live animal attractions early or late in the day.

The very best time to see the animals, especially the ones in the Kilimanjaro Safaris, is when it's cool, overcast, or raining. Obviously, this isn't ideal for vacationers, but the animals tend to come out and be far more visible and lively.

Virtually all of the live animals you'll be seeing at Disney's Animal Kingdom are wild. They have not been trained or domesticated. They are kept in habitats designed to simulate their natural environments as closely as possible. All of the animals are kept on strict diets in order to keep them healthy. Thus, while as a guest at Disney's Animal Kingdom you can purchase all sorts of food and snacks for yourself, it's critical that you do not share your food or beverages with any of the animals, no matter how tempting it might be to toss a few pieces of popcorn, for example, to one of the animals you encounter.

## ☰FAST FACT

Admission to Disney's Animal Kingdom requires a ticket. For details about the various ticket and pricing options for visiting Disney's Animal Kingdom and all of the theme parks within The WDW Resort, see Chapter 3.

### Same Day Re-entry

As you leave Disney's Animal Kingdom, be sure to have your hand stamped as you exit in order to be granted readmission into the park later that day or evening. In addition to the hand stamp, be sure to retain your ticket stub. The hand stamps are designed to be water-resistant, so don't worry if your hand gets wet if you choose to return to your hotel in the middle of the day to go swimming, and then want to return to Disney's Animal Kingdom later that evening. Try to refrain, however, from scrubbing your hands clean with soap until your day's visit to Disney's Animal Kingdom is complete.

### What to Bring

Make sure you wear comfortable shoes, because you'll be doing a tremendous amount of walking! Much of your time will be spent outdoors while visiting this theme park, so depending on the weather, you might also want to take along a jacket (you can always store it in a locker). Sunglasses, a cap (with a visor), and sunblock are also important items to have with you, especially if the weather is sunny.

Try to avoid carrying too much stuff with you. You'll enjoy your visit more if your hands are as free as possible. Don't forget to bring your camera, along with plenty of film and batteries. Avoid having to purchase high-priced film, batteries, or camera supplies in the park.

In case of rain, plan on getting a bit wet. Wear a raincoat or purchase a Mickey Mouse poncho (for about $5). Avoid bringing an umbrella into the park. You'll find it frustrating trying to walk around the crowded park with an open umbrella. During a rainstorm, crowds will be less; however, some outdoor shows and attractions will be closed or cancelled.

## The Information Board

Located next to the Creature Comforts shop inside the park is one of the park's Attraction Information Boards. A second board is located outside the Disney Outfitters store, across from the Island Mercantile. These boards list the current wait times for all of the major attractions in Disney's Animal Kingdom, and also list the show times for the various parades and stage performances.

Stationed at each board is a Disney cast member who is in constant contact with the operators of all of the park's major attractions. Accurate wait times for each ride and attraction are posted, so you can better plan your day at Disney's Animal Kingdom. If you have any questions about planning your day at the park, the cast members overseeing the Attraction Information Board will be able to provide answers. Other Disney cast members who are always in the know are those roaming the park carrying walkie-talkies.

The Disney cast members manning the Information Board will be able to assist you in determining how early you should arrive to the shows and how long you'll have to wait for the various attractions.

## ≡FAST FACT

While it's critical that guests refrain from feeding any of the animals that live within Disney's Animal Kingdom (because each animal has a very specialized diet), the team of animal experts that care for the animals feeds them over three tons of food per day.

## Transportation

Located just outside the main entrance of Disney's Animal Kingdom is a 6,000-car parking lot. There is a daily parking fee if you're not a guest of a WDW Resort hotel. Guests can also be dropped off and picked up right near the park's main entrance when they use the WDW buses. When using the complimentary bus service, plan on spending thirty to sixty minutes each way getting to and from the park from any location within The WDW Resort complex.

While waiting for the bus (outside of the park's main entrance) to take you back to your hotel or to another Disney theme park, there are no nearby benches, telephones, and rest rooms, so take advantage of these facilities before leaving the park. You could wind up waiting between twenty and thirty minutes for the right bus to take you where you want to go. The bus stop is, however, covered, so you'll remain pretty sheltered during bad weather.

A faster, but more expensive, mode of transportation for getting to and from Disney's Animal Kingdom is taking a taxi. Guests will, however, ultimately save a tremendous amount of commuting time by renting a car for the duration of their vacation at The WDW Resort. (Renting a car from the Orlando International Airport is cheaper than taking taxis within The WDW Resort and much faster and less frustrating than dealing with the WDW bus.)

## Tours

For an additional fee, private and small group tours are available that will give you a special behind-the-scenes look at **Disney's Animal Kingdom.** These tours are given by people who are extremely knowledgeable about the animals, and are designed for teens and adults. For more information about the tours that are available, call ✆ (407) WDW-TOUR. Since the tours are limited to small groups, make your reservations as early as possible. Discounts are given if you use your American Express Card to pay for the tours.

## Mickey's Jammin' Jungle Parade

All of the Disney theme parks are known for their daytime, character-oriented parades. Disney's Animal Kingdom is now the home to Mickey's Jammin' Jungle Parade, a fifteen-minute extravaganza featuring Mickey, Minnie, Rafiki, thirteen other Disney characters, and a cast of over sixty dancers and performers. Complete with an African jungle theme, this parade features original music and a format that encourages guest participation along the parade route. Mickey's Jammin' Jungle Parade is definitely suitable for the entire family.

The parade route begins at the Tusker House Gate at Harambe Village, then winds through Disney's Animal Kingdom (around Discovery Island) and returns to the Tusker House Gate. During the parade, it becomes extremely difficult for guests to leave the theme park (because the parade route blocks the entrance/exit), so plan your exit accordingly. Also, be prepared for large groups of people to leave the park immediately after this parade.

##  TRAVEL TIP

For parade times, see the *Disney's Animal Kingdom Guide Map.* If the parade is being held around sunset, be sure the spot you choose to watch the parade is away from the setting sun. You don't want to be watching the oncoming parade and staring directly into the sun. If you're taking pictures during the parade, Mickey makes an appearance on the last float.

## The Disney Wildlife Conservation Fund

The underlying theme of the rides, shows, and attractions at Disney's Animal Kingdom is to promote the conservation of animal habitats around the world. The Disney Wildlife Conservation Fund promotes global wildlife conservation by working directly with scientists, educators, and organizations that are committed to preserving Earth's biodiversity. The Fund provides financial support and resources to over 200 programs in over twenty-four different countries. To help raise money and awareness for this fund, each of the gift shops located in Disney's Animal Kingdom encourages guests to make a $1 donation to the fund when they make a purchase. All of the contributions are combined with the funds of the Walt Disney Company Foundation and are distributed to the wildlife conservation programs that the Disney Wildlife Conservation Fund supports. To obtain a list of these organizations, write to: **The Disney Wildlife Conservation Fund** c/o Conservation Initiatives, Walt Disney World Co., ▣ P.O. Box 10,000, Lake Buena Vista, Florida 32830.

## ══FAST FACT

Walt Disney's love for animals began when he was four years old. His family moved from Chicago to a forty-five-acre farm in Marceline, Missouri. Growing up, Walt helped to care for the animals on the farm and learned how to draw them.

## The Rating System

To help you choose which rides and attractions are most worth seeing while visiting Disney's Animal Kingdom, this book offers star-based ratings for each ride and attraction based on the age group each will most appeal to. Each ride and attraction has earned between one and three stars.

★ = Rides and attractions that earned just one star aren't worth waiting for and could be skipped, especially if your time within the theme park is limited.

★★ = Rides and attractions that earned two stars are good, but they don't fall into the "must-see" category.

★★★ = The rides and attractions that earned three stars are definitely worth seeing and should not be missed.

N.S. = This denotes rides and attractions that are "Not Suitable" for a specific age group.

## The Oasis

The Oasis is a park area that separates Entrance Plaza from the rest of the Animal Kingdom. As you walk through this area, you'll see exotic plants as well as colorful birds in the trees. It's about a three-minute walk from the main entrance to Discovery Island.

# Discovery Island

 This island is the hub from where you'll depart on your animal-based adventures. The centerpiece of this island is the Tree of Life, which is the home of It's Tough to Be a Bug!

### The Tree of Life

Not only is the Tree of Life the centerpiece of Disney's Animal Kingdom, it's also a stunning work of art. A picture of the people you're traveling with standing in front of this tree will make the perfect addition to your vacation photo album.

> **Here's the scoop on this manmade masterpiece:**
> **Animal Carvings:** 325 animals
> **Chief Sculptor:** Zsolt Hormay and a team of three Native American artists, plus artists from France, Ireland, Indianapolis, and Central Florida. It took eighteen months to create the carvings on the Tree of Life.
> **Height:** 145 feet (14 stories tall)
> **Number of Branches:** 8,000
> **Number of Leaves:** 103,000
> **Trunk Width:** 50 feet
> **Width at Root Base:** 170 feet

### The Tree of Life Garden

Pathways have been created throughout Safari Village so guests can wander around and enjoy the landscaping and wildlife.

### It's Tough to Be a Bug!

| | |
|---|---|
| Ages 2–4: | ★ |
| Ages 5–10: | ★★★ |
| Ages 11–15: | ★★★ |
| Ages 16–Adult: | ★★★ |
| Senior Citizens: | ★★★ |

When you enter the theater (located in the trunk of the Tree of Life), you become an honorary bug and begin to see the world from a bug's point of view. Not only is this a 3-D movie with incredibly lifelike special effects, but the entire theater becomes part of the adventure, so expect to see, hear, and feel what's happening. As you enter into the theater, the best seats are in the sixth or seventh row close to the center. As you enter the theater, you'll be given a pair of 3-D glasses. Don't put the glasses over your eyes until you're seated and the Audio-Animatronic character who hosts the show (a bug, of course) tells you to put on the glasses.

The theater holds 430 guests and shows are presented continuously throughout the day. This is, however, one of the most popular attractions in the park, so be prepared to wait in line. It's Tough to Be a Bug! appeals to people of all ages, whether they like real-life bugs or not. Like all of the attractions at Disney's Animal Kingdom, this one has a positive message. Because this 3-D movie takes place within a custom-built theater that's interactive, young children (under the age of eight) may get frightened by some of the special effects.

 This is a must-see attraction.

## ⊕ HOT SPOT

> Throughout the day, bands and other forms of live entertainment perform at various locations around Safari Village. Kick back, relax, and enjoy the show!

# Africa

 Just in case you haven't yet traveled to Africa and experienced a real-life safari, Disney has brought Africa to Orlando. Everyone from the performers to the cast members will be dressed in African fashions, while the architecture and atmosphere in this area of the park are all authentically African.

### Harambe

This area is designed to replicate a port in East Africa. The restaurants, shops, and entertainment all help guests feel like they've traveled across the world.

## Kilimanjaro Safaris

| | |
|---|---|
| Ages 2–4: | ★★ |
| Ages 5–10: | ★★★ |
| Ages 11–15: | ★★★ |
| Ages 16–Adult: | ★★★ |
| Senior Citizens: | ★★★ |

You came to Disney's Animal Kingdom to see animals, and that's exactly what you'll see when you experience this safari ride. You'll ride on a thirty-two-passenger camouflage safari truck with a tour guide as this true-life adventure unfolds on over one hundred acres of savanna, rivers, and rocky hills. Antelope, giraffes, zebras, baboons, rhinos, elephants, crocodiles, lions, hippos, and other animals roam freely. As a result, what you see and where and when you see it will be different every time you experience this tour.

Some of the animals will come within a few feet of your vehicle. The best time to experience Kilimanjaro Safaris is in the morning or late afternoon, because that's when the animals are most active. During the hottest times of the day, many of the animals take naps in the shade. As you see the animals, the tour guide talks about animal poachers and how some species of animals are becoming extinct. Throughout this ride, keep your camera ready. There's no telling when a perfect photo opportunity will happen.

Throughout the safari, you'll see many different animals, so don't use up all of your film early on. Kilimanjaro Safaris will appeal to people of all ages and is one of this park's very best and most popular attractions. It shouldn't be missed! Each time you visit this safari, your experience will be different, because you'll see different animals and sites. Thus, if you have time to experience the Kilimanjaro Safaris twice during your visit, it's well worth it.

 This is a must-see attraction.

## 📁 TRAVEL TIP

To save time waiting in line for Kilimanjaro Safaris, be sure to take advantage of FASTPASS.

### Pangani Forest Exploration Trail

| | |
|---|---|
| Ages 2–4: | ★★ |
| Ages 5–10: | ★★★ |
| Ages 11–15: | ★★★ |
| Ages 16–Adult: | ★★★ |
| Senior Citizens: | ★★★ |

Take a walking tour through a park-like environment and see a troop of gorillas, colorful African birds, and even a few hippos. You can walk through this area at your own pace, so the lines are usually minimal. On hand near each of the exhibits are experts who will answer questions about the animals. About halfway through this exhibit is a small building that contains computers that guests can use to learn more about naked mole rats (also on exhibit within this building). As you make your way through the Pangani Forest Exploration Trail, be sure to look up into the trees to see about thirty-five different species of exotic birds.

## ⊕ HOT SPOT

Disney "Streetmosphere" performers take on the roles of Harambe citizens who are very pleased to have you as a guest in their African village. Guests are invited to interact with the citizens of Harambe while enjoying the live musical performances from an African contemporary band.

### Wildlife Express to Conservation Station

| | |
|---|---|
| Ages 2–4: | ★ |
| Ages 5–10: | ★★ |
| Ages 11–15: | ★★★ |
| Ages 16–Adult: | ★★★ |
| Senior Citizens: | ★★ |

A short train ride takes you partway through the 100-acre savanna where you'll catch glimpses of some of the same animals you'll see on the Kilimanjaro Safaris. You'll also see some of the buildings where the animals are kept at night. Your destination is Disney's Conservation Station, where animals are cared for. As you ride the train, keep your camera handy. There are some excellent photo opportunities along the way.

There may be a wait to board and ride the train to and from

Conservation Station, but once you're there, you're can roam freely and see things at your own pace. Thus, the waits to see the various attractions and exhibits at Conservation Station are kept to a minimum. The round-trip train ride to and from Conservation Station is 1.2 miles long.

# DinoLand U.S.A.

 This area of Disney's Animal Kingdom is somewhat kid-oriented; however, it's here that you'll find the most exciting thrill-ride in the park, which is far more suitable for teens and adults than it is for young kids. In this area, you'll also see life-size replicas of dinosaur skeletons and discover how fossils are found and prepared for display.

Anyone who is fascinated by dinosaurs will want to explore DinoLand U.S.A., which is sponsored by McDonald's. In this case, you'll see some innovative, educational, and highly entertaining attractions, shows, exhibits, and rides. The best time to check out this area is in the morning when the park opens.

## Dinosaur!

| | |
|---|---|
| Ages 2–4: | N.S. |
| Ages 5–10: | ★★ |
| Ages 11–15: | ★★★ |
| Ages 16–Adult: | ★★★ |
| Senior Citizens: | ★ |

This is a highly turbulent ride that takes you back in time to see a group of life-size, very realistic, Audio-Animatronic dinos. After watching a preshow movie, you'll climb aboard a twelve-person vehicle that'll transport you back to prehistoric times. Much of the ride itself takes place in dark surroundings as the vehicles follow an extremely bumpy track and travel at high speeds. Thus, young children may find it scary and senior citizens may find Dinosaur! too turbulent. As for everyone else, this is an awesome ride with spectacular special effects.

For the most thrilling ride, as you climb aboard your vehicle, try to grab a seat that's in the back row and on the left side of the vehicle. Be sure to safely stow loose items like hats, purses, and cameras in the seat pockets in front of you before the ride begins.

 This is a must-see attraction.

## ═FAST FACT

Beginning in late 2001, with the opening of TriceraTop Spin (which is similar to the Dumbo ride within The Magic Kingdom, but with a dinosaur twist), several new kid-oriented rides and attractions are being created for this area of the park. In 2002, Primeval Whirl! will open, giving young guests a roller-coaster experience with a primeval twist.

## The Boneyard

| | |
|---|---|
| Ages 2–4: | ★★★ |
| Ages 5–10: | ★★★ |
| Ages 11–15: | ★★ |
| Ages 16–Adult: | N.S. |
| Senior Citizens: | N.S. |

Designed for young people, the Boneyard offers a preview of what it's like to be an archeologist or paleontologist. Best described as a huge sandbox, in this attraction, young guests get to dig for dino bones.

## Cretaceous Trail

Guests of all ages can take a walking tour (at their own pace) and explore an outdoor exhibit of plants and animals that have survived on this planet since the days of the dinosaurs.

## Tarzan Rocks!

| | |
|---|---|
| Ages 2–4: | ★★★ |
| Ages 5–10: | ★★★ |
| Ages 11–15: | ★★ |
| Ages 16–Adult: | ★ |
| Senior Citizens: | ★ |

One of Disney's recent animated films comes to life on stage during this fun-filled musical. Swing your way right into a rockin' show that's definitely on the wild side and of particular interest to kids. The show is filled with all kinds of extreme stunts and live music from the film's soundtrack. Tarzan Rocks! takes place several times throughout the day within the 1,500-seat Theatre in the Wild (found near DinoLand U.S.A.). For the best seats, arrive between fifteen and thirty minutes prior to show time. This is an excellent family-oriented show, especially if you're traveling with kids.

## TriceraTop Spin

| | |
|---|---|
| Ages 2–4: | ★★ |
| Ages 5–10: | ★★★ |
| Ages 11–15: | ★★★ |
| Ages 16–Adult: | ★ |
| Senior Citizens: | ★ |

This is the newest ride within Disney's Animal Kingdom and part of DinoLand U.S.A.'s new kid-oriented area. Up to four guests ride in triceratops-shaped vehicles that rise and tilt as they spin around a giant top while cartoon comets whiz past and playful dinosaurs pop up. This ride is very much like Dumbo the Flying Elephant (a popular kids' ride found within The Magic Kingdom's Fantasyland); however, instead of being shaped like an elephant, the vehicles resemble dinosaurs.

## TRAVEL TIP

It's possible this ride will support FASTPASS. If this is the case, you'll definitely want to take advantage of FASTPASS to experience it. As with any kid-oriented ride within a Disney theme park, the lines always tend to be shorter late in the day and during peak mealtimes.

## Chester & Hester's Primeval Whirl

| | |
|---|---|
| Ages 2–4: | ★★ |
| Ages 5–10: | ★★★ |
| Ages 11–15: | ★★ |
| Ages 16–Adult: | ★ |
| Senior Citizens: | ★ |

Slated to open in 2002, this kid-oriented roller coaster will feature free-spinning cars that travel along a twisting track of tight loops and short drops. It's being designed to offer a mild thrill-ride experience for young children. Since this will be a new and definitely popular ride when it opens, be prepared for a wait.

 This is a must-see attraction.

## Chester & Hester's Dino-Rama!

As a whole, the Dino-Rama area contains TriceraTop Spin and Primeval Whirl!, in addition to a handful of classic carnival games (all of which have a dinosaur twist). Young players can win prizes for playing the carnival games, but there is an additional charge to participate.

# Camp Minnie-Mickey

 Disney's Animal Kingdom is the largest Disney theme park at The WDW Resort in Orlando, yet it's only in this area of the park where you'll get to meet some of the popular Disney characters, like Mickey and Minnie (dressed in safari attire). This area of the park is also where you'll see several different live shows.

### Character Meet-and-Greet Areas

Located across from where *Festival of the Lion King* is presented are several trails that lead to secluded character meeting areas. Get your camera ready, because throughout the day, this is where you and your kids will get to meet Mickey Mouse and his pals up close and in person. If you're traveling with kids, make sure that they have their autograph books with them, since young people enjoy collecting the signatures of the Disney characters. (Official Disney autograph books are sold at many of the gift shops for about $5.)

### Festival of the Lion King

| | |
|---|---|
| Ages 2–4: | ★★★ |
| Ages 5–10: | ★★★ |
| Ages 11–15: | ★★★ |
| Ages 16–Adult: | ★★★ |
| Senior Citizens: | ★★★ |

Out of all the shows and parades featured at Disney's Animal Kingdom and the other Disney theme parks, this one is the best! This live show is presented several times throughout the day, and is one of the most popular attractions at the park for people of all ages (although kids in particular will love this thirty-minute musical show.)

The theater in which this show is presented is a covered "fresh-air" amphitheater that holds about 1,000 guests. The seating is on benches that are divided into four sections. All sections offer an equally good view, although, if you're traveling with kids, you'll want to sit as close to the front (near the stage) as possible, since as part of the show's finale, kids are invited onto the stage to join the show.

"Festival of the Lion King" features human actors along with costumed characters and Audio-Animatronic characters, and includes nonstop singing and dancing. Several of the popular songs from Disney's *The Lion King* are performed live; however, new music has also been incorporated into this show, which is very different from the animated movie, the Legend of the Lion King Audio-Animatronic puppet show presented at The Magic Kingdom, and *The Lion King: The Broadway Show* (at the New Amsterdam Theatre on Broadway in New York City).

 This is a must-see attraction.

## ⊕ HOT SPOT

Moving scenery, 136 colorful costumes, and acrobatic circus acts make this a fun-filled show. Since the theater is covered, you'll be out of the Florida sun and have an opportunity to sit down and relax while you're entertained.

## Pocahontas and Her Forest Friends

| | |
|---|---|
| Ages 2–4: | ★★★ |
| Ages 5–10: | ★★★ |
| Ages 11–15: | ★★ |
| Ages 16–Adult: | ★ |
| Senior Citizens: | ★ |

Unlike Festival of the Lion King, which features a large cast of characters, this show stars a human actress who portrays Pocahontas, a life-size Audio-Animatronic tree (Grandmother Willow), and several real-life animals. The show, designed primarily for young guests, talks about the importance of preserving the planet's forests and runs about twelve minutes. It is presented throughout the day in an outdoor theater that holds 350 guests. Be sure to arrive at the theater between thirty and forty-five minutes prior to the posted show time in order to ensure yourself a seat for the performance of your choice. No food or beverages are allowed in the theater.

# Rafiki's Planet Watch

 Especially for young people (age fifteen and under) this area of Disney's Animal Kingdom will encourage education and exploration. The focus is on conservation and protecting our planet and its wildlife. People of all ages, however, will find much of what this area offers to be interesting.

## The Conservation Station

This facility combines hands-on displays, live animal displays, and a chance to see some of the park's veterinary facilities, animal nurseries, and even where some of the food for the animals in the park gets prepared. Upon arriving at Conservation Station, guests can roam freely and see everything at their own pace. Plenty of animal experts are on hand to answer questions and conduct various types of demonstrations.

## ═FAST FACT

This is one of the most educational areas of Disney's Animal Kingdom. Some of the live animals you'll see include aardvarks, chinchillas, a miniature donkey, great horned owls, porcupines, guinea pigs, and a rock hyrax. Young guests can also pet some of the animals; however, feeding them is strictly prohibited.

## Affection Section

| | |
|---|---|
| Ages 2–4: | ★★ |
| Ages 5–10: | ★★★ |
| Ages 11–15: | ★★ |
| Ages 16–Adult: | ★ |
| Senior Citizens: | ★ |

Designed for young children, Affection Section is a petting zoo where guests can get up close to animals, pet them, and have pictures taken with them. Guests are welcome to spend as much time as they'd like in this area and proceed at their own pace. Kids who will be interacting with the animals are encouraged to wash their hands both prior to and after touching the animals. For parents, this area offers wonderful photo opportunities.

## Look Backstage!

| | |
|---|---|
| Ages 2–4: | ★ |
| Ages 5–10: | ★★ |
| Ages 11–15: | ★★ |
| Ages 16–Adult: | ★★ |
| Senior Citizens: | ★★ |

Inside the Hall of Animal Care, guests get to see many animal experts, including vets, researchers, and keepers, work with live animals. This is an educational area where the animals are the stars. Animal experts are always on hand to answer questions. One of the favorite parts of this exhibit is the baby mammal nurseries.

## ⊕ HOT SPOT

There are interactive exhibits that allow guests of all ages to use touch-screen computers and learn more about animals and their habitats.

# Asia

This is the newest area of Disney's Animal Kingdom. It features one of the most popular thrill rides in the park— Kali River Rapids: Whitewater Adventure.

## Flights of Wonder at Caravan Stage

| | |
|---|---|
| Ages 2–4: | ★ |
| Ages 5–10: | ★★★ |
| Ages 11–15: | ★★★ |
| Ages 16–Adult: | ★★ |
| Senior Citizens: | ★★ |

Presented several times throughout the day, this live show features human bird handlers and a cast of over twenty species of trained exotic birds from around the world, some of which fly out into the audience. The Caravan Stage is an outdoor theater that holds about 1,250 guests. No food or beverages are allowed in the theater. Be sure to arrive between twenty and thirty minutes prior to a posted show time to guarantee yourself a seat for the performance of your choice.

This show presents a story about a character named Luke who is in search of lost treasures. Kids especially will enjoy this show, although it is entertaining for people of all ages. The show itself lasts about twenty-five minutes.

## Maharajah Jungle Trek

Here's an opportunity to wander down jungle paths, explore temple ruins, and see some of the world's most exotic and powerful animals—Bengal tigers, Komodo Monitor Dragons, gibbons, and an assortment of other wild animals that are native to Asia. There are some excellent photo opportunities along this trail.

## Kali River Rapids: A Whitewater Adventure

| | |
|---|---|
| Ages 2–4: | N.S. |
| Ages 5–10: | ★★★ |
| Ages 11–15: | ★★★ |
| Ages 16–Adult: | ★★★ |
| Senior Citizens: | ★ |

In addition to Dinosaur!, Kali River Rapids represents a second thrill ride that's designed for teens and adults. Guests ride in six-passenger rubber rafts and slide down a raging and windy river through rapids and waterfalls. This is definitely one of the most popular attractions at Disney's Animal Kingdom, so be prepared to wait in line to experience it. Also, be prepared to get soaked! (If you're carrying items that aren't waterproof, be sure to store them in lockers, leave them with someone not riding this attraction, or use the watertight storage compartment on the raft.) Guests must be at least 40 inches tall to experience this rather turbulent ride.

 This is a must-see attraction.

##  TRAVEL TIP

To save time waiting in line for Kali River Rapids, be sure to take advantage of FASTPASS. If you have one of the Disney ponchos, be sure to wear it on this ride to help you stay dry. As a bystander, it's possible to shoot water at guests experiencing the ride.

## Shopping at the Animal Kingdom

Like all of the Disney theme parks, you'll find many gift shops and souvenir kiosks scattered throughout Disney's Animal Kingdom. Sure, you'll find a wide assortment of Disney's Animal Kingdom logo merchandise, along with plenty of T-shirts, plush toys, and other items featuring Mickey dressed in a safari outfit, but you'll also find a great assortment of non-Disney-based items that make excellent souvenirs or great gifts.

All of the gift shops accept cash, credit cards, checks, debit cards, traveler's checks, and Disney Dollars, along with your hotel room charge card (your room key, if you're staying at a Disney Resort hotel). The souvenir kiosks and carts accept cash, checks, and traveler's checks only.

Keep in mind that much of the merchandise sold at these shops is available only within this park and can't be purchased at the shops in **Downtown Disney,** from the **Disney Stores,** or through the **Disney Catalog.** You can, however, purchase most items sold exclusively at the park by telephone by calling ✆ (407) 363-6200 during business hours. You must, however, know exactly what item(s) you want to purchase and be willing to pay by credit card.

When you make a purchase, you can take your merchandise with you (and carry it around the park), arrange to have it delivered to the park's exit so that you can pick up your purchases on your way out, arrange to have the purchase delivered to your WDW Resort hotel, or, for an additional fee, you can have your purchases shipped anywhere in the world. If you arrange to have your packages delivered to the park's exit, keep in mind that on busy days, it could take up to ninety minutes for your packages to arrive, so plan accordingly. Likewise, if you're having packages shipped, even if you pay FedEx charges, it might take up to several weeks for your purchases to actually get shipped.

## Dining at the Animal Kingdom

Like all of the Disney theme parks, Disney's Animal Kingdom offers a selection of fast-food and full-service dining establishments that serve everything from snack foods to full multicourse meals. No matter where you eat within the park, it's not going to be cheap, but if you're hungry, you'll find many different food and drink choices available. One of Disneyland's most popular treats (previously unavailable at the WDW theme parks), chocolate-covered frozen bananas, is available from many of the ice-cream carts throughout Disney's Animal Kingdom.

### ⊕ HOT SPOT

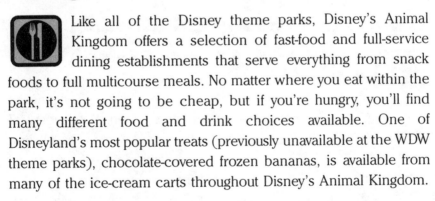

If you're looking for an animal-themed dining experience where you're surrounded by waterfalls, tropical plants, and an exciting atmosphere for lunch or dinner, you'll want to experience the Rainforest Café, located in Entrance Plaza. A second Rainforest Café is located within Downtown Disney.

# Disney's Water Parks

FOR PEOPLE WHO ENJOY THE WATER, The WDW Resort offers three full-size water parks, all of which contain various kid- and family-oriented activities that are water based. So, if visiting one or more of these water parks is on your vacation itinerary, plan on packing bathing suits, plenty of sunblock, and beach shoes.

## Water Park Information

 If you're staying at any of the Disney resorts, you're entitled to take advantage of the swimming pools and beaches at any of Disney's resorts. Many of the resorts offer multiple pools, whirlpools, water slides, and kid-oriented areas. The WDW Resort also offers three exciting water parks—Blizzard Beach, Typhoon Lagoon, and River Country—that have become favorite attractions of families traveling with kids.

Families can easily spend at least one full day at Blizzard Beach or Typhoon Lagoon. River Country provides more like a half day's worth of fun and excitement. These parks are always busiest in the mornings, so if you have a multiday Park Hopper Plus Pass, plan on arriving around lunchtime to avoid the heavy morning crowds. Spend the morning at The Magic Kingdom,

Epcot, The Disney-MGM Studios, or Disney's Animal Kingdom, then cool off at one of the refreshingly wet and wildly exciting water parks.

For female guests, wearing a one-piece bathing suit is highly recommended, due to the "rough water" and "waves" you'll be encountering. These water parks offer family-oriented entertainment with kids and teens in mind. Older guests traveling alone will probably prefer to spend their vacation participating in other types of activities or relaxing by the pool at their hotel.

## ≡FAST FACT

Being able to swim is a prerequisite for some, but not all, of these water-based attractions. Keep in mind, Disney's water parks are either open seasonally or have limited hours during off-peak times of the year.

### Hours of Operation

All of these water parks are somewhat seasonal and are open during nice weather only. Typically, the hours of operation are between 10:00 A.M. and 5:00 P.M. (with extended hours during the peak summer months). Be sure to call ✆ (407) 824-4321 to ensure that the water parks will be open during your visit and to confirm exact operating hours. All of the water parks can be reached using the WDW Transportation Bus system.

### Guest Services

At all of the water parks, showers, and rest rooms are available. Lockers may be rented on a daily basis. Life jackets are available for free, but a $25 refundable deposit is required. Towels can be rented at the various water parks for $1 each, or you can bring your own from your hotel room (but you must also return them to your hotel room at the end of the day).

## Admission to the Water Parks

Admission to the three Disney water parks is included in the price of the multiday Park Hopper Plus tickets. You can, however, also purchase one-day admission tickets or annual passes for each of the water parks separately. See Chapter 3 for details. As you'll soon discover, each of the water parks has a totally different theme and a different set of activities and attractions.

# Blizzard Beach

Blizzard Beach opened in 1995 and has a winter, ski slope theme. If a 66-acre ski slope existed in the middle of Orlando, what would happen if all of a sudden the weather went from below freezing to the mid-80s and all of the snow on the mountain started to melt? That's the premise for many of the attractions at Blizzard Beach, which features some of the world's fastest water slides. The attractions include:

**Cross Country Creek**—If high-speed, turbulent tube rides aren't your thing, you can relax and enjoy a one-mile lazy tube ride around the entire Blizzard Beach park.

**Downhill Double Dipper**—Ride along a twin tube run and race against others as you travel at speeds of up to 25 miles per hour.

**Melt-Away Bay**—Take a dip in a one-acre wave pool.

**Run-Off Rapids**—Ride a tube along flume runs filled with wet and wild surprises.

**Ski Patrol Training Camp**—This area of Blizzard Beach is designed specifically for preteens.

**Slush Gusher**—This is a fast-paced and exciting slide experience that sends guests down through a snow-banked gully.

**Snow Stormers**—A toboggan flume ride.

**Steamboat Springs**—This is the longest and most exciting man-made family white-water raft ride in the world. Groups of people travel down 1,200 feet of twisting rapids while riding in six-passenger tube rafts.

**Summit Plummet**—Take a plunge down the world's tallest free-fall speed slide. This is a 120-foot, nearly vertical drop that allows guests to reach speeds of up to 50 miles per hour. This has been called the fastest water slide in America.

**Tike's Peak**—This kid-oriented area of Blizzard Beach offers thrill rides that younger kids will enjoy.

**Toboggan Racer**—Ride on foam toboggan-like sleds along an eight-lane run that goes down a water-slick mountain.

##  TRAVEL TIP

Since you'll be outside in direct sunlight, be sure to apply plenty of waterproof sunblock, even in overcast weather conditions. Plan on spending between three hours and an entire day at any of Disney's water parks.

# Typhoon Lagoon

 When visiting Typhoon Lagoon, guests are asked to imagine a small resort village that just got hit by a typhoon. While if this happened in real-life it would be a disaster, when it's done Disney style, the result is a 56-acre water park that offers a splashing good time.

The main Typhoon Lagoon swimming area is a massive wave pool that contains almost 3 million gallons of water. Along the coast of this pool is a sandy white beach. Meanwhile, Castaway Creek is a 2,100-foot-long river that allows guests to enjoy a fun-filled tubing ride that takes them through a series of themed areas. In all, this ride takes about thirty minutes to complete.

Gangplank Falls, Keelhaul Falls, and Mayday Falls are the thrill rides offered at Typhoon Lagoon. Guests ride on various types of tubes as they plummet down waterfalls and other white-water terrain.

Water slides at Typhoon Lagoon provide for extremely wet and fast-paced experiences that nobody who rides them will soon forget. Humunga Kowabunga is a 214-foot slide that includes a 51-foot drop, allowing guests to travel upward of 30 miles per hour. The Storm Slides are a bit tamer, but not much. These fiberglass slides are 300 feet long and allow guests to slide down at 20 miles per hour.

For some snorkeling fun, check out Shark Reef (snorkeling equipment is provided) and explore a made-made coral reef where you'll come face-to-face with friendly Leopard, Nurse, and Bonnethead sharks, plus schools of exotic and colorful fish.

Ketchakiddee Creek is a water park unto itself, but it's designed only for people under four feet tall.

## ⊕ HOT SPOT

Surfers (or wanna-be surfers) can obtain top-notch instruction and then experience two and a half hours of surfing at Typhoon Lagoon before the park opens to the general public. The fee (which includes the instruction) is $125 per person. Reservations are required for this Surfer's Secret package. Call ☎ (407) WDW-PLAY.

# River Country

 River Country first opened in 1973 and was inspired by Tom Sawyer's swimmin' hole. The biggest swimming area at River Country is called Bay Cove (or Ol' Swimmin' Hole). It's a 330,000-gallon swimming pool. This pool, and the others in this theme park, offer all sorts of water slides and flume rides. River Country is the smallest of the water parks and the quaintest. Nearby picnic tables are provided so you can enjoy a leisurely lunch. (Don't forget to wait about thirty minutes to digest after eating before going back into a pool or swimming.) Keep in mind, this water park is typically closed between early September and mid-March.

River Country's attractions include:

**Cypress Point Nature Trail**—When you're done swimming, you can enjoy a short hike that takes you through a scenic wilderness area filled with cypress trees.

**Kiddy Area**—This is a separate area designed for kids that offers small water slides and other water activities.

**Slippery Slide Falls**—Two exciting slides send guests plummeting into the oversize pool.

**White Water Rapids**—Enjoy a slow-paced and relaxing tube ride along rather calm rapids.

**Whoop-N-Holler Hollow**—Two corkscrew slides wind up in the heart of Bay Cove.

## Other Area Water Parks

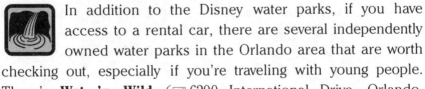

In addition to the Disney water parks, if you have access to a rental car, there are several independently owned water parks in the Orlando area that are worth checking out, especially if you're traveling with young people. There's **Wet 'n Wild** (⌨ 6200 International Drive, Orlando, ✆ (407) 351-WILD, ✍ *www.wetnwild.com*) as well as **Water Mania** (⌨ 6073 West Irlo Bronson Highway, Kissimmee, ✆ (407) 396-2626, ✍ *www.watermania-florida.com*).

For people who enjoy scuba diving and would love a chance to swim with dolphins, SeaWorld's Discovery Cove offers a once-in-a-lifetime experience. See Chapter 18 for details.

# Disney Nightlife

SO, WHAT'S THERE TO DO AFTER DARK at The WDW Resort? Well, for adults, there is an abundance of activities, clubs, shops, and restaurants within the Downtown Disney, Pleasure Island, and Disney's West Side areas. There's also Disney's BoardWalk area, which offers an exciting nightlife for adult vacationers.

## Nighttime Entertainment Overview

 Downtown Disney has three unique areas: Pleasure Island, the Marketplace, and Disney's West Side. Starting at around 7:00 P.M. and going until 1:00 A.M. (or 2:00 A.M., depending on the season) every night, there's plenty to experience.

While both Downtown Disney and Disney's BoardWalk offer some family-oriented activities, several of the nightclubs are restricted to those over twenty-one years of age, since alcoholic beverages are served. After spending an exciting day at the park with the family, you might consider leaving your young kids with a baby-sitter and experiencing Disney's nightlife.

Everyone in the family will enjoy exploring the Downtown Disney area in the late afternoon and evening, but after dark, Pleasure Island especially becomes a place designed with adults in mind. If you're visiting The WDW Resort for multiple nights, plan on spending at least one night at Pleasure Island (which has an admission fee) and at least one additional evening/night exploring everything that the Marketplace and Disney's West Side have to offer.

## Getting to Downtown Disney

Plenty of free parking is available in front of Disney's West Side, Pleasure Island, and the Marketplace. Valet parking (daily between 5:30 P.M. and 2:00 A.M.) is also available for $6 (or free to guests with physical disabilities). Free valet parking is also provided to WDW Resort hotel guests. From anywhere in The WDW Resort, follow the signs to Downtown Disney/Pleasure Island.

Buses run constantly to and from Disney's resort hotels and theme parks to Pleasure Island, the Marketplace, and Disney's West Side areas.

If you're staying at Disney's Dixie Landings, Disney's Old Key West Resort, the Disney Institute, or Disney's Port Orleans, complimentary boat launches are available that drop off and pick up passengers from the docks located at the Marketplace.

For a fee, taxi service is available to take you back to your hotel or anywhere in the Orlando area. Taxis can be hailed at any of the exits of the Downtown Disney area. This, however, is a costly option.

## Admission Information and Prices

While there is no charge to shop and explore the Marketplace or Disney's West Side, there is an admission charge to enter Pleasure Island after 7:00 P.M. This admission fee gives you unlimited access (for the night) to all of the area's nightclubs, including:

- Adventurers Club
- BET SoundStage Club
- Comedy Warehouse
- 8Trax
- Mannequins Dance Palace
- Motion

- Pleasure Island Jazz Company
- Rock N Roll Beach Club

You'll also get to see the live entertainment presented outside at the West End Stage, which includes a nightly New Year's Eve celebration at midnight that features fireworks. Drinks and food are not included in the admission price. Adult admission to Pleasure Island after 7:00 P.M. is $19.81 per night. An annual pass to Pleasure Island costs $54.95. Disney Club members receive a discount off of this admission price. Admission to Pleasure Island is included with a multiday Park Hopper Plus pass and the WDW Premium Annual Pass.

People under the age of eighteen will not be permitted into Pleasure Island after 7:00 P.M. unless accompanied by a parent or guardian. No alcoholic beverages will be served to anyone under the age of twenty-one. People under the age of twenty-one will not be admitted into Mannequins Dance Palace (and some of the other clubs) under any circumstances. Be prepared to show a valid passport, U.S. (or foreign) driver's license with a photo, or a U.S. military ID to be served alcohol or be admitted into the adults-only clubs.

##  TRAVEL TIP

If you're spending three or more days (and nights) at The WDW Resort and plan on returning to Pleasure Island during each of those nights, consider purchasing an annual pass in order to save yourself some cash.

## Guest Services

A Guest Services office is available at the Marketplace and also inside the AMC 24 Theater building. At various locations within the Downtown Disney area you'll find ATM machines, restrooms (containing baby-changing facilities), and public telephones. If any type of first aid is required, contact any Disney cast member for assistance. For additional information about the **Downtown Disney** area, call ☏ (407) 934-7781.

## Dining Reservations

Reservations are recommended for many of the full-service restaurants located in **Pleasure Island,** the **Marketplace,** and **Disney's West Side.** Check with the restaurant of your choice directly, or call ☏ (407) WDW-DINE. Without a reservation, be prepared to wait up to two hours to be seated. Most of the full-service restaurants will give you a beeper, allowing you to walk around the area and shop until your table is ready.

## ≡FAST FACT

Pleasure Island, the Marketplace, and Downtown Disney West Side are all vacation areas, so while you're not expected to dress up in formal attire to dine or go dancing, some type of shirt and shoes must be worn at all times.

# Disney's West Side

This is the newest addition to Disney's nighttime entertainment complex, and while all of the listed restaurants, shops, and activities are now open (or scheduled to open in the near future), this area is constantly being expanded. There is no charge to visit Disney's West Side area; however, there is an admission fee to several of the shows, movies, and attractions. The shops in this area open at 11:00 A.M. daily and remain open until 11:00 P.M. Many of the restaurants serve until midnight.

## AMC Theaters

Currently the largest movie theater complex in the Southeast, the AMC 24 Theaters offers twenty-four screens, all showing the hottest new movies in theaters with state-of-the-art sound systems.

## Bongos Cuban Café

Gloria Estefan and husband Emilio are the owners of this 550-seat family restaurant that serves authentic Cuban cuisine in a two-story building that's decorated with colorful hand-painted mosaic murals that depict Old World Cuba in the 1940s and 1950s. Seating is available both inside and outside, and live entertainment is presented throughout the night. The main performer each night is Desi Arnaz (well, he's an incredibly talented impersonator who looks and sounds just like the real Desi).

Like all of the full-service restaurants located at The WDW Resort, this one isn't cheap, but the food is delicious! In a typical night, Bongos Cuban Café serves up to 3,000 people. If you're planning to drop in to enjoy the restaurant's three fully stocked bars, plan on paying a $15 cover charge, which includes one drink and plenty of live entertainment and dancing.

Bongos Cuban Café is open daily from 11:00 A.m. to 2:00 A.M. "We specifically created Bongos Cuban Café for the entire family so they may enjoy the festive Cuba that once was—and will be again," said Emilio Estefan.

## ⊕ HOT SPOT

Designer sunglasses and prescription eyewear are available at Celebrity Eyeworks Studio. Included in this shop's inventory are replicas of sunglasses worn in recent hit films.

## Cirque du Soleil: La Nouba

Within the 70,000-square-foot, custom-designed, state-of-the-art theater that's located at the end of Disney's West Side is the permanent U.S. home of Cirque du Soleil. This theater holds 1,650 guests per performance and was designed to actually be part of the show itself.

Cirque du Soleil is a nontraditional French-Canadian circus that includes specialty acts the likes of which you've probably never seen before (even if you've seen a touring Cirque du Soleil show or one of the shows in Las Vegas). Circus acts are mixed with special effects, colorful and unusual costumes, and wonderful music. This is a wonderful, memorable, and breathtaking show for people of all ages.

Two performances are held Thursday through Monday evenings at 6:00 P.M. and 9:00 P.M. The show lasts about ninety minutes and contains no intermission. Ticket prices are $67 (adults) and $39 (children, ages three to nine). Tickets can be purchased at the box office located within the theater itself, or by calling ✆ (407) 939-7600. This is a popular show, so once you know your travel schedule, reserve your tickets as far in advance as possible, especially during peak travel times. For more information about this highly unique show, visit the Cirque du Soleil Web site at ✍ www.cirquedusoleil.com.

## DisneyQuest

This interactive, high-tech attraction provides fun and exciting entertainment and dining opportunities for the whole family. When guests step into this flashy-looking 100,000-square-foot pavilion, they're taken on a virtual journey to places that could only be dreamed of.

Combining video games, virtual reality, motion simulator rides, and other high-tech forms of entertainment, DisneyQuest is an indoor theme park unto itself that will appeal mainly to teenage guys and younger kids.

## ⊕ HOT SPOT

Cappuccino, espresso, smoothies, juice, and an assortment of other drinks and yummy desserts are available at Forty Thirst Street between 7:00 A.M. and 2:00 A.M. daily.

Admission to DisneyQuest is included with a multiday Park Hopper Plus ticket or the WDW Premium Annual Pass. Otherwise, there's a per-day entrance fee of $29 (adults) and $23 (children). An annual pass for DisneyQuest can be purchased for $79 (adults) or $63 (children).

## Disney's Candy Cauldron

If you're in the mood to sample a wide range of candy and other treats that are guaranteed to satisfy your sweet tooth, drop into this shop for the perfect snack or after-lunch/dinner dessert.

## Guitar Gallery

This is a music shop for serious guitarists and amateur musicians alike. Guitar Gallery offers a wide selection of guitars and accessories from all major manufacturers. You'll also find very rare instruments of interest to serious collectors.

## House of Blues

As you've probably guessed, the Downtown Disney complex has become a mecca of themed restaurants. House of Blues serves lunch and dinner daily, between 11:00 A.M. and 2:00 A.M. in the dining room. The BB Blues Bar offers live entertainment and a fully stocked bar that's open every evening.

There's also an official House of Blues merchandise shop attached to the restaurant. In the dining room, authentic Mississippi Delta cooking is served as live blues, R&B, jazz, country, and gospel music are performed nightly. Specialties of the house include jambalaya, etouffee, gumbo, and bread pudding.

The restaurant's concert hall features regular performances by big-name recording artists, so be sure to check the schedule to see who's performing during your stay at The WDW Resort. For concert information, call ✆ (407) 934-2222 or on the Internet, visit the House of Blues Web site at ✍ *www.hob.com.*

## Hoypoloi

This gallery/gift shop offers a large assortment of highly unusual non-Disney gift items, jewelry, and art. Tabletop fountains, wind chimes, mini Zen gardens, and other tastefully displayed items make this an extremely interesting store to browse through, especially for adults.

## Magic Masters

Want to amaze and astound your friends and family members? Learn how to perform magic tricks just like a professional magician. This store is staffed by highly skilled magicians who offer demonstrations and perform short magic shows. Even if you don't plan on shopping here, it's a great place to visit for a few minutes if you want to enjoy watching magic tricks and illusions performed right before your eyes.

## Magnetron

Magnets, magnets, and more magnets, of every shape, size, and color, are what you'll find at this small shop. Whether you're a collector or someone looking for a new magnet for your refrigerator, you'll find what you're looking for. Even the salespeople have magnetic personalities.

## ⊕ HOT SPOT

Mickey's Groove is a Disney-owned shop offering an assortment of Disney-themed merchandise, including apparel.

## Planet Hollywood

As you approach Disney's West Side, you can't miss seeing Planet Hollywood, the giant globe-shaped restaurant that's jam-packed with Hollywood memorabilia, movie props, posters, photos, costumes, and giant monitors that constantly show music videos and movie clips.

This is the hip family-oriented, Hollywood-themed restaurant chain owned by some of Hollywood's biggest stars. Menu entrees range in price from about $10 to $20 each, and include salads, pizzas, burgers, steaks, pastas, and a wide assortment of desserts. Planet Hollywood also offers a fully stocked bar and nonstop entertainment.

It's a complete interactive and highly entertaining experience, so be sure to bring your camera. Also, don't be surprised if you run into a popular celebrity or pop star dining right along with you.

## Planet Hollywood on Location

In addition to being the home of the world's largest Planet Hollywood restaurant, Disney's West Side also features two Planet Hollywood merchandise shops. This is where you can pick up official Planet Hollywood Orlando and Planet Hollywood America apparel, toys, and other logoed merchandise. You'll discover that some of the limited-edition clothing is endorsed by big-name recording artists and pop groups. To see a preview of the merchandise, visit ✎ *www.PlanetHollywood.com.*

## ⊕ HOT SPOT

Hand-rolled fresh cigars and other smoking accessories are available at Sosa Family Cigars. You'll find a knowledgeable staff on hand to answer your questions and make recommendations.

## Starabilias

This unusual antique and collectibles showroom and store allows you to take home valuable pieces of authentic pop culture and history. Whether or not you consider yourself a collector, Starabilias is a fun place for adults and teens to explore.

Here, you'll find genuine items such as an antique Coca-Cola vending machine (which can be yours for $8,995), a 1930s Texaco gas pump (suggested retail price $10,000), and a Ty Cobb–autographed baseball bat (which you can own for $10,000). A wide range of autographed memorabilia from politicians, recording artists, Hollywood's superstars, and other historical figures is available.

The inventory of this store changes regularly. In addition to high-priced collectibles, you'll also find a selection of inexpensive toys and collectibles. For a preview of the items you'll find at

Starabilias, or to place an order online, you can visit the company's Web site at ◁ *www.Starabilias.com.*

## Virgin Megastore

Three massive floors in this store offer thousands upon thousands of music CDs, cassettes, videos, laser discs, DVD movies, computer games, video games, magazines, music accessories, and books. There's even a Virgin Megastore café located on the top floor. Throughout this store, you'll find CD-listening stations, computers to try out the hottest new games, and over twenty video/laser stations for previewing movies. Live musical performances, author appearances, and other special events are held regularly at this store.

## Wolfgang Puck Café

Spago's is a premier restaurant in Hollywood where the biggest stars go for dinner and to be seen. Owner/chef Wolfgang Puck has also created the California Pizza Kitchen (CPK) restaurants (now located throughout the country), as well as the Wolfgang Puck Cafés. This chain can best be described as a pricey, albeit extremely trendy, CPK restaurant. Pizzas and California cuisine are what's offered on the menu. A basic four-cheese ten-inch pizza (which will feed one or two people max) is priced at $9.95. Reservations are strongly recommended, so call ✆ (407) 939-3463.

# Pleasure Island

Most people think of Pleasure Island as a Magic Kingdom for adults who enjoy dancing, drinking, and having fun. Whether you like disco dancing or dancing to the latest hits, there's a dance club at Pleasure Island that'll appeal to you.

There are also clubs that allow you to enjoy comedy shows, live jazz performances, and rhythm and blues music. One flat nightly admission fee gives you unlimited access to all of the clubs within Pleasure Island. (All food and drinks are extra.) In addition to the various nightclubs, Pleasure Island offers carnival-like games and several unique shops, not to mention a nonstop street-party atmosphere that doesn't end until 1:00 A.M. or 2:00 A.M. (depending on the season). Pleasure Island offers "the largest nightly street party on the planet."

## ≡FAST FACT

Every night at 11:45 P.M., live dancers appear on the West End Stage, inviting guests to participate in an outdoor New Year's Eve celebration that's complete with a short fireworks show at exactly midnight. Throughout the night, live music is performed on the West End Stage, while elsewhere (outside) you'll hear a live DJ playing all of the hottest dance music.

### 8Trax

Disco is back and at 8Trax, you can boogie down to the hottest hits from the 1970s. Disco lights surround the dance floor and fully stocked bar. There are also video monitors located throughout the club that continuously show classic music videos from the disco era. There's always a party atmosphere here as you're taken back in time.

### Adventurers Club

Modeled after an adventurers club from the 1930s, this club features live stage shows and actors who roam around (in character) and mingle with the crowds. The humor is a bit dry and rather sophisticated, and the décor of this club is rather unusual. Full bar service is available. This club tends to attract an older (thirty-plus) crowd.

### The Comedy Warehouse

One of the funniest thirty to forty minutes you'll spend at The WDW Resort will be at the Comedy Warehouse, where a troupe of five improvisational comedians and a piano/keyboards player perform five off-the-wall shows per night. Since this is improvisational comedy, the show is totally based around comments and suggestions from the audience. The more creative the audience's input is, the funnier the show itself will be.

The Comedy Warehouse holds a large audience, but seating is on a first-come basis, so arrive at least thirty minutes prior to show time to ensure you'll get a seat. (If Pleasure Island is extremely crowded, arrive forty-five minutes to one hour early.) All seating is on bar stools, except for a few small tables in front near the stage. Shows earlier in the evening tend to be less crowded than the ones presented between 11:00 P.M. and 1:00 A.M.

## DTV

Character-based Disney merchandise, clothing, and souvenirs are sold here. If you happen to need an aspirin, you can purchase personal care items from any checkout counter/cashier within this store.

## ⊕ HOT SPOT

One of the newest additions to Pleasure Island is the BET SoundStage Club, a rhythm-and-blues club that offers live DJs playing dance music, as well as live entertainment.

### Hub Video Stage

Located opposite the DJ tower is this small stage that features a large video wall, where music videos are played in conjunction with the music that's heard throughout the outdoor area of Pleasure Island. Live performances are also presented here.

### Island Depot

Near the Rock N Roll Beach Club building, stroller and wheelchair rentals, along with the Pleasure Island lost and found, are located here. You can also purchase a selection of official Pleasure Island merchandise at the shop in this building. An ATM is nearby.

## Mannequins Dance Palace

This is Pleasure Island's premier dance club. It features a rotating dance floor, a state-of-the-art lighting and sound system, live DJs, and plenty of nonstop popular dance music. The club was recently renovated to maintain its cutting-edge atmosphere. You must be twenty-one years or older to enter into Mannequins, which offers a fully stocked bar and small cocktail tables. Throughout the night, Pleasure Island's Explosion Dancers perform.

## Pleasure Island Jazz Company

Live jazz music is performed throughout the night in this club, which also sells cigars and offers a full bar service. The crowd tends to be a bit older and more sophisticated compared to the people you'll find at the other clubs. Plenty of small tables and chairs are available, so plan on relaxing, having a few drinks, and enjoying some extremely good classic jazz.

## ⊕ HOT SPOT

A variety of carnival-like games are offered at Pleasure Island near Motion. Large plush toys are awarded as prizes. There's an additional fee to try your luck or show off your skills on games.

## Motion

Pleasure Island's newest club offers nonstop Top-40 music. This club features a casual party atmosphere and live DJs. Local Orlando residents, off-duty Disney cast members, and tourists alike gather here for great nighttime entertainment. While Mannequins Dance Palace appeals to a slightly older crowd (twenty-one-plus), those over eighteen will find that this club offers a great atmosphere for socializing and dancing.

## Portobello Yacht Club

For a fine-dining experience, Portobello Yacht Club is one of the few nontrendy, nonthemed restaurants located in the Downtown Disney area. While the food is a bit pricey (between $21 and $35 per person), what you'll find is award-winning Northern Italian cuisine that includes seafood, pasta, and chicken dishes, along with wood-burning oven pizzas and some incredible desserts. Lunch is served starting at 11:30 A.M., and dinner is served until midnight daily.

## Reel Finds

Genuine celebrity autographs and photos are sold in this shop. If you're looking for an autographed picture of a cast member from *Star Trek: The Next Generation, Start Trek Voyager,* or *Star Trek: Deep Space Nine,* you'll find it here for $180 and up, depending on the individual cast member you're looking for. A photo of the entire *Diff'rent Strokes* cast, for example, sells for $220. Dozens of other photos and movie scripts are also available, so if you're a movie buff, you'll enjoy checking this place out.

# ═FAST FACT

Disney animation cells, collectible figurines, and Disney poster artwork is sold at the Suspended Animation gallery. Some of the stuff sold here is rather expensive, but it's fun to browse, especially if you enjoy Disney's classic animated movies. A limited number of autographed animation cells are also available.

## Rock N Roll Beach Club

Nonstop rock and roll music from the past and present is played continuously throughout the evening and late into the night. This club has a beach-party theme and features a mix of live performances and talented DJs who keep cranking out the music. Snacks and full bar service are available.

## Superstar Studios

If you've ever had dreams of becoming a recording artist, here's your chance to star in your own music video. Take the videocassette of your performance home with you as a souvenir (for a fee, of course) and show it to your friends and family—it'll be good for a laugh.

# The Marketplace

This entire shopping area is dedicated to everything Disney, but there are also plenty of shops that offer very unique non-Disney merchandise. At all of the Disney-owned shops, Disney Club members receive a 10 percent discount on their purchases. It's easy to spend an evening browsing, shopping, and enjoying the festive atmosphere, whether or not you plan on making purchases.

In addition to the shops, restaurants, and activities available at the Marketplace, there are also dozens of kiosks that sell unique handcrafted souvenirs and snacks. The Marketplace is open daily from 9:30 A.M. to 11:00 P.M. Most of the full-service restaurants open at 10:30 A.M. and serve until 11:00 P.M.

## 2R's Reading & Riting

Are you looking for a good novel to enjoy while relaxing at the pool of your hotel? Perhaps you're more interested in a book about the history of The WDW Resort, or you want to pick up a Disney storybook for your kids. Books, stationery, greeting cards, and other gifts are sold here. Soda, cappuccino, and espresso can also be purchased and enjoyed while you browse.

## Art of Disney

Connected to 2R's Reading & Riting is an upscale gallery that sells high-priced Disney animation and artwork. Some of the pieces on display here are absolutely stunning. Less expensive Disney posters and figurines issued by the Walt Disney Collector's Society are also available.

## Boating at Cap'N Jack's Marina

During the day, a selection of boats can be rented here by the half hour or by the hour. Guests must be twelve years of age or older to rent a boat. Water sprites, canopy boats, and pontoon boats are available. For more information, call ✆ (407) 828-2204.

## Cap'N Jack's Oyster Bar Restaurant

Located along the coast of Buena Vista Lagoon, this restaurant features seafood dishes, including shrimp, clam chowder, and oysters, served daily between 11:30 A.M. and 10:30 P.M. Several non-seafood dishes are also available, although if you're not looking for seafood, there are plenty of other dining options available to you elsewhere.

## ⊕ HOT SPOT

Three hundred and sixty-five days a year, it's always the Christmas holiday season in Disney's Days of Christmas, a lovely shop that sells Christmas tree ornaments and other Disney-themed holiday merchandise like animated Disney character statues.

## Disney at Home

Here's your opportunity to take some of the magic of Walt Disney World home with you. Disney-themed furniture, kitchen accessories, bathroom fixtures, and household accessories (even bed sheets and pillowcases) are sold here. A woven Mickey Mouse–themed throw rug (47" × 68") is available for $55. A Mickey Mouse wing chair, perfect for any living room or study, sells for $695.

## Eurospain

Lovely handmade glass and crystal merchandise is sold here,

and not all of it has a Disney theme. This is a beautiful shop to browse through, but keep a close eye on your kids. The items on display here are extremely fragile. Many of the gift items can be engraved while you wait. In the center of this shop is an area where a glassblower demonstrates how some of the products in this shop are made.

## Fishing at Cap'N Jack's Marina

Grab a reel, rod, and some bait (supplied when you arrive at the dock) and climb aboard a boat for a two-, three-, or four-hour fishing trip. Up to five people can participate in each relaxing fishing cruise. All fish that are caught must be released. Reservations are required. For rates and information, call ✆ (407) 828-2461.

## Fulton's Crab House

Lunch and dinner are served daily. This is the place to eat if you're looking for an upscale environment and fresh seafood from around the world. The food here is rather expensive, but delicious. You and your children can also join popular Disney characters at Fulton's Crab House for breakfast every morning between 8:00 A.M. and 10:00 A.M. Lunch is served from noon to 5:00 P.M. Dinner is served from 5:00 P.M. until midnight.

## Ghirardelli Soda Fountain & Chocolate Shop

This ice-cream parlor serves a tasty selection of shakes, ice-cream sundaes, and chocolates. It's the perfect place to drop in for a midday (or midnight) snack, especially if you're in the mood for something sweet. Indoor and nearby outdoor tables are available.

## Gourmet Pantry

You'll find all sorts of kitchen goodies here, most with a Disney theme. Cookbooks, aprons, Mickey Mouse cutting boards, coffee mugs, dinner plates, pot holders, and even Mickey Mouse–shaped ice trays can be purchased here. If you want to make Mickey Mouse–shaped sandwiches (like grilled cheese) at home, the

Mickey & Minnie Sandwich Maker costs $59.95. This shop also offers a full deli and bakery where you can grab a snack and eat on the go as you shop.

## LEGO Imagination Center

This colorful LEGO superstore and activity center is like a magnet for young people. Throughout the store (and outside) are giant statues made from LEGOs. In the courtyard that's just outside this shop, kids can walk up to the various kiosks and build their own LEGO creations. The LEGO playground is a great place for young people to hang out and have a blast (as long as they're supervised by a parent or guardian). This is one of the coolest shops/activities for kids in the Downtown Disney area. Here you can purchase virtually every LEGO play set currently available, plus LEGO-themed clothing and souvenirs.

## ≡FAST FACT

A Guest Services desk is located at Dock Stage. You can get your questions answered, make dinner reservations, or learn about special events taking place at Downtown Disney during your visit.

## McDonald's

This is the first McDonald's restaurant opened on Disney property. This inexpensive fast-food establishment offers a large play area for kids, plus a full menu of McDonald's favorites, like Big Macs, Chicken McNuggets, french fries, and Happy Meals. The Golden Arches are located in the heart of the Marketplace. There's virtually always a crowd here, so expect a slight wait to order your food.

## The Rainforest Café

Why travel to a tropical rain forest when you can enjoy a wild meal in a rain forest setting, complete with live wildlife and Audio-

Animatronic creatures. Inside the restaurant you'll find huge salt-water fish tanks. Lunch and dinner are served daily (between 10:30 A.M. and 11:00 P.M.).

This is an extremely popular restaurant at the Marketplace, so be prepared to add your name to the waiting list and then have plenty of time to shop before your table becomes available. The prices here are reasonable, and a wide assortment of American cuisine and seafood is offered. This is a wonderful family-oriented restaurant that's unique and offers a very different dining experience from the many themed restaurants located nearby.

## Sand Street Station

This is an outdoor playground area for young people. While this is an area in which kids can climb, run around, and have fun, they should never be left unsupervised, here or anywhere else within The WDW Resort.

## Studio M

In case you were wondering what the "M" stands for, simply step foot into this shop and there will be no doubt in your mind. Studio M is divided up into small areas, each offering something unique, like Disney-themed airbrushed T-shirts created while you wait by robots (priced between $23 and $42).

You can also pick up a Mickey Mouse mug with your name on it, or meet and greet Mickey Mouse in person and have your photo taken with him. The cost of the Mickey photo session is $29.95 and includes one 8" × 10", two 4" × 5", and four wallet-size color photos of you (or your kids) and Disney's main mouse.

## Team Mickey's Athletic Club

All sorts of Disney-themed sports-related apparel and sporting equipment is for sale at this shop. Mickey Mouse tennis balls, Disney-character golf balls, and Disney-themed golf bags from Belding Sports (ranging in price from $210 to $285) are among the most popular items.

## ⊕ HOT SPOT

Pooh Corner offers all sorts of Winnie the Pooh merchandise, from clothing to storybooks. This charming shop isn't just for kids.

## Toys Fantastic

Presented by Mattel, you'll find all sorts of Barbie dolls, Hot Wheels, and other toys for sale here. Regular Barbie dolls as well as collectible Barbies are available. The Disney Fun Barbie (wearing Mickey ears) sells for about $25. Walt Disney World Barbie (a special-edition doll) is priced around $20. Mickey's Toontown Stacie doll sells for about $20. Young girls and Barbie collectors of all ages will love this store.

## Wolfgang Puck Express

This is fast food, Wolfgang Puck style. The prices here are lower than at the Wolfgang Puck Café located at Disney's West Side. Lunch and dinner are served daily. Outdoor, but covered, seating is available. Gourmet pizzas are the specialty here, although salads, sandwiches, and baked goods are also available. While this is fast food, the prices aren't too cheap. McDonald's might not be as tasty, but it's a far less expensive, fast-food alternative.

## World of Disney

You're about to experience the world's largest Disney Store, featuring all sorts of Disney clothing, toys, gifts, souvenirs, plush toys, collectibles, kitchen items, and other Disney character-based products. This store is divided into twelve different (and very large) rooms. In the center of the store there's an information booth manned by Disney cast members who can help you locate any type of Disney merchandise available anywhere at The WDW Resort, The Disney Stores, and the Disney Catalog.

# Disney's BoardWalk

 Located a short walk from Epcot (and several of The WDW Resort hotels), Disney's BoardWalk offers another alternative for adult-oriented evening and nighttime entertainment. There is no admission charge to enter the BoardWalk area, although several of the clubs have a small cover charge.

This half-mile stretch of nightclubs, restaurants, shops, and activities is located along Crescent Lake and is modeled after the boardwalks of the 1920s and 1930s. While the shops and restaurants in this area are open during the day, Disney's BoardWalk is most enjoyable after dark, so you can experience the lights and festive atmosphere. If you happen to be a guest at Disney's BoardWalk Villas hotel, then the excitement of Disney's BoardWalk will happen all around you.

# ⊕ HOT SPOT

Listen to a ten-piece swing band perform hits from the 1940s to today, and strut your stuff on the ballroom dance floor of the Atlantic Dance Club. You must be twenty-one years old or older to get into this club. There is an admission charge, and special events are held here on holidays.

An ATM is located in the main courtyard area of the BoardWalk, behind the hotel (near Wyland Galleries). For additional information about **Disney's BoardWalk,** call ✆ (407) 939-5100. Don't forget to bring your passport, U.S. (or foreign) driver's license with photo, or U.S. Military ID in order to show proof of age, required for entry into some of the clubs. The hours of operation for each of the restaurants and clubs listed are subject to change based on the season.

## Big River Grille & Brewing Works

Lunch and dinner entrees (ranging in price from $12.95 to $15.95), along with sandwiches, appetizers, salads, and desserts, are available, but the main draw to this dining establishment is the assortment of specialty beers that are served. Operating hours are from 10:00 A.M. to 2:00 A.M. daily.

## BoardWalk Bakery

An assortment of freshly baked goodies is available here, along with cappuccino and espresso. All items are served to go, but if you choose, you can hang out and watch the bakers at work in the kitchen.

## Disney Vacation Club Information Center

In case you're interested in learning about the Disney Vacation Club time-sharing facilities offered at The WDW Resort, you can drop into this information office to schedule an appointment or obtain literature. Time-share vacation opportunities are extremely popular in the Orlando area, so be prepared to hear a sales pitch.

## The ESPN Club

Sports fans will feel like they're in heaven when they step foot into this giant sports bar, which offers dozens of sporting events shown on monitors throughout the club. Live ESPN radio and television broadcasts originate from here, so guests often get to meet their favorite ESPN personalities and sportscasters. A full and pretty inexpensive menu and bar service are available. Food entrees range in price from $7.95 to under $15, and include burgers, hot dogs, tuna salad, and Caesar salad.

There's no admission charge to hang out at the ESPN club. Operating hours are from 11:00 A.M. to 2:00 A.M. If there's a big sporting event taking place, like the Super Bowl or World Series, this club will be packed with sports fans. This club is, however, packed pretty much every evening and night.

After hanging out at the ESPN Club, you can purchase official ESPN merchandise at the nearby shop. Glasses, sports clothing, and caps with the ESPN logo are among the offerings.

# 🌐 HOT SPOT

Open daily for dinner only, the Flying Fish Café serves fine American cuisine including seafood and steak entrees. This is the most classy and expensive restaurant in the BoardWalk area. Reservations are recommended. Call ☎ (407) WDW-DINE.

## Jellyrolls

If you're in the mood for some lighthearted musical entertainment, often with a comedy twist, drop into Jellyrolls. This is a dueling piano bar, where two extremely talented singers/musicians entertain guests simultaneously in a casual and cozy bar atmosphere. The performers change every hour or so, and each pair has its own repertoire of music. Of course, audience participation is expected, so be prepared to sing and clap along, plus request your favorite songs.

To ensure that the performers will honor your song request, write it down on a cocktail napkin and take it up onto the small stage, accompanied by a tip. Even if you don't drink, you'll easily be able to spend a very enjoyable hour or two watching the performances. There's a small admission fee ($4 or less) to enter Jellyrolls, and the drink prices are reasonable.

You must be twenty-one years old or older to be admitted into this piano bar. If you do nothing else during your visit to the BoardWalk, drop into Jellyrolls to experience the live entertainment. Of course, Jellyrolls T-shirts and other souvenirs are available near the exit.

## Leaping Horse Libations

Open from 11:00 A.M. until dusk, this poolside bar offers a small menu of inexpensive food items. Relax by the pool and enjoy your favorite alcoholic or nonalcoholic beverage, along with a burger, hot dog, french fries, or ice cream. This area is mainly for guests of the BoardWalk Inn hotel, but it's open to everyone.

## ⊕ HOT SPOT

At the Screen Door General Store, you'll find groceries, snack items, canned and bottled beverages, and other items that can be brought back to your hotel room in case you experience the late-night or early-morning munchies.

### Seashore Sweets

Styled after an old-fashioned sweet shop, you'll find a delicious assortment of cookies, candies, taffy, hand-dipped gelato, and flavored coffees served here between 11:00 A.M. and 2:00 A.M. A limited number of small tables are available.

### Souvenir Kiosks

Along with the shops, throughout the BoardWalk area you'll encounter many souvenir kiosks that offer a variety of unique products and services, such as face painting (a favorite among kids). There's also a hair wrap kiosk (also popular among young girls). At the Design Your Own Cap kiosk, you can have a baseball cap embroidered with a name or design, while you wait. Another interesting souvenir is your hand in wax, which is created by dipping your hand in hot wax. There's usually a small crowd around this kiosk because watching the hand-dipping process is somewhat interesting. A box for your wax creation is provided for easy transport home.

## ⊕ HOT SPOT

Men's and women's fashions, resort apparel, and swimwear are sold at Thimbles and Threads, and not all of the clothing has a Disney character imprinted on it.

## Wyland Galleries

Wyland is a world-renowned artist who specializes in painting and drawing dolphins, whales, and other sea life. You can see (and purchase) his work at this stunning gallery located in the heart of Disney's BoardWalk. The art on display is beautiful, so be sure to drop in to browse. Another Wyland Gallery is located in Celebration, Florida (the city that Disney built). If you can't afford the actual artwork, postcards, posters, books, and other merchandise featuring Wyland's work are also on sale.

# A High Seas Adventure

THE MAGIC AND WONDER of a Walt Disney World vacation no longer has to end in Orlando. Disney's Imagineers have dreamed up a way for people of all ages, traveling with or without children, to enjoy a cruise to the Bahamas that's unlike what any other cruise-ship line has to offer.

## Disney Cruise Lines

 Disney Cruise Lines features two state-of-the-art ships, offering three-, four-, and seven-night cruises from Cape Canaveral (located near Orlando) to Nassau and Disney's own private island, called Castaway Cay. While these may sound like fun-filled and exotic destinations (which they are), getting there is more than half the fun, because the Disney Cruise Line ships offer all kinds of activities and world-class service that will make your cruise a vacation you'll remember for a lifetime. In most cases, you can combine your Disney cruise with a several-day visit to The WDW Resort, thus creating the ultimate all-inclusive Disney vacation package.

The vacations available through Disney Cruise Lines are offered at a variety of prices (with special package deals always being made available through travel agents, online travel services, and directly through Disney Cruise Lines). Since this is a family-oriented cruise ship, accommodations are available that cater to guests of all ages.

When you board either the *Disney Magic* or the *Disney Wonder,* you will find in your cabin a daily itinerary for what's happening aboard the ship. Each evening, the next day's itinerary will be delivered to your cabin.

## ≡FAST FACT

If you're leaving from The WDW Resort to the cruise ship, your baggage will be picked up at your hotel early in the morning on your day of departure and be delivered directly to your stateroom aboard the ship. The bus ride from The WDW Resort to Cape Canaveral is about one hour and fifteen minutes. During the bus ride, an entertaining video will introduce you to shipboard activities and prepare you for your journey.

## Meet Disney Characters

What would a Disney vacation be without seeing Mickey, Minnie, and the other Disney characters? Well, while sailing aboard either of Disney's cruise ships, you'll meet up with all of your favorite Disney characters many times. Plenty of photo opportunities are available. The majority of character appearances are pre-planned and listed with your itinerary.

## Extra Charges

While the majority of activities and the dining are all included within your cruise package, alcoholic beverages, bottled water, and soft drinks cost extra. (Soda and water are served free of charge within the dining rooms, however.) There's also a charge to play Bingo onboard (because cash prizes are awarded), and separate charges apply for land-based excursions and tours when the ship stops at Nassau and Castaway Cay. All charges can be billed to your room (just like at The WDW Resort), so unless you leave the ship in Nassau, there's no need to carry cash.

### Castaway Cay

One of the highlights of a Disney Cruise Line vacation is the stop the ship makes at Disney's Castaway Cay, a 1,000-acre private island in the Abacos. During the one-day stop at this private tropical island paradise, guests enjoy an authentic island experience that features the Bahamas' best attributes, such as a half-mile-long beach area and a wide range of water sports and activities for families. There's also a secluded mile-long pristine beach that provides the ideal place to relax and unwind, plus an adults-only beach, where older people can go to enjoy quiet time. Snorkeling, sailboat and kayak rentals, bike riding, massages on the beach, and live entertainment are among the ways guests spend their time on the island.

 **TRAVEL TIP**

Kids and teens in particular will enjoy having their hair braided with beads while on the island (for an additional fee). If you want to have this done, don't wait until the end of the day. The line gets long in the afternoon, and the braiders stop taking new people about one hour before the ship's scheduled departure.

## The *Magic* and the *Wonder*

 If you and your family have already experienced a Disney World vacation and you're looking for something new, different, but equally exciting, set sail aboard the *Disney Magic* or *Disney Wonder* cruise ships.

Disney Cruise Line's first ship, *Disney Magic*, began service in mid-1998, with its cruises leaving from the $27 million glass-towered Disney terminal in Port Canaveral, Florida. On August 15, 1999, *Disney Wonder* made its maiden voyage. Both ships are similar and hold between 1,760 and 2,400 guests per voyage.

Both *Disney Magic* and *Disney Wonder* are 85,000-ton ships that were built at the Fincantieri Shipyards in Ancona and Marghera, Italy. Each ship was designed to cater to the vacation demands of four distinct audiences: kids, teens, families, and adults. Instead of relying on ship designers from Fincantieri Shipyards to design and then build the two ships, Disney tapped the talent of its own Imagineers, giving them the task of creating a totally unique cruise ship design that would result in guests experiencing a cruise vacation that only Disney could offer. *Disney Magic* and *Disney Wonder* are two of the most technologically advanced ships afloat.

## ⊕ HOT SPOT

If you're interested in experiencing the many different treatments and massages available within the onboard day spa, be sure to make your appointment within several hours of first boarding the ship. Appointments for massages, facials, and other treatments fill up immediately.

The ships offer 875 staterooms (73 percent of which offer outside views) featuring more space and attention to detail than any other cruise ship in existence. Even the smallest of the ship's staterooms will easily accommodate three guests, with many staterooms designed for families of up to six people (using bunk beds). The staterooms aboard both the *Magic* and the *Wonder* are 25 percent larger than the current industry average and have been designed to offer more storage and usable space than any other cruise ship accommodations. Many of the staterooms also feature a bathroom-and-a-half, featuring separate bath facilities. About 44 percent of the staterooms feature private verandas.

# Pricing Your Vacation

 The pricing structure for the various cruise packages is divided up much like that of the The Walt Disney World Resort hotels. For example, *Disney Magic* offers twelve different stateroom categories to make it easy to choose the perfect accommodations for your family or the people you're traveling with.

Disney Cruise Line's vacation packages include airfare from major U.S. cities. Based on the package you choose, the package might also include three or four days' worth of hotel accommodations, plus unlimited admission to The WDW Resort's theme parks and other land-based recreational activities, such as ninety-nine holes of golf (on six courses).

Prices for the seven-night theme park/cruise vacation packages range from $829 per person (based on double occupancy) to as high as $4,799 per person, depending on the level of hotel and stateroom accommodations guests desire (these are 2002 prices). Three-night cruise-only vacation packages start at $439 per person (based on double occupancy) and go as high as $2,649 per person. The four-night cruise-only packages average between $100 and $200 higher per person than the three-night packages. When traveling with at least one adult, kids and teens receive highly discounted rates (starting at $199 per child).

## ═FAST FACT

> Every night, a different Broadway-style show is presented that's suitable for the entire family. For the eighteen and over crowd, however, the nightlife aboard the ship includes dance clubs and an improv comedy club (where every show is totally different).

Using an online service, such as Travelocity.com, discounted rates for nonpeak travel periods can be found for Disney Cruise Lines. For example, one "online only" deal on Travelocity.com offered a three-night cruise aboard the *Disney Wonder* starting at $379 per person (for a January 2002 sailing).

For additional information about **Disney Cruise Lines,** to request a free vacation-planning brochure, or to make a reservation, call ☎ (407) 566-7000 or ☎ (800) WDW-CRUISE, visit any travel agent, or check out the Disney Cruise Line's Web site at ✎ *www.disneycruise.com.* Be sure to inquire about early-booking discounts that could save you hundreds of dollars per stateroom for some of the cruises scheduled to take place during nonholiday periods. Special honeymoon packages are also available.

# Children's Space

 In order to cater to the unique needs of young guests, 15,000 square feet of the ship have been set aside as dedicated children's space. The kid- and teen-oriented areas of the ship are staffed by more than forty professional counselors, who personalize each guest's experience. Kids and teens are encouraged to participate in a wide range of organized camplike activities.

# Adult Activities

 While the children are enjoying the personalized attention and the dozens of activities designed specifically for them, parents and adults traveling without children will be able to enjoy the ship's adults-only areas, including a nighttime entertainment complex that offers three themed nightclubs and shopping. There's a rock and roll club, a comedy club, and a piano/cappuccino club. A special adults-only alternative restaurant, a separate adults-only swimming pool, and a fully equipped day spa facility (offering the most modern exercise equipment and spa treatments, as well as educational and enrichment programs) are offered.

When parents want to leave their children and experience the nightlife aboard the ship, private baby-sitting service is available (for an additional fee). No matter what time it is, day or night, unlimited room service is available (and all food is included in the cruise package).

## Family Time

 During times when parents and children want to spend time together, many family-oriented activities are also available on Disney Cruise Line's ships. Each ship offers three family-oriented restaurants, snack bars, a buffet, and multiple bars. Each night, guests experience a different restaurant with a different theme, but the entire waitstaff remains the same, so your waiter will quickly get to know your personal preferences and accommodate your every need.

### ≡FAST FACT

Throughout the year, Disney Cruise Lines hosts special theme cruises, with celebrity guests making appearances, performing concerts, conducting workshops, and interacting with guests.

Of course, since The Walt Disney Company specializes in family-oriented entertainment, there is no shortage of Disney-style entertainment aboard the cruise ship. There's a 1,040-seat theater that features one of the most sophisticated show settings in the world. This theater is the home of three different Broadway-style shows. Each evening, the cruise line offers a uniquely themed production, including Disney classics and newly created shows that combine storytelling and music.

Throughout each day, the Buena Vista Theater (a 270-seat full screen cinema with state-of-the-art Dolby Sound) shows a variety of Disney's animated classics and first-run movie releases. For less formal entertainment, the ships offer multiple lounges and the ESPN Sports Club. In this sports club, multiple screens continuously broadcast all of the latest sports news and events from around the world.

## Dining Experiences

Out of all the dining experiences on the ships, the Animator's Palate offers the most unique dining experience. When guests first enter into this dining room, everything is in black and white. As guests dine on California cuisine, the entire room begins to change—colors begin to appear on the walls, on the ceiling, and at each table. As the meal proceeds, the entire restaurant undergoes a complete transformation that's synchronized with light and sound. At the end of the meal, diners are treated to an appearance from a few surprise guests who participate in a musical finale.

The Palo restaurant (which requires separate reservations) definitely offers the most spectacular view aboard the ship, not to mention incredible food, mouthwatering desserts, and an impressive wine list. If you're celebrating a special occasion, want to enjoy a romantic dinner, or just want to relax and experience an awesome dining experience, make plans to dine at least one evening at this onboard restaurant. As a guest aboard Disney Cruise Lines, you'll automatically be invited to dine at the ships' regular restaurants. A reservation for Palo must be requested.

## Guest Services

As if having the facilities and built-in entertainment venues and offering countless activities isn't enough, each ship is operated by a crew of almost 1,000 people (representing over fifty countries) who are totally dedicated to providing superior Disney-style service to all guests.

Other services aboard the ships include self-service launderettes, complete photographic services, complete laundry and dry-cleaning services, satellite telephone service, modern medical facilities, a twenty-four-hour front desk service, fax and secretarial service, and conference facilities for groups of up to 120 people.

When traveling on Disney Cruise Lines, satellite telephones are available in every stateroom; however, the price per minute for making calls is extremely high. Public phones are available in Nassau; however, making an international call to the United States, even if you're using a calling card, is both expensive and time-consuming. So, plan on sending postcards rather than calling your friends and family back home.

A somewhat less expensive alternative is to visit the onboard Internet Café and send e-mail home to friends, coworkers, and relatives. There's a seventy-five-cent-per-minute charge to surf the Web while aboard the ship; however, for a flat fee of $39.99 (for a three- or four-night cruise) or $89.99 (for a seven-night cruise), unlimited Internet access is available.

Disney Cruise Lines offers a structured land and sea vacation experience. Guests can choose from one of three primary itineraries, including a three-, four-, or seven-night cruise. Some of the cruise packages include several days at The WDW Resort as well.

##  TRAVEL TIP

Once you book your cruise, pay attention to the two-suitcase (plus one carry-on) baggage limitation per person and pack accordingly. Leave space for your souvenirs! Be sure to keep any medications, tickets, your passport, a change of clothes, and toiletries with you in a carry-on.

CHAPTER 14

# The Universal Orlando Resort

FOLLOWING IN THE FOOTSTEPS of The WDW Resort, The Universal Orlando Resort (also referred to as Universal Studios Escape) is quickly becoming a vacation destination unto itself, complete with resort hotels, theme parks, and a unique restaurant/shopping area.

## Overview of the Resort

 Once you arrive at Universal Studios Escape, plan on spending at least one full day at each of the theme parks, plus your evenings/nights at CityWalk. While both theme parks are family-oriented, each offers a totally different overall theme and atmosphere.

### ≡FAST FACT

Universal Studios Escape has multiple on-site ATMs. At Universal Studios Florida, there's a full-service bank on the property. The First Union National Bank offers traveler's check cashing, cash advances from credit cards, and currency exchanges.

## The Theme Parks

Universal Studios Florida (like its counterpart in Hollywood, California) offers rides, shows and attractions based on blockbuster movies like *Twister, E.T. – The Extraterrestrial, The Blues Brothers, Jaws, Beetlejuice, King Kong, Men in Black, Back to the Future,* and *Terminator 2.* The majority of these aren't traditional thrill rides, yet they offer an interactive and often exciting way to experience the story behind each of these movies in a whole new way. Hence, the overall theme of this park (as well as its advertising slogan) is "Ride the Movies!"

Universal Studios Florida is divided into various themed lands. Woody Woodpecker's KidZone, for example, is a kid-oriented area. Another favorite among the younger crowd is Nickelodeon Studios. This is where some of the most popular shows from the Nickelodeon television network are filmed. For families and adults, Production Central, New York, San Francisco/Amity, The World Expo, and Hollywood are the other themed areas of Universal Studios Florida, each of which offers its own rides, shows, attractions, shops, and dining options (all described in the next chapter).

The second theme park within Universal Studios Escape is Islands of Adventure. Also divided into a series of themed areas, this park offers more traditional roller coasters and thrill rides, each with its own storyline. Here, Seuss Landing and Toon Lagoon offer an assortment of kid-oriented rides, shows, and attractions (plus shops and dining options), while the Lost Continent, Jurassic Park, and Marvel Super Hero Island will appeal more to teens and adults. Everything that Islands of Adventure has to offer is described within Chapter 16.

## CityWalk

Located between these two exciting theme parks is CityWalk, a unique dining and shopping area that by day is family-oriented, but by night offers exciting nightlife activities for adults, featuring dance clubs, bars, live entertainment, and an overall party atmosphere. In addition to a state-of-the-art movie theater, CityWalk offers a handful of themed restaurants, plus several fine-dining restaurants, mixed with unique shops. Somewhat similar in concept to Disney's Pleasure Island (and Downtown Disney area), you can learn all about CityWalk in Chapter 17.

## ═FAST FACT

Universal Studios offers a variety of discounts for members of AARP, HIA, and the Orlando MagiCard. Occasionally, Florida-resident discount offers are available. For more information, contact the park's Guest Services office at ☎(407) 224-6356.

## Driving Directions

 Once you're in the Orlando area, you'll find this theme park located near the intersection of Interstate 4 (I-4) and the Florida Turnpike. Depending on where you're coming from, follow these driving directions:

- From the **Orlando International Airport:** Take 528 West (the Bee-Line Expressway) toward Tampa. Watch for signs to Interstate 4 East (to Orlando). From Interstate 4 East, take Exit #29B (Universal Boulevard). Take a left onto Universal Boulevard and follow the signs to Universal Studios Escape.
- **Traveling East on I-4** (from the Tampa area): Exit I-4 at Exit #30A (Universal Boulevard). Take a left onto Universal Boulevard and follow the signs to Universal Studios Escape.
- **Traveling North on the Florida Turnpike** (from the Miami/Ft. Lauderdale area): Take Exit #259 (the second of the Orlando exits) and follow the signs to the I-4 Tampa exit. Exit I-4 at Exit #29B. Take a right onto Hollywood Way and follow the signs to Universal Studios Escape.
- **Traveling South on the Florida Turnpike** (from the Wildwood/Ocala area): Take Exit #259 and follow the signs

to the I-4 Tampa exit. Exit I-4 at Exit #29B. Take a right onto Hollywood Way and follow the signs to Universal Studios Escape.

- **Traveling West on I-4** (from the Daytona/Jacksonville area): Exit I-4 at Exit #29B. Take a right onto Hollywood Way and follow the signs to Universal Studios Escape.
- When driving from **The Walt Disney World Resort:** Take I-4 to Exit #30A (Universal Boulevard). Take a left onto Universal Boulevard and follow the signs to Universal Studios Escape. Driving time is about twenty minutes from most areas within The WDW Resort.

## ≡FAST FACT

Shuttle buses are available from many non-Disney hotels in the Orlando area, especially those along International Drive and surrounding areas. If you're staying at The WDW Resort, however, the cheapest and fastest way to get to Universal Studios Escape is by renting a car, although taxi and shuttle bus service is available. If you need shuttle bus service, contact Mears Transportation at ☎(407) 839-1570 or ☎(407) 699-9999.

## Parking at Universal Studios Escape

Most people arrive at Universal Studios Escape (Universal Studios Florida, Islands of Adventure, and CityWalk) traveling by car. The theme park offers an enclosed parking garage that is equipped with a 200-camera security system, moving sidewalks, escalators and elevators, on-site wheelchair rental, and an on-site kennel. Daily parking for cars, vans, and motorcycles is $7 per vehicle. Daily parking for RVs and trailers is $8 per vehicle.

Vehicles can leave the garage and return the same day by stopping at the toll plaza upon re-entry and presenting their original parking ticket. Valet parking is available for cars and vans at a charge of $14 per day.

Taxis, buses, limousines, and shuttles to hotels and other area destinations are available outside the main entrance at the Transportation Center of the parking structure. For schedule information, contact the Guest Services office.

The distance between the Universal Studios Escape parking complex and the theme parks is considerable. While moving walkways and escalators are used to make the trip to and from your car easier, the commute takes about twenty minutes on foot and involves walking. Much of this commute is outdoors, so if it's raining, you're going to get wet.

##  TRAVEL TIP

Show your AAA membership card when purchasing tickets or making a purchase at gift shops or restaurants within Universal Studios Escape and receive up to a 10 percent discount.

# Admission to Universal Studios Theme Parks

 As you'll see, depending on your length of stay and which park(s) you plan on visiting, there is a variety of different ticket options available. If you'll be in the Orlando area for multiple days (and you plan to visit Universal Studios Florida and Islands of Adventure), you can save money by purchasing a multiday/multipark pass.

After purchasing your admission ticket, if you decide you want to stay longer or upgrade your admission for additional days, special discounts are offered at the Customer Service counter near the entrance of the park. You must upgrade your ticket the day it's purchased, however.

### Orlando FlexTicket

In addition to the multiday passes for the Universal Studios Escape theme parks, the Orlando FlexTicket offers a way to see multiple Orlando-based attractions and theme parks, and save money. The 5-Park Orlando FlexTicket provides unlimited admission for fourteen consecutive days to all of the following theme parks:

- Busch Gardens (located in Tampa Bay)
- SeaWorld Orlando
- Universal Studios Florida
- Universal Studios Islands of Adventure
- Wet 'N Wild

## ⹀FAST FACT

While the Orlando FlexTicket does not include admission to any of the Disney-owned theme parks, this ticket option offers a significant savings over the single-day admission price to each participating park.

### Same Day Theme Park Re-entry

As you leave either of the Universal Studios Escape theme parks, be sure to have your hand stamped as you exit in order to be granted readmission into that park later in the day or evening. In addition to the hand stamp, be sure to retain your ticket stub. The hand stamps are designed to be water-resistant, so don't worry if your hands get wet if you choose to return to your hotel in the middle of the day to go swimming, and then want to return to Universal Studios Florida later that evening. Try to refrain, however, from scrubbing your hands clean with soap until your day's visit to the theme park is complete.

## Universal Studios Florida VIP Tours

 If you're pressed for time and want to ensure that you see and do the best of what Universal Studios Florida has to offer, consider participating in a VIP Tour. This walking tour of the park lasts about five hours, departs at either 10:00 A.M. or noon (daily), and ensures that participants get to experience eight of the park's most popular shows and attractions—without waiting in lines.

Advanced reservations are required. Call ☏ (407) 363-8295 during normal business hours. The cost of the VIP Tour is $120 per person. Rides and attractions participants get to experience include:

- Back to the Future: The Ride
- Earthquake–The Big One
- E.T. Adventure
- The FUNtastic World of Hanna-Barbera
- Jaws
- Kongfrontation
- Terminator 2: 3-D
- Twister–Ride It Out

## Exclusive VIP Tours

This eight-hour walking tour is private and can accommodate up to fifteen people. These tours are scheduled at your convenience and will ensure that you and your group have the opportunity to see and do exactly what you want within the Universal Studios Florida park—without waiting in lines. Priority seating is provided at select restaurants and shows. The cost of this exclusive private tour is $1,700 for the entire group.

 **TRAVEL TIP**

If you plan to stay at one of the on-property Universal Studio Escape hotels or resorts, special package deals including hotel accommodations and admission to the theme parks are available. For more information, call Universal Studios Vacations at ☏(800) 711-0080 or ☏(407) 224-7000. You can also visit ✎ *www.usf.com*.

## Ultimate Escape Tours

This two-day private tour offers a true insider's perspective of Universal Studios Florida and also brings to life the stories behind Islands of Adventure. This two-day tour gives you unlimited park-to-park priority entrance to rides, shows, and attractions, plus preferred seating for the attractions of your choice. The cost is $3,000 for the entire group (up to fifteen people).

## Islands of Adventure VIP Tours

Thrill Seeker VIP Tours are available (for an additional fee) that ensure you get to experience all of the thrill rides Islands of Adventure has to offer—with little or no waiting.

The Thrill Seekers VIP Tour departs daily at 10:00 A.M. and noon. The price of this tour is $120 per person. It includes a five-hour walking tour (nonprivate) of the Islands of Adventure theme park. Participants receive priority entrance and preferred seating for approximately eight popular attractions, including:

- The Amazing Adventures of Spider-Man
- Dudley Do-Right's Ripsaw Falls
- Dueling Dragons
- The Eighth Voyage of Sindbad
- Incredible Hulk Coaster
- Jurassic Park River Adventure
- Poseidon's Fury: Escape from the Lost City

The Universal Studios Islands of Adventure Family Adventure VIP Tour (also priced at $120 per person) is very much like the Thrill Seekers tour; however, the emphasis is on family-oriented rides and attractions. This tour is recommended for families traveling with children. It includes priority entrance and preferred seating for the following attractions:

- Camp Jurassic
- Caro-Seuss-el

- The Cat in the Hat
- The Eighth Voyage of Sindbad
- Jurassic Park Discovery Center
- One Fish Two Fish Red Fish Blue Fish
- Pandemonium Cartoon Circus

## ≡FAST FACT

Reservations for all tours should be made in advance by calling ☎(888) U-ESCAPE or ☎(407) 363-8295. Reservations are accepted between 9:00 A.M. and 6:00 P.M. (EST), Monday through Friday only.

## Guest Services

 Located just inside the main entrance of each of the theme parks is the Guest Services office. Here you can take advantage of special services for guests with disabilities. Printed disability tour guides, TDD, assisted listening devices, and wheelchairs are available. Tour maps are also available in French, German, Japanese, Portuguese, and Spanish. Each park's lost and found, stroller rental desk, wheelchair rental counter, foreign money exchange, ATM, pay lockers, and mail drop-off are all located at or near Guest Services.

## Getting the Most out of Your Day

 Just like when you're visiting one of the Disney theme parks, it's always a good idea to save the most popular attractions for lunch time or dinner time, when many guests take a break to eat. At these times (between 11:30 A.M. and 1:00 P.M., and 5:00 P.M. to 6:00 P.M.), the lines are somewhat shorter. The lines for the popular attractions also tend to be shorter late in the day, since many guests try to experience the hottest rides and attractions as soon as they arrive.

If the weather is bad and it's raining, you can count on shorter-than-average lines, no matter when you visit this theme park. You'll want to wear lightweight rain gear (such as a rain poncho, which can be purchased at the various Universal Studios shops) and refrain from carrying an umbrella. Navigating through the park in crowds when you're carrying an open umbrella is difficult, and if it's windy, you won't stay dry. Also, when you enter into a ride or attraction, there's often nowhere to stow your wet umbrella.

During periods of rain, you have two options. You can choose to get wet and see the rides and attractions that require you to wait outside, or you can follow the crowds and head for the indoor rides and attractions. During periods of rain, outdoor shows and attractions will be cancelled or postponed.

 **TRAVEL TIP**

To find out the television and motion picture production schedule at Universal Studios during the time you'll be visiting, drop by the Studio Audience Center located to the right of the main entrance turnstiles to Universal Studios Florida. You can also call the Studio Audience Center at ☏(407) 224-6355 or Nickelodeon's Production Hotline at ☏(407) 363-8586.

# The Universal Studios Florida Theme Park

WHAT STARTED OUT AS A WORKING TELEVISION and motion picture studio in Orlando has developed into an extremely popular tourist destination. Universal Studios Florida offers guests a chance to see what happens behind the scenes in television and movie production, as well as a chance to "Ride the Movies."

## Park Information

 Designed to provide at least one full day's worth of entertainment for the entire family, the majority of things to see and do at this park are suitable for people of all ages. Universal Studios Florida opens every day at 9 A.M. Closing times vary, based on the season. For the exact hours of operation during your planned visit, call ✆ (407) 363-8000.

| USEFUL PHONE NUMBERS |
| --- |
| **General Information:** ✆(407) 363-8000 |
| **Hearing Impaired TDD:** ✆(407) 224-4414 |
| **Merchandise Sales & Information:** ✆(407) 363-8320 |
| **Universal Studios Florida Guest Services:** ✆(407) 224-6350 |
| **Universal Studios Florida Lost & Found:** ✆(407) 224-6355 |
| **Vacation Information:** ✆(800) 711-0080 or ✆(407) 224-7000 |

# The Rating System

 Not all of the rides, shows, and attractions at Universal Studios Florida are suitable or designed for everyone. To help you choose which rides and attractions are most worth seeing while visiting Universal Studios Florida, this book offers star-based ratings for each ride and attraction, based on the age group each will most appeal to. Each ride and attraction has earned between one and three stars.

★ = Rides and attractions that earned just one star aren't worth waiting for and could be skipped, especially if your time within the theme park is limited.

★★ = Rides and attractions that earned two stars are good, but they don't fall into the "must-see" category.

★★★ = The rides and attractions that earned three stars are definitely worth seeing and should not be missed.

N.S. = This denotes rides and attractions that are "Not Suitable" for a specific age group.

## Choose a Place to Meet

As soon as you arrive at Universal Studios Florida, choose a place where you'll meet up with the other people in your group if you happen to get separated. Two ideal meeting places are in front of Guest Services (near the entrance) and in front of Back to the Future . . . The Ride. Arrange to meet on the half hour if you become separated.

## ══FAST FACT

Award-winning producer and director Steven Spielberg is one of this theme park's creative consultants. He's worked hands-on in the development of several of the park's most popular rides, shows, and attractions.

# The Rides

 The slogan for this theme park is "Ride the Movies," and that's exactly what you'll do when you experience the various rides at Universal Studios Florida. All of the rides and attractions are based on popular motion pictures and television shows produced by Universal Studios. Many of these rides are cutting-edge and can't be experienced anywhere else (except in some cases at Universal Studios Hollywood in California).

## Back to the Future . . . The Ride

| | |
|---|---|
| Ages 2–4: | N.S. |
| Ages 5–10: | ★★★ |
| Ages 11–15: | ★★★ |
| Ages 16–Adult: | ★★★ |
| Senior Citizens: | ★★ |

Location within the park: **The World Expo**

This ride is absolutely awesome, so expect to wait for up to an hour (or longer) to experience it. About 90 percent of your waiting time will be under a covered awning or inside.

Once inside the ride's building, you'll see the preshow on video monitors. This preshow stars several actors from the *Back to the Future* movie trilogy, including "Doc Brown" and "Biff," although you won't see Michael J. Fox's character. Just before boarding the ride, you'll see a second four-minute preshow, which is shown to you in a small room.

As you climb aboard the actual ride, you'll step into a time-traveling vehicle, which is Doc Brown's latest invention (just like the one in the movie), except this model holds eight passengers. As the ride itself begins, prepare yourself for four minutes of turbulent excitement as you race through time.

Using state-of-the-art flight simulator, audio, and Omnimax movie technology, your vehicle will move and bounce around in a way that's perfectly synchronized with the Omnimax movie shown on a massive 80-foot-tall projection screen in front of you. You'll hear (and feel) the realistic sound effects through the 300 speakers that surround you.

To make the experience even more realistic, smoke and other special effects are used. Back to the Future . . . The Ride was two years in the making and cost over $16 million to create. This ride is as turbulent as a roller coaster, although there are no real drops (but it feels like there are).

👍 This is a must-see attraction.

## E.T. Adventure

| | |
|---|---|
| Ages 2–4: | ★ |
| Ages 5–10: | ★★★ |
| Ages 11–15: | ★★★ |
| Ages 16–Adult: | ★★★ |
| Senior Citizens: | ★★★ |

Location within the park: **Woody Woodpecker's KidZone**

Only Steven Spielberg himself (in conjunction with Universal Studios' attraction designers) could have created this ride, which is absolutely charming. Guests sit on moving bicycle-shaped vehicles that roll and eventually fly while being piloted by E.T. himself. The visuals throughout this ride experience are stunning and realistic. As a passenger, guests have the opportunity to visit E.T.'s home planet. At the very end, E.T. even says "good-bye" to each passenger by saying his or her name (something kids absolutely love). E.T. Adventure is loosely based on the movie *E.T.: The Extra-Terrestrial*.

## ═FAST FACT

John Williams, the composer who created the original soundtrack for the *E.T.* motion picture, also created an original score for this ride. Steven Spielberg created several new characters that appear during the ride.

This is one of the most popular attractions within this park, so be prepared for a wait. Virtually all of the waiting, however, is inside, as guests wind around a maze and have a chance to see lifelike Animatronic re-creations of E.T.'s friends and relatives. Sure,

E.T. Adventure is somewhat kid-oriented, but just like the movie itself, it'll appeal to everyone and shouldn't be missed.

👍 This is a must-see attraction.

## Earthquake: The Big One

| | |
|---|---|
| Ages 2–4: | N.S. |
| Ages 5–10: | ★★ |
| Ages 11–15: | ★★★ |
| Ages 16–Adult: | ★★★ |
| Senior Citizens: | ★★ |

Location within the park: **San Francisco/Amity**

Using highly realistic sets and special effects, guests feel like they're trapped within San Francisco's Embarcadero subway station during an earthquake that measures 8.3 on the Richter scale. In other words, there's a whole lot of shaking going on. Don't worry, this ride is perfectly safe, although you will bounce around a bit in the vehicle you're traveling in, while 65,000 gallons of water rush past you (you'll stay dry, however).

The Hollywood-style special effects used in this ride are impressive. This attraction is based on the 1974 movie *Earthquake*, which starred Charlton Heston and Ava Gardner. Young children might get frightened by this ride, so you might want to have them sit this one out. The ride itself lasts about six minutes.

## ⟶FAST FACT

If the earthquake visitors experience in this attraction were real, it would register 8.3 on the Richter scale. To make this attraction more realistic, over 65,000 gallons of water are released and recycled every six minutes.

## Jaws

| | |
|---|---|
| Ages 2–4: | N.S. |
| Ages 5–10: | ★★ |
| Ages 11–15: | ★★★ |
| Ages 16–Adult: | ★★★ |
| Senior Citizens: | ★★ |

Location within the park: **San Francisco/Amity**

Located in the area of Universal Studios Florida that re-creates the small town of Amity in which the movie *Jaws* took place, there's an exciting and somewhat scary ride/attraction starring Jaws himself. While guests remain dry (for the most part), everyone winds up face-to-face with a very lifelike Animatronic shark. The 32-foot-long creature weighs three tons and is made of steel and fiberglass, but even up close, he looks very real and very hungry. The shark travels at a rate of 20 feet per second around the attraction's manmade 5-million-gallon, 7-acre lagoon. This ride is so realistic, young children may get frightened.

## Kongfrontation

| | |
|---|---|
| Ages 2–4: | N.S. |
| Ages 5–10: | ★★ |
| Ages 11–15: | ★★★ |
| Ages 16–Adult: | ★★★ |
| Senior Citizens: | ★★ |

Location within the park: **New York**

As you experience Kongfrontation, a helicopter flies overhead, warning you to stay clear of King Kong who is approaching. The helicopter, however, winds up crashing right before your eyes, with the help of King Kong, of course. You'll then be greeted by a 32-foot-tall, not-so-friendly ape, who has a 54-foot arm span (and he wants to give you a hug!). All sorts of special effects and high-tech robotics are used to create the illusion that King Kong has escaped captivity and is loose.

Just when you think it's totally safe, the tram you're riding on will make a sudden drop, which lasts about one second, but creates 1.75 Gs of acceleration that you will feel throughout your entire body. Young kids might find this ride/attraction scary and a bit too realistic.

# ≡FAST FACT

The King Kong that appears in this attraction was created using several tons of steel, plastic, fabric, and 7,000 pounds of fur. He stands four stories tall, weighs six tons, and has an arm span of 54 feet. This character is one of the largest animated figures ever created.

## The FUNtastic World of Hanna-Barbera

| | |
|---|---|
| Ages 2–4: | ★ |
| Ages 5–10: | ★★★ |
| Ages 11–15: | ★★★ |
| Ages 16–Adult: | ★★★ |
| Senior Citizens: | ★★ |

Location within the park: **Production Central**

Aside from E.T. Adventure, this is the most lighthearted and fun-filled ride at Universal Studios Florida. The FUNtastic World of Hanna-Barbera puts you into a cartoon that stars some of Hanna-Barbera's most popular characters, including the Flintstones and the Jetsons. After seeing a preshow video featuring Bill Hanna and Joseph Barbera, guests move into a specially built theater. What's different about this theater is that the seats are divided into groups, and each group of seats is on a separate set of hydraulic lifts. Thus, the seats move in conjunction with the movie, making guests feel like they're actually part of the cartoon. The best seats are in the center section of the theater. The ride itself is pretty turbulent, so make sure you stow any loose articles of clothing, as well as cameras, purses, etc. Even if you're not a big cartoon fan, this ride is entertaining for people of all ages, although it's been around for over a decade and the preshow especially could use a bit of updating.

For older guests (and those who don't like turbulent rides), special stationary seats are available, so you can watch the movie without experiencing the physical aspect of the ride.

👍 This is a must-see attraction.

## ≡FAST FACT

Working together for over fifty years, Bill Hanna and Joe Barbera were pioneers in the art of animation. Together, Hanna and Barbera created over 300 animated specials, series, and films, plus 3,000 thirty-minute cartoons. Their work has won seven Oscars and eight Emmys.

## Men in Black: Alien Attack

| | |
|---|---|
| Ages 2–4: | N.S. |
| Ages 5–10: | N.S. |
| Ages 11–15: | ★★★ |
| Ages 16–Adult: | ★★★ |
| Senior Citizens: | ★★ |

Location within the park: **World Expo**

Guests team up to save Earth from alien terrorists. While riding in special vehicles through a simulated New York City, riders directly affect the environment around them as they try to shoot and capture aliens roaming freely. Each rider is equipped with a "Series IV Alienator" device with which to shoot aliens (who will also be shooting at the vehicles guests are traveling in). This exciting ride offers twelve different endings, from a hero's welcome to an embarrassing defeat. It's based on the popular *Men in Black* motion picture.

 This is a must-see attraction.

## Curious George Goes to Town

| | |
|---|---|
| Ages 2–3: | N.S |
| Ages 4–10: | ★★★ |
| Ages 11–15: | ★ |
| Ages 16–Adult: | N.S. |
| Senior Citizens: | N.S. |

Location within the park: **Woody Woodpecker's KidZone**

This attraction takes the popular children's books and brings them to life in an area that kids can interact within. Kids can climb, explore, play, and even get a little wet (if they choose to). This area is not suitable for children under age three. Parents should maintain constant supervision over their kids while they play in this innovative playground area.

## Woody Woodpecker's Nuthouse Coaster

| | |
|---|---|
| Ages 2–4: | N.S. |
| Ages 5–10: | ★★★ |
| Ages 11–15: | ★★ |
| Ages 16–Adult: | ★ |
| Senior Citizens: | N.S. |

Location within the park: **Woody Woodpecker's KidZone**

This kid-oriented roller coaster offers an 800-foot-long track that travels through a factory filled with gears and gadgets. The coaster is a mild thrill ride that lasts for about ninety seconds. It's for young people, so don't expect any big drops, sharp turns, loops, or other surprises. The highest point on the ride is 28 feet off the ground. Guests must be at least three years old and able to sit upright to ride this coaster. Kids under 48 inches tall must be accompanied by an adult.

☞ This is a must-see attraction.

## A Day in the Park with Barney

| | |
|---|---|
| Ages 2–4: | ★★★ |
| Ages 5–10: | ★★★ |
| Ages 11–15: | ★ |
| Ages 16–Adult: | ★ |
| Senior Citizens: | ★ |

Location within the park: **Woody Woodpecker's KidZone**

If you're traveling with kids (ages ten and under), one of the stops you'll definitely want to make while visiting this park is to see Barney, who performs in live shows throughout the day. After each show, kids get to meet their favorite purple dinosaur.

The preshow stars one of Barney's human friends, Mr. Peekaboo, but once you enter into the main theater, the main show stars Barney, Baby Bop, and BJ from the PBS television series *Barney and Friends*. Kids are invited to sing and clap along as Barney performs popular songs that kids know and love. This show is presented in a specially built indoor theater that contains a 360-degree stage (that resembles a park) and offers benches for kids (and their parents) to sit on. All of the seats in the theater offer an excellent view.

The theater itself holds 350 people. During the actual performance, no flash photography is permitted; however, during the meet-and-greet session after each performance, you're welcome to take photographs of Barney shaking hands with or hugging your child. While many adults find Barney annoying, this show is actually rather charming. Young kids will absolutely love it, and most parents will find it tolerable.

 This is a must-see attraction.

# ⊕ HOT SPOT

After the show, guests exit the theater into an adjoining gift shop that sells all sorts of Barney merchandise, so be prepared to either spend money or have to explain to your child why he or she can't have whatever Barney toy catches his or her attention. Also near the exit to the theater is a Barney-themed playground that kids will love exploring.

## Animal Planet Live!

| | |
|---|---|
| Ages 2–4: | ★★ |
| Ages 5–10: | ★★★ |
| Ages 11–15: | ★★★ |
| Ages 16–Adult: | ★★ |
| Senior Citizens: | ★★ |

Location within the park: **Woody Woodpecker's KidZone**

Based on programming from the Animal Planet television cable network, as the name suggests, this is a totally live, twenty-minute stage show featuring real animal trainers and a cast of animals you've seen on popular television shows and in movies. Exotic birds, trained monkeys, snakes, and famous dogs are among the animals that perform in a show that can best be described as extremely cute and enjoyable.

This is a highly entertaining and rather humorous show that young kids in particular will enjoy. However, it's definitely suitable for and appealing to people of all ages. The theater in which this show is presented is large, so there's seldom a wait, assuming you arrive about fifteen minutes before a scheduled show time. Show times are posted in front of the theater, on the information board locations throughout the park, and in the printed park schedule available from the ticket booths. The theater itself is covered, so you'll be sheltered from direct sunlight or rain.

After each performance, some of the animals and their trainers remain onstage to meet and greet young audience members. This provides for an excellent photo opportunity.

 This is a must-see attraction.

## Fievel's Playland

| | |
|---|---|
| Ages 2–4: | ★★★ |
| Ages 5–10: | ★★★ |
| Ages 11–15: | ★★★ |
| Ages 16–Adult: | N.S. |
| Senior Citizens: | N.S. |

Location within the park: **Woody Woodpecker's KidZone**

This fun-filled playground is for children only. It's based on the animated movie *An American Tail* and features all sorts of activities for young kids to experience, like slides, a water flume, and a massive jungle gym. There's also a shooting fountain that allows kids to get wet and cool off on a hot day. As you make your way to or from A Day in the Park with Barney and/or E.T. Adventure, you might want to drop by this playground with your kids.

 This is a must-see attraction.

##  TRAVEL TIP

For parents, there are nearby benches where you can relax while your kids play. While sitting on a nearby bench, however, keep a constant eye on the young people you're with.

## Universal Studios Florida . . . Take 3!

In addition to the awesome rides, you won't want to miss these highly entertaining shows, many of which feature talented live performers (who don't lip-synch). For the majority of these shows, the wait is minimal, especially if you time your arrival to the appropriate theater correctly. On the days when the park isn't totally jammed, arrive at the appropriate theater about fifteen minutes before the posted show time. Arrive thirty minutes prior to a show if the park is crowded and you want to be assured a good seat.

When you arrive at Universal Studios Florida and purchase your ticket, you'll be given a full-color guide booklet that lists all show times and show locations. While some shows are continuous, others are presented only a few times each day, at specific times.

Some of the shows/attractions listed here, like Terminator 2: 3-D and Twister, are extremely popular, so you might want to see these shows between 11:30 A.M. and 1:00 P.M., or around 5:00 P.M., when many guests take a lunch or dinner break. Another ideal time to catch these two popular attractions is during the Dynamite Nights Stuntacular show that's held every evening.

## Alfred Hitchcock: The Art of Making Movies

| | |
|---|---|
| Ages 2–4: | N.S. |
| Ages 5–10: | N.S. |
| Ages 11–15: | ★★ |
| Ages 16–Adult: | ★★ |
| Senior Citizens: | ★★ |

Location within the park: **Production Central**

If you've ever wondered how special effects are created for motion pictures, this guided tour/presentation will answer your questions, using scenes from some of Alfred Hitchcock's most famous horror films as examples. This show is presented continuously throughout the day; however, since scary scenes from Hitchcock's movies are shown, it's not suitable for children (under age thirteen). Teens and adults, however, will find this presentation entertaining. The show takes place in an air-conditioned theater, so it offers an excellent way to get out of the sun and relax, and be entertained at the same time.

## Beetlejuice's Graveyard Revue

| | |
|---|---|
| Ages 2–4: | ★ |
| Ages 5–10: | ★★★ |
| Ages 11–15: | ★★★ |
| Ages 16–Adult: | ★★ |
| Senior Citizens: | ★★ |

Location within the park: **San Francisco/Amity**

Several times throughout the day, a group of Universal Studios' official monsters get together for a fun-filled concert, featuring adaptations of popular rock and roll songs. This twenty-five-minute show is suitable for the entire family, and features a cast of talented performers who perform all of the songs live. Join Dracula, the Phantom of the Opera, the Wolfman, the Bride of Frankenstein, and Frankenstein himself in a lighthearted musical extravaganza.

## Dynamite Nights Stuntacular

| | |
|---|---|
| Ages 2–4: | N.S. |
| Ages 5–10: | ★★ |
| Ages 11–15: | ★★ |
| Ages 16–Adult: | ★★ |
| Senior Citizens: | ★★ |

In the center of Universal Studios Florida is an eight-acre, manmade lagoon that holds 13,850,000 gallons of water. Every evening, this lagoon is the stage of an awesome show featuring high-speed powerboats, jet skis, and other aquatic vehicles performing a stunt show that's accompanied by a flashy pyrotechnics demonstration (lots of explosions).

 **TRAVEL TIP**

If you don't want to see this show, while it's going on is an excellent time to experience some of the other popular attractions. If you choose to see this show, there are excellent viewing locations all around the perimeter of the lagoon. Some of the best spots to watch this show from are along the Embarcadero, in the Central Park area, or along Exposition Boulevard.

This show will appeal to guests of all ages and offers some pretty incredible and rather dangerous stunts. Dynamite Nights Stuntacular is presented once each evening (around 6:00 P.M.) during good weather conditions only.

## Lucy: A Tribute

| | |
|---|---|
| Ages 2–4: | N.S. |
| Ages 5–10: | N.S. |
| Ages 11–15: | ★ |
| Ages 16–Adult: | ★★ |
| Senior Citizens: | ★★ |

Location within the park: **Hollywood**

This museumlike exhibit offers a salute to Lucy. It will appeal to fans of the *I Love Lucy* sitcom. This self-paced, walk-through exhibit features a handful of interactive displays, TV show clips, props from *I Love Lucy,* and other memorabilia.

## Gory, Gruesome & Grotesque Horror Make-Up Show

| | |
|---|---|
| Ages 2–4: | N.S. |
| Ages 5–10: | N.S. |
| Ages 11–15: | ★★ |
| Ages 16–Adult: | ★★ |
| Senior Citizens: | ★★ |

Location within the park: **Hollywood**

Do you like scary movies? Watch a live demonstration of how an actor is transformed into a monster using makeup and special effects. A scene from *An American Werewolf in London* is used in this demonstration.

## ⊕ HOT SPOT

Stage 54 is a soundstage that houses actual props, sets, and memorabilia from a popular (current) motion picture. The interactive exhibit changes every few months, but it offers an up close and behind-the-scenes look at how a movie is made. This is a self-paced walking tour of a soundstage (a large, indoor building where movies are actually filmed).

Also, discover how decapitations, severed limbs, bullet holes, stab wounds, and other special effects are incorporated into TV shows and movies. This show is both entertaining and educational (especially if you're a horror movie buff).

The show takes place in an air-conditioned theater and utilizes special fog effects. The Gory, Gruesome & Grotesque Horror Make-Up Show is not suitable for kids under the age of thirteen.

## Terminator 2: 3-D

| | |
|---|---|
| Ages 2–4: | N.S. |
| Ages 5–10: | ★★ |
| Ages 11–15: | ★★★ |
| Ages 16–Adult: | ★★★ |
| Senior Citizens: | ★★★ |

Location within the park: **Hollywood**

You can experience every single ride, show, and attraction at The Magic Kingdom, Epcot, The Disney-MGM Studios, Universal Studios Florida, and at every other theme park and tourist attraction in the Orlando area, but you won't see anything as incredible as Terminator 2: 3-D . . . it's that good! This 3-D movie/attraction cost over $60 million to produce, and reunited Arnold Schwarzenegger, Linda Hamilton, Edward Furlong, and director James Cameron in a truly spectacular twelve-minute-and-forty-one-second film that's presented in 3-D.

This attraction is much more than simply a 3-D movie. The theater in which it is presented was custom built just for this presentation, and the entire theater becomes part of the show. Three 23-foot-high by 50-foot-wide movie screens are used to project the 3-D movie, while lasers, smoke, robots, special effects, and moving seats in the theater itself all add to the overall experience. Live actors (stunt doubles) literally go from the stage and leap into the movie screens using effects never used before in a theme park attraction. The story itself takes audience members from the present to the year 2029.

Whatever you do, don't leave Universal Studios Florida without experiencing Terminator 2: 3-D, no matter how long the wait is. Young children might find this movie a bit scary. This show/3-D movie is equivalent to a rated PG-13 movie that you'd see in a regular theater in terms of suitability for kids.

☞ This is a must-see attraction.

## The Wild, Wild, Wild West Stunt Show

| | |
|---|---|
| Ages 2–4: | N.S. |
| Ages 5–10: | ★★ |
| Ages 11–15: | ★★ |
| Ages 16–Adult: | ★★ |
| Senior Citizens: | ★★ |

Location within the park: **San Francisco/Amity**

Hollywood stuntpeople put on Western costumes and demonstrate how fight scenes and stunts are choreographed for television shows and movies. These scenes, of course, look totally real, but nobody gets hurt. This show is suitable for all ages and combines comedy with high-action stunts. The Wild, Wild, Wild West Stunt Show is presented at specific times throughout the day.

## Twister . . . Ride It Out

| | |
|---|---|
| Ages 2–4: | N.S. |
| Ages 5–10: | ★★★ |
| Ages 11–15: | ★★★ |
| Ages 16–Adult: | ★★★ |
| Senior Citizens: | ★★★ |

Location within the park: **New York**

The blockbuster movie *Twister* has been developed into another stunning special-effects-intensive attraction at Universal Studios Florida that's almost as awesome as Back to the Future . . . the Ride and Terminator 2: 3-D. You'll actually experience a real-life twister from only 20 feet away and see firsthand how incredibly treacherous a tornado can be. In this case, a five-story-tall tornado is created inside this 25,000-square-foot attraction.

## ≡FAST FACT

This attraction blasts wind in your face and sends cows flying through the air, and to add to the realism, 150,000 gallons of recycled water are used as part of this attraction each day.

While a real tornado is actually created, guests remain totally safe as they watch this awe-inspiring spectacle. You'll see the tornado consume everything in its path, shatter windows, lift up and hurl life-size trucks, crush enormous signs, and ultimately burst into a massive funnel of fire. Like Earthquake and Jaws, this attraction is highly realistic and might be too scary for young people (under the age of six). For teens and adults, however, it shouldn't be missed and is well worth the wait! This attraction will blow your mind, and might get you a little wet (but not drenched). The preshow features actors from the movie *Twister* but is a bit dull.

👍 This is a must-see attraction.

## Universal Studios Florida . . . Take 4!

Along with the rides and shows, there are also plenty of interactive entertainment opportunities available throughout this theme park. There's an additional charge to participate in some of these activities. These attractions aren't anywhere near as entertaining or exciting as the rides and shows, but if you have some free time, they're worth checking out.

**Amity Pitch & Skill Games**—Play an assortment of carnival-like games that require both skill and luck. These games can be found near the entrance of the Jaws ride. The cost to participate is $1 per try. Prizes are awarded to winners.

**AT&T at the Movies**—Learn about the history and future of moviemaking from this interactive attraction.

**Caricature Artist**—Located at kiosks throughout the theme park are artists who will create caricatures of guests while they wait. There is a charge to take home this personalized souvenir.

**Sega's Coney Island Arcade**—Check out some of the hottest new arcade games here. Just like in any arcade, be prepared to pay for each game you want to play.

**Sega's Space Station Arcade**—This is a second arcade located in the Universal Studios Florida park.

### Nickelodeon Studios Florida

Location within the park: **Production Central**

The most popular cable network for kids, Nickelodeon, has a full production facility located in the heart of Universal Studios Florida. Special forty-five-minute, kid-oriented guided tours of this studio complex are given throughout the day. Kids get a chance to see some of their favorite Nickelodeon shows in production.

At the entrance to this studio area is a 17-foot green slime geyser (instead of a fountain). The Nickelodeon Studios Tour is included in the general admission price to Universal Studios Florida. In addition to seeing the sets of popular Nickelodeon shows (and maybe even having the opportunity to see actors and actresses from those shows), free tickets for kids to be in the audience during show tapings are often available. To find out if any shows will be in production during your visit, call ☎ (407) 363-8586.

Kids of all ages will enjoy this fun-filled and informative tour of Nickelodeon Studios, which includes a stop at the gack kitchen, where guests learn how green slime is created. Special Nickelodeon merchandise is sold near the exit of the Nickelodeon Studios. If you're traveling with kids, plan on spending at least two hours exploring the Nickelodeon Studios, experiencing the Game Lab, and taking the guided tour.

## ═FAST FACT

Throughout the year, Universal Studios Florida hosts a variety of theme-oriented special events including Mardi Gras (which runs for forty-four nights in early Spring) and the Halloween Horror Nights (which run throughout October).

## Meet the Characters

 At Universal Studios Florida, kids have the chance to meet some of their favorite animated idols, who roam around the park continuously and participate in special meet-and-greet sessions held at specific times and locations in the park throughout the day.

Some of the characters you're apt to meet at Universal Studios Florida include Boo Boo Bear, Yogi Bear, Scooby Doo, Fred Flintstone, Frankenstein, Harry Henderson, George Jetson, Fievel Mousekewitz, Rocky and Bullwinkle, Barney Rubble, Winnie Woodpecker, and Woody Woodpecker. Oh, and kids also get a chance to meet and greet that lovable purple dinosaur . . . Barney! As you explore Universal Studios, you'll also meet celebrity look-alikes ranging from Beetlejuice and Charlie Chaplin to Groucho Marx and Marilyn Monroe.

If you're traveling with kids, be sure to take photos of them meeting these characters and celebrity look-alikes. They'll make a perfect addition to your family photo album. You'll also want to bring along an autograph book so that your children can collect the autographs of the "celebrities" they meet. Autograph books are an inexpensive souvenir that kids really appreciate and look forward to taking home to show their friends.

# Dining Opportunities

 Whether you're looking for a quick bite or a full sitdown lunch or dinner, there are many dining opportunities available in the main Universal Studios Florida theme park area, plus plenty of other restaurants in the CityWalk area. Reservations are accepted at some of the Studios' full-service restaurants.

**Animal Crackers**—Hot dogs, chicken fingers, and smoked sausage hoagies are among the fast-food and snack options served here.

**Beverly Hills Boulangerie**—Sandwiches, pastries, and cappuccino are among the popular menu selections. Counter service and nearby tables are offered.

**Boardwalk Funnel Cake Co.**—Funnel cakes and soft drinks make up the menu here.

**Brody's Ice Cream Shop**—Ice cream, sundaes, and floats are the dessert and snack items you can purchase and enjoy on a hot day.

**Café LaBamba**—Rotisserie chicken, burgers, sandwiches, and BBQ ribs are the popular entrees served. Counter service and nearby seating are offered.

**Captain Quint's Seafood and Chowder House Restaurant**—Enjoy a fresh selection of coastal seafood and chowder.

**Chez Alcatraz**—Hot dogs, shrimp cocktail, clam chowder, and sandwiches are served. Counter service and nearby seating are offered.

**Finnegan's Bar & Grill**—This is a full-service restaurant that serves traditional Irish-American food and beverages. Live entertainment and a fully equipped bar are provided for your pleasure. During mealtimes, be prepared to wait for a table.

**The Fudge Shop**—The name says it all. Homemade fudge is created daily.

**International Food Bazaar**—Everything from pizza to fried chicken, tacos, burgers, sweet-and-sour chicken, and a wide range of desserts is offered. Counter service with nearby seating is offered.

**Lombard's Landing**—At this full-service restaurant, you'll find seafood dishes like fresh lobster, as well as steak, pasta, and sandwiches. During lunch and dinner periods, expect to wait for a table.

**Louie's Italian Restaurant**—Pizza, pasta, Italian desserts, and a full espresso bar are offered. Counter service and nearby tables are provided.

**Mel's Drive-In**—This 1950s diner offers burgers, fries, shakes, and other popular diner entrees. Limited indoor table service is offered.

While you eat, you'll be entertained by a disc jockey who plays popular 1950s and 1960s music. Outside seating is more readily available. This is one of the better mid-priced eating places within the park.

**Midway Grill**—Sausage hoagies, Philly cheese steaks, and beer are served.

**Schwab's Pharmacy**—In addition to ice cream, the specialty at this eating establishment is hand-carved turkey and ham sandwiches that are really tasty. Limited table service is available.

**Universal Studios Classic Monster Café**—Salads, pizza, and other lunch items are served.

# Shopping

 Now that you've gotten a behind-the-scenes look at how movies and T.V. shows are made and you've had a chance to "Ride the Movies," you'll probably want to take home a few souvenirs from your trip to Universal Studios Florida. There are dozens of stores, gift shops, and souvenir kiosks located in the main theme park area.

# Special Events

 Throughout the year, Universal Studios Florida hosts popular themed events. For example, during the month of October, at night Universal Studios Florida hosts Halloween Horror Nights (targeted primarily to teenagers). On July 4th and New Year's Eve, Universal Studios Florida presents a gala fireworks spectacular, combining pyrotechnics with lasers and synchronized music. Every spring (early February through late March), there's also a Mardi Gras celebration, and for the Christmas holidays, you can expect to see the park decked out with festive décor.

# Universal Escape's Islands of Adventure

THE ISLANDS OF ADVENTURE THEME PARK offers traditional amusement park thrill rides, spread out over a series of themed areas. These themes encompass every aspect of the park, from the rides, shows, and attractions to the architecture, the landscaping, and the music you'll hear in the background. The result is a truly immersive adventure.

## Park Overview

 Islands of Adventure is a 100-acre park designed to be a theme park for the new millennium. Many of the rides and attractions are truly state-of-the-art and offer full entertainment experiences, not just basic rides. For example, even the roller coasters have a story line.

When visiting Islands of Adventure, be prepared for a full day (and evening) of walking, so wear comfortable shoes. If you want to experience the rides that involve getting wet, seriously consider bringing along a change of clothes and storing it in a locker. Ride all of the water-based rides in a row and then change into dry clothes before continuing your day.

For more information about **Islands of Adventure,** be sure to check out the park's Web site at *www.uescape.com* or

🖉 *www.universalstudios.com* before you leave home. You can also make reservations and purchase admission tickets online in order to save time once you arrive at the park.

## Layout of the Park

From the Port of Entry, which is the main entrance to Islands of Adventure (accessed by walking through CityWalk), all of the themed islands surround a large lake. Moving counterclockwise, first as you enter into the park is Seuss Landing, a 10-acre area designed specifically for young people (and those who are young at heart). The Lost Continent is the next island of adventure and features rides, shows, and attractions for teens and adults alike.

As guests continue their island-hopping adventure, Jurassic Park is next. Based on the movies, this area features the Jurassic Park River Adventure along with an assortment of other dinosaur-themed rides and attractions suitable for people of all ages. Comic strips come alive within Toon Lagoon, where characters like Popeye, Dudley Do-Right, and Beetle Bailey are the basis for a handful of whimsical rides, shows, and attractions.

Finally, for comic-book fans of all ages, Marvel Super Hero Island is where you'll find two of the park's most popular thrill rides, The Incredible Hulk Coaster and Doctor Doom's Fearfall.

## 🧳 TRAVEL TIP

To avoid the longest lines, the best times to visit Islands of Adventure are during the winter (January through March), the month of May, or in the fall (September through mid-December). These periods offer the mildest weather and allow you to avoid peak tourist traffic.

By combing thrill rides with family-oriented entertainment, shops, restaurants, and attractions, Islands of Adventure offers something for everyone in a not-so-traditional theme park atmosphere that rivals anything The Walt Disney World Resort has to offer. Whether you're traveling alone, with fellow adults, or with a family, plan on spending at least one full day exploring Islands of Adventure.

# The Rating System

Not all of the rides, shows, and attractions at Islands of Adventure are suitable or designed for everyone. To help you choose which rides and attractions are most worth seeing during your visit to Islands of Adventure, this book offers star-based ratings for each ride and attraction, based on the age group each will most appeal to. Each ride and attraction has earned between one and three stars.

★ = Rides and attractions that earned just one star aren't worth waiting for and could be skipped, especially if your time within the theme park is limited.

★★ = Rides and attractions that earned two stars are good, but they don't fall into the "must-see" category.

★★★ = The rides and attractions that earned three stars are definitely worth seeing and should not be missed.

N.S. = This denotes rides and attractions that are "Not Suitable" for a specific age group.

## Restrictions

Islands of Adventure contains multiple adult-oriented thrill rides, plus separate rides and attractions designed specifically for young kids. Certain rides and attractions have height restrictions. For example, people under 54 inches tall are not permitted to ride Dueling Dragons or The Incredible Hulk Coaster. Those under 52 inches tall cannot ride Doctor Doom's Fearfall, and those under 48 inches tall won't be allowed to experience Popeye and Bluto's Bilge-Rat Barges. Visitors must be over 42 inches tall to experience Dudley Do-Right's Ripsaw Falls and over 40 inches tall to experience Jurassic Park River Ride and the Amazing Adventures of Spider-Man. Finally, children must be at least 36 inches tall to ride the Pteranodon Flyers.

Due to the turbulent nature of the above-mentioned rides, expectant mothers and people with certain physical disabilities or limitations should not experience these rides either. For additional information about special accommodations for people with physical disabilities, contact the Guest Services office located near the main entrance of the park.

## ≡FAST FACT

The hours of operation for Universal Escape's Islands of Adventure vary by season. The park typically opens at 9:00 A.M. and remains upon until between 6:00 P.M. and 8:00 P.M. For the hours of operation during your planned visit, call (800) 711-0080.

## Port of Entry

 Upon passing through CityWalk, you'll find yourself at Port of Entry, the main entrance to Islands of Adventure. This area contains a handful of shops, a package pickup station, plus a few snack areas. Port of Entry is an ideal meeting spot if you and the people you're traveling with happen to become separated. In the Port of Entry, you'll also find rest rooms, lockers, ATMs, public telephones, the lost and found, and Guest Services. Stroller and wheelchair rentals are also available.

### Shopping

The shops you'll find in the Port of Entry area include:

**De Foto's Expedition Photography**—Film, camera supplies, batteries, and anything else you'll need to take vacation pictures can be found here. As you enter into Islands of Adventure, professional photographers will be on hand, snapping pictures and welcoming guests. If you choose to purchase the picture taken of you (or the people you're traveling with), you can pick it up at this location.

**Island Market and Export**—Candy, gourmet foods, and gift baskets are among the edible offerings sold.

**Ocean Trader Market**—Carver and loom artists sell their crafts.

**Port Provisions**—T-shirts, caps, rain ponchos, and souvenirs are sold.

**Silk Road Clothiers**—Travel wear, leather bags, jewelry, gifts, and souvenirs are sold at this shop. Any of your purchases made within the park can also be delivered to this location (near the entrance/exit of Islands of Adventure).

 **TRAVEL TIP**

Once you've explored some of the shops, it's time to travel toward the various islands. You'll probably want to travel to the right if you're with young kids, or to the left if you're traveling with teens and/or adults. You can also climb aboard the Island Skipper Tour boat and experience a sea voyage that takes you directly to Jurassic Park.

## Dining

**Confisco Grille** (and **Backwater Bar**) is a full-service restaurant featuring personal pizzas, pasta, fresh seafood, grilled meats, specialty burgers, and fresh desserts. Reservations are accepted. Get autographs and photos with some of your favorite Universal Escape's Islands of Adventure characters during the **Confisco Grille Character Lunch.** There's no extra charge—just the normal cost of your menu selections. The **Confisco Grille** is open every Monday through Friday from noon until 2:00 A.M.

Other dining options within the Port of Entry area include: **Arctic Express** (featuring fruit-topped funnel cakes, Belgian waffles, waffle-cone sundaes), **Croissant Moon Baker** (fresh-baked pastries and desserts, coffee, cappuccino, espresso, latte, beer, wine, and soda), and **Spice Island Sausages** (grilled Italian sausage sandwiches, jumbo hot dogs, corn dogs, fresh-cut french fries, beer, wine, and soda).

## Seuss Landing

 For kids (and those who are young at heart), there's Seuss Landing. This colorful area offers rides, shows, and attractions based on some of Dr. Seuss's famous and beloved characters and children's books. This entire area is designed to make visitors feel as if they've stepped into the pages of a Dr. Seuss story. All of the buildings and surroundings are painted in pastel colors.

Costumed characters taken from the pages of Dr. Seuss's popular books can be seen roaming around this area of the park and are available for pictures and autographs. Weather permitting, there's also the *Seuss Street Show,* a live music show presented several times daily. This show is suitable for young children, ages twelve and under. Shows typically begin midmorning and continue every hour or two throughout the afternoon. For exact show times, refer to the free *Adventure Guide* given to all visitors entering the park.

## ⊕ HOT SPOT

The Green Eggs & Ham Café serves an array of meal and snack items, but the specialty of the house is green eggs and ham. This is a fun place for a family with young children to eat breakfast, lunch, or an early dinner. It's also ideal for a midday snack. Hamburgers and chicken fingers are among the other main entrees available.

## Caro-Seuss-el

| | |
|---|---|
| Ages 2–4: | ★★★ |
| Ages 5–10: | ★★★ |
| Ages 11–15: | ★★ |
| Ages 16–Adult: | ★★ |
| Senior Citizens: | ★★ |

This is no ordinary merry-go-round. It features the colors, characters, and music that Dr. Seuss made famous. Ride around in circles on the back of a popular character. Some of the characters move up and down, while other are stationary on the turning merry-go-round.

## The Once-Ler's House

This interactive area comes straight from the pages of one of Dr. Seuss's popular stories. Listen on the Whisper-ma-phone as the Once-Ler tells you the story of the Lorax. Guests can also stand on the stone podium where, by the seat of his pants, the Lorax lifted himself through a hole in the clouds.

## One Fish, Two Fish, Red Fish, Blue Fish

| | |
|---|---|
| Ages 2–4: | ★★★ |
| Ages 5–10: | ★★★ |
| Ages 11–15: | ★★ |
| Ages 16–Adult: | ★ |
| Senior Citizens: | ★ |

Steer your flying fish up, down, around and around as you avoid shooting water. This ride has its own catchy theme song that will certainly put even the most serious adults in a lighthearted, childish mood. If you're traveling with young kids, this is one ride that shouldn't be missed. Riders can fly 15 feet into the air as they travel in the Seussian fish vehicle. Topping off the center pedestal of the rise is an 18-foot-tall sculpture of the star-belly fish featured in the Dr. Seuss book *One Fish Two Fish Red Fish Blue Fish*.

👍 This is a must-see attraction.

### The Cat in the Hat

| | |
|---|---|
| Ages 2–4: | ★★★ |
| Ages 5–10: | ★★★ |
| Ages 11–15: | ★★★ |
| Ages 16–Adult: | ★★★ |
| Senior Citizens: | ★★★ |

Thanks to Animatronics, the pages of Dr. Seuss's most famous book, *The Cat in the Hat*, come to life. Visitors ride in moving vehicles that take them through scenes lifted directly from the storybook. The scenes, however, are depicted in 3-D using life-size characters and colorful sets. This ride is lighthearted and recommended for people of all ages. Although it's not a thrill ride, it's definitely one of the most impressive, original, and imaginative attractions within Islands of Adventure.

 This is a must-see attraction.

## 🌐 HOT SPOT

For a more elaborate, sit-down meal in a theme-oriented dining area, kids will enjoy chowing down on fried chicken, lasagna, spaghetti, and pizza at Circus McGurkus Café Stoopendous. Special kids' meals are available.

### If I Ran the Zoo

| | |
|---|---|
| Ages 2–4: | ★★ |
| Ages 5–10: | ★★★ |
| Ages 11–15: | ★★ |
| Ages 16–Adult: | N.S. |
| Senior Citizens: | N.S. |

This is an interactive play area that tells the story of Gerald McGrew and his quest to create a totally different zoo of strange and unusual animals. This attraction is divided into three distinct areas: Hedges, Water, and New Zoo.

 This is a must-see attraction.

### Shopping with Seuss

The shops within Seuss Landing include:

- **Cats, Hats & Things**—All kinds of clothing, gifts, and toys based on *The Cat in the Hat* can be purchased here. As you exit The Cat in the Hat ride, you'll find yourself within this colorful shop.
- **Dr. Seuss's All the Books You Can Read**—This bookshop offers a complete library of Dr. Seuss books, videocassettes, CDs, and computer software.
- **Mulberry Street Store**—Merchandise featuring all of your favorite Dr. Seuss characters can be found here.
- **Picture This!**—Purchase a unique photo of yourself (or your children) within the pages of a popular Dr. Seuss story.
- **Snookers & Snookers Sweet Candy Cookers**—A large selection of candy will satisfy your sweet tooth, while the gifts sold here make excellent souvenirs.

## ⊕ HOT SPOT

At the Hop on Pop food kiosk, guests can create their own sundae on a stick. Banana splits and ice cream served in waffle cones are also available. If you're really thirsty and don't want soda, check out Moose Juice Goose Juice, a drink kiosk that serves juices, fruit cups, and other beverages.

# The Lost Continent

 This area of Islands of Adventure houses one of the most thrilling roller coasters in Orlando—the Dueling Dragons. Out of all the areas within Islands of Adventure, the Lost Continent is the smallest. It'll appeal mainly to people in their teen or early-adult years looking for the thrill of a roller-coaster ride they won't soon forget.

## Poseidon's Fury: Escape from the Lost City

| | |
|---|---|
| Ages 2–4: | ★ |
| Ages 5–10: | ★ |
| Ages 11–15: | ★★ |
| Ages 16–Adult: | ★★ |
| Senior Citizens: | ★★ |

Explore the relics of a once-glorious civilization as you tour the ruins of a mysterious lost city. This city isn't totally dead, however. After eons, something may have survived. You'll find out what when Poseidon himself opens a portal to the underseas through a 42-foot swirling vortex of water. This is the gateway to Atlantis! During your adventure, Zeus suddenly appears and challenges Poseidon on your behalf. Watch out, or you could get caught in the deadly battle between the gods!

## Dueling Dragons

| | |
|---|---|
| Ages 2–4: | N.S. |
| Ages 5–10: | N.S. |
| Ages 11–15: | ★★★ |
| Ages 16–Adult: | ★★★ |
| Senior Citizens: | N.S. |

You'll soar up to 125 feet in the air and travel at speeds of 55 miles per hour on one of two distinct, yet simultaneously running tracks that put you perilously close to collision. At one point, the two tracks bring riders within a foot of each other. No matter which track you experience, this is an inverted coaster, so your legs will be dangling freely.

## ≡FAST FACT

According to the coaster's designers, the tracks of Dueling Dragons feature one Immelmann, a 70-degree inclined loop, two vertical loops, one cobra roll, one 45-degree inclined loop, one "zero g" roll, a flat spin, and two interlocked flat rolls. This is the world's first inverted dueling coaster.

Dueling Dragons is a thrill ride in every sense of the term, so if you don't like high-speed and turbulent roller coasters, you'd best skip it. Since this is one of the most popular attractions within the park, expect a long line. It's best to check this coaster out first thing in the morning or during peak mealtimes. The coaster has a capacity of 3,264 riders per hour, so while the line may seem long, it moves constantly. It's a favorite among thrill seekers!

👍 This is a must-see attraction.

## The Eighth Voyage of Sindbad

| Ages 2–4: | N.S. |
|---|---|
| Ages 5–10: | ★ |
| Ages 11–15: | ★★ |
| Ages 16–Adult: | ★★ |
| Senior Citizens: | ★★ |

This is a live-action stunt show presented several times throughout each day, typically every two hours in the afternoon. During peak vacation times, the show is presented more frequently. Check the *Adventure Guide* (available free of charge at the ticket window) for exact show times. The show itself features fifty pyrotechnic effects, including a 10-foot-tall circle of flames.

## The Flying Unicorn

| Ages 2–4: | N.S. |
|---|---|
| Ages 5–10: | ★★★ |
| Ages 11–15: | ★★★ |
| Ages 16–Adult: | ★ |
| Senior Citizens: | ★ |

This nonthrill ride offers a gentle, yet exciting ride through an enchanted forest. The ride simulates flying on a unicorn and is cute and rather kid-oriented.

## Dine with the Gods

Within the Lost Continent, you'll find several places to grab a bite to eat. Several of these places offer indoor seating, which provides an excellent opportunity to get out of the sun, sit down, and take a break.

**The Enchanted Oak Tavern (and Alchemy Bar)**—Within this "buffeteria," hickory-smoked barbecue chicken and ribs, roasted corn on the cob, chicken salad, kids' meals, and soda are served. The adjoining bar features fifty brands of bottled beers.

**Fire-Eater's Grill**—Sausages are served in a roll or on a stick. Grab an order of fresh fries to round out the meal. Soda, beer, and wine are also served.

**Frozen Desert**—Soft-serve ice cream and sundaes are guaranteed to cool you down on a hot day. Fresh fruit cups, cookies, and an assortment of candy items are also available.

**Mythos Restaurant**—This is a full-service restaurant. Menu items include appetizers, fresh seafood, grilled meats, entree salads, gourmet wood-oven pizzas, pasta, and desserts. There's also a full bar and an extensive wine menu. Reservations are accepted.

**Oasis Coolers**—If you're in the mood for a snack or refreshing drink while on the go, check out this food kiosk for lemonade, soda, nachos, pretzels, and fruit cups.

# ≡FAST FACT

If you return home and wish you had purchased an item you saw at any of the shops within Islands of Adventure, you can order merchandise by phone. Call ☎ (800) 354-8157.

## Shopping for Treasures

Souvenirs are plentiful within the Lost Continent. Here's a sampling of what treasures you'll encounter:

**The Coin Mint**—Choose from one of several dozen designs and watch as your selected design gets minted on a metal coin right before your eyes. This is a personalized and rather unique souvenir you can actually watch being made.

**The Dragon's Keep**—If you survive the coaster, you might want to pick up a Dueling Dragons T-shirt or souvenir. Dragons are the theme behind the merchandise sold.

**Garlands**—Handmade silk garlands and satin garters will make any woman feel like a princess.

**Metal Smith**—Bronze and copper items are available. There's also a selection of handcrafted pottery.

**Shop of Wonders**—Silks, copper, brass, woven rugs, travel bags, leather, and cotton goods are among the offerings at this shop. There's also an extensive jewelry selection.

**Treasures of Poseidon**—Themed merchandise from the Poseidon's Fury: Escape from the Lost City attraction is sold.

## ⊕ HOT SPOT

If you want to know what your future holds, visit with the psychic who's on duty within the Shop of Wonders area.

# Jurassic Park

 Steven Spielberg's motion pictures come to life within this area of Islands of Adventure. If you thought dinosaurs were extinct, think again! This area offers activities and attractions for young kids, and more thrill-oriented rides for teens and adults—all with a dinosaur theme. The state-of-the-art Animatronic creatures look and act extremely real, which adds to the overall ambiance of this area. This is the largest of the areas within the Islands of Adventure theme park.

## Camp Jurassic

| | |
|---|---|
| Ages 2–4: | ★ |
| Ages 5–10: | ★★★ |
| Ages 11–15: | ★★★ |
| Ages 16–Adult: | N.S. |
| Senior Citizens: | N.S. |

Kids can make their way through this prehistoric playground/maze that offers volcanoes and cascading water-falls. The play area is filled with secret caves and an amber mine to explore. Visitors can also climb along dinosaur capture-nets, ride down slides, and cross suspension bridges. This play area is a self-paced attraction for kids only. Parents can watch from nearby, but will be too large to fit in some parts of this play area.

As a parent, if you're looking to rest your feet, let your kids roam freely in this area while you park yourself at a nearby bench and act as a spectator. Needless to say, never leave your child unattended within this or any other area of a theme park.

## Pteranodon Flyers

| | |
|---|---|
| Ages 2–4: | N.S. |
| Ages 5–10: | ★★ |
| Ages 11–15: | ★★ |
| Ages 16–Adult: | ★ |
| Senior Citizens: | ★ |

Riders will feel like they've been grabbed by a flying pteranodon as they soar through the air and take an all-too-quick tour of the Jurassic Park area. This ride is most suitable for kids.

 TRAVEL TIP

While kids will enjoy this swing ride around Jurassic Park, the wait is typically extremely long, but the ride itself is rather short. Unless you happen to be visiting Jurassic Park on an unusually quiet day, you probably don't want to spend too much time waiting to experience this ride. Adults traveling without kids will most likely want to skip it.

## Jurassic Park River Adventure

| | |
|---|---|
| Ages 2–4: | N.S. |
| Ages 5–10: | ★ |
| Ages 11–15: | ★★★ |
| Ages 16–Adult: | ★★★ |
| Senior Citizens: | ★ |

Pass through the grand gates of this prehistoric theme park (just like in the movie) and travel within a riverboat as you see firsthand the scientific marvels that brought dinosaurs back to roam the earth.

While the initial part of your river journey will be quiet, peaceful, and rather beautiful, just like in the movie, things don't always go as planned. In fact, you'll soon discover deadly 'raptors and venomous spitters that don't appreciate you visiting their territory. As if that weren't bad enough, a raging T-Rex has gotten loose, and this creature is hungry.

Just when you think you're safe, grab onto your personal belongings and prepare for an 85-foot plunge into total darkness for the conclusion of your adventure. This exciting and somewhat scary ride ultimately ends with a splash, so be prepared to get wet. (Also, be sure to protect your valuables, such as cameras and camcorders, from the water.)

 This is a must-see attraction.

## ═FAST FACT

Over 1.5 million gallons of water are used to create this manmade river ride that ends with a splash!

## Jurassic Park Discovery Center

| | |
|---|---|
| Ages 2–4: | N.S. |
| Ages 5–10: | ★★ |
| Ages 11–15: | ★★ |
| Ages 16–Adult: | ★★ |
| Senior Citizens: | ★★ |

Within the hands-on interactive exhibits and displays that make up this attraction, you can examine the massive fossilized remains of a T-Rex. Visitors can also join the activity in the nursery, where you might see a velociraptor hatching from its egg. Taken from the movie, visitors along this self-paced walking tour can see how dinosaurs were brought back to life and how they're being raised within Jurassic Park.

## Triceratops Encounter

| | |
|---|---|
| Ages 2–4: | N.S. |
| Ages 5–10: | ★★★ |
| Ages 11–15: | ★★★ |
| Ages 16–Adult: | ★★ |
| Senior Citizens: | ★★ |

Thanks to the latest in Audio-Animatronic technology, an extremely lifelike (not to mention life-size) triceratops is part of this unique interactive attraction. This 24-foot-long and 10-foot-tall beast is friendly and outgoing. As guests visit, this creature will snort, blink, flinch, and even make sounds. Visitors are allowed to pet the triceratops and take pictures. (If this creature were really alive, it would weigh more than two full-size elephants.)

 **TRAVEL TIP**

While Triceratops Encounter is somewhat entertaining, if you're pressed for time or there's a long wait, skip it in favor of the more popular and exciting rides and attractions that Islands of Adventure has to offer.

## Dining with the Dinos

If encountering dinosaurs makes you hungry, there are several snack shops and dining areas within Jurassic Park that will help you quench your hunger or thirst.

**The Burger Digs**—The name says it all. Burgers and chicken sandwiches are among this dining area's primary offerings.

**Pizza Predattoria**—Personal pan pizzas, sandwiches, salads, dessert items, along with soda, beer, and wine are served.

**Thunder Falls Terrace**—Rotisserie chicken, baby back ribs, beef kabobs, and roasted corn are among the entrees available.

**The Watering Hole**—For adult visitors, an assortment of alcoholic beverages is served, including coolers, margaritas, and rum runners.

### Bring Home a Dino-Size Souvenir

Dinosaurs don't make the best pets, but you can pick up a wide range of dinosaur-themed gifts and souvenirs at these shops located within Jurassic Park:

**Camp Jurassic Outpost**—Youth survival gear and Jurassic Park–themed merchandise are among the offerings.

**Dinostore**—If it has to do with dinos, you'll find it here. Toys, books, plush toys, and plenty of educational (and not so educational) souvenirs are available—all with a dinosaur theme.

**Jurassic Outfitters**—After experiencing Jurassic Park River Adventure, you can see the look on your own face (and take it home with you) because your photo gets taken as you experience that massive drop at the end of the ride. This personalized souvenir is available for purchase at this shop. Here, you'll also find a wide range of Jurassic Park and Islands of Adventure souvenirs.

# Toon Lagoon

 Take your favorite comic strip characters, add some water, and you have the makings of some lighthearted fun that's suitable for the entire family. All of the rides in this area are family-oriented and aren't really considered thrill rides (with the possible exception of Dudley Do-Right's Ripsaw Falls, which ends in a mighty splash).

Keep in mind, many of the rides and attractions within Toon Lagoon are water-based, so be prepared to get wet (and possibly soaked).

## Dudley Do-Right's Ripsaw Falls

| | |
|---|---|
| Ages 2–4: | N.S. |
| Ages 5–10: | ★★ |
| Ages 11–15: | ★★★ |
| Ages 16–Adult: | ★★★ |
| Senior Citizens: | ★ |

Based on *Rocky and Bullwinkle*, the popular cartoon from the 1960s, guests who experience this water-flume ride embark on a wild and wet adventure around a 400,000 gallon lagoon. This ride ends with a major splash, so be prepared to get wet. Also, be sure to protect your camera, camcorder, and other valuables from the water when you experience this ride.

## ⊕ HOT SPOT

On the bridge that overlooks Dudley Do-Right's Ripsaw Falls, passersby have a chance to squirt water at those brave enough to experience this water flume firsthand.

## Popeye & Bluto's Bilge-Rat Barges

| | |
|---|---|
| Ages 2–4: | N.S. |
| Ages 5–10: | ★★★ |
| Ages 11–15: | ★★★ |
| Ages 16–Adult: | ★★★ |
| Senior Citizens: | ★★ |

This wet and wild water raft ride has its turbulent moments, but overall it's suitable for people of all ages who don't mind getting wet. Twelve people at a time ride in specially designed rafts that travel along the manmade river at about 16 feet per second. If you're carrying valuables or other items you want to keep dry, consider putting them in lockers or within the center (watertight) compartment of the raft before the ride begins.

While this is a fun-filled and rather exciting ride, if the weather is chilly or you don't want to get drenched, consider skipping this attraction. It does, however, offer an awesome way to cool off on a hot and sunny day. As if the water along the ride weren't enough, people on land (exploring Popeye's boat) have a chance to squirt water at those aboard the rafts.

## Me Ship, The Olive

| | |
|---|---|
| Ages 2–4: | N.S. |
| Ages 5–10: | ★★★ |
| Ages 11–15: | ★★★ |
| Ages 16–Adult: | ★ |
| Senior Citizens: | N.S. |

Popeye the Sailor Man invites guests (primarily younger ones) to climb aboard his three-story boat and partake in a fun-filled exploration. From bow to stern, the boat is loaded with interactive activities and things to do. There are water cannons to shoot, whistles to blow, organs to play, bells to clang, and plenty of things to crawl and climb through. If you're traveling with kids, this will be a fun-filled stop. For adults traveling alone, keep on trekking.

## Pandemonium Cartoon Circus

Within this amphitheater, live shows and special events are held throughout the day. To find out what live shows are being presented during your visit, check the *Adventure Guide* booklet offered at all ticket windows.

##  TRAVEL TIP

Along the street that winds through Toon Lagoon, be on the lookout for comic strip captions hanging overhead. Find an appropriate message and have the person or people you're traveling with stand under these signs for a funny photo opportunity.

## Dine with Your Favorite Toons

Kick back, relax, read a comic strip, and have some food. The following are the dining options available within Toon Lagoon. If you're looking for a more formal, sit-down meal, consider one of the full-service restaurants located within CityWalk.

**Blondie's Home of the Dagwood**—This kitchen-style deli offers a 3-foot-long Dagwood sandwich, chicken noodle soup, jumbo smoked turkey sandwiches, kosher deli dogs, veggie sandwiches, kids' meals, chef salads, apple pie, soda, beer, and wine.

**Comic Strip Café**—This buffeteria offers American, Mexican, Italian, and Chinese fast food. Soda, beer, and wine are available for toon-loving adults.

**Cathy's Ice Cream**—Hot fudge sundaes, waffle-cone sundaes, and soda are what's served here. If you're looking for a cool snack, this is the place to visit.

**Wimpy's**—If you're looking for a place to break for lunch, Wimpy's offers charbroiled burgers and cheeseburgers, jumbo hot dogs, spinach salad, kids' meals, fries, onion rings, fresh fruit cups, soda, beer, and wine.

## ⊕ HOT SPOT

Located near the Pandemonium Cartoon Circus theater and the Comic Strip Café, you'll find public restrooms and public phones. Every island area within Islands of Adventure offers these amenities.

### Shopping in Toon Lagoon

For those who love reading the Sunday comics or have a special affinity for a specific comic strip character, chances are you'll find a souvenir at one of these shops located within Toon Lagoon:

**Gasoline Alley**—Comic strip and Islands of Adventure–themed souvenirs are sold here.

**Photo Funnies**—One-of-a-kind, personalized souvenirs are created while you wait. Photo Funnies allows guests to have their picture taken and then incorporated into a comic strip that costars some of their favorite characters.

**Toon Extra**—A selection of clothing, accessories, gifts, and souvenirs, all with a toon theme are sold here. You can also pick up personalized gifts and limited-edition collectibles featuring Betty Boop, Popeye, and Beetle Bailey. Some of these items will appeal more to adults and collectors than to kids.

**Toon Toys**—Nostalgic toys and novelty gifts from sipper straws to plush toys, costumes to candy, activity sets to stationery are what you'll find at this shop. Adults more than kids will find Toon Toys a fun place to visit.

**WossaMotta U**—Fans of Dudley Do-Right and Rocky and Bullwinkle will find a selection of merchandise including clothing, accessories, watches, backpacks, totes, activity sets, rubber stamps, glassware, and collectibles featuring these and other popular characters.

## Marvel Super Hero Island

 Rounding out Islands of Adventure is an area designed for teens, young adults, and Marvel comic book fans of all ages. This entire area focuses on characters and themes from Marvel comics, so don't be surprised if you run into the X-Men, Spider-Man, the Incredible Hulk, or other characters as you explore this area.

The main rides within Marvel Super Hero Island are considered thrill rides and aren't suitable for young kids or many senior citizens. If you're a comic book collector, you'll definitely want to check out some of the shops within this area and take a look at the collectibles offered.

## The Amazing Adventures of Spider-Man

| | |
|---|---|
| Ages 2–4: | N.S. |
| Ages 5–10: | ★★★ |
| Ages 11–15: | ★★★ |
| Ages 16–Adult: | ★★★ |
| Senior Citizens: | ★★★ |

The Amazing Adventures of Spider-Man combines moving vehicles with filmed 3-D action and special effects, resulting in a visually stunning attraction/ride that most visitors want to experience multiple times. Upon boarding, guests get a tour of the *Daily Bugle* (the newspaper where Peter Parker, a.k.a. Spider-Man, works). It's a typical day for Peter until he discovers that evil villains, including Doctor Octopus, are using an antigravity gun to steal the Statue of Liberty. This is where the action heats up. You, along with Spider-Man, experience an action-packed adventure worthy of any superhero.

 This is a must-see attraction.

## ══FAST FACT

While this ride is somewhat turbulent, most of the thrill-ride elements are created using visual special effects. This ride isn't suitable for toddlers, but everyone else will enjoy it. Expect a wait to experience this ride, but it's well worth it.

## Doctor Doom's Fearfall

| | |
|---|---|
| Ages 2–4: | N.S. |
| Ages 5–10: | N.S. |
| Ages 11–15: | ★★★ |
| Ages 16–Adult: | ★★★ |
| Senior Citizens: | N.S. |

What goes up, must come down. That's the premise behind this free-fall ride that takes guests up a 200-foot tower and then drops them.

 This is a must-see attraction.

## Incredible Hulk Coaster

| | |
|---|---|
| Ages 2–4: | N.S. |
| Ages 5–10: | N.S. |
| Ages 11–15: | ★★★ |
| Ages 16–Adult: | ★★★ |
| Senior Citizens: | N.S. |

Perhaps the most popular ride in all of the Islands of Adventure, this roller coaster allows riders to experience the same thrust as the pilot of a real-life U.S. Air Force F-16 fighter attack jet experiences. The ride starts with a blast (from zero to 40 miles per hour in less than two seconds) and continues with a series of loops, twists, turns, and flips. The ride lasts two minutes and fifteen seconds, but is one that won't soon be forgotten.

As with any thrill ride, this one isn't suitable for young children. Be prepared for a long wait because this ride is so popular, but if you're a roller-coaster fanatic, it's well worth the wait.

 This is a must-see attraction.

## ===FAST FACT

The Incredible Hulk Coaster features one cobra roll, one weightless roll, one 360-degree carousel, two loops, one inclined loop, one high-speed carousel, and two flat spins. According to the ride's designers, the track measures 3,800 feet in length and includes two subterranean enclosures, one under water and one under land.

## Storm Force Acceleration

| | |
|---|---|
| Ages 2–4: | N.S. |
| Ages 5–10: | ★ |
| Ages 11–15: | ★★★ |
| Ages 16–Adult: | ★★★ |
| Senior Citizens: | ★ |

If you thought the Mad Tea Party (Tea Cups) ride at The Magic Kingdom took you for a spin, just wait until you experience this faster-spinning thrill ride. Here, Storm faces Magneto in a ride that features sound and visual effects, plus a whole lot of spinning. It's certainly not for young kids or those who have just eaten.

## ⊕ HOT SPOT

A selection of the most popular video arcade games is offered at Kingpin's Arcade. Your admission ticket to Islands of Adventure does not include the cost of these arcade games.

## Recharge Your Super Powers

You don't have to be a superhero or a notorious villain trying to take over the world to work up an appetite. The following are your dining options within Marvel SuperHero Island:

**Café 4**—This Italian buffeteria's menu includes minestrone soup, Caesar salads, pizza by the slice, spaghetti, fettuccini, Italian hoagies, sausage sub sandwiches, kids' meals, desserts, soda, beer, wine, espresso, and cappuccino.

**Captain America Diner**—Charbroiled burgers and cheeseburgers, chicken sandwiches, kids' meals, onion rings, apple pie a la mode, shakes, and soda are among the offerings served.

**Chill**—Soft-serve ice cream, sundaes, and other treats are available.

**Cotton Candy**—Freshly made cotton candy, snacks, soda, and other items that will satisfy your sweet tooth are available.

**Freeze**—Snow cones, snacks, and soda are available from this kiosk located in the heart of Marvel Super Hero Island.

**Fruit**—Whole fruit, fresh fruit cups, snacks, and juice are served here and give health-conscious visitors an alternative to junk food when they're ready for a snack.

## Take the Comics Home with You

Marvel Super Hero Island offers the following shops. You can purchase a wide range of toys, comic books, clothing, and other themed merchandise based on Marvel comic book characters.

**Arcade News**—Here you'll find Dr. Doom merchandise, much of which isn't available anywhere else.

**Comics Shop**—As the name suggests, comic books and trading cards, plus other comic book–related items for the casual and serious collector, are available.

**Hulk Photo**—For those who experience the Incredible Hulk Coaster and don't think they'll remember the experience without a photo, personalized photos can be purchased near the ride's exit. (Photos of every rider are taken.)

**The Marvel Alterniverse Store**—Higher-priced collectibles, clothing, jewelry, and other items (all based on Marvel comics) are available at this shop.

**Spider-Man Shop**—Fans of this popular Marvel superhero will find toys, clothing, and other merchandise all based on Spider-Man.

# *Universal CityWalk*

BY DAY, CITYWALK CONTAINS AN ARRAY of themed, family-oriented dining and shopping experiences, while at night, this area transforms into an adult-oriented party scene, complete with restaurants, cafés, shops, nightclubs, movie theaters, bars, and plenty of live entertainment.

## An Overview of CityWalk

 Even if you've been to CityWalk at Universal Studios Hollywood, this CityWalk offers a very different nighttime entertainment experience, primarily targeted to adults. During the day, however, people of all ages are invited to experience one of several theme-oriented restaurants located within CityWalk, plus explore the unique shops within this area. During the days, street performers are often on hand (weather permitting), entertaining passersby. CityWalk is a 30-acre entertainment complex unto itself. After 6:00 P.M. there is no charge for parking.

Admission to CityWalk is free; however, there may be a cover or admission charge for the nightclubs and/or for special events. A separate admission is required to see a movie at the Universal Cineplex (a twenty-screen movie theater).

## ≡FAST FACT

For a flat fee of $7.95 per person, unlimited access to all of CityWalk's clubs and bars is available. For $11.95, admission to the clubs and bars is included, along with one Universal Cineplex movie ticket.

# The Restaurants

 The restaurants within CityWalk typically serve both lunch and dinner; however, many are open late and are ideal for late-night snacks or meals (after visiting a club or seeing a movie). If you're traveling with children or underaged teens, arrange for baby-sitting services at your hotel so that the adults you're traveling with can enjoy the nightlife offered at CityWalk.

### The Hard Rock Café

This is the world's largest Hard Rock Café. It offers seating for 2,200 people and often features live entertainment by top-name artists. Of course, this Hard Rock Café also offers an extensive rock memorabilia collection. The dining room is open from 11:00 A.M. to midnight daily. Don't forget to drop into the gift shop for official Hard Rock Café Orlando merchandise.

The Hard Rock Café Live arena offers seating for 2,500 and live entertainment nightly. There is a cover charge to see the Hard Rock Live house band. The ticket prices vary for national acts that perform at this venue (primarily on the weekends).

While dining, be sure to explore the multilevel dining room and check out the over 1,000 pieces of music memorabilia. For more information, visit the **Hard Rock Café Web site** at *www.hardrock.com*. For dining reservations at this or any CityWalk restaurant, call (407) 363-8000.

## Jimmy Buffett's Margaritaville

This is a family-oriented restaurant by day, but at night, adults will enjoy the three full-service bars. The menu offers a combination of Key West and Caribbean-style foods, known as Floribbean cuisine. Fruits, vegetables, and seafood are the various entrees' main ingredients. Open from 11:00 A.M. to 2:00 A.M. daily. There's a $3.25 cover charge after 10:00 P.M. Live musical performances begin at 10:00 P.M. For reservations and live entertainment information, call ☎ (407) 224-2155.

## Emeril's Restaurant Orlando

You've seen Emeril Lagasse on TV's Food Network as the host of *Emeril Live*. Now, this world-renowned chef has a permanent home in Orlando, where New Orleans Creole-based cuisine is served. The wine cellar houses over 12,000 selections. Lunch is served daily from 11:30 A.M. to 2:00 P.M. Dinner begins at 5:30 P.M. and is served until 10:00 P.M. (Sunday through Thursday) and until 11:00 P.M. (Fridays and Saturdays). Within the restaurant is a gift shop that sells Emeril's New Orleans Cooking and Louisiana Real & Rustic cookbooks, plus his own line of spices and plates.

The restaurant also houses a cigar bar containing a wall-sized humidor. The dining room seats 250 people. This restaurant will appeal mainly to adults.

 TRAVEL TIP

While the food is top-notch, the prices at this award-winning restaurant are rather steep. Due to the restaurant's popularity (and Emeril's huge fan base), reservations are an absolute must to avoid a several-hour wait. Call ☎ (407) 224-2424.

## Bob Marley–A Tribute to Freedom

Set in a Jamaican atmosphere, this one-of-a-kind restaurant celebrates the music, style, and philosophy of Bob Marley. The venue is part museum (featuring over 100 photographs and portraits of Marley), part restaurant, and part nightclub.

On the menu, you'll find Jamaican jerk chicken and roasted plantains. Live reggae music is presented nightly. The full-service bar offers island drinks and Red Stripe beer. Dinner is served nightly (Mondays through Fridays), between 5:00 P.M. and 1:30 A.M. On weekends, the restaurant is open 11:00 A.M. to 1:30 A.M. There's a $4.25 cover charge after 8:00 P.M. to enter the bar. Live musical performances begin at 8:00 P.M. This restaurant/bar will appeal mainly to adults. To learn more about this restaurant, visit its Web site at ✎ *www.bobmarley.com*. The dining room offers an adult-oriented atmosphere.

## NBA City

NBA City is a colorful, basketball-themed restaurant endorsed and licensed by the National Basketball Association. This is a joint venture between the Hard Rock Café and the NBA/WNBA, so you know it offers a hip place to eat for basketball fans of all ages. The menu offers a wide range of entrees from burgers to sandwiches. Open from 11:00 A.M. to 2:00 A.M., this is definitely a family-oriented restaurant that also contains a gift shop that sells official NBA and WNBA merchandise.

## Patamoré

This open-air marketplace café environment offers authentic Italian cuisine served a la carte or family style. Open from 8:00 A.M. to midnight (marketplace area) and 5:00 P.M. to midnight (restaurant area), pizzas, grilled chicken, and steaks, plus pasta, pastries, and sandwiches are served. Full bar service is available.

## The Motown Café

Music and memorabilia from top Motown artists are what you'll hear and see throughout this unique restaurant. Get a behind-the-scenes look at the Supremes, the Temptations, and other music legends as you enjoy slow-cooked American cuisine and live entertainment. An in-house singing group performs many of Motown's classic hits live on stage every twenty minutes.

This restaurant will definitely appeal more to adults with an appreciation for Motown's music and history. Open Sundays through Thursdays between 5:00 P.M. and midnight, and Fridays and Saturdays between 5:00 P.M. and 2:00 A.M. There's a $5.25 per-person cover charge to visit the bar after 9:00 P.M.

## ⊕ HOT SPOT

To learn more about this restaurant, visit the official Motown Web site at 🖉 *www.motown.com*.

### The NASCAR Café

No matter how old you are, if you're a NASCAR racing fan, you'll appreciate this themed restaurant. It's jam-packed with NASCAR memorabilia that's displayed throughout the dining room and all public areas. In addition, there are full-size stock cars on display, plus video monitors showing NASCAR racing highlights.

Open from 10:00 A.M. to 10:00 P.M., in addition to the dining room, this restaurant offers an arcade area and a gift shop. Like the Hard Rock Café and NBA City, this is a fun, family-oriented restaurant that tends to get crowded during lunchtime and early evenings (for dinner).

### Pat O'Brien's

Modeled after the famous New Orleans watering hole, every evening guests are entertained by dueling pianos and sing-alongs. A full-service bar is offered. Pat O'Brien's is suitable for adults, over the legal drinking age. Dining hours are between 11:00 A.M. and 1:00 A.M. daily in the main bar and courtyard. Guests must be over the age of twenty-one to enter after 7:00 P.M. There's a small cover charge to enter the dueling piano bar, which is open (and features live music) between 6:00 P.M. and 2:00 A.M.

## The Latin Quarter

This area offers food and entertainment inspired by twenty-one Latin American nations. Dining and dancing is offered late into the night as guests are entertained by music from Central America, South America, Mexico, and the Caribbean. Open from 11:00 A.M. to 1:30 A.M. There's a small cover charge after 10:00 P.M.

## ≡FAST FACT

In addition to the themed restaurants, CityWalk contains a unique assortment of shops. Whether you're looking for something to do for an hour or an entire evening, chances are you'll be pleased with what's offered at CityWalk.

# The Universal Cineplex

 After a day of roller coasters, rides, and shows, perhaps you'll want to kick back and enjoy one of Hollywood's latest blockbuster films. The Universal Cineplex within CityWalk features twenty screens, all offering stadium seating, cutting-edge projection equipment, state-of-the-art sound systems, and air-conditioning. For show times and movie listings, call ✆ (407) 354-3374.

On bad-weather days and evenings, or when a hit movie first opens, expect larger-than-normal crowds here. The good news is that when a blockbuster film first opens, it'll typically be shown on multiple screens to accommodate the larger crowds.

# CityJazz

 This jazz center features ongoing live performances (nightly) in a nightclub setting. It's also the home of the Down Beat Jazz Hall of Fame, which was established in 1952 and features such distinguished jazz luminaries as Louis Armstrong, Ella Fitzgerald, and Dave Brubeck.

Over 500 pieces of memorabilia are on display. A light menu

is served daily between 8:30 P.M. and 1:00 A.M. The Down Beat Jazz Hall of Fame museum is open from 3:00 P.M. to 6:00 P.M. There's a small cover charge after 8:30 P.M. (which includes the live entertainment).

# The Groove

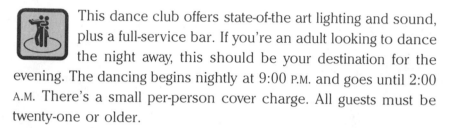

This dance club offers state-of-the art lighting and sound, plus a full-service bar. If you're an adult looking to dance the night away, this should be your destination for the evening. The dancing begins nightly at 9:00 P.M. and goes until 2:00 A.M. There's a small per-person cover charge. All guests must be twenty-one or older.

# CityWalk Shopping

Throughout the day and into the night, a handful of unique shops are available within CityWalk. Shop here for souvenirs, collectibles, and a wide range of unusual merchandise. Shops include:

**All-Star Collectibles**—Autographed sports memorabilia and other collectibles are on display and can be purchased.

**Captain Crackers**—Step back into the disco era. Toys, T-shirts, and other items based on a disco theme are available.

**Cigarz at CityWalk**—Here, cigar aficionados can find an unparalleled assortment of cigars and accessories, plus a knowledgeable staff.

**Dapy**—Novelty items for kids and adults are available. This is a chain store found in many malls.

**Elegant Illusions**—Inexpensive replicas of fine jewelry are sold here.

**Endangered Species**—A wide range of merchandise, toys, and clothing based on wild animals and the rainforest are available. This is a fun place to shop, especially with children.

**Fossil**—Fine leather goods, watches, apparel, and sunglasses are what's ticking at this shop.

**Glow!**—This shop sells items that glow in the dark, reflect, and/or illuminate.

**Quiet Flight**—Surf and beachwear from well-known labels and designers is sold.

**Silver**—This jewelry shop offers a wide range of merchandise created from sterling silver. The prices are reasonable and the selection is impressive for this type of shop.

**Tabasco Country Store**—Sample a wide range of Tabasco products inspired by the Tabasco Pepper Sauce. Sportswear, Cajun and Creole foods, and household items are offered.

**The Universal Studios Store**—If you didn't pick up a souvenir at Universal Studios Florida or Islands of Adventure, you'll find a large selection of merchandise, clothing, and toys.

# SeaWorld and Discovery Cove

LOCATED JUST MILES AWAY FROM THE WDW RESORT and Universal Studios Escape is another extremely popular, family-oriented theme park—SeaWorld Orlando. In the past few years, this park has undergone a massive redesign and expansion. It now offers a full day's worth of activities, rides, and shows suitable for everyone.

## Park Overview

 While Disney's Animal Kingdom offers guests an up close look at land-based animals living in their natural habitats, SeaWorld offers a look at sea creatures and combines that experience with rides, shows, and other attractions. In addition, a second theme park, called Discovery Cove, offers an even more personalized look at some of the ocean's most amazing creatures, including dolphins.

SeaWorld is a 200-acre park that's open year-round, from 9:00 A.M. to 7:00 P.M. (with extended hours during the summer months and holiday periods). To truly see the majority of what SeaWorld has to offer, you'll need at least eight hours. If you haven't visited this park in a while and you have an extra day in your travel itinerary, it's well worth experiencing, especially if you're traveling with kids and teens.

Both **SeaWorld** and **Discovery Cove** are owned and operated by Anheuser-Busch. For more information about these two theme parks, call ✆ (800) 4-ADVENTURE or ✆ (407) 351-3600. You can also visit the SeaWorld Web site at ✑ *www.seaworld.com.*

## ═FAST FACT

Like any theme park or tourist attraction, gift shops, snack shops, and restaurants are all in abundance throughout the SeaWorld park. Guest services such as wheelchair rentals, locker rentals, kennels, first aid, ATMs, and a foreign currency exchange are all available within the park.

## Tours

In addition to the exciting rides, shows, and attractions that bring guests closer to understanding the mysteries of the ocean and the exotic creatures that live within the sea, SeaWorld offers a series of highly educational tours and programs, including the Dolphin Interaction Program ($159 per person) and the Trainers for a Day Program ($349 per person). In addition, less expensive tours are available to small groups of guests for an additional fee of $6.95 (adults) or $5.95 (kids) each. **To the Rescue, Sharks!** and the **Polar Expedition Tour** each last about one hour. These tours and programs must be reserved in advance. For more information, call ✆ (407) 370-1382 or ✆ (407) 370-1385.

## Admission

Like all theme parks, there is an admission fee for SeaWorld and a separate admission fee for Discovery Cove. If you're staying in the Orlando area for several days and want to see more than the Disney theme parks, you can save money by purchasing the Orlando FlexTicket. This one ticket offers unlimited admission to five non-Disney theme parks, including SeaWorld, Universal Studios Florida, Islands of Adventure, Busch Gardens, and Wet 'N Wild, over a fourteen-day period. Admission to Discovery Cove is not included. For more information, call ☎ (800) 224-2828.

## ═FAST FACT

SeaWorld charges a daily parking fee of $5 per car or $7 per RV or camper. If you're staying at a non-Disney hotel, consider utilizing shuttle bus service to the SeaWorld theme park. Ask your hotel's front desk attendant or concierge for details.

### Getting to SeaWorld

SeaWorld is located at the intersection of Interstate 4 (I-4) and the Bee-Line Expressway (approximately ten minutes south of downtown Orlando and fifteen minutes from the Orlando International Airport).

The easiest way to reach SeaWorld (from the airport, The WDW Resort, or Universal Studios Escape) is via car; however, taxi service and shuttle buses are available.

## The Rating System

 To help you choose which rides and attractions are most worth seeing while visiting SeaWorld, this book offers star-based ratings for each ride and attraction, based on the age group each will most appeal to. Each ride and attraction has earned between one and three stars.

| ★ | = | Rides and attractions that earned just one star aren't worth waiting for and could be skipped, especially if your time within the theme park is limited. |
| ★★ | = | Rides and attractions that earned two stars are good, but they don't fall into the "must-see" category. |
| ★★★ | = | The rides and attractions that earned three stars are definitely worth seeing and should not be missed. |
| N.S. | = | This denotes rides and attractions that are "Not Suitable" for a specific age group. |

## SeaWorld Highlights

 SeaWorld offers a wide range of rides, shows, and attractions, most of which cater to a family audience. Perhaps the most popular show at this theme park is *The Shamu Adventure*, a fun-filled live show starring killer whales interacting with their trainers. The nighttime version of this show, *Shamu Rocks America*, features SeaWorld's trainers and whales performing with rock music in the background.

| | |
|---|---|
| Ages 2–4: | ★★ |
| Ages 5–10: | ★★★ |
| Ages 11–15: | ★★★ |
| Ages 16–Adult: | ★★★ |
| Senior Citizens: | ★★★ |

Check with the park's ticket office or customer relations desk for daily show times. Shows are presented on a weather-permitting basis. Be sure to arrive at least fifteen to thirty minutes early to the show in order to ensure admission and good seats, especially during peak vacation periods. For kids especially, there's a section of seats within Shamu Stadium that guarantees audience members will get splashed by the performing whales.

 This is a must-see attraction.

##  TRAVEL TIP

To learn more about Shamu and SeaWorld's killer whales, visit the Shamu Web site at *www*.shamu.com.

## Kraken

| | |
|---|---|
| Ages 2–4: | N.S. |
| Ages 5–10: | N.S. |
| Ages 11–15: | ★★ |
| Ages 16–Adult: | ★★★ |
| Senior Citizens: | N.S. |

This is the new flagship roller coaster at SeaWorld. It's also the tallest, fastest, longest, and only floorless roller coaster in Orlando. It will take you to the height of a fifteen-story building and turn you upside down seven times, all at speeds reaching 65 miles per hour.

Kraken is named after a legendary sea monster—a massive, mythological underwater beast. As you experience this coaster, your feet will dangle as you sit on open-air, pedestal-like seats with nothing around you except shoulder restraints. There's no one to hold on to, nothing in front of you, and nothing below you. There's only sky above and the wind in your face.

This is a must-see attraction.

## Clyde and Seamore Take Pirate Island

| | |
|---|---|
| Ages 2–4: | ★ |
| Ages 5–10: | ★★ |
| Ages 11–15: | ★★★ |
| Ages 16–Adult: | ★★ |
| Senior Citizens: | ★★ |

Sea lions, otters, and walrus perform with trainers in this rather lighthearted "adventure" designed for kids and teens. While the story line is a bit childish, this show features a cast of well-trained sea lions interacting with their trainers and the audience.

## Journey to Atlantis

| | |
|---|---|
| Ages 2–4: | N.S. |
| Ages 5–10: | N.S. |
| Ages 11–15: | ★★★ |
| Ages 16–Adult: | ★★★ |
| Senior Citizens: | ★ |

As you kick off your adventure to the lost city of Atlantis, you'll be traveling on water and high-speed rails. Evil spirits will try to keep you from your destination, but your bravery and sheer guts will keep you one step ahead. Along your journey, you never know what's around the next corner or the next drop. Oh, and there are drops. In fact, one drop is 60 feet long and goes nearly straight down. Journey to Atlantis is a thrill ride that nicely combines special effects, the excitement of a roller coaster, and the thrills of a turbulent water ride.

## Shamu's Happy Harbor

| | |
|---|---|
| Ages 2–4: | ★★★ |
| Ages 5–10: | ★★★ |
| Ages 11–15: | N.S. |
| Ages 16–Adult: | N.S. |
| Senior Citizens: | N.S. |

For young kids, this is a freestyle play area filled with giant pink flamingos and palm trees. Young guests are encouraged to run, jump, and climb as they explore four stories of nets, shoot through tunnels, cool down in a splashy water maze, and slip down nine slippery slides.

## Pets Ahoy!

| | |
|---|---|
| Ages 2–4: | ★★★ |
| Ages 5–10: | ★★★ |
| Ages 11–15: | ★★ |
| Ages 16–Adult: | ★★ |
| Senior Citizens: | ★★ |

This is a fun-filled and funny live show starring a cast of trained dogs, cats, birds, rats, pot-bellied pigs, and other animals performing a series of entertaining skits. Nearly all of the cast members were rescued from local animal shelters. Kids in particular will enjoy this show; however, it's definitely suitable for the entire family.

## Cirque de la Mer

| | |
|---|---|
| Ages 2–4: | N.S. |
| Ages 5–10: | ★ |
| Ages 11–15: | ★★★ |
| Ages 16–Adult: | ★★★ |
| Senior Citizens: | ★★★ |

Acrobatics, athleticism, modern dance, and special effects are used to create a fun-filled but nontraditional circus (sort of like Cirque du Soleil). The show comprises several specialty circus acts, featuring performers from around the world.

## Terrors of the Deep

| | |
|---|---|
| Ages 2–4: | ★★ |
| Ages 5–10: | ★★ |
| Ages 11–15: | ★★ |
| Ages 16–Adult: | ★★ |
| Senior Citizens: | ★★ |

Travel through the world's largest underwater acrylic tunnel and find yourself just inches away from dangerous predators like eels, barracuda, venomous fish, and sharks. This is a large and beautiful coral reef habitat.

## The Intensity Water Ski Show

| | |
|---|---|
| Ages 2–4: | N.S. |
| Ages 5–10: | ★★★ |
| Ages 11–15: | ★★★ |
| Ages 16–Adult: | ★★★ |
| Senior Citizens: | ★★★ |

Champion water skiers perform stunts and tricks live. The show features a twenty-person cast, composed of world-class wake boarders and record-holding skiers from across America.

## Key West Dolphin Fest

| | |
|---|---|
| Ages 2–4: | N.S. |
| Ages 5–10: | ★★ |
| Ages 11–15: | ★★ |
| Ages 16–Adult: | ★★ |
| Senior Citizens: | ★★ |

Guests have a chance to see Atlantic bottlenose dolphins perform live with their trainers in an entertaining, family-oriented show. SeaWorld also offers a pool area where guests can see, feed, and pet dolphins. (This is not an opportunity to actually swim with dolphins, however.)

## Wild Arctic

| | |
|---|---|
| Ages 2–4: | N.S. |
| Ages 5–10: | ★ |
| Ages 11–15: | ★★★ |
| Ages 16–Adult: | ★★★ |
| Senior Citizens: | ★★ |

This motion-simulator-based thrill ride takes guests on a helicopter journey to the frozen north for an Arctic exploration that's filled with surprises. The photography and overall realism is highly impressive. You're about to preview a part of the world that few see firsthand.

## Shamu Close Up

| | |
|---|---|
| Ages 2–4: | ★★ |
| Ages 5–10: | ★★★ |
| Ages 11–15: | ★★★ |
| Ages 16–Adult: | ★★ |
| Senior Citizens: | ★★ |

This 1.7-million-gallon pool features a killer whale habitat that guests can see up close. Throughout the day, trainers and caretakers interact with the whales.

### Manatees: The Last Generation?

| | |
|---|---|
| Ages 2–4: | ★★ |
| Ages 5–10: | ★★ |
| Ages 11–15: | ★★★ |
| Ages 16–Adult: | ★★★ |
| Senior Citizens: | ★★★ |

This exhibit allows guests to see Florida manatees up close and learn about the dangers this species is currently facing. It's both educational and entertaining, like all of the shows and exhibits at SeaWorld that involve live animals.

### Tropical Rain Forest

| | |
|---|---|
| Ages 2–4: | ★★ |
| Ages 5–10: | ★★ |
| Ages 11–15: | ★★ |
| Ages 16–Adult: | ★★ |
| Senior Citizens: | ★★★ |

SeaWorld's own Tropical Rain Forest is one of the park's most beautiful areas. This is a walk-through attraction featuring dozens of exotic birds, 30-foot-tall bamboo trees, exotic banyan trees, and many other plants and trees commonly found in the world's rain forests. Some excellent photo opportunities are offered.

### Pacific Point Preserve

| | |
|---|---|
| Ages 2–4: | N.S. |
| Ages 5–10: | ★★★ |
| Ages 11–15: | ★★★ |
| Ages 16–Adult: | ★★ |
| Senior Citizens: | ★★ |

Sea lions and fur seals living in a 2.5-acre naturalistic environment that replicates the rocky northern Pacific coast are the stars of this exhibit. Young people, in particular, will enjoy this zoo-like attraction.

## Getting Hungry?

SeaWorld offers nine restaurants, ranging from full-service to cafeteria-style. For families looking for an entertaining dinner show, the nightly **Aloha Polynesian Luau Dinner and Show** features traditional music, song, dance, and food from the islands of Hawaii. The show includes the famous **Samoan Fire Knife Dance,** performed by Viliami Netane Jr. The Fire Knife skills showcased by Viliami Netane Jr. are passed down from generation to generation. Viliami began his training at the age of six. Reservations are required. Call ✆ (800) 227-8048.

## ═FAST FACT

There are a handful of other activities and exhibits at SeaWorld. For example, the Penguin Encounter is an exhibit featuring penguins, while the Dolphin Nursery offers a look at dolphin moms and their calves.

## Become an Animal Trainer

 After seeing some of the live animal shows at SeaWorld, many people are inspired to become animal trainers. Now, SeaWorld offers a once-in-a-lifetime chance to experience this dream firsthand. In fact, A&E ranked this experience as one of the best animal adventures in the world.

When you participate in this program, you'll spend an entire day with the animal training staff at SeaWorld and interact one-on-one with the animals. You'll be involved with the care, feeding, and ongoing training of the animals, including the whales from the Shamu show. Your supplied wardrobe for the day will be a wetsuit.

While this is an incredible experience, especially for teens and adults, it's rather expensive. The cost is $349 per person. Because the program is an upclose, intimate experience, only three people at a time can be a "Trainer for a Day." Participants must be in good physical condition and need to be at least thirteen years old. For more information, call the **"Trainer for a Day"** hotline at ✆ (407) 370-1382.

## Kids and SeaWorld

 Since SeaWorld combines fun with wildlife education, the theme park's animal trainers offer these suggestions to parents regarding how to enhance a child's experience while visiting this theme park:

- At the end of each day, encourage your kids to draw pictures or write short stories about the favorite parts of their day at SeaWorld.
- Take lots of pictures, with a focus on your kids interacting with the various animals. Later, spend time reviewing the photos (or video) with your kids.
- Throughout your vacation, keep a "memory bag" close by. A "memory bag" can be a purse, pocket, or a backpack pouch reserved for holding fun keepsakes that your kids collect (or purchase).
- While the trip is still fresh in their minds, ask your children what they learned during their trip and what they would like to do next time.

## ═FAST FACT

At SeaWorld, more than 200 programs designed for various age groups are offered year-round and include day camps, resident camps, sleepovers, family camps, teacher camps, and group programs. To learn more about the special programs offered, call ☎(866) GO-TO-CAMP or☎(407) 370-1380. To make a camp reservation, call ☎(800) 406-2244 or ☎(407) 363-2380.

## Discovery Cove

Located adjacent to SeaWorld is Discovery Cove, which opened in Summer 2000. This truly unique theme park recreates an exotic tropical island, complete with sandy beaches. Unlike most theme parks, however, only a limited number of visitors are granted admission each day to Discovery Cove. Advanced reservations are definitely required.

Instead of rides, shows, and attractions, Discovery Cove offers a one-on-one, up close, and hands-on look at marine wildlife, including dolphins. The park is staffed by a team of highly trained and knowledgeable animal trainers and caregivers who work directly with guests to provide an extremely personalized experience that includes interacting one-on-one with dolphins and other sea creatures. This park is designed for guests over the age of six. Younger children will be limited in terms of what activities they can participate in.

Discovery Cove offers snorkeling in a manmade coral reef, lagoon, and tropical river; the chance to swim and interact with dolphins; and a lovely manmade beach. Best of all, this park is open to only 800 to 1,000 people per day, so there are never any long lines or crowds.

Visiting Discovery Cove is an all-day experience (with lunch included). The package includes:

- A reserved dolphin swim experience.
- Unlimited access to snorkeling in the coral reef.
- Unlimited access to wade and swim in the ray pool.
- Unlimited access to the free-flight bird aviary, the resort pool, and the tropical river.
- A freshly prepared meal for lunch.
- Use of a mask, snorkel, swim vest, towels, lockers, and other amenities.
- All-day self-parking.
- A seven-day pass to SeaWorld Orlando.

The all-inclusive admission price for Discovery Cove is $199 per person (this includes the dolphin swim experience). If you decide to skip the dolphin experience, the admission price is $109 per person. Anyone who has ever thought about swimming or interacting with dolphins, or who wants to try snorkeling in a 100 percent safe and supervised environment, will definitely enjoy this experience.

The only drawback to this park is that the souvenir photographs taken of guests by the on-staff professional photographer are rather expensive, yet this is a special personalized keepsake that virtually all guests wind up purchasing.

For more information about Discovery Cove, call ☎ (877) 4-DIS-COVERY or visit the park's Web site at ✍ *www.discoverycove.com*.

## ≡FAST FACT

Discovery Cove is home to Atlantic bottlenose dolphins, stingrays, over 10,000 tropical fish, barracuda, sharks, and more than 300 exotic birds.

# *Exploring Greater Orlando*

IF YOU CHOOSE TO EXPLORE MORE of the nearby Greater Orlando area, you'll find literally hundreds of other family-oriented activities that offer more than another theme park experience. This chapter will highlight some of the non–theme park activities you'll find at resort hotels and throughout Orlando.

## Resort Hotel Activities

 If you're staying at one of The WDW Resort hotels, each hotel offers activities that range from swimming and boat rentals to biking, shopping, and tennis. Health clubs and full-service day spas are also offered at several of The WDW Resort hotels (as well as independent resort hotels, such as the Wyndam Palace Resort).

### Golf

The WDW Resort offers ninety-nine holes of what Disney calls the world's greatest golf. The resort offers five championship eighteen-hole courses and a nine-hole walking course, including:

**Eagle Pines** Par: 72/6,772 yards  Rating: 72.3  Slope: 131
**Lake Buena Vista** Par: 72/6,820 yards  Rating: 72.7  Slope: 128

**Magnolia**  Par: 72/7,190 yards  Rating: 73.9  Slope: 133
**Oak Trail**  Par: 72/582b Rating: 68.2 Slope: 123
**Osprey Ridge**  Par: 72/7,101 yards  Rating: 73.9  Slope: 135
**Palm**  Par: 72/6,957 yards  Rating: 73.0  Slope: 133

In addition to the golf courses, The WDW Resort contains three full-service pro shops, four driving ranges, and four practice putting greens. If you don't feel like packing up your own clubs and bringing them with you to Orlando, all Disney courses rent Callaway golf clubs and Footjoy shoes. Private golf instruction from Disney's PGA Professional staff is available by appointment, but you'll want to schedule your lessons as far in advance as possible. Keep in mind, proper golf attire is required on all of Disney's golf courses. Shirts with collars and Bermuda-length shorts are part of the dress code.

WDW Resort guests can reserve tee times up to ninety days in advance, and day guests can reserve up to thirty days in advance by calling ✆ (407) WDW-GOLF (939-4653). All reservations must be guaranteed with a major credit card.

## ≡FAST FACT

Complimentary taxi vouchers (through Yellow Cab) are provided for Walt Disney World Resort guests who are coming to play golf at one of Disney's golf courses. The valet/concierge desk or Bell Services will summon a cab for you. The Pro Shop at the golf course will assist you in returning to your resort.

For more information about the golfing opportunities available at The WDW Resort and for current rates, call ✆ (407) WDW-GOLF, or visit the special Web site at ✎ *www.golf.disneyworld.com*. Special golf vacation packages are also offered throughout the year. Call ✆ (407) 939-7677 for travel package information. January through April is the busiest golfing season at Disney.

If miniature golf is more your thing, there are several miniature golf courses on WDW Resort property. For example, there's the family-oriented Fantasia Gardens Miniature Golf and Garden Pavilions, which offers two whimsical eighteen-hole miniature golf courses and a 22,000-square-foot outdoor meeting facility located near Epcot and The Disney-MGM Studios.

## Calling All Sports Fans!

In addition to the ESPN Club and ESPN Store at Disney's BoardWalk, The WDW Resort also offers the Disney's Wide World of Sports complex, which hosts all sorts of professional and amateur sporting events throughout the year and is the permanent training location for the Harlem Globetrotters. Tickets to the "premium" sporting events that take place at this complex can be obtained by calling TicketMaster at ✆ (407) 839-3900.

Disney's Wide World of Sports is a 200-acre complex that contains sports fields, baseball diamonds, tracks, tennis courts, basketball courts, and a 7,500-seat baseball stadium, designed to accommodate professional teams and amateurs alike in more than thirty different sports.

A flat one-price daily admission gives guests access to watch as many "nonpremium" events as they'd like throughout the day and tour the complex. For ticket prices and admission information, see Chapter 3.

## ⊕ HOT SPOT

The NFL Experience is an exciting attraction for football fans of all ages. This interactive football playground allows fans to kick the ball through uprights, throw footballs at targets, and test their speed in the 40-yard dash.

To reach Disney's Wide World of Sports, take the WDW bus service, or by car, take I-4 to The Magic Kingdom exit (#25), then follow signs. Parking is free. The D-Sports Shop located in the complex sells a wide range of official NBA, NFL, MLB, and NHL merchandise and clothing. There are also several other sports-oriented shops that sell equipment, apparel, memorabilia, and souvenirs.

## Drive a Race Car

Champion driver Richard Petty has teamed up with Disney to offer the Richard Petty Driving Experience at the Walt Disney World Speedway. Now you can experience what it's like to drive an actual two-seat stock car around a professional track at speeds of up to 145 miles per hour.

The basic Riding-Along Experience ($89 to $125) allows you to be in the passenger seat of a two-seat stock car as a professional driver takes you for three laps around the track. The Rookie Experience ($349 to $499) puts you in the driver's seat for eight laps around the one-mile tri-oval track, in a car that can reach 125 miles per hour. This is a three-hour program. The upgraded King's Experience ($749 to $1,199) offers sixteen laps of driving divided into two eight-lap sessions. The Experience of a Lifetime ($1,199 to $1,249) allows you to participate in a thirty-lap program (which is divided into three ten-lap sessions). You'll receive professional instruction designed to teach you the basics of racing.

The Walt Disney World Speedway is open to spectators, who can watch nonprofessional races, free of charge, between 9:00 A.M. and 5:00 P.M. daily (weather permitting). For more information about the **Richard Petty Driving Experience,** call ✆ (800) BE-PETTY or visit the Web site at ✍ *www.1800bepetty.com.*

## Tennis Anyone?

Disney's Wide World of Sports complex offers eleven clay courts, plus there are over twenty-five additional courts located at the various WDW Resort hotels. Disney's Racquet Club at the Contemporary Resort offers six courts, plus a pro shop and private instruction. Court time can be reserved between 8:00 A.M. and 8:00 P.M. daily. Some lighted courts are available and are open until 9:00 P.M.

Other court locations include: Disney Institute (four clay courts), Disney's Grand Floridian Resort & Spa (two clay courts),

Disney's Fort Wilderness Campground (two hard courts), Disney's Yacht Club Resort and Disney's Beach Club Resort (two hard courts), and Disney's Old Key West Resort (three hard courts). All are lighted for night play.

For the best court times, you'll have to plan ahead. Reservations are taken up to one year in advance for the courts at Disney's Racquet Club, as well as at many of the other WDW Resort hotel locations. For many of the courts, the rental fee is $15 per hour; however, some of them are free of charge.

For more information about Disney's Racquet Club and where you can play tennis at The WDW Resort, call ✆ (407) 824-3578. For information about any of the tennis courts at The WDW Resort, call ✆ (407) WDW-PLAY.

## ═ FAST FACT

Private tennis lessons, with a U.S. Tennis Association–certified instructor, are available at Disney's Racquet Club for $50 per hour. To play against a pro, without receiving instruction, that costs $45 per hour. Racquets and ball machines can both be rented for an additional fee.

## Row, Row, Row Your Boat

At various locations throughout The WDW Resort, you can rent various types of boats by the half hour or by the hour. Renting a boat is a wonderful and relatively inexpensive way to spend a morning or afternoon enjoying the outdoors, without dealing with crowds at one of the Disney theme parks.

Boats available for rent include: canoes, canopy boats, pedal boats, pontoon boats, sailboats, and speedboats. You can also go parasailing or waterskiing. Many of these boating activities can be done from the various hotels located along the Seven Seas Lagoon, Crescent Lake, or Buena Vista Lagoon. To rent any of the boats at The WDW Resort, you must be a guest at any WDW Resort hotel and have a valid driver's license or passport. No privately owned boats are allowed to be used anywhere on WDW property. Some restrictions apply in regard to minors' renting boats. Check with any WDW Resort hotel for details or to reserve a boat.

## There's Even Bass Fishing

Back in the mid-1960s, Bay Lake, which is located on Disney property, was stocked with 70,000 bass. Well, those fish have multiplied, making for a wonderful fishing opportunity. If you want to partake in the fishing activities, you must sign up for one of the **Fishing Excursions** that take place throughout the day. Reservations are required. Call ✆ (407) 828-2204 (**Fort Wilderness Fishing Excursion**), ✆ (407) 934-5409 (**Dixie Landings Fishing Excursion**), or ✆ (407) 824-2621 (**Yacht & Beach Club Fishing Excursion**).

All fish that are caught must be released. Fishing equipment is provided. The price for a two-hour Fishing Excursion ranges from about $50 to $70 per person. Up to five people can participate in each excursion. The cost of a five-person tour is $160, with a departure in early morning, midmorning, or afternoon.

## Other Activities at The WDW Resort

Some of the other activities you can participate in at The WDW Resort include:

- Basketball
- Biking
- Health clubs
- Hiking
- Horseback riding
- Inline skating
- Jogging
- Playgrounds
- Rock climbing
- Swimming
- Video arcades
- Volleyball

## 📎 TRAVEL TIP

For information about these activities, many of which are free of charge, call ☎ (407) WDW-PLAY, or speak with a Disney cast member at whichever WDW Resort hotel you're staying at during your vacation. Equipment needed to participate in the above activities is provided (or can be rented).

# The Town of Celebration

 When Walt Disney first began designing Disneyland and later The Walt Disney World Resort, he dreamed of creating an actual town. Well, in 1996, Walt's dream became a reality when the town of Celebration, Florida, was officially founded. The first phase of this massive construction project included 350 residences, two office buildings, fourteen businesses in the town center, a 150-bed medical center, a school, a teaching academy, and a golf course (which is open to the public). Since the completion of this first phase, additional phases were subsequently built, transforming this into a community.

While Celebration is a private residential community, tourists are invited to the downtown area to explore the unique shops and restaurants, and to take in the atmosphere of this storybook-like community. Yes, there's even upbeat music piped into the streets through hidden speakers as you walk through the downtown area.

There are several restaurants and shopping opportunities in Celebration. There's also a full-service bank and a post office located in the downtown area, as well as an AMC movie theater, live entertainment in the streets, and paddleboat and sailboat rentals on the lake that's adjacent to downtown Celebration.

Celebration, Florida, covers 4,900 acres and is surrounded by 4,700 acres of protected greenbelt near the intersection of I-4 and U.S. 192 (about a ten-minute drive from The WDW Resort). Located just outside of Celebration is Orlando's largest indoor shopping mall.

## 🧳 TRAVEL TIP

If you're interested in possibly purchasing some real estate in Celebration and making this town your home, be sure to visit the Celebration Preview Center (open 10:00 A.M. to 6:00 P.M. daily). It's located in the heart of downtown Celebration. To reach Celebration Realty, call ☏(407) 566-4663.

## Tourist Information

When you arrive in Orlando, visit any tourist information center or the front desk of virtually any hotel, and you'll be able to pick up brochures or additional information about the various attractions in the Orlando area, many of which are conveniently located just minutes (by car) from The WDW Resort or Universal Studios Florida. Special savings coupons are available for many of these attractions in the Orlando edition of the Entertainment Book or from the various tourist books available free of charge from hotels and tourist information desks.

Central Florida Tourist Information Centers, located throughout the Orlando area, are excellent places to visit for ideas on how to spend your time as well as to receive all sorts of money-saving coupons and special offers. Call ☏ (800) 396-1883 (or check out their Web site at ✐ *www.orlandovisitor.com*) for the location nearest to where you'll be staying. The Official Visitor Center (located at ▣ 8723 International Drive, Suite 101, at the corner of International Drive and Austrian Court) is one place you can pick up discount tickets for many of Orlando's top attractions. Call ☏ (407) 363-5872 for more information, or check out its Web site at ✐ *www.goflorida.com/orlando.*

*See Orlando* is a complimentary quarterly publication from SEE Florida Magazines, Inc. This full-color publication includes ads and information about tourist attractions, plus offers dozens of money-saving coupons for the attractions and nearby restaurants. You can pick up this publication at many hotels and tourist information offices, as well as at the Information Desk located at the Orlando International Airport.

## Orlando-Area Activities

 Located in the Orlando, Kissimmee, and Lake Buena Vista area, in between The WDW Resort and Universal Studios Florida, there are literally dozens of smaller, independent attractions designed to appeal to tourists of all ages. There are water parks, animal parks (both zoos and shows), unique shopping opportunities, dinner shows, theatrical performances, theme restaurants, fine-dining restaurants, family-oriented (inexpensive) restaurants, boat rides, helicopter tours, and all sorts of other ways to spend a few hours or an entire day having nonstop fun in Florida's sun.

 **TRAVEL TIP**

If the weather's bad and you're looking for indoor activities, or you have an afternoon or evening free that you'd like to spend outside of a theme park, consider taking a drive along International Drive in Orlando. In addition to finding literally hundreds of restaurants and stores, you'll also find many popular tourist attractions and activities suitable for the entire family.

The following are just a few of the many Orlando-area attractions designed for families that are available outside of The WDW Resort (many of which are located along International Drive). These attractions are listed in alphabetical order. Call each attraction directly for driving directions and admission prices.

**Air Florida Charter, Inc.,** ☎ (407) 888-4114
Aerial sightseeing flights that include a bird's-eye viewing of The WDW Resort, SeaWorld, and Universal Studios Florida are offered. All tours are narrated and provide excellent photo opportunities.

**Arabian Nights,** ☎ (800) 553-6116

This family-oriented dinner show features a cast of over fifty of the world's most famous horses in an indoor twenty-five-act equestrian show. Reservations are required.

**Balloons by Renee,** ☎ (407) 422-3529

Hot-air balloon rides at sunrise are offered.

**Belz Factory Outlet World,** ☎ (407) 352-9600

This shopping center features 170 outlet shops in one location. Save up to 75 percent off of retail prices.

**Boggy Creek Airboat Rides,** ☎ (407) 344-9550

Explore some of Florida's wetlands with a professional guide, while traveling at speeds of up to 50 miles per hour. You might even see alligators in their natural habitat.

**Busch Gardens,** ☎ (888) 800-5447, ✍ *www.buschgardens.com*

Located in Tampa, Florida (about a sixty-minute drive from The WDW Resort), this is an entirely different theme park experience that features some of the best thrill rides you'll find anywhere on the East Coast. Busch Gardens also features a world-famous wildlife animal park and a water park.

**Church Street Station,** ☎ (407) 422-2434

Restaurants, shops, and bars make up this entertainment location that's one of Orlando's hottest night spots. Live musical performances and plenty of unique eating and drinking opportunities await you here every night.

**Cinemark USA, Inc.,** ☎ (407) 351-3117

In the Orlando area, moviegoers have a selection of state-of-the-art theaters to choose from. Watching a movie is a relatively inexpensive yet entertaining activity.

**Colonial Lanes** (Bowling), ☎ (407) 894-0361

This bowling alley, located at 400 North Primrose in Orlando, features thirty-two Brunswick lanes and a game room. It's open daily between 9:00 A.M. and midnight.

**Fighter Pilots USA,** ☎ (800) 568-6748, ✑ *www.fighterpilotsusa.com*
Experience an air combat mission with an F-16 fighter pilot in a Merchetti fighter trainer. No experience is necessary.

**The Florida Mall,** ☎ (407) 851-6255
This is the largest indoor mall in the Orlando area. What you'll find here are over 200 specialty stores, five department stores, and restaurants.

**Gatorland,** ☎ (407) 855-5496, ☎ (800) 393-JAWS, ✑ *www.gatorland.com*
See live alligator wrestling, along with many alligators up close. This zoolike attraction also features all sorts of exotic snakes and a special kids area/petting zoo.

**Golf**
If you have a passion for golf, there are dozens of public and members-only golf courses throughout the Orlando area. For a complete listing of golf courses, driving ranges, and pro shops, check the Greater Orlando Yellow Pages, found at most public telephones and within the majority of hotel rooms.

**Green Meadows Petting Farm,** ☎ (407) 846-0770
Designed with kids in mind, this petting zoo allows young people to get close to the animals. Visitors can interact with ostriches, ducks, pot-bellied pigs, peacocks, sheep, cows, donkeys, an American bison, and other farm animals.

**Guinness World Records Experience,** ☎ (407) 248-8891,
✑ *www.guinnessattractions.com*
This interactive museum (located at 8437 International Drive) takes the *Guinness Book of World Records* and transforms it into a hands-on attraction that features the "Ride the Records" motion-simulator ride and many interactive exhibits.

**Jungleland Zoo,** ☎ (407) 396-1012
See hundreds of rare and exotic animals (over 500 in all). Several live animal shows are also presented throughout the day. This outdoor zoo is located at ▱ 4580 West Irlo Bronson Highway in Kissimmee.

**KartWorld,** ☎ (407) 396-4800
Take a few laps in a high-powered go-kart. The track at this driving facility is almost one mile long. The cost is $3.50 per lap. Bumper boats and other activities can also be experienced here for an additional fee.

**Kennedy Space Center,** ☎ (321) 449-4444
Located about one hour outside of Orlando, this attraction allows you to learn about the history of space travel, NASA, and the space shuttle program. There are plenty of hands-on exhibits, as well as replica space shuttles and genuine NASA equipment on display.

**Kissimmee Billie Swamp Safari,** ☎ (800) 949-6101
The Seminole Tribe of Florida invites guests to their reservation for a fun-filled day of air boat rides, swamp buggy eco-tours, reptile and alligator exhibits, hiking tours, and other family-oriented activities.

**Masters of Magic Show,** ☎ (407) 352-3456,
✎ *www.mastersofmagic.net*
Your family will enjoy this ninety-minute magic show, complete with Las Vegas–style special effects and breathtaking illusions.

**Medieval Times Dinner and Tournament,** ☎ (407) 396-1518
This dinner show transports guests back to the medieval era, a time when knights were revered as heroes. While guests enjoy a multicourse feast, eaten without benefit of utensils, a cast of 100 knights on horseback (and other costumed characters) participate in an interactive show that kids and teens in particular will enjoy. The show includes authentic jousting matches, hand-to-hand combat, and a rather lighthearted story line.

**Orlando Science Center,** ☎ (407) 896-7151
If you're looking for an educational and fun indoor activity to experience with your kids, visit Orlando's Science Center, which offers many fully interactive exhibits, plus a planetarium and laser shows.

**Ripley's Believe It or Not! Museum,** ☎ (407) 363-4418,
✎ *www.ripleysorlando.com*
See, hear, and experience a museum full of the strange, wacky, and totally outrageous.

**Skycoaster,** ☎ (407) 397-2509
Most people have heard of bungee jumping and sky diving; Skycoaster is a spin-off of these sports. It allows brave riders to soar through the air at speeds of up to 70 miles per hour while strapped into a harness that's held by a giant rubber band and that swings freely from a tall tower.

**Skyventure,** ☎ (407) 903-1150
This is a skydiving wind tunnel that allows nonexperienced and experienced skydivers alike to experience the thrill of skydiving without jumping out of a plane. Instead, riders fly on a 120-mile-per-hour column of air.

**Speed Wavzzz,** ☎ (407) 390-0201
Rent Waverunners, paddle boats, ski tubes, and a variety of other boats by the half hour or hour.

**Splendid China,** ☎ (800) 244-6226
This attraction features over sixty detailed replicas of China's famous landmarks, as well as a live animal show featuring tigers. There's also "The Mysterious Kingdom of the Orient" acrobatic show presented every evening, as well as shops and dining opportunities.

**Titanic: Ship of Dreams,** ☎ (407) 248-1166 ext: 3103,
✎ *www.titanicshipofdreams.com*
This museum is designed primarily for teens and adults. The exhibit features over 200 priceless artifacts from the Titanic as well as multimedia documentaries and interactive exhibits that retell the story of this infamous cruise ship.

**Water Mania,** ☎ (407) 396-2626
Fans of water parks will enjoy the various fun-filled water slides and water-based attractions at this park.

**Wet 'N Wild,** ☎ (407) 351-1800
This water park features all sorts of water slides, pools, and fun-filled activities for the entire family. Wet 'N Wild also offers a huge video arcade.

**WonderWorks,** ☎ (407) 351-8800

This high-tech arcade and entertainment center offers a variety of cutting-edge arcade games, virtual reality attractions, and motion-simulator rides. Also featured is what WonderWorks calls the world's largest Laser Tag Arena and a virtual reality attraction that allows guests to "create" their own virtual roller coaster and then ride it.

**World of Orchids,** ☎ (407) 396-1887

If you enjoy gardening, flowers, and nature, World of Orchids offers the largest permanent indoor display of flowering orchids, as well as exotic fish, birds, African chameleons, and more.

# The Orlando FlexTicket

 Universal Escape, SeaWorld, Wet 'N Wild, and Busch Gardens Tampa Bay have teamed up to offer the Orlando FlexTicket. The 5-Park Orlando FlexTicket, which includes unlimited admission to Busch Gardens Tampa Bay, SeaWorld, Universal Studios Florida, Islands of Adventure, and Wet 'N Wild for up to fourteen consecutive days, is priced at $196.95 (plus tax) per adult, or $157.95 (plus tax) per child, ages three to nine. This ticket also includes free ground transportation between Orlando and Tampa Bay. Ask about AAA-member discounts when purchasing FlexTickets.

An additional parking fee is required, but only once per day. The Orlando FlexTicket can be purchased at any of the attractions listed, or at many of the Orlando-area tourism offices. The Orlando FlexTicket offers a wonderful money-saving opportunity.

##  TRAVEL TIP

For other money-saving opportunities, call the Tampa Bay Visitors Association at ☎(800) 44-TAMPA.

CHAPTER 20

# *Planning Your Trip*

IT'S A WISE IDEA to do a bit of preplanning in order to help ensure you make the most of your vacation and stay within your allocated budget. After all, unless you'll be staying in Orlando for a long period of time, it's impossible to see and do everything. Thus, you need to make decisions about how you'll spend your time.

## Plan Accordingly

As you plan your itinerary, make sure to obtain input from everyone you'll be traveling with. Also, leave plenty of flexibility in each day's schedule. Allow ample time to explore and enjoy experiences as they happen, without worrying too much about staying on a timetable and getting to the next preplanned activity. In most cases, creating an itinerary with plans down to the hour or minute might make you more organized, but it will also create a tremendous level of stress during your vacation as you run around trying to stick to your schedule. Be sure to leave time in your schedule for travel (between destinations, such as theme parks), meals, rest/relaxation, etc.

For the purposes of preplanning your itinerary and visiting theme parks, it's best to divide your day into three chunks of time: morning, afternoon, and nighttime. Use the following Travel Itinerary worksheets to help preplan your itinerary, keeping in mind that you'll most likely be altering this itinerary once you arrive in Orlando and start actually experiencing your vacation. Use these worksheets to guide you in scheduling the things you believe you (and the people you're traveling with) will most enjoy based on the time you have available.

# Airline Information

Departing date:

Departing time:

Airline:

Flight number(s)/connecting cities:

Departing airport:

Arriving airport:

Arrival time:

Seat assignment(s):

Returning date (to go home):

Departing time:

Airline:

Flight number(s)/connecting cities:

Departing airport:

Arrival time (to home city):

Seat assignment(s):

Travel agency used:

Travel agent/airline phone number(s):

Parking lot name/number at airport:

Location/aisle:

# Airport Ground Transportation Information

Getting to the airport:

Taxi/limo service name:

Phone number:

Reservation number:

Pickup date/time:

Pickup location:

Getting home from the airport:

Taxi/limo service name:

Phone number:

Reservation number:

Pickup date/time:

Pickup location:

# Rental Car Information

Rental car company:

Confirmation number:

Daily rate:

Pickup location:

Rental car company phone number:

Type of car reserved:

# Accommodation Information

Hotel/resort name:

Phone number:

Reservation number:

Check-in date:

Checkout date:

Type of accommodations reserved:

# *Important Phone Numbers*

THE FOLLOWING ARE MANY OF THE PHONE numbers listed within this book that will help you learn more about the various theme parks and other activities within the Greater Orlando area.

**Accommodations Express:** ☎(800) 444-7666
**AeroMexico:** ☎(800) 237-6639
**Air Canada:** ☎(800) 247-2262
**Air Florida Charter, Inc.:** ☎407) 888-4114
**AirJamaica:** ☎(800) 523-5585
**AirTran Airways:** ☎(800) AIR-TRAN
**Alamo Car Rental:** ☎(800) 354-2322
**American Airlines:** ☎(800) 433-7300
**American Automobile Association (AAA):** ☎(800) AAA-HELP
**American Express Travel:** ☎(800) 346-3607
**AmericaWest Airlines:** ☎(800) 235-9292
**Amtrak:** ☎(800) USA-RAIL
**ANA:** ☎(800) 235-9262
**Arabian Nights:** ☎(800) 553-6116
**Avis Car Rental:** ☎(800) 331-1212
**Bahamasair:** ☎(800) 222-4262
**Balloons by Renee:** ☎(407) 422-3529

Belz Factory Outlet World: &(407) 352-9600

Black Bear Golf Club: &(800) 4-BEAR-18

Boggy Creek Airboat Rides: &(407) 344-9550

British Airways: &(800) AIR-WAYS

Budget Car Rental: &(800) 527-0700

Busch Gardens: &(888) 800-5447

Carnival: &(800) 274-6140

Celebration Golf Club: &(407) 566-GOLF

Celebration Health: &(407) 303-4000

Celebration Hotel, The: &(407) 566-6000, (888) 499-3800

Centra Care: &(407) 239-7777

Central Florida Tourist Information Centers: &(800) 396-1883

Central Reservation Service: &(800) 548-3311

Check-In Reservation Services: &(800) 237-1033

Church Street Station: &(407) 422-2434

Cinemark USA, Inc.: &(407) 351-3117

Cirque du Soliel Box Office: &(407) 939-7600

Colonial Lanes (Bowling): &(407) 894-0361

ComAir: &(800) 354-9822

Continental: &(800) 523-3273

Delta Airlines/Delta Express: &(800) 221-1212

Destinations Travel Service: &(407) 859-3501

Diamondback Golf Club: &(800) 222-5629

Discovery Cove Information: &(800) 224-2828

Disney Catalog: &(800) 237-5751

Disney Club, The: &(800) 654-6347

Disney Club Membership Information: &(800) 49-DISNEY

Disney Cruise Lines: &(888) DCL-2500, v(407) 566-7000

Disney's All-Star Movies Resort: &(407) 939-7000

Disney's All-Star Music Resort: &(407) 939-6000

Disney's All-Star Sports Resort: &(407) 939-5000

Disney's Animal Kingdom Lodge: &(407) 934-7639

Disney's Beach Club: &(407) 934-8000

Disney's BoardWalk Inn: &(407) 939-5100

Disney's BoardWalk Nightlife Information: &(407) 939-5100

Disney's BoardWalk Villas: (407) 939-6200

Disney's Caribbean Beach: (407) 934-3400

Disney's Contemporary Resort: (407) 824-1000

Disney's Coronado Springs Resort: (407) 939-1000

Disney's Fort Wilderness Resort & Campground: (407) 824-2900

Disney's Grand Floridian Resort & Spa: (407) 824-3000

Disney's Old Key West Resort: (407) 827-7700

Disney's Polynesian Resort: (407) 824-2000

Disney's Port Orleans Resort–French Quarter: (407) 934-5000

Disney's Port Orleans Riverside: (407) 934-6000

Disney's Wilderness Lodge: (407) 824-3200

Disney's Yacht Club: (407) 934-7000

Disney World Merchandise Hotline: (407) 363-6200

Disney World Theme Park Tour Information: (800) WDW-TOUR

Doctors-On-Call: (407) 399-3627

Dollar Car Rental: (800) 800-4000

Downtown Disney Information: (407) 934-7781

Dream Cars Unlimited: (866) 624-6396

El Al: (800) 223-6700

Emeril's Restaurant: (407) 224-2424

Enterprise Car Rental: (800) 736-8227

Entertainment Book, The: (800) 933-2605

Eventures Unlimited, Inc.: (800) 356-7891

Fighter Pilots USA: (800) 568-6748

Florida Mall, The: (407) 851-6255

Gatorland: (407) 855-5496, (800) 393-JAWS

Glen Abbey Golf Club: (407) 668-4209

Green Meadows Petting Farm: (407) 846-0770

Greyhound Bus: (407) 292-3440, (407) 847-3911

Guinness World Records Experience: (407) 248-8891

Hard Rock Café Restaurant: (407) 363-8000

Hard Rock Hotel, The: (888) 322-5541

Hertz Car Rental: (800) 654-3131

Hertz Gold Club Reservations Car Rental: (800) CAR-GOLD

Hotel Reservations Network, The: (800) 511-5321

House of Blues Concert Information: ☎(407) 934-2222

Icelander: ☎(800) 223-5500

International Golf Club: ☎(407) 239-6909

Jet Blue: ☎(800) 538-2583

Jungleland Zoo: ☎(407) 396-1012

KartWorld: ☎(407) 396-4800

Kennedy Space Center: ☎(321) 449-4444

KinderCare Daycare Center: ☎(407) 827-5437

KinderCare In-Room Babysitting: ☎(407) 827-5444

Kissimmee Billie Swamp Safari: ☎(800) 949-6101

Kissimmee Convention & Visitors Bureau: ☎(407) 847-5000

Kodak Film Customer Service: ☎(800) 242-2424

LTU: ☎(800) 888-0200

Masters of Magic Show: ☎(407) 352-3456

Mears Motor Shuttles: ☎(407) 423-5566

Mears Transportation: ☎(407) 839-1570, ☎(407) 699-9999

Medieval Times Dinner & Tournament: ☎(407) 396-1518

MetroWest Country Club: ☎(407) 299-1099

Midway: ☎(800) 44-MIDWAY

Mortinair: ☎(800) 627-8462

National Car Rental: ☎(800) 227-7368

Nickelodeon's Production Hotline: ☎(407) 363-8586

Northwest Airlines/KLM: ☎(800) 225-2525

Official Visitor Center: ☎(407) 363-5872

Orange Bowl Lanes, The: ☎(407) 847-2866

Orlando Convention & Visitors Bureau: ☎(407) 363-5871

Orlando International Airport: ☎(407) 825-2001

Orlando Science Center: ☎(407) 896-7151

Payless Car Rental: ☎(800) PAY-LESS

Portofino Bay Hotel, The: ☎(888) 322-5541

Priceline.com: ☎(800) 774-2354

Rent A Wreck Car Rental: ☎(407) 823-8388

Richard Petty Driving Experience: ☎(800) BE-PETTY

Ripley's Believe It or Not! Museum: ☎(407) 363-4418

Royal Pacific Resort: ☎(888) 322-5541

Sandlake Hospital: ☎(407) 351-8500

Saudia: ☎(800) 472-8342

SeaWorld & Discovery Cove Reservations: ☎(800) 4-ADVENTURE

Shades of Green on Walt Disney World Resort: ☎(407) 824-3600

Skycoaster: ☎(407) 397-2509

Skyventure: ☎(407) 903-1150

Southwest Airlines: ☎(800) 435-9792

Speed Wavzzz: ☎(407) 390-0201

Spirit Airlines: ☎(800) 772-7117

Splendid China: ☎(800) 244-6226

Summerfield Suites: ☎(800) 833-4353

SunTrust Bank: ☎(407) 237-4786

Tampa Bay Visitors Association: ☎(800) 44-TAMPA

Thrifty Car Rental: ☎(800) 367-2277

Ticketmaster: ☎(407) 839-3900

Titanic: Ship of Dreams: ☎(407) 248-1166 ext. 3103

United: ☎(800) 241-6522

Universal Cineplex Movie Listings: ☎(407) 354-3374

Universal Studios Audience Tickets: ☎(407) 224-6355

Universal Studios Escape Guest Services: ☎(407) 224-6356

Universal Studios Escape Hours of Operation: ☎(407) 363 8000, ☎(800) 711-0080

Universal Studios Escape Reservations: ☎(888) U-ESCAPE, ☎(407) 363-8295

Universal Studios Lost & Found: ☎(407) 224-6355

Universal Studios Vacations: ☎(800) 711-0080, ☎(407) 224-7000

Universal Studios VIP Tours: ☎(407) 363-8295

US Airways: ☎(800) 428-4322

US Airways Vacation Packages: ☎(800) 455-0123

Vanguard Airlines: ☎(800) 826-4827

Varig Brazil: ☎(800) 468-2744

Villas at the Disney Institute: ☎(407) 827-1100

Virgin Atlantic: ☎(800) 862-8621

Walt Disney Dining Reservations: ☎(407) WDW-DINE

Walt Disney Dolphin & Swan Resorts: ☎(407) 934-4000

Walt Disney Travel Company: ✆(407) 939-7675, ✆(800) 225-2024

Walt Disney World Activities Information: ✆(407) WDW-PLAY

Walt Disney World Golf Information: ✆(407) WDW-GOLF

Walt Disney World Guest Relations: ✆(407) 824-4321

Walt Disney World Park Operating Hours: ✆(407) 824-4321

Walt Disney World Resort Reservations: ✆(407) W-DISNEY

Walt Disney World Tennis Reservations: ✆(407) WDW-PLAY

Walt Disney World Weather Forecast: ✆(407) 824-4104

Water Mania: ✆(407) 396-2626

WDW In-Room Babysitting Service: ✆(407) 939-3463

Wet 'N Wild: ✆(407) 351-1800

Windermere Golf Center: ✆(407) 654-0200

WonderWorks: ✆(407) 351-8800

World of Orchids: ✆(407) 396-1887

Wyndam Palace Resort: ✆(407) 827-2727, ✆(800) WYNDHAM

# *Attraction Selection Worksheet*

THE FOLLOWING IS A WORKSHEET that will help you choose which rides, shows, and attractions you and the people you're traveling with will want to experience once you arrive at each of the Disney theme parks. Place a checkmark in the appropriate column next to each listed ride, show, and attraction.

# The Magic Kingdom

Rate the rides, shows, and attractions, listed here in alphabetical order, on the following scale:

1=Must see            2=Experience if time permits
3=Already experienced  4=No interest

| Attraction Name | 1 | 2 | 3 | 4 |
|---|---|---|---|---|
| Ariel's Grotto | ☐ | ☐ | ☐ | ☐ |
| Astro Orbiter | ☐ | ☐ | ☐ | ☐ |
| Barnstormer at Goofy's Wiseacre Farm, The | ☐ | ☐ | ☐ | ☐ |
| Big Thunder Mountain | ☐ | ☐ | ☐ | ☐ |
| Buzz Lightyear's Space Ranger Spin | ☐ | ☐ | ☐ | ☐ |
| Cinderella's Castle | ☐ | ☐ | ☐ | ☐ |
| Cinderella's Golden Carrousel | ☐ | ☐ | ☐ | ☐ |
| Cinderella's Surprise Celebration | ☐ | ☐ | ☐ | ☐ |
| City Hall | ☐ | ☐ | ☐ | ☐ |
| Country Bear Jamboree | ☐ | ☐ | ☐ | ☐ |
| Diamond Horseshoe Saloon Revue, The | ☐ | ☐ | ☐ | ☐ |
| Disney Gallery, The | ☐ | ☐ | ☐ | ☐ |
| Donald's Boat | ☐ | ☐ | ☐ | ☐ |
| Dumbo the Flying Elephant | ☐ | ☐ | ☐ | ☐ |
| Enchanted Tiki Room, The | ☐ | ☐ | ☐ | ☐ |
| ExtraTERRORestrial Alien Encounter | ☐ | ☐ | ☐ | ☐ |
| Fairytale Garden | ☐ | ☐ | ☐ | ☐ |
| Fantasy in the Sky (Nighttime) | ☐ | ☐ | ☐ | ☐ |
| Fantasyland Character Festival | ☐ | ☐ | ☐ | ☐ |
| Frontier Shootin' Arcade | ☐ | ☐ | ☐ | ☐ |
| Galaxy Palace Theater | ☐ | ☐ | ☐ | ☐ |
| Hall of Presidents, The | ☐ | ☐ | ☐ | ☐ |
| Haunted Mansion, The | ☐ | ☐ | ☐ | ☐ |
| It's a Small World | ☐ | ☐ | ☐ | ☐ |

| Attraction Name | 1 | 2 | 3 | 4 |
|---|---|---|---|---|
| Judge's Tent | ☐ | ☐ | ☐ | ☐ |
| Jungle Cruise | ☐ | ☐ | ☐ | ☐ |
| Legend of the Lion King | ☐ | ☐ | ☐ | ☐ |
| Liberty Square Riverboat | ☐ | ☐ | ☐ | ☐ |
| Mad Tea Party | ☐ | ☐ | ☐ | ☐ |
| Magic Carpets of Aladdin, The | ☐ | ☐ | ☐ | ☐ |
| Many Adventures of Winnie the Pooh, The | ☐ | ☐ | ☐ | ☐ |
| Mickey's Country House | ☐ | ☐ | ☐ | ☐ |
| Minnie's Country House | ☐ | ☐ | ☐ | ☐ |
| Peter Pan's Flight | ☐ | ☐ | ☐ | ☐ |
| Pirates of the Caribbean | ☐ | ☐ | ☐ | ☐ |
| Share A Dream Come True (Daytime Parade) | ☐ | ☐ | ☐ | ☐ |
| Snow White's Scary Adventures | ☐ | ☐ | ☐ | ☐ |
| Space Mountain | ☐ | ☐ | ☐ | ☐ |
| SpectroMagic Parade (Nighttime) | ☐ | ☐ | ☐ | ☐ |
| Splash Mountain | ☐ | ☐ | ☐ | ☐ |
| Swiss Family Treehouse | ☐ | ☐ | ☐ | ☐ |
| Timekeeper, The | ☐ | ☐ | ☐ | ☐ |
| Tomorrowland Arcade | ☐ | ☐ | ☐ | ☐ |
| Tomorrowland Indy Speedway | ☐ | ☐ | ☐ | ☐ |
| Tomorrowland Stage | ☐ | ☐ | ☐ | ☐ |
| Tomorrowland Transit Authority | ☐ | ☐ | ☐ | ☐ |
| Tom Sawyer Island | ☐ | ☐ | ☐ | ☐ |
| Toontown Hall of Fame Tent | ☐ | ☐ | ☐ | ☐ |
| Town Square Exposition Hall | ☐ | ☐ | ☐ | ☐ |
| Walt Disney's Carousel of Progress | ☐ | ☐ | ☐ | ☐ |
| Walt Disney World Railroad | ☐ | ☐ | ☐ | ☐ |
| Other:_____ | ☐ | ☐ | ☐ | ☐ |
| Other:_____ | ☐ | ☐ | ☐ | ☐ |
| Other:_____ | ☐ | ☐ | ☐ | ☐ |
| Other:_____ | ☐ | ☐ | ☐ | ☐ |

# Epcot

Rate the rides, shows, and attractions, listed here in alphabetical order, on the following scale:

1=Must see      2=Experience if time permits
3=Already experienced      4=No interest

| Attraction Name | 1 | 2 | 3 | 4 |
|---|---|---|---|---|
| Canada | ☐ | ☐ | ☐ | ☐ |
| China | ☐ | ☐ | ☐ | ☐ |
| France | ☐ | ☐ | ☐ | ☐ |
| Germany | ☐ | ☐ | ☐ | ☐ |
| IllumiNations (Nighttime) | ☐ | ☐ | ☐ | ☐ |
| Imagination! | ☐ | ☐ | ☐ | ☐ |
| Innoventions East | ☐ | ☐ | ☐ | ☐ |
| Innoventions West | ☐ | ☐ | ☐ | ☐ |
| Italy | ☐ | ☐ | ☐ | ☐ |
| Japan | ☐ | ☐ | ☐ | ☐ |
| Land, The | ☐ | ☐ | ☐ | ☐ |
| Leave A Legacy | ☐ | ☐ | ☐ | ☐ |
| Living Seas, The | ☐ | ☐ | ☐ | ☐ |
| Mexico | ☐ | ☐ | ☐ | ☐ |
| Mission: SPACE | ☐ | ☐ | ☐ | ☐ |
| Morocco | ☐ | ☐ | ☐ | ☐ |
| Norway | ☐ | ☐ | ☐ | ☐ |
| Spaceship Earth | ☐ | ☐ | ☐ | ☐ |
| Tapestry of Dreams Parade (Daytime) | ☐ | ☐ | ☐ | ☐ |
| Test Track | ☐ | ☐ | ☐ | ☐ |
| United Kingdom | ☐ | ☐ | ☐ | ☐ |
| Universe of Energy | ☐ | ☐ | ☐ | ☐ |
| U.S.A.: The American Adventure | ☐ | ☐ | ☐ | ☐ |
| Wonders of Life | ☐ | ☐ | ☐ | ☐ |
| Other:_____ | ☐ | ☐ | ☐ | ☐ |
| Other:_____ | ☐ | ☐ | ☐ | ☐ |
| Other:_____ | ☐ | ☐ | ☐ | ☐ |

# The Disney-MGM Studios

Rate the rides, shows, and attractions, listed here in alphabetical order, on the following scale:

1=Must see      2=Experience if time permits
3=Already experienced    4=No interest

| Attraction Name | 1 | 2 | 3 | 4 |
|---|---|---|---|---|
| 100 Years of Magic Disney Stars and Motor Cars Parade (Daytime) | ☐ | ☐ | ☐ | ☐ |
| Beauty and the Beast–Live on Stage | ☐ | ☐ | ☐ | ☐ |
| Discover the Stories Behind the Magic | ☐ | ☐ | ☐ | ☐ |
| Disney-MGM Studios Backlot Tour | ☐ | ☐ | ☐ | ☐ |
| Disney's The Hunchback of Notre Dame–A Musical Adventure | ☐ | ☐ | ☐ | ☐ |
| Fantasmic! (Nighttime) | ☐ | ☐ | ☐ | ☐ |
| Great Movie Ride, The | ☐ | ☐ | ☐ | ☐ |
| Honey, I Shrunk the Kids Movie Set Adventure | ☐ | ☐ | ☐ | ☐ |
| Indiana Jones Epic Stunt Spectacular | ☐ | ☐ | ☐ | ☐ |
| Jim Henson's Muppet*Vision 3-D | ☐ | ☐ | ☐ | ☐ |
| Magic of Disney Animation, The | ☐ | ☐ | ☐ | ☐ |
| Playhouse Disney–Live on Stage | ☐ | ☐ | ☐ | ☐ |
| Radio Disney Studios | ☐ | ☐ | ☐ | ☐ |
| Rock 'n' Roller Coaster Starring Aerosmith | ☐ | ☐ | ☐ | ☐ |
| Sounds Dangerous–Starring Drew Carey | ☐ | ☐ | ☐ | ☐ |
| Star Tours | ☐ | ☐ | ☐ | ☐ |
| Tower of Terror, The | ☐ | ☐ | ☐ | ☐ |
| Voyage of the Little Mermaid | ☐ | ☐ | ☐ | ☐ |
| Walt Disney: One Man's Dream | ☐ | ☐ | ☐ | ☐ |
| Who Wants To Be A Millionaire–Play It! | ☐ | ☐ | ☐ | ☐ |
| Other: _____ | ☐ | ☐ | ☐ | ☐ |
| Other: _____ | ☐ | ☐ | ☐ | ☐ |
| Other: _____ | ☐ | ☐ | ☐ | ☐ |

# Disney's Animal Kingdom

Rate the rides, shows, and attractions, listed here in alphabetical order, on the following scale:

1=Must see  2=Experience if time permits
3=Already experienced  4=No interest

| Attraction Name | 1 | 2 | 3 | 4 |
|---|---|---|---|---|
| Affection Section | ☐ | ☐ | ☐ | ☐ |
| Boneyard, The | ☐ | ☐ | ☐ | ☐ |
| Chester & Hester's Dino-Rama! | ☐ | ☐ | ☐ | ☐ |
| Chester & Hester's Primeval Whirl! | ☐ | ☐ | ☐ | ☐ |
| Conservation Station | ☐ | ☐ | ☐ | ☐ |
| Dinosaur! | ☐ | ☐ | ☐ | ☐ |
| Dino-Sue | ☐ | ☐ | ☐ | ☐ |
| Discover the Stories Behind the Magic | ☐ | ☐ | ☐ | ☐ |
| Discovery Island Trails | ☐ | ☐ | ☐ | ☐ |
| Festival of the Lion King | ☐ | ☐ | ☐ | ☐ |
| Flights of Wonder | ☐ | ☐ | ☐ | ☐ |
| Habitat Habit! | ☐ | ☐ | ☐ | ☐ |
| It's Tough to Be a Bug! | ☐ | ☐ | ☐ | ☐ |
| Kali River Rapids | ☐ | ☐ | ☐ | ☐ |
| Kilimanjaro Safaris | ☐ | ☐ | ☐ | ☐ |
| Look Backstage! | ☐ | ☐ | ☐ | ☐ |
| Maharajah Jungle Trek | ☐ | ☐ | ☐ | ☐ |
| Mickey's Jammin' Jungle Parade | ☐ | ☐ | ☐ | ☐ |
| Pangani Forest Exploration Trail | ☐ | ☐ | ☐ | ☐ |
| Pocahontas and Her Forest Friends | ☐ | ☐ | ☐ | ☐ |
| Tarzan Rocks! | ☐ | ☐ | ☐ | ☐ |
| Tree of Life, The | ☐ | ☐ | ☐ | ☐ |
| TriceraTop Spin | ☐ | ☐ | ☐ | ☐ |
| Wildlife Express Train | ☐ | ☐ | ☐ | ☐ |
| Other:_____ | ☐ | ☐ | ☐ | ☐ |
| Other:_____ | ☐ | ☐ | ☐ | ☐ |
| Other:_____ | ☐ | ☐ | ☐ | ☐ |

# *Daily Itinerary*

## Travel Itinerary

Make a copy of this worksheet for each day of your vacation; then use the completed worksheet as a guide for scheduling the things you believe you (and the people you're traveling with) will most enjoy based on the time you have available.

## DAY 1

Date: _____

Day of week: _____

### Morning Activities

| Time | Location | Activity Description |
|------|----------|----------------------|
|      |          |                      |
|      |          |                      |
|      |          |                      |
|      |          |                      |
|      |          |                      |
|      |          |                      |

Breakfast restaurant: _____

Reservation time: _____

Restaurant phone number: _____

### Afternoon Activities

| Time | Location | Activity Description |
|------|----------|----------------------|
|      |          |                      |
|      |          |                      |
|      |          |                      |
|      |          |                      |
|      |          |                      |
|      |          |                      |

Lunch restaurant: _____

Reservation time: _____

Restaurant phone number: _____

## DAY 1

### Evening/Nighttime Activities

| Time | Location | Activity Description |
|------|----------|---------------------|
|      |          |                     |
|      |          |                     |
|      |          |                     |
|      |          |                     |
|      |          |                     |
|      |          |                     |

Dinner restaurant: _____

Reservation time: _____

Restaurant phone number: _____

### Other

_____

_____

_____

_____

_____

_____

_____

_____

_____

_____

_____

_____

## DAY 2

Date: _____

Day of week: _____

### Morning Activities

| Time | Location | Activity Description |
|------|----------|----------------------|
|      |          |                      |
|      |          |                      |
|      |          |                      |
|      |          |                      |
|      |          |                      |
|      |          |                      |

Breakfast restaurant: _____

Reservation time: _____

Restaurant phone number: _____

### Afternoon Activities

| Time | Location | Activity Description |
|------|----------|----------------------|
|      |          |                      |
|      |          |                      |
|      |          |                      |
|      |          |                      |
|      |          |                      |
|      |          |                      |

Lunch restaurant: _____

Reservation time: _____

Restaurant phone number: _____

## DAY 2

### Evening/Nighttime Activities

| Time | Location | Activity Description |
|------|----------|---------------------|
|      |          |                     |

Dinner restaurant: 

Reservation time: 

Restaurant phone number: 

### Other

## DAY 3

Date: _____

Day of week: _____

## Morning Activities

| Time | Location | Activity Description |
|------|----------|----------------------|
|      |          |                      |
|      |          |                      |
|      |          |                      |
|      |          |                      |
|      |          |                      |
|      |          |                      |

Breakfast restaurant: _____

Reservation time: _____

Restaurant phone number: _____

## Afternoon Activities

| Time | Location | Activity Description |
|------|----------|----------------------|
|      |          |                      |
|      |          |                      |
|      |          |                      |
|      |          |                      |
|      |          |                      |
|      |          |                      |

Lunch restaurant: _____

Reservation time: _____

Restaurant phone number: _____

## DAY 3

### Evening/Nighttime Activities

| Time | Location | Activity Description |
|------|----------|---------------------|
|      |          |                     |
|      |          |                     |
|      |          |                     |
|      |          |                     |
|      |          |                     |
|      |          |                     |

Dinner restaurant:

Reservation time:

Restaurant phone number:

### Other

## DAY 4

Date: _____

Day of week: _____

## Morning Activities

| Time | Location | Activity Description |
|------|----------|---------------------|
|      |          |                     |
|      |          |                     |
|      |          |                     |
|      |          |                     |
|      |          |                     |

Breakfast restaurant: _____

Reservation time: _____

Restaurant phone number: _____

## Afternoon Activities

| Time | Location | Activity Description |
|------|----------|---------------------|
|      |          |                     |
|      |          |                     |
|      |          |                     |
|      |          |                     |
|      |          |                     |

Lunch restaurant: _____

Reservation time: _____

Restaurant phone number: _____

## DAY 4

### Evening/Nighttime Activities

| Time | Location | Activity Description |
| --- | --- | --- |
| | | |
| | | |
| | | |
| | | |
| | | |
| | | |

Dinner restaurant: _____

Reservation time: _____

Restaurant phone number: _____

### Other

_____

_____

_____

_____

_____

_____

_____

_____

_____

_____

_____

_____

## DAY 5

Date: _____

Day of week: _____

## Morning Activities

| Time | Location | Activity Description |
|------|----------|----------------------|
|      |          |                      |
|      |          |                      |
|      |          |                      |
|      |          |                      |
|      |          |                      |
|      |          |                      |

Breakfast restaurant: _____

Reservation time: _____

Restaurant phone number: _____

## Afternoon Activities

| Time | Location | Activity Description |
|------|----------|----------------------|
|      |          |                      |
|      |          |                      |
|      |          |                      |
|      |          |                      |
|      |          |                      |
|      |          |                      |

Lunch restaurant: _____

Reservation time: _____

Restaurant phone number: _____

## DAY 5

### Evening/Nighttime Activities

| Time | Location | Activity Description |
|------|----------|---------------------|
|      |          |                     |
|      |          |                     |
|      |          |                     |
|      |          |                     |
|      |          |                     |

Dinner restaurant: _____

Reservation time: _____

Restaurant phone number: _____

### Other

_____

_____

_____

_____

_____

_____

_____

_____

_____

_____

_____

_____

## DAY 6

Date: _____

Day of week: _____

## Morning Activities

| Time | Location | Activity Description |
| --- | --- | --- |
| | | |
| | | |
| | | |
| | | |
| | | |

Breakfast restaurant: _____

Reservation time: _____

Restaurant phone number: _____

## Afternoon Activities

| Time | Location | Activity Description |
| --- | --- | --- |
| | | |
| | | |
| | | |
| | | |
| | | |

Lunch restaurant: _____

Reservation time: _____

Restaurant phone number: _____

## DAY 6

### Evening/Nighttime Activities

| Time | Location | Activity Description |
|------|----------|----------------------|
|      |          |                      |
|      |          |                      |
|      |          |                      |
|      |          |                      |
|      |          |                      |

Dinner restaurant:

Reservation time:

Restaurant phone number:

### Other

## DAY 7

Date: _____

Day of week: _____

### Morning Activities

| Time | Location | Activity Description |
|------|----------|---------------------|
| | | |
| | | |
| | | |
| | | |
| | | |
| | | |

Breakfast restaurant: _____

Reservation time: _____

Restaurant phone number: _____

### Afternoon Activities

| Time | Location | Activity Description |
|------|----------|---------------------|
| | | |
| | | |
| | | |
| | | |
| | | |
| | | |

Lunch restaurant: _____

Reservation time: _____

Restaurant phone number: _____

## DAY 7

### Evening/Nighttime Activities

| Time | Location | Activity Description |
|------|----------|---------------------|
|      |          |                     |

Dinner restaurant:

Reservation time:

Restaurant phone number:

### Other

# Index

2R's Reading & Riting, 255
8Trax, 251

## A

Accommodations, 39–68. *See also*
  Hotels
Admissions, 69–89. *See also* specific
  parks
Adult attractions, 112, 143, 261–65,
  335–42. *See also* Epcot; Pleasure
  Island
Adventureland, 116, 120–23, 136–37
Adventurers Club, 251
Affection Section, 231
Africa, 214, 222–25
Air Florida Charter, Inc., 363
Airlines
  airfares, 15–21
  arrival information, 20
  list of, 18–20
  online reservations, 32–33
  record of information, 370
  security issues, 20–21, 66–67
Alfred Hitchcock: The Art of Making
  Movies, 298
All-Star Resorts, 44
Amazing Adventures of Spider-Man, 330
AMC Theaters, 243, 244

American Adventure, 177–78
American Film Institute Showcase, 194
Amtrak, 21
AnaComical Players Theater, 164
Animal Kingdom. *See* Disney's Animal
  Kingdom
Animal Planet Live!, 296–97
Annual passes, 73
Arabian Nights, 364
Art of Disney, 255–56
Asia, 214, 231–33
Astro Orbiter, 131, 151
Atlantic Dance Club, 261
Attire, 65–66, 103–4, 156, 187, 216–17,
  236, 244
Attraction selection worksheet, 379–84
Auto clubs, 22, 23, 33, 57
Automated teller machines (ATMs),
  82, 157, 277, 285, 344

## B

Baby care services, 82–83, 157
Babysitting services, 83
Back to the Future, 289
Balloons by Renee, 364
Barbera, Joe, 294
Barnstormer at Goofy's Wiseacre
  Farm, 149

Bay Cove, 239
Beach Club Resort, 44–45, 359
Beauty and the Beast, 194–95
Beetlejuice's Graveyard Revue, 299
Belz Factory Outlet World, 364
Big River Grille & Brewing Works, 261–62
Big Thunder Mountain Railroad, 123, 139, 151
Big Thunder Shooting Arcade, 124
Blizzard Beach, 235, 237–38
  admission prices, 71, 73
  description of, 13
Boarding pets, 86
BoardWalk
  description of, 14, 80, 241, 261
  dining options, 261–63
  shopping, 262–65
BoardWalk Bakery, 262
BoardWalk Inn, 45, 80, 261–65
BoardWalk Villas, 45–46
Boating, 256, 359–60
Bob Marley—A Tribute to Freedom, 337–38
Body Wars, 165–66
Boggy Creek Airboat Rides, 364
Boneyard, the, 226
Bongos Cuban Café, 245
Budget
  checklist, 29–30
  money-saving tips, 28–29
  planning, 13, 27–30, 369
Buena Vista Lagoon, 359
Bus service, 21, 39, 48, 101–3, 174, 218, 280
Busch Gardens, 282, 364, 368
Buzz Lightyear's Space Ranger Spin, 133, 139, 151


**C**

Camp Jurassic, 322
Camp Minnie-Mickey, 214, 228–30
Campground facilities, 41

Campsites, 48–49
Canada pavilion, 181
Cap'N Jack's Marina, 256, 257
Cap'N Jack's Oyster Bar, 256
Capellas, Michael, 184
Car rentals
  companies, 24–25
  insurance, 23–24
  luxury cars, 24–25
  rates, 22–23, 218
  record of information, 371
  special services, 25–26
  tips on, 26–27
Caribbean Beach Resort, 46–47
Caro-Seuss-el, 315
Carousel of Progress, 131–32
Carriages, 119
Carry-on bags, 66–67
Castaway Cay, 269
Castaway Creek, 238
Cat in the Hat, 316
Celebration, Florida, 97, 361–62
Celebration Hotel, 53
Cellular phone rentals, 25
Chester & Hester's Dino-Rama!, 228
Chester & Hester's Primeval Whirl!, 226, 227
Child care services, 82–83
China pavilion, 173–74
Church Street Station, 364
Cinemark USA, Inc., 364
Cinderella's Castle, 142
Cinderella's Golden Carrousel, 143
Cinderella's Surprise Celebration, 142
Cinemark USA, Inc., 364
Circle of Life, 161
Cirque de la Mer, 348
Cirque du Soleil: La Nouba, 245–46
CityJazz, 340–41
CityWalk, 335–42
  admission to clubs, 336
  description of, 278–79, 335
  dining options, 336–40
  parking, 280–81
  shopping, 341–42

Climate considerations, 64–65, 81, 187, 208, 238, 286, 363

Clyde and Seamore Take Pirate Island, 347

Colonial Lanes, 364

Comedy Warehouse, 251–52

Conservation Station, 230

Contemporary Resort, 47

Coronado Springs Resort, 47

Counterfeit passes, 74–75

Country Bear Jamboree, 124, 151

Cranium Command, 165

Crescent Lake, 359

Cretaceous Trail, 226

Cross Country Creek, 237

Cruises, 267–75. *See also* Disney cruises

Curious George Goes to Town, 294

Cypress Point Nature Trail, 240

**D**

Daily itinerary, 385–99

Davy Crockett Keel Boats, 126

Day in the Park with Barney, A, 295–96

Del Frisco's Steak House, 98–100

Diamond Horseshoe Saloon Revue, 126

Dining options, 91–100. *See also* specific parks

Dino-Rama!, 228

DinoLand U.S.A., 214, 225–28

Dinosaur!, 225–26

Disabled assistance, 87–88

Discovery Cove, 240, 352–54

Discovery Island, 73, 214, 221–22

Disney at Home, 256

Disney Bus Service, 39, 48, 218

Disney Catalog, 34, 134

Disney characters, meeting, 113, 122, 150–51, 202, 228, 268, 304–5

Disney Club, 34, 70, 134

Disney cruises, 267–75

adult activities, 272–73

children's space, 272

cruise lines, 267–70

dining, 274

extra charges, 268–69

family time, 273

guest services, 274–75

luggage limitations, 275

preparations for, 268

prices, 271–72

Disney hotels, 44–58

benefits of, 14, 42–43, 54

discounts, 34

rates, 41–42

reservations, 40, 43

transportation, 39

Disney Institute, 51, 358

*Disney Magic* cruise ship, 268–70

Disney-MGM Studios, 185–212

admission prices, 72, 73

admission to, 186

attire for, 187

attraction selection, 383

attractions, 189–204

backstage studio tours, 202–4

description of, 14, 185–89

dining options, 204–7

directions to, 186

guest services, 82–89, 157

hours of operation, 187

map of, *4–5*

meeting place, 188–89

overview of, 185–89

rating system, 189

re-entry, 186–87

shopping, 207–12

snack shops, 206–7

tip board, 188, 195

*Disney-MGM Studios Guide Map*, 201

Disney Radio Studios, 197

Disney restaurants, 15, 34, 91–92

Disney Stars and Motor Cars Parade, 199

Disney Store, 34, 134

Disney Vacation Club Information
   Center, 262
Disney vacation preparations, 13–38.
   *See also* Vacation preparations
Disney, Walt, 97, 132, 200–201, 220, 361
Disney Wildlife Conservation Fund,
   219–20
*Disney Wonder* cruise ship, 268–70
Disney World resort. *See* Walt Disney
   World (WDW) Resort
Disney's Adult Discoveries, 112
Disney's Animal Kingdom, 213–34
   admission prices, 72, 73
   admission to, 216
   animal care and viewing, 215
   areas of, 214
   attire for, 216–17
   attraction selection, 384
   conservation fund, 219–20
   description of, 14, 53, 213–20
   dining options, 234
   guest services, 82–89, 157
   information center, 217
   map of, *6*
   overview of, 213–20
   parades, 218–19
   rating system, 220
   re-entry, 216
   shopping, 233–34
   tours, 218
   transportation, 217–18
*Disney's Animal Kingdom Guide Map*,
   219
Disney's Animal Kingdom Lodge, 53
Disney's Beach Club Resort, 44–45, 359
Disney's BoardWalk
   description of, 14, 80, 241, 261
   dining options, 261–63
   shopping, 262–65
Disney's BoardWalk Inn, 45, 80,
   261–65
Disney's BoardWalk Villas, 45–46
Disney's Candy Cauldron, 247
Disney's Old Key West Resort, 50, 359

Disney's Racquet Club, 359
Disney's Vacation Club, 14
Disney's West Side, 244–50
   description of, 14, 241, 242
   dining options, 244, 249–50
   shopping, 245, 247–50
   snack shops, 246
Disney's Wide World of Sports Complex
   admission prices, 72, 73, 74
   description of, 14, 357–58
Disney's Wilderness Lodge, 52
Disney's Yacht Club Resort, 44–45, 359
DisneyQuest, 72, 73, 74, 246–47
DisneyStore.com, 34
DisneyWorld.com, 65, 70
DiveQuest, 163
Dixie Landings Fishing Excursion, 360
Doctor Doom's Fearfall, 330
Dolphin Fest, 349
Dolphin Nursery, 351
Dolphins in Depth program, 163
Dolphins, swimming with, 240, 352–53
Donald's Boat, 148
Double-decker buses, 174
Down Beat Jazz Hall of Fame, 341
Downhill Double Dipper, 237
Downtown Disney
   admission to, 242–43
   description of, 80, 241
   dining reservations, 244
   directions to, 242
   entertainment, 243
   guest services, 243
   map of, *7*
DTV, 252
Dudley Do-Right's Ripsaw Falls, 325, 326
Dueling Dragons, 318–19
Dumbo the Flying Elephant, 143
Dynamite Nights Stuntacular, 299–300

**E**

Earthquake: The Big One, 291
Eighth Voyage of Sindbad, 319

Electronic convenience vehicles, 81, 88, 211
Emergency services, 83–84
Emeril's Restaurant Orlando, 337
Enchanted Tiki Room, 122
Entertainment Books, 22, 34–35
Epcot, 153–84
   admission prices, 72, 73
   admission to, 155
   attire for, 156
   attraction selection, 382
   country showcases, 170–82
   description of, 14, 153–57
   dining options, 168–69, 171
   directions to, 154–55
   future of, 183–84
   Guest Relations, 157
   guest services, 82–89, 157
   hours of operation, 155–56
   legacies, 182–83
   map of, 2–3
   meeting place, 156–57
   memory tiles, 183
   overview of, 153–57
   rating system, 157–58
   re-entry, 155
   for seniors, 81
   shopping, 170, 175
   tip board, 159
   tours, 161–63
ESPN Club, 262, 357
Estefan, Gloria, 245
E.T. Adventure, 290–91
Eurospain, 256–57
Expedia.com, 32
ExtraTERRORestrial Alien Encounter, 129, 151

**F**

*Fantasia*, 195
Fantasmic!, 197
Fantasyland, 116, 141–47
FASTPASS, 75–78, 139, 168, 223, 227, 233
Ferryboats, 101, 186
Festival of the Lion King, 228–29
Fievel's Playland, 297
Fighter Pilots USA, 365
Fine-dining experiences, 98–100
Fireworks, 118, 195, 307
Fishing, 257, 360
Five-Day Park Hopper Plus passes, 73
Flights of Wonder at Caravan Stage, 232
Florida Mall, 365
Flying Fish Café, 263
Flying Unicorn, 319
Food Rocks, 161
Foreign currency exchange, 82, 277, 285, 344
Fort Wilderness Fishing Excursion, 360
Fort Wilderness Resort & Campground, 14, 48–49, 359
Four-Day Park Hopper passes, 72
Fourth of July Fireworks, 307
France pavilion, 179–80
Frequent-flyer program, 22, 23
Frontierland, 116, 123–25, 137–38
Fulton's Crab House, 257
FUNtastic World of Hanna-Barbera, 293–94
Future World, 158–70

**G**

Galaxy Palace Theater, 133
Gangplank Falls, 239
Gatorland, 365
Germany pavilion, 174–76
Ghirardelli Soda Fountain & Chocolate Shop, 257
Golf courses, 13–14, 80, 355–56, 365
Gory, Gruesome & Grotesque Horror Make-Up Show, 300–301
Gourmet Pantry, 257–58
Grand Floridian Resort and Spa,

49–50, 80, 358
Great Movie Ride, 191, 193
Green Meadows Petting Farm, 365
Green Thumb Emporium, 161
Greyhound, 21
Groove Club, 341
Guest Relations, 88, 157
Guest services, 82–89, 157, 243,
    274–75, 277, 285, 344
*Guidebook for Guests with
    Disabilities, The*, 88
Guinness World Records Experience,
    365
Guitar Gallery, 247

**H**

Hall of Flags, 177
Hall of Presidents, 127
Halloween Horror Nights, 304, 307
Hanna, Bill, 294
Hanna-Barbera, 293–94
Harambe, 222
Hard Rock Café, 336
Hard Rock Hotel, 56
Haunted Mansion, 127–28, 139, 151
Health-related services, 83–84
Heat concerns, 81
Holiday lights, 202, 307
Hollywood, 278, 300, 301
Hollywood Boulevard, 189–90
Holzberg, Roger, 200
Honey, I Shrunk the Audience Show,
    166–67
Honey, I Shrunk the Kids Movie Set
    Adventure, 193
Hotels
    Disney-owned hotels, 14, 34, 39–58
    non-Disney hotels, 28–29, 40, 57–64
    rates, 40–42, 55, 58–63
    record of information, 372
    reservations, 31, 33, 38, 40, 43
    tips on, 28–29, 40–41
House of Blues, 247

Hoypoloi, 247–48
Hub Video Stage, 252
Humunga Kowabunga, 239
Hunchback of Notre Dame: A Musical
    Adventure, 196

**I**

If I Ran the Zoo, 316
IllumiNations, 181–82
Imagination!, 166–67
Incredible Hulk Coaster, 331
Indiana Jones Epic Stunt Spectacular,
    194
Indy Speedway, 132–33, 151
Information Center, 117
Information Desk/Wait Board, 36
Information Line, 89
Innoventions, 159–60
Innoventions Fountain, 168
Intensity Water Ski Show, 349
International dining options, 92
International Gateway, 154
Island Depot, 252–53
Islands of Adventure, 309–33
    admission to, 281–82, 368
    description of, 278, 309–10
    dining options, 313–14, 316, 319–20,
        324–25, 327–28, 332
    games, 332
    hours of operation, 312
    layout, 310–11
    map of, *10–11*
    overview of, 278, 309–10
    parking, 280–81
    rating system, 311
    restrictions, 311–12
    shopping, 312–13, 317, 320–21, 325,
        328–29, 332–33
    snack shops, 317
    tours, 284–85
    transportation, 313
*Islands of Adventure Guide*, 327
It's a Small World, 141, 144

It's Tough to Be a Bug!, 221–22
Italy pavilion, 176
Itinerary, planning, 369–72, 385–99

# J

Japan pavilion, 178
Jaws, 292
Jazz Hall of Fame, 341
Jellyrolls, 263
Jim Henson's Muppet*Vision 3-D, 191
Jimmy Buffett's Margaritaville, 337
Journey into Your Imagination, 166
Journey to Atlantis, 347
July 4th Fireworks, 307
Jungle Cruise, 121, 139
Jungleland Zoo, 365
Jurassic Park, 321–25
    description of, 278, 310
    dining options, 324–25
    shopping, 325
Jurassic Park Discovery Center, 323–24
Jurassic Park River Adventure, 323

# K

Kali River Rapids, 79, 232–33
KartWorld, 366
Keelhaul Falls, 239
Kennedy Space Center, 366
Kennel rentals, 86, 344
Ketchakiddee Creek, 239
Key West Dolphin Fest, 349
Kid Switch Policy, 106
Kilimanjaro Safaris, 215, 223
Kissimmee Billie Swamp Safari, 366
Kissimmee, Florida
    activities, 363–68
    hotels, 58–63
    restaurants, 94–95
Kongfrontation, 292–93
Kraken, 346–47

# L

Lagasse, Emeril, 337
Lake Buena Vista, Florida
    activities, 363–68
    hotels, 58–63
    restaurants, 94–95
Land, the, 160
Land's Greenhouses, 161
LastMinuteTravel.com, 17, 33
Latin Quarter, 340
Leaping Horse Libations, 263
Legend of the Lion King, 141, 147
LEGO Imagination Center, 258
Length of Stay pass, 74
Liberty Square, 116, 125–28, 138–39
Liberty Square Riverboat, 126–27
Limousines, 281
Lines for attractions, 36, 75–78, 104,
    106, 139, 142, 155, 285, 310
Living Seas, 162
Living with the Land, 160
Locker rentals, 85, 157, 285, 344
Look Backstage!, 231
Lost and found services, 85
Lost children, 83, 104, 156–57, 188–89
Lost Continent, 317–21
    description of, 278, 310
    dining options, 319–20
    shopping, 320–21
Lucas, George, 129, 192
Lucy: A Tribute, 300
Luggage, 66–67

# M

Mad Tea Party, 145
Magic Carpets of Aladdin, 123, 151
Magic Kingdom, 101–39
    admission prices, 72, 73
    admission to, 103
    attire for, 103–4
    attraction selection, 380–81
    description of, 14, 115–16

dining options, 106–12
directions to, 101–3
exploring, 115–39
fireworks, 118
guest services, 82–89, 157
information center, 117
information desk, 36
introduction to, 101–14
for kids, 141–51
map of, 1
meeting place, 104
opening of, 116
overview of, 115–16
parades, 119–20
rating system, 104–5
restaurants, 110–12
rides, 151
shopping, 134–39, 150
snack shops, 107–10
theme lands, 116–39
tours, 112–14
transportation, 118–19
*Magic Kingdom Guide Map, The*, 122,
     130, 133, 148, 151
Magic Masters, 248
Magic of Disney Animation, 203
Magnetron, 248
Maharajah Jungle Trek, 232
Main Street, U.S.A., 116–20, 135–36
Manatees: The Last Generation?, 350
Mannequins Dance Palace, 253
Many Adventures of Winnie the Pooh,
     139, 141, 146
Mardi Gras, 304, 307
Marketplace
     description of, 241, 242
     dining options, 244, 256–60
     shopping, 255–60
Marvel Super Hero Island, 329–33
     description of, 278, 310
     dining options, 332
     shopping, 332–33
Masters of Magic Show, 366
Mayday Falls, 239

McDonald's, 258
Me Ship, the Olive, 327
Medical services, 83–84
Medieval Times Dinner and
     Tournament, 366
Melt-Away Bay, 237
Men in Black: Alien Attack, 294
Mexico pavilion, 171–72
Mickey's Country House and Judge's
     Tent, 148–49
Mickey's Jammin' Jungle Parade,
     218–19
Mickey's Sorcerer's Hat, 198
Mickey's Toontown Fair, 116, 147–50
Miniature golf courses, 356–57
Minnie's Country House, 149
Mission: SPACE, 183–84
Monorail, 39, 101, 154
Morocco pavilion, 178–79
Motion Club, 253
Motown Café, 338
Mr. Toad's Wild Ride, 145

## N

NASCAR Café, 339
NBA City, 338
Netane, Viliami, Jr., 350–51
NeverLost device, 27
New Year's Eve Fireworks, 307
New York, 278, 292, 302
NFL Experience, 357
Nickelodeon Studios, 278, 304
Nightlife, 241–65, 335–42
Norway pavilion, 172–73

## O

Oasis, the, 214, 220
Old Key West Resort, 50, 359
Once-Ler's House, 315
One-day/one-park passes, 69, 70,
     71–72
One Fish, Two Fish, Red Fish, Blue

Fish, 315
Online reservations, 32–33
Orbitz.com, 17, 32
Orlando FlexTicket, 281–82, 368
Orlando, Florida
  activities, 363–68
  climate considerations, 64–65, 363
  exploring, 355–68
  flying to, 15–21
  hotels, 57–64
  map of, *12*
  restaurants, 93–100
  tourist information, 58, 362–63
Orlando International Airport
  airlines, 18–19
  directions from, 19, 279
  information desk, 363
  shuttle services, 19–20
Orlando/Orange County Convention &
  Visitors Bureau, 58
Orlando Science Center, 366
Osborne Family Spectacle of Lights,
  202

**P**

Pacific Point Preserve, 350
Package Express Service, 85–86
Pandemonium Cartoon Circus, 327
Pangani Forest Exploration Trail, 224
Parades, 36, 119–20, 182, 199, 218–19
Park Hopper passes, 69, 70, 73–74
Park Hopper Plus passes, 70, 73–74
Passes, 69–74
Pat O'Brien's, 339
Patamoré, 338
Peak season, 35, 37
Penguin Encounter, 351
Pet care services, 86
Pet kennels, 86, 344
Peter Pan's Flight, 139, 145, 151
Pets Ahoy!, 348
Petty, Richard, 358
Phone numbers, 373–78

Pirates of the Caribbean, 121
Planet Hollywood, 248–49
Planet Hollywood on Location, 249
Playhouse Disney—Live on Stage!, 201
Pleasure Island, 250–55
  admission prices, 71, 73, 74
  description of, 14–15, 241
  dining options, 244, 254
  entertainment, 250–55
  shopping, 252–54
Pleasure Island Jazz Company, 253
Pocahontas and Her Forest Friends,
  229–30
Polar Expedition Tour, 344
Polynesian Resort, 50–51
Pop Century Resort, 54
Popeye & Bluto's Bilge-Rat Barges, 326
Port of Entry
  description of, 310, 312
  dining options, 313–14
  shopping, 312–13
Port Orleans Resort-French Quarter, 51
Port Orleans Riverside, 47–48
Portobello Yacht Club, 254
Portofino Bay Hotel, 55–56
Poseidon's Fury: Escape from the Lost
  City, 318
Premium Annual passes, 70, 73–74
Priceline.com, 17, 33
Primeval Whirl!, 226, 227
Production Central, 278, 293, 298, 304
Pteranodon Flyers, 322
Public telephones, 86–87, 157, 243
Public transportation. *See*
  Transportation
Puck, Wolfgang, 250, 260

**R**

Race car driving, 132–33, 167, 358
Racquet Club, 359
Rafiki's Planet Watch, 214, 230–31
Rainforest Café, 258–59
Red-eye flights, 16

Reel Finds, 254
Religious services, 84–85
Restaurants, 15, 34, 91–100. *See also*
    specific parks
    attire for, 244
    calculating tips, 97–98
    reservations for, 87, 244, 336–40
Richard Petty Driving Experience, 358
Ripley's Believe It or Not! Museum,
    366
River Country, 235, 239–40
    admission prices, 71, 73
    description of, 15
Rock 'n' Roller Coaster Starring
    Aerosmith, 197–98
Rock N Roll Beach Club, 254
Royal Pacific Resort, 56–57
Run-Off Rapids, 237


# S

Safari Village, 214, 221
San Francisco/Amity, 278, 291, 292,
    299, 302
Sand Street Station, 259
Scams, 74–75
Seashore Sweets, 264
SeaWorld, 343–52
    admission to, 282, 344–45, 368
    animal training, 351
    camps, 352
    description of, 343–45
    dining options, 350
    directions to, 345
    guest services, 344
    highlights of, 346–50
    kids and, 351
    overview of, 343–45
    parking, 345
    programs, 352
    rating system, 345
    tours, 344
SeaWorld's Discovery Cove, 240,
    352–54

Security
    on airlines, 20–21, 66–67
    at Walt Disney World Resort, 66, 131
*See Orlando*, 362
Senior travelers, 80–81
Seuss Landing, 314–17
    description of, 278, 310
    dining options, 314
    shopping, 317
    snack shops, 317
Seven Seas Lagoon, 101, 359
Shades of Green on Walt Disney
    World Resort, 52–53
Shamu Close Up, 349
Shamu's Happy Harbor, 348
Sharks!, 344
Ships, 126
Shopping, 364, 365. *See also* specific
    parks
Shuttle services, 17, 19–20, 280, 281
Single travelers, 80
Ski Patrol Training Camp, 237
Skycoaster, 367
Skyventure, 367
Slippery Slide Falls, 240
Slush Gusher, 237
Snorkeling, 239
Snow Stormers, 237
Snow White's Scary Adventures, 146,
    151
Sorcery in the Sky Fireworks
    Spectacular, 195
Sounds Dangerous: Starring Drew
    Carey, 198–99
Space Mountain, 130–31, 139, 151
Spaceship Earth, 158–59
Speed Wavzzz, 367
Spielberg, Steven, 288, 290, 321
Splash Mountain, 124–25, 139, 151
Splendid China, 367
Sporting events, 357–61
Stage 54, 300
Star Tours, 192
Starabilias, 249–50

Steamboat Springs, 238
Storm Force Acceleration, 331
Storm Slides, 239
Streetmosphere performers, 196, 224
Stroller rentals, 89, 211, 285
Studio Backlot Tour, 203–4
Studio M, 259
Stunt shows, 299–300, 302
Summit Plummet, 238
Sun protection, 81
Superstar Studios, 255
Surfing, 239
Swimming, 235, 236, 238, 239
Swimming, with dolphins, 240, 352–53
Swiss Family Treehouse, 122, 151

**T**

Tampa Bay, Florida, 282, 368
Tapestry of Dreams, 182
Tarzan Rocks!, 226–27
Taxi services, 19–20, 218, 281, 356
Teacups, the, 145
Team Mickey's Athletic Club, 259
Telephone numbers, 373–78
Telephone services, 86–87, 157, 243
Tennis, 358–59
Terminator 2: 3-D, 301
Terrors of the Deep, 348
Test Track, 167
Theme dining, 92
Ticket and Transportation Center
    (TTC), 101, 102
Tike's Peak, 238
Time-share packages, 14, 64, 75
Timekeeper, 129–30
Tips, calculating, 97–98
Titanic: Ship of Dreams, 367
To the Rescue, 344
Toboggan Racer, 238
Tom Sawyer Island, 125, 151
Tomorrowland, 116, 128–34
Tomorrowland Indy Speedway, 132–33,
    151

Tomorrowland Transit Authority, 132
Toon Lagoon, 325–29
    description of, 278, 310, 325
    dining options, 327–28
    shopping, 328–29
Toon Park, 149
Toontown Fair Hall of Fame, 150
Toontown Fair Railroad Station, 150
Tourist information, 362–63
Tours
    Disney's Animal Kingdom, 218
    Epcot, 161–63
    Magic Kingdom, 112–14
    SeaWorld, 344
    Star Tours, 192
    Studio Tours, 202–4
    Universal Studios Florida, 282–85,
        298, 300, 304
Toys Fantastic, 260
Train service, 21, 150
Translator devices, 157
Transportation
    airlines, 15–21
    bus service, 21, 39, 48, 101–3, 174,
        218, 280
    car rentals, 22–27, 218
    ferryboats, 101, 186
    limousines, 281
    monorail, 39, 101, 154
    record of information, 371
    shuttle services, 17, 19–20, 280, 281
    taxi services, 19–20, 218, 281, 356
    train service, 21, 150
    water taxis, 174, 186
Travel agents, 17–18, 31, 33
Travel budget, 27–30
Travel itinerary, 369–72, 385–99
Travel options, 15–30
TravelHub.com, 33
Travelocity.com, 17, 32
Tree of Life, 214, 221
Tree of Life Garden, 221
TriceraTop Spin, 226, 227
Triceratops Encounter, 324

Trip, planning, 369–72. *See also*
  Vacation preparations
Trolleys, 119
Tropical Rain Forest, 350
Twilight Zone: Tower of Terror, 190–91
Twister . . . Ride It Out, 302–3
Typhoon Lagoon, 235, 238–39
  admission prices, 71, 73
  description of, 15

**U**
Ultimate Escape Tours, 284
Ultimate Park Hopper pass, 74
United Kingdom pavilion, 180–81
Universal Cineplex, 335, 340
Universal CityWalk, 335–42. *See also*
  CityWalk
Universal Studios Escape, 309–33
  admission to, 281–82, 368
  description of, 277–79, 309–10
  dining options, 278–79, 313–14, 316,
    319–20, 324–25, 327–28, 332
  directions to, 279–80
  discounts, 279, 281
  games, 332
  guest services, 277, 285
  hotels, 54–57
  hours of operation, 312
  layout, 310–11
  map of, *8–9, 10–11*
  overview of, 277–79, 309–10
  parking, 280–81
  rating system, 311
  re-entry, 282
  restrictions, 311–12
  shopping, 278–79, 312–13, 317,
    320–21, 325, 328–29, 332–33
  snack shops, 317
  theme parks, 278
  transportation, 313
Universal Studios Florida, 287–307
  admission to, 281–82, 368
  attractions, 289–304

  description of, 278
  dining options, 305–7
  fireworks, 307
  games, 303
  guest services, 277
  information center, 287
  meeting place, 288
  overview of, 278
  parking, 280–81
  phone numbers, 287
  production schedule, 286
  rating system, 288
  re-entry, 282
  shopping, 307
  special events, 307
  theme parks, 278
  tours, 282–85, 298, 300, 304
Universe of Energy, 163

**V**
Vacation Club at Eagle Pines, 54
Vacation Club Time-Share, 14
Vacation packages, 18, 33, 74
Vacation preparations, 13–38
  insurance information, 84
  itinerary, 369–72, 385–99
  before leaving home, 67–68
  luggage, 66–67
  online reservations, 32–33
  packing, 64–66
  planning, 15, 79–80, 369–72
  prescriptions, 84
Villas at the Disney Institute, 51–52
VIP Tours, 283–85
Virgin Megastore, 250
Voyage of the Little Mermaid, 193

**W**
Walt Disney Dolphin and Swan
  Resorts, 48
Walt Disney: One Man's Dream,
  200–201

Walt Disney Travel Company, 18, 70

Walt Disney World (WDW) Resort.
  *See also* specific parks
  admission to, 69–89
  attire, 65–66, 103–4, 156, 187, 216–17,
    236, 244
  busiest days, 35, 37
  climate considerations, 64–65, 81,
    187, 208, 238, 286
  description of, 13–15
  hours of operation, 37–38
  lines for attractions, 36, 75–78, 104,
    106, 139, 142, 155, 285, 310
  nightlife, 241–65
  off-season, 36
  opening of, 116
  peak season, 35, 37
  phone numbers, 89, 373–78
  sporting events, 357–61
  tours, 112–14
  Web site, 65, 70

Walt Disney's Carousel of Progress,
  131–32

Water Mania, 240, 367

Water parks, 235–40. *See also* Blizzard
  Beach; River Country; Typhoon
  Lagoon
  admission prices, 71
  admission to, 237
  attire for, 236
  hours of operation, 236
  in Orlando area, 240
  services for, 236
  transportation, 236

Water taxis, 174, 186

Weiss, Al, 183

Welcome Center, 120

Wet 'n Wild, 240, 282, 367, 368

Wet rides, 79, 125. *See also* Water
  parks

Wheelchair rentals, 81, 88, 173, 211,
  285, 344

White Water Rapids, 240

Who Wants to Be a Millionaire—Play

It!, 199–200

Whoop-N-Holler Hollow, 240

Wild Arctic, 349

Wild, Wild, Wild West Stunt Show,
  302

Wilderness Lodge, 52

Wildife Express to Conservation
  Station, 224–25

Williams, John, 290

Wolfgang Puck Café, 250

Wolfgang Puck Express, 260

Wonders of Life, 164–65

WonderWorks, 368

Woody Woodpecker's KidZone, 278,
  290, 294, 295, 296, 297

Woody Woodpecker's Nuthouse
  Coaster, 295

World Expo, 278, 289, 294

World of Disney, 260

World of Orchids, 368

World Showcase, 154, 170–82

Wyland Galleries, 265


## Y

Yacht & Beach Club Fishing
  Excursion, 360

Yacht Club Resort, 44–45, 359

Yahoo! Travel, 32

# We Have EVERYTHING!

Everything® **After College Book**

Everything® **American History Book**

Everything® **Angels Book**

Everything® **Anti-Aging Book**

Everything® **Astrology Book**

Everything® **Astronomy Book**

Everything® **Baby Names Book**

Everything® **Baby Shower Book**

Everything® **Baby's First Food Book**

Everything® **Baby's First Year Book**

Everything® **Barbecue Cookbook**

Everything® **Bartender's Book**

Everything® **Bedtime Story Book**

Everything® **Bible Stories Book**

Everything® **Bicycle Book**

Everything® **Breastfeeding Book**

Everything® **Budgeting Book**

Everything® **Build Your Own Home Page Book**

Everything® **Business Planning Book**

Everything® **Candlemaking Book**

Everything® **Car Care Book**

Everything® **Casino Gambling Book**

Everything® **Cat Book**

Everything® **Chocolate Cookbook**

Everything® **Christmas Book**

Everything® **Civil War Book**

Everything® **Classical Mythology Book**

Everything® **Coaching and Mentoring Book**

Everything® **Collectibles Book**

Everything® **College Survival Book**

Everything® **Computer Book**

Everything® **Cookbook**

Everything® **Cover Letter Book**

Everything® **Creative Writing Book**

Everything® **Crossword and Puzzle Book**

Everything® **Dating Book**

Everything® **Dessert Cookbook**

Everything® **Diabetes Cookbook**

Everything® **Dieting Book**

Everything® **Digital Photography Book**

Everything® **Dog Book**

Everything® **Dog Training and Tricks Book**

Everything® **Dreams Book**

Everything® **Etiquette Book**

Everything® **Fairy Tales Book**

Everything® **Family Tree Book**

Everything® **Feng Shui Book**

Everything® **Fly-Fishing Book**

Everything® **Games Book**

Everything® **Get-A-Job Book**

Everything® **Get Out of Debt Book**

Everything® **Get Published Book**

Everything® **Get Ready for Baby Book**

Everything® **Get Rich Book**

Everything® **Ghost Book**

Everything® **Golf Book**

Everything® **Grammar and Style Book**

Everything® **Great Thinkers Book**

Everything® **Guide to Las Vegas**

Everything® **Guide to New England**

Everything® **Guide to New York City**

Everything® **Travel Guide to The Disneyland Resort®, California Adventure®, Universal Studios®, and the Anaheim Area**

Everything® **Travel Guide to Walt Disney World®, Universal Studios®, and Greater Orlando, 3rd Edition**

Everything® **Guide to Washington D.C.**

Everything® **Guide to Writing Children's Books**

Everything® **Guitar Book**

Everything® **Herbal Remedies Book**

Everything® **Home-Based Business Book**

Everything® **Homebuying Book**

Everything® **Homeselling Book**

Everything® **Horse Book**

Everything® **Hot Careers Book**

Everything® **Hypnosis Book**

Everything® **Internet Book**

Everything® **Investing Book**

Everything® **Jewish Wedding Book**

Everything® **Judaism Book**

Everything® **Job Interview Book**

Everything® **Knitting Book**

Everything® **Lawn Care Book**

Everything® **Leadership Book**

Everything® **Learning French Book**

Everything® **Learning Italian Book**

Everything® **Learning Spanish Book**

Everything® **Low-Carb Cookbook**

Everything® **Low-Fat High-Flavor Cookbook**

Everything® **Magic Book**

Everything® **Managing People Book**

Everything® **Meditation Book**

Everything® **Menopause Book**

Everything® **Microsoft® Word 2000 Book**

Everything® **Money Book**

Everything® **Mother Goose Book**

Everything® **Motorcycle Book**

Everything® **Mutual Funds Book**

Everything® **Network Marketing Book**

Everything® **Numerology Book**

Everything® **One-Pot Cookbook**

Everything® **Online Business Book**

Everything® **Online Genealogy Book**

Everything® **Online Investing Book**

Everything® **Online Job Search Book**

Everything® **Organize Your Home Book**

Everything® **Pasta Book**

Everything® **Philosophy Book**

Everything® **Pilates Book**

Everything® **Playing Piano and Keyboards Book**

Everything® **Potty Training Book**

Everything® **Pregnancy Book**

Everything® **Pregnancy Organizer**

Everything® **Project Management Book**

Everything® **Puppy Book**

Everything® **Quick Meals Cookbook**

Everything® **Resume Book**

Everything® **Romance Book**

Everything® **Running Book**

Everything® **Sailing Book, 2nd Ed.**

Everything® **Saints Book**

Everything® **Scrapbooking Book**

Everything® **Selling Book**

Everything® **Shakespeare Book**

Everything® **Slow Cooker Cookbook**

Everything® **Soup Cookbook**

Everything® **Spells and Charms Book**

Everything® **Start Your Own Business Book**

Everything® **Stress Management Book**

Everything® **Study Book**

Everything® **T'ai Chi and QiGong Book**

Everything® **Tall Tales, Legends, and Other Outrageous Lies Book**

Everything® **Tarot Book**

Everything® **Thai Cookbook**

Everything® **Time Management Book**

Everything® **Toasts Book**

Everything® **Toddler Book**

Everything® **Total Fitness Book**

Everything® **Trivia Book**

Everything® **Tropical Fish Book**

Everything® **Vegetarian Cookbook**

Everything® **Vitamins, Minerals, and Nutritional Supplements Book**

Everything® **Weather Book**

Everything® **Wedding Book, 2nd Edition**

Everything® **Wedding Checklist**

Everything® **Wedding Etiquette Book**

Everything® **Wedding Organizer**

Everything® **Wedding Shower Book**

Everything® **Wedding Vows Book**

Everything® **Weddings on a Budget Book**

Everything® **Weight Training Book**

Everything® **Wicca and Witchcraft Book**

Everything® **Wine Book**

Everything® **World War II Book**

Everything® **World's Religions Book**

Everything® **Yoga Book**

To order, call 1-800-872-5627
or visit everything.com

# We Have
# EVERYTHING!®

# For Travel!

## The Everything® Guide to New York City

### Rich Mintzer

The Everything® Guide to New York City features all of New York's best-loved attractions, from Battery Park to Museum Mile. Starting with the must-see landmarks—the Statue of Liberty and Empire State Building—to surprising secret treasures that are off the beaten path, this book includes information on where to stay and eat, neighborhood explorations, shows and attractions, New York after dark, and more.

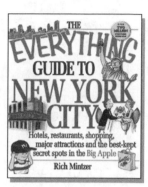

1-58062-314-X, $12.95

## The Everything® Guide to Washington D.C.

### Lori Perkins

1-58062-313-1, $12.95

The Everything® Guide to Washington D.C. captures the spirit and excitement of this unique city, from important historical showpieces such as the White House and the Smithsonian, to the best museums, galleries, and family activities. You'll find up-to-date reviews for tons of hotels and restaurants, guided tours, loads of attractions and activities, museums for every interest, and more!

**To order, call 800-872-5627 or visit everything.com**